THE SHADOW PRESIDENTS

Also by Michael Medved:
What Really Happened to the Class of '65?
(With David Wallechinsky)

THE SHADOW PRESIDENTS

The Secret History of the
Chief Executives
and Their Top Aides

MICHAEL MEDVED

Times
BOOKS

Published by TIMES BOOKS, a division
of Quadrangle/The New York Times Book Co., Inc.
Three Park Avenue, New York, N.Y. 10016

Published simultaneously in Canada by
Fitzhenry & Whiteside, Ltd., Toronto

Library of Congress Cataloging in Publication Data

Medved, Michael.
  The Shadow Presidents.

  Bibliography: p. 367
  Includes index.
  1. Presidents—United States—Staff—Biography.
  2. United States—Politics and government—19th century.
  3. United States—Politics and government—20th century.
  I. Title.
  E176.47.M42 1979   353'.03' 130922   78-20682
  ISBN 0-8129-0816-3

      Manufactured in the United States of America.

FOR NANCY

רַבּוֹת בָּנוֹת עָשׂוּ חָיִל
וְאַתְּ עָלִית עַל כֻּלָּנָה

PROVERBS 31:29

ACKNOWLEDGMENTS

This is the sort of project that requires considerable hubris: in the course of a few hundred pages I have tried to review more than a century of political history and some fifty personalities—including Presidents and their chief aides—who ran the operations of the White House. The ambitious scope of this attempt may be seen as the product of youthful enthusiasm—I was 26 when I began the book some three and a half years ago. Today, notably older and wiser, I am acutely conscious of the limitations of this volume. In no sense is it intended as a substitute for detailed biographies of individual Presidential assistants. For a handful of aides, such biographies already exist and for the others, I hope they will be written in years to come. The one message that emerged from my research more clearly than any other was how much we still have to learn about the private interaction between chief executives and the staff members closest to them. This book marks a beginning.

I am not a professional historian and have relied frequently on the assistance of others. My original research, conducted at Presidential libraries, university collections, and the Library of Congress, would have been impossible without three gifted associates: Gail Dickersin at the University of Buffalo; Dan Wicks of the University of California at Berkeley; and Mel-Erik Morton, a skeptical Englishman and Oxonian with a fine eye for the foibles of his adopted homeland. Patrick Anderson, who wrote an excellent book on the modern White House staff (*The President's Men,* 1968) gave generously of his time in answering my questions and suggesting approaches for my final chapters. Several individuals helped with sympathetic readings of the manuscript and made valuable suggestions for its improvement. They include my parents, David and Renate Medved; my precocious kid brother, Harry Medved; and my friends Rabbi Daniel Lapin, Joseph Telushkin, and John Rothmann. I owe special debts to my agent, Artie Pine, who stood by this project through some difficult times, to my resolute and incisive editor, Roger Jellinek, who helped it to find its current form and to Pam Lyons of Times Books, whose patient assistance made possible the publication of the photographs. I must also express appreciation to the Wallaces, who encouraged the book from the beginning and who provided advice and moral support at several points along the way.

The patient cooperation of several distinguished Americans contributed immeasurably to the portions of this volume dealing with the White House staff since 1945. Clark Clifford, Sherman Adams, Theodore C. Sorensen, Bill Moyers, H. R. Haldeman, and Richard Cheney all gave personal interviews and invaluable information and insights. I also spoke at great length with four current and former aides to President Jimmy Carter who provided most of the material on which the final chapter is based. I would like to thank each of them by name, but, true to the style of the present administration, they have requested that they not be identified as my sources.

Finally, I must express formally my gratitude to my wife, Nancy Medved. It has become a commonplace for the writer of a history book to thank his spouse at the conclusion of a long list of acknowledgments, and after finishing this project I can understand why. By its very nature, research work puts a premium on endurance and persistence—qualities that would be far more difficult to muster outside of the context of a rewarding marriage. In this case, my wife provided practical services that went far beyond the intangibles of emotional support. She spent months as a research assistant in various libraries, edited the manuscript at every stage, and provided an unerring source of common sense and good judgment. In this book about "Shadow Presidents" she must rightfully be acknowledged as my "Shadow Author."

Venice,
California
January 1979

CONTENTS

(Illustrations follow page 212.)

RAISING THE CURTAIN

In December of 1977, Hamilton Jordan, ranking aide to the President of the United States attended an ''off the record'' dinner party hosted by Barbara Walters. According to numerous eyewitnesses, Jordan, who had been drinking heavily, made a loud and vulgar remark about the wife of the Egyptian ambassador. In the days that followed, rumors of the incident began appearing in the press, the White House issued a formal denial, the Egyptian government chose not to force a diplomatic crisis and Hamilton Jordan nursed a throbbing headache. The entire episode might have been quickly forgotten except for another embarrassing night on the town some six weeks later. On that Friday evening Jordan visited Sarsfield's, a popular Washington singles bar, and allegedly spat his drink at a young lady who resisted his advances. In the commotion that followed, the President's assistant had to leave the bar without paying his bill.

None of this blended smoothly with the image of born-again virtue the Carter administration was trying so strenuously to project. Columnists and congressmen began questioning Jordan's mental health and calling for his resignation. Though Jimmy Carter never wavered in support of his beleaguered aide, many Americans found his commitment difficult to understand. What unique abilities made Hamilton Jordan worth the embarrassment that he caused his President? Unlike Carter's other troublesome friend Bert Lance, Jordan had never achieved a distinguished career or a position of power on his own. The only talent he had ever displayed was one for serving Jimmy Carter—and even that ability could be seriously questioned. Long before his mauling of the social graces made national headlines, Jordan had drawn fire for sloppy administrative methods in the White House. Out of 220 million Americans, surely the President could find another man who would help him at least as effectively as Hamilton Jordan. Why should he risk continued criticism and humiliation by keeping the controversial aide at his right hand?

It would be fruitless to approach that question without a sense of historical perspective. Jimmy Carter is hardly the first of our chief executives to display stubborn loyalty to an embattled assistant when it made little political sense for him to do so. Abraham Lincoln, Andrew Johnson, U. S. Grant, William Howard Taft, Calvin Coolidge, Franklin Roosevelt, Harry Truman, Dwight

3

Eisenhower, and Richard Nixon all suffered setbacks, major and minor, in defending aides who had become targets for the opposition. Their behavior reflects the curiously intense relationship that inevitably grows up between a president and his principal assistant. Bob Haldeman, who ought to know, compares that intimacy to the connection that develops between men who face combat together. As in combat, the nature of their personal interaction can change the course of battle—in this case affecting the success of a Presidency and the fate of a nation.

A brief note of autobiography is appropriate here. This book, like most others, was written to satisfy the author's personal curiosity. In 1970, as a 21-year-old dropout from Yale Law School, I worked as head speechwriter for a major party nominee for the U.S. Senate. I began by helping my candidate put his own thoughts into words, but after a few months it became impossible to tell which ideas were his and which were mine. An extraordinary interdependence developed. In the course of laboring sixteen hours a day in his behalf, I actually took on some of my boss's gestures and habits of speech. I spent many evenings sleeping on the couch at his home. Eventually, he came to view me as a reliable extension of his own personality. By the end of the campaign, I had been given the authority to issue statements in his name through our press office even if he had never seen the material before its release. It was an eerie feeling to read in the newspapers "the candidate said today . . ." and to know that all the press was really reporting were words that a totally obscure, totally inexperienced 21-year-old aide had put into the candidate's mouth. The public, as usual, never knew the difference.

After the election (we lost) I worked as a freelance speechwriter for enough Congressmen and Senators to learn that they depended on their key aides at least as thoroughly as my candidate had depended on me. This observation led to some interesting speculation. If so many of a legislator's day-to-day decisions were made for him by an invisible assistant, then how much of the complex business of the White House is actually transacted by a "Shadow President"? The Watergate revelations provided a startling answer to that question. During the Senate hearings and other public investigations, we heard again and again that H. R. Haldeman, now fallen onto dismal circumstances, had once intimidated everyone else in government and ruled the White House with an iron hand. Yet few citizens of the Republic knew much about him when his name first surfaced in the midst of the scandal. Anti-Nixon partisans viewed Haldeman's behind-the-scenes power as a departure from tradition, another original sin by Richard the Rogue, but such claims flew in the face of common sense. Knowing what I did about the emotional and practical demands of high public office, it seemed inconceivable that previous chief executives had operated without the support of similar aides, guiding the President's hand and acting boldly in his name. This book was written to tell the stories of all those Haldemans of the past, both the heroes and the scoundrels, who did not have the bad luck to be flushed out of the shadows by a well-publicized scandal during their years of service.

Many of these men remain mysterious figures to this day. Richard Cheney, who followed Haldeman and served with distinction as Chief of Staff to President Gerald Ford, managed to duplicate the anonymity associated with aides of previous generations. Even if you happen to know the Presidents by heart, how many White House aides can you name from the years before 1933? Woodrow Wilson's celebrated companion Colonel Edward M. House comes readily to mind, but very few others. In fact, ten of the individuals described in this book—all of them top aides to Presidents of the United States—are not listed in the supposedly comprehensive *Dictionary of American Biography*. Despite contributions both positive and negative, their names have been virtually erased from the history books.

This anonymity is no accident: it has resulted from conscious cooperation between the Presidents and the assistants themselves. It hardly makes sense for a chief executive to reveal to the public his dependence on a personal aide. He has nothing to gain and much to lose by such exposure. Calvin Coolidge felt so strongly on this point that as a condition for the employment of C. Bascom Slemp as his chief aide at the White House, Coolidge extracted a promise that he would keep no notes, copy no papers, and write no intimate memoirs. Slemp lived up to both the letter and the spirit of the agreement and, like most of his colleagues, proved adept at covering his tracks. Like courtiers in every era, these men have learned that publicity only alarms the sovereign and limits their room for maneuver.

In the past, reporters and historians have been all too willing to cooperate in protecting the low profile of Presidential aides. Heroes make good copy, and political conflicts come into sharper focus when described as a clash of larger-than-life personalities. This sort of colorful, simplistic canvas, particularly popular in the early years of this century, leaves little room for consideration of the subtle and complex interaction that goes on within a staff. For years, most Americans believed that the White House was occupied by a series of demigods who performed miracles in "splendid isolation." The clichés about "the loneliest job in the world" obscured the fact that a President can hardly go to the bathroom without some aide on hand to take orders or offer advice.

During the Franklin Roosevelt administration, a more accurate view of the White House at long last began to emerge, due at least in part to public fascination with the flamboyant antics of the President's friend Harry Hopkins. For the first time, the average informed American came to recognize what Washington insiders had known for generations—that members of the White House staff play at least as important a governmental role as Cabinet officers or Congressmen. Because this discovery coincided with a dramatic increase in the size of the Presidential staff and sweeping executive reorganization, it produced a major misunderstanding. Many observers reached the mistaken conclusion that the development of powerful White House aides had been another New Deal innovation. According to this view, pre-Roosevelt assistants deserved their obscurity. It became part of the conventional wisdom that the long line of

Presidential shadows who toiled in the White House before 1933 included nothing more than paper pushers and glorified clerks with little influence on events. How then can we explain the astonishing incident of 1870 in which a free-wheeling personal aide to President Grant, without authorization from the State Department or anyone else, personally negotiated a sweeping treaty providing for U.S. annexation of the island of Santo Domingo? Basic arithmetic shows that the impact of a single assistant may have been even greater in the nineteenth century than in today's White House. An aide to President Carter, no matter how important or influential, is one of more than 600 members of the White House staff. On the other hand, John Nicolay, who worked for Abraham Lincoln, was one of only two federal employees assigned to serve the President fulltime. Lincoln's dependence on this individual aide exceeded anything a contemporary President might experience. As far back as 1881, President James A. Garfield recognized that his appointment of a principal assistant might be the most crucial decision of his political life. "The position ought to be held in higher estimation than Secretary of State . . ." he declared in a letter to a friend. "The man who holds that place can do very much to make or mar the success of an administration."

Certainly it is more than coincidence that all of our most distinguished Presidents of both the recent and distant past (Lincoln, Cleveland, TR, Wilson, FDR, Truman, JFK) have enjoyed the services of exceptionally talented aides. Conversely, the most disappointing of our Presidents (Andrew Johnson, Grant, Benjamin Harrison, Taft, Harding, Nixon) have all relied on incompetent or morally flawed assistants. On occasion, highly capable aides have been associated with Presidents (McKinley, Coolidge, Ford) usually counted as mediocre and have contributed substantially to raising the quality of those administrations. For years, Americans have played the diverting game of rating our Presidents according to "greatness." Presidential assistants deserve no less. Not only will it help us to understand the past, but it can provide a useful tool in predicting Presidential performance for the future. In every election, millions of voters allow a candidate's selection of a Vice-Presidential running mate to influence their decision. His selection of a top White House assistant, however, will surely have a greater impact on the conduct of his administration. As Niccolò Machiavelli observed long ago: "The first impression that one gets of a ruler and of his brains is from seeing the men that he has about him."

The intimate portraits that make up this book begin in the year 1857, when Congress first appropriated government funds for the creation of a White House staff. For each administration from that time to the present, one Shadow President has been selected. In most cases the choices have been clear-cut, but occasionally a President may rely on several powerful aides in succession. Under these circumstances, the assistant with the greatest impact on the overall record of the administration will be the one featured in the book. For two Presidents—Chester Arthur and Woodrow Wilson—talented outsiders who happened to be personal friends became their principal lieutenants, with the regular staff relegated to lesser duties. Despite their absence from government payrolls, these unofficial advisors have found a place in the chapters that lie ahead. Cabinet members, on the other hand, have not been considered. These officials invariably become the protectors of the departments they head, with their own bureaucratic priorities and responsibilities. The members of the White House staff remain the only personnel in the executive branch whose sole constituency is the President. They owe no allegiance to government agencies, special interest groups, or the voting public. Their performance need satisfy only a single human being.

No attempt has been made here to present a comprehensive view of the programs and policy decisions of each administration. This is not a book about politics. It is a book about people. The focus in each chapter is on the special, often mysterious chemistry between a President and his top aide. In his thoughtful essay *Decision Making in the White House,* Ted Sorensen writes that "a President's evaluation of any individual's advice is dependent in part on the human characteristics of both men. Personalities play an intangible but surprisingly important role."

It is the hope of the author that the personalities encountered on these pages will become better known. Taken as a group, these men are considerably more fascinating, flawed, and various than the Presidents they served. Unlike the chief executives, they never submitted to an electoral winnowing process and most of them could never have come to power on their own. Their number includes a German immigrant, a British immigrant, one-and-a-half Jews, a secretive Italian-American, an alcoholic, a well-known lothario, a possible suicide, a possible homosexual, a private detective, a social worker, a sand and gravel salesman, an advertising man, a graduate student in history, two ordained ministers, two Army officers, three newspapermen, and six sufferers from bleeding ulcers.

The power of such characters in the White House should surprise none of us who have grown up with *The Wizard of Oz.* We all remember that exquisite moment when Dorothy and her friends finally arrive for their long-awaited interview with the Wizard. Fire flashes, thunder rumbles, and an enormous disembodied face scowls down at them. Naturally, they tremble in fear until, quite by accident, a little dog pulls aside a decorative curtain in one corner of the chamber. Behind this veil sits an odd little man who pulls the levers that control the great image before them. He is a singularly unimpressive fellow and no one in the Land of Oz has ever seen him before. Dorothy and company will never again look upon the Wizard as an omnipotent giant, but they are better off for knowing the truth.

In the same sense, the American public and political professionals alike will be better off for recovering the lost history of the White House and for meeting some of the odd little men who stand behind those noble Rushmore faces. In the chapters that follow, we will pull aside the curtain.

CHAPTER ONE

NOBLE BEGINNINGS

The White House Before Lincoln

Before 1857, if a President of the United States wanted help in running the White House he had to arrange for it privately. The Congress refused to make even the most minimal appropriation to provide secretarial assistance. The members of the Cabinet were supposed to give the chief executive all the advice he needed, so other Presidential attendants were deemed to be unnecessary. As to the daily trivia of his exalted office—receiving callers, answering the mail, reviewing and signing countless official documents, arranging state dinners and receptions—the chief executive was left to fend for himself.

George Washington proved unusually successful in handling the situation. In 1786 the wealthy plantation owner hired a bright young man named Tobias Lear to help him organize his business affairs. When he became President three years later, Washington brought Lear along with him to the federal capital in New York. The young man assumed the imposing title "Personal Secretary to His Excellency the President of the United States"—a position which lacked all official sanction, but his methodical work consistently pleased his employer. At the end of his first term, Washington declared his aide to be "a person who possesses my entire friendship and support" and the two men remained intimate friends for the rest of the general's life. During Washington's final illness in 1799, Lear sat for hours beside the sickbed, holding the great man's hand until the end. Washington's last words, "'Tis well," were addressed to Lear. After the former President expired, the faithful secretary performed one last service to his employer and to posterity: he lovingly measured George Washington's body so that future generations would know the precise physical dimensions of the father of their country.

Washington's successors, lacking the general's personal wealth and heroic reputation, found it difficult to attract helpers of Lear's caliber. Many of them turned in desperation to unemployed relatives. Nearly every Presidential family included some young man at loose ends who, in return for food and lodging at the White House, would be willing to assist the chief executive in attending to his duties. Presidents John Quincy Adams and John Tyler relied on their sons; James Monroe retained the services of his younger brother and two sons-in-law. James K. Polk succeeded in recruiting a nephew while Zachary Taylor persuaded his brother-in-law, an Army colonel stationed in Washington, to

11

help out at the White House in his spare time. When such attendants received salaries at all, they were paid from the President's own pocket.

Andrew Jackson rebelled against this precedent and devised a roundabout method to put his aide and nephew, Andrew Jackson Donelson, on the government payroll. He appointed Donelson clerk of the General Land Office, but saw to it that he spent most of his time at the White House. Other chief executives tried to follow this example—borrowing clerks and stenographers from various corners of the federal bureaucracy—but these arrangements remained decidedly unsatisfactory. After six months in office, Jackson described his job as "a situation of dignified slavery." Martin Van Buren found the office to be filled with "toilsome and anxious probation." Polk wrote in his diary that his service as President had been a time "of incessant labour and anxiety and great responsibility. I am heartily rejoiced that my term is so near its close." He looked forward to a peaceful retirement but died just 103 days after leaving office—fatally weakened by four years of overwork.

In 1825 the outgoing President James Monroe became the first of our chief executives to lodge a formal complaint with Congress about the lack of proper staff support at the White House. The higher duties of the office, he insisted, "are sufficient to employ the whole mind and unceasing labors, of any individual. . . ." Absorption with petty detail prevented the President from exercising leadership in the broader sense. How could he consider ambitious goals if he spent most of his time writing out letters, statements, and speeches in his own hand? The situation reduced the dimensions of the office and encouraged some of the early incumbents to view the Presidency as a glorified clerkship.

The experience of John Quincy Adams, Monroe's successor, highlighted another failing in the unhappy staff arrangements: the absence of a buffer between the President and the outside world. In our own era, H. R. Haldeman drew widespread criticism for the "Berlin Wall" he erected around Richard Nixon, but Adams' situation showed the perils of the other extreme. Idle visitors and total strangers streamed into his office every day simply for the privilege of shaking the President's hand. Occasionally, persistent callers caused Adams more serious annoyance. His diary tells the story of one such visitor: an early American crackpot named Dr. George P. Todson.

Todson, recently court-martialed from his post as an assistant surgeon in the Army, first appeared at the White House on December 16, 1826, to ask for a reinstatement. Adams had already reviewed the proceedings twice, declined to reverse the verdict, and learned from the good doctor's attorney "that Todson had come to the most cool and inflexible determination to murder me." Needless to say, the chief executive felt a certain discomfort in the presence of this visitor but refused to budge, even under threat of assassination. After a lengthy interview Todson left the White House, only to return five days later. This time he announced that his former intention to kill the President had been "absurd" since he now understood that Adams entertained kindly feelings toward him. As *proof of those feelings, he wanted the chief executive to give him money for passage to New Orleans. The President politely declined the request for a personal loan. On March 15, Todson made another appearance with the new demand that the government return his court-martial fee of $47. On March 21 he requested additional favors and received Adams' suggestion that he return to the practice of medicine. On the 27th he returned to the President with a joyous announcement: he was close to "forming a matrimonial connection with a young lady." The girl's parents, however, would not approve the match unless Adams agreed to reverse the court-martial conviction. The President held his ground and Todson disappeared for two months, only to shatter the President's hopes in May by showing up once again. This time he demanded appointment to a vacant clerkship in the War Department. Adams referred him to the Secretary of War who, not surprisingly, denied Todson the job. Nearing the end of his patience at last, the President in June recommended Todson to the Navy as a surgeon accompanying a boat-load of freed American blacks on their way to Africa. With some reluctance, the Naval officials agreed to the President's urgent request and sent the doctor across the Atlantic. When Todson returned after six months, he made a personal report to the President and offered a glowing account of his own achievements. Adams, no doubt impressed, wasted no time in finding the doctor another crucial assignment: traveling into uncharted western wilderness with a band of displaced Indians. This last errand worked out entirely to the President's satisfaction since he never heard from Todson again. Such was the burden one private citizen could place upon a defenseless chief executive.*

It took thirty more years of administrative chaos before Congress finally tried to remedy the situation. In 1857 the national legislature authorized the princely salary of $2,500 a year to pay for a private secretary for the President, $1,200 for a steward to take charge of the White House domestic establishment, and $900 for a part-time messenger. It would have confirmed the worst fears of these tight-fisted lawmakers to know that within 120 years of this initial breakthrough the White House staff would employ more than 600 individuals and require an annual expenditure in excess of $20 million.

James Buchanan, the first President to enjoy the services of an officially financed and recognized staff, hardly knew what to make of his opportunity. In the time-honored tradition, he appointed a nephew as his private secretary, in this case 23-year-old James Buchanan Henry. An orphan since age 10, Henry relied on his uncle for financial support throughout adolescence while he studied at Princeton and prepared for a career as a lawyer. Apparently one of the bachelor President's chief motivations in bringing his ward to Washington was a desire to keep close watch on the young man. Henry had displayed a distressing tendency for the wrong sort of feminine companionship, and as it turned out, he left the White House shortly before the end of his uncle's term for a marriage Buchanan vigorously condemned. Prior to this family disaster the youthful Henry had the chance to define for the first time the duties of the newly created post of President's Private Secretary. From 8 in the morning until Buchanan took his daily stroll at 5, the secretary made himself available for various stenographic services. Henry also had charge of paying the steward and the household staff, ordering coal for heating and oil for lamps, administering the White House library, and keeping the President's personal accounts. His greatest achievement as a White House aide involved the organization of a set of books to keep track of all correspondence received and the answers provided. "Such letters as the President ought to see I folded and briefed and took them to him every morning at eight o'clock and received his instructions as to the answer I should make." Once a day he sent a large envelope to each of the Cabinet Departments containing letters for their attention. When messages and executive communications went to the Congress, Henry delighted in delivering them personally. On each of these occasions he delivered what one reporter described as "a little set speech of tiresome uniformity."

If his job seemed less than exciting, then it reflected the timid goals of a caretaker Presidency. No one ever accused James Buchanan of bold leadership or sweeping historical vision. The President seemed content to preside quietly over the dissolution of the Union while his nephew and secretary, absorbed with the gay social life of the capital and copying letters in a large flowery hand, took scant interest in the political developments around him. A visitor to the Buchanan White House, noting the slow pace of the principals, could never have predicted the changes that would be brought about by the challenges of the Civil War and by three remarkable personalities in the next administration. Those individuals radically altered the conception of the White House staff and demonstrated the full potential of the fledgling institution.

John George Nicolay:
Lincoln's Shadow

The low-hanging clouds dropped rain and then snow on the crowd that gathered at Springfield's red-brick prairie station. Inside the waiting room the President-elect relied on a wood-burning stove to keep warm, as his Illinois neighbors filed past to shake his hand and say goodbye. At exactly 7:55 A.M., a station bell warned the Presidential party to board the special train. Abraham Lincoln wrapped himself in a shawl and the crowd opened a path for him to step outside. He had not planned to speak, but as he mounted the rear platform of the flag-draped train, with the bell ringing insistently and the locomotive coughing smoke into the morning air, he took off his top hat and looked over the crowd. Silently, the men in the audience removed their own hats, despite the snowflakes that gathered on their hair. Lincoln's high-pitched tenor voice seemed abnormally husky as he began to speak:

> My friends—no one not in my situation can appreciate my feeling of sadness at this parting. To this place, and the kindness of these people, I owe everything. Here I have lived for a quarter of a century, and have passed from a young to an old man. Here my children have been born, and one is buried. I now leave, not knowing when, or whether ever, I may return, with a task before me greater than that which rested on Washington. Without the assistance of that Divine Being, who ever attended him, I cannot succeed. With that assistance I cannot fail. Trusting in Him, who can go with me, and remain with you and be everywhere for good, let us confidently hope that all will be well. To His care commending you, as I hope in your prayers you will commend me, I bid you an affectionate farewell.

The wheels began to turn, the train pulled away, and the little knot of umbrellas and watching faces shrank and disappeared. But no sooner had Lincoln settled himself in his specially furnished car than a breathless reporter pushed up to him. The newspaperman had been impressed by the extemporaneous farewell speech and insisted that the President-elect write it down for the press before its noble words were lost forever. Lincoln, who was still in a somber and quiet mood, sat down resignedly and tried to write. He managed to scrawl only the first four sentences before a young man with a scraggly beard and long, sober face came up to snatch the pencil out of his hand. The President-elect seemed genuinely relieved when this trusted assistant took up the chore and wrote out the rest of the speech as he remembered it. It seemed entirely appropriate to their relationship that one of

Lincoln's most celebrated public utterances should come down to us through this intermediary—through the careful, quiet hand of John George Nicolay.

There is something vaguely disturbing in the notion that Abraham Lincoln, of all people, should have relied so heavily on the services of this near-invisible aide. Generations of historians have idolized Lincoln and down-played Nicolay's role, which is very much the way Nicolay himself would have wanted it. He was, as the Clerk of the Senate remembered him, "a man without excitement or emotions . . . absorbed in the President and seeing that the executive business was well done . . . coming and going about the Capitol like a shadow."

This shadow to the most classically American of all our Presidents was born in Germany in 1832, and came to the U.S. with his parents when he was 5. Nicolay's only formal education came at an immigrant school in Cincinnati where English and German were taught side by side. When John George was 14, his father died, leaving him a penniless orphan on the edge of the frontier. The young man worked at a series of odd jobs before settling down as a printer's devil, for the Pike County *Free Press* in Pittsfield, Illinois. By the time he was 22, he had worked his way through sweeping the office, typesetting, reporting, and editing, to be editor in chief and sole owner of the newspaper. This sounds very impressive until one looks more closely at the *Free Press*; it was a crude frontier weekly that offered news, chitchat, political opinions, and advertisements, all in the course of four pages. On one occasion, the *Free Press* waited two weeks before announcing the death of Czar Nicholas of Russia, explaining to its readers that the news had been previously omitted because of "lack of space."

Young Nicolay did most of the writing for the *Free Press* himself, including the unsigned romantic little poems that appeared from time to time. He also took a strong interest in local politics. Passionately opposed to slavery, he used the pages of his newspaper to boost candidates with similar convictions. By 1857, the 25-year-old editor was so thoroughly swept up in the excitement of the brand-new Illinois Republican Party that he decided to sell his paper and take his chances with full-time political work. He soon won himself a job as clerk to the Illinois secretary of state. It was hardly a top-level position, but it allowed Nicolay to move to Springfield—the bustling capital and center of the state's political life.

Part of his job involved supervision of the State Library—a single room in the old Statehouse crammed with several thousand volumes. Nicolay spent many hours sitting there alone, sorting through materials or reading law books. By 1859 he had learned enough law to be admitted to the bar, but he never practiced. The other benefit of his connection with the library eventually proved more important to him—it was in that quiet book-lined room that he first got to know Abraham Lincoln.

According to popular myth, Lincoln at the time was just a humble prairie lawyer, with no thought of his own future greatness; in reality, he was a veteran vote-chaser whose political career had suffered a series of temporary setbacks but who continued to harbor the most intense personal ambitions. He spent much of his free time in the State Library, carefully studying election statistics from every county, trying to plan political strategy for himself and for his party. Nicolay helped him find and analyze material, and soon came to worship Lincoln as a hero and a father figure. His real father had died when Nicolay was 14, and the frail, awkward clerk—who at 5'9" never weighed more than 125 pounds—felt powerfully drawn to the rugged, protective company of the older man.

In 1858, Lincoln's patience was rewarded when he won the Republican nomination for U.S. Senator. This meant the chance to take on Stephen A. Douglas, the nation's leading Democrat and the likely Presidential nominee two years later. Nicolay did his part for the Lincoln campaign, writing in pamphlet form an effective partisan hatchet job entitled "The Political Record of Stephen A. Douglas." Though Lincoln lost the Senate race, his strong showing established his national reputation. In an editorial which first appeared in the Chicago *Tribune* in February 1860, the loyal Nicolay formally suggested "FOR PRESIDENT —HON. ABRAHAM LINCOLN." It may have been the first public suggestion of a Lincoln candidacy.

When Lincoln won the Republican nomination on the third ballot at the convention, Nicolay felt certain that he would be given an important role in the campaign. The job he coveted had more to do with literary than with political ambitions: Nicolay wanted to write the official campaign biography of the candidate. When that assignment went to another man—William Dean Howells, who later established himself as one of America's premier men of letters—Nicolay was bitterly disappointed. He aired that disappointment with one of his colleagues at the state capitol and suddenly found himself at the point of tears. His friend shook his head and laid a friendly hand on the clerk's arm. "Never mind," he whispered. "You are to be Private Secretary!"

That report proved accurate: as soon as Lincoln began to organize his campaign, he asked Nicolay to join him as his only full-time aide. Letters were pouring in at the rate of nearly a hundred a day, and Lincoln needed someone bright and reliable to answer them. He also needed a man who could help him organize his time and deal with the impossible demands placed on a Presidential candidate, even in the year 1860.

In that era it was considered somewhat undignified for a Presidential nominee to stump the country in his own behalf, so Lincoln stayed home at Springfield while reporters, political leaders, and plain citizens came to visit him by the hundreds.

Nicolay helped receive visitors and handled correspondence while living alone in a hotel room that Lincoln provided for him. Officially, he was engaged to be married to a docile, diminutive girl he had met during his newspaper days back in Pittsfield, but at the time of the Presidential election, the engagement had already dragged on for four years. Part of the reason for the delay was financial: Therena Bates was the daughter of a prosperous merchant, and even as Lincoln's private secretary, Nicolay never earned more than the barest subsistence wages. More importantly, his time and energy were so totally taken up in the service of Lincoln that there was little room for a personal life.

On election night, Nicolay wrote to his fiancée that the jubilant Lincoln partisans lit all the candles in the Representatives Hall of the Statehouse. "It was filled all night by a crowd shouting, yelling, singing, dancing, and indulging in all sorts of demonstrations of happiness as the news came in. Across the street, in an ice cream saloon kept by a Republican, a large number of Republican ladies had a table spread with coffee, sandwiches, cake, oysters and other refreshments for their husbands and friends. It was 'happy times' there also. I did not go to bed until half after four in the morning, and then couldn't sleep for the shouting and firing of guns."

In the last few months before the President-elect left for Washington, the volume of mail swelled to such an extent that Nicolay could no longer handle it on his own. Fortunately, one of his best friends from Pittsfield happened to be in town studying law with a well-known local firm. After the election, this young friend volunteered to help Nicolay in attending to Lincoln's business. John Hay was only 22 at the time, but as a graduate of Brown University he had an air of worldliness and sophistication that both Lincoln and Nicolay lacked. By the end of his life, Hay would be widely recognized as one of the most remarkable Americans of his century. He was destined to become a distinguished poet, a first-rate novelist, a brilliant diplomat, a bestselling biographer, and a great Secretary of State under Presidents McKinley and Theodore Roosevelt. To get some idea of John Hay's extraordinary breadth and stature, you would have to imagine the careers of Carl Sandburg and Henry Kissinger somehow merged into one, But back in 1860 he was still a nervous youth with red cheeks and sparkling dark eyes, full of wit, good humor, and dreams of glory. His high spirits provided the perfect balance to Nicolay's methodical solemnity, and Nicolay came to rely on him as much for his company as for his abilities as an assistant secretary.

When the time neared for the journey to Washington, Nicolay found it unthinkable that Hay might be left behind. He approached Lincoln one afternoon and requested that Hay be appointed as number two man on the Presidential staff. An expression of amused perplexity crossed Lincoln's face as he pondered the suggestion. "But I can't take all of Illinois with me!" the President-elect protested. When Nicolay insisted, Lincoln finally relented. "Well, let Hay come," he said. The fact that Hay's family was not at all pleased with this turn of events may indicate the low esteem in which a job as Presidential aide was held at the time. They objected to young Hay's service in the White House because such a move would "necessarily interfere with his law studies."

It seems likely that neither Hay's parents nor his new employers knew all the unorthodox details of the young man's recent past at Brown University. It comes as something of a shock, even today, to learn that this outstanding nineteenth-century statesman was a hundred years ahead of his time in his undergraduate experimentation with drugs. In 1857, at age 18, Hay became so enthusiastic over a poem entitled "The Hasheesh-Eater" that he resolved to try the drug and reported that he found it a "marvelous stimulant to the imagination." In a letter to a friend some months after graduation, Hay described his college experience as a "far off mystical Eden'' and lamented the departure of those days when he ''used to eat Hasheesh and dream dreams.'' Just three years later, this same young man was working at Lincoln's side in the White House.

For both Hay and Nicolay, their tour of duty began as an adventure. ''The first official act of Mr. Lincoln after inauguration,'' Nicolay wrote proudly to his fiancée, ''was to sign my appointment as Private Secretary. . . . John Hay and I are both staying here in the White House. We have very pleasant offices and a nice large bedroom, though all of them sadly need new furniture and carpets. That too we expect to have remedied after a while.'' His optimism proved unwarranted: the appointments were never changed, and after four years' residence in the dreary executive mansion, Nicolay was notably less tolerant of the situation. He came to describe the White House as ''an ill-kept dirty rickety concern'' and wondered ''how much longer a great nation, as ours is, will compel its ruler to live in such a small and dilapidated old shanty, and in such shabby-genteel style.''

Nicolay's office was located on the second floor of the White House, directly adjoining the President's. Lincoln kept a bell cord at his desk so that he could summon his assistant at any time for a question or a command. On most occasions, however, the President preferred to walk directly into Nicolay's office, sit down for a moment with his long legs stretched in front of him, and chat with his aide about the business at hand. At times, he also used his secretary's chambers as an escape hatch: if he wanted to avoid the visitors who swarmed the halls and waited to see him at all times, he would disappear into Nicolay's office and from there make his way quietly to the more private parts of the mansion.

Nicolay estimated that three quarters of Lincoln's waking hours were taken up in meeting people. The Civil War brought to Washington unprecedented hordes of adventurers, office-seekers, soldiers, inventors, ''experts'' of every description, worried mothers, and sweethearts, all of whom had only one point in common —they wanted a few minutes of the President's time. In the midst of this tumult Abraham Lincoln was expected to run the country and save the Union. It was only to be expected that Nicolay took more liberties than any previous White House clerk in guarding access to the President. He became known as the ''impassable Mr. Nicolay'' who cast his cold, disapproving eye not only on cranks and common citizens, but on haughty Congressmen as well. Self-important Senators, who in all previous administrations had been accustomed to striding unchallenged through crowded anterooms and going directly to the President, developed a strong resentment for ''this mere boy from the West'' who forced them to await his permission. Nicolay's blunt and businesslike manner didn't help matters. He was, as one of his friends recalled, ''decidedly German in his habit of telling men what he thought of them.''

Both Nicolay and his even more youthful assistant, John Hay, were soon written down by official Washington as ''snobby and unpopular.'' As might be expected, no one was more easily offended by them than Lincoln's old cronies from Illinois politics. Lincoln's former campaign manager, David Davis, personally forwarded to the President a complaint from a member of Congress that the presuming youngsters in the White House deliberately prevented important letters from reaching the President. Like all other communications, this complaint crossed Nicolay's desk, and without a moment's hesitation, the secretary brought it directly to Lincoln. The President appears to have dismissed the matter without a second thought, but Nicolay could not resist firing off a quick and rather testy reply. "A moment's reflection will convince you that the President has not time to read all the letters he receives," he snapped, and then added at the bottom of the note: "I have shown this letter to the President, and have his permission to send it." Davis remained undaunted, however, and several months later he was still insisting that Lincoln read more of the mail himself. He sent to the White House a fifteen-page letter from the president of the University of Michigan, with the following endorsement: "This letter is an elaborate one, written in good temper and from the Christian character of the author entitled to be read." When Nicolay dutifully left it on Lincoln's desk, the President sent it back to his aide with a hasty note scrawled across the back: "Mr. Nicolay, please run over this and tell me what is in it."

From our contemporary perspective, it is difficult to understand the great importance attached to their daily mail by Presidents in the mid-nineteenth century. Before the invention of the telephone, this constant flow of letters to and from the White House was the President's chief means of contact with the outside world. Nicolay's supervision of these communication lines constituted an enormous responsibility. At any hour of the day or night he might be found hunched behind his desk—an enormous Victorian contraption with four wings, a built-in safe, fifteen drawers, and thirty-three square feet of flat top. Two large wicker baskets stood at either side of the desk, and received most of each day's mail as quickly as the hate letters and crank suggestions could be sorted out. In those cases in which the letter was deserving of a response, the reply usually came over Nicolay's signature with the introduction, "the President has instructed me to write . . ." In only a tiny minority of these instances was Lincoln actually consulted.

The President's other most significant line of contact involved personal messengers and emissaries, and here too, Nicolay played the leading role. His emaciated, unsmiling figure became a familiar sight on Capitol Hill and all the executive departments as he established the rule that "a President's Private Secretary could not be detained one moment. . . . He must be seen at once, no matter who else had to wait." Nicolay was also sent on crucial political errands outside Washington wherever the President needed a personal representative. The secretary was called upon to mediate a bitter patronage dispute which threatened to split the New York Republican Party; he was dispatched to Minnesota to help avert an Indian war; he was Lincoln's personal observer at the Republican convention of 1864 at which the President was renominated. The delicate nature of many of Nicolay's missions is reflected in the written instructions the President provided him for one such occasion. "Ascertain what he wants," Lincoln ordered. ". . . Tell him my motto is 'Fairness to All,' but commit me to nothing."

Lincoln was no more immune to newspaper criticism than any other President, and he came to rely on Nicolay as his watchdog of the press. With the demands of wartime administration, it was impossible for the President to review the newspapers himself, so Nicolay and Hay began preparing brief summaries of the most important stories from all the major journals. These press digests have become a fixture in most Presidential administrations down to the present day.

Nicolay was also an innovator in his attempts to influence the press behind the scenes. From the White House, and presumably with the President's approval, he sent letters to newspaper editors complaining about what he considered unfair treatment. In 1864, during a visit to New York on other political business, the President's secretary went so far as to summon Horace Greeley of the New York *Tribune* to his hotel room to protest a "villainous, unfair and untrue" editorial. Under Nicolay's persistent badgering, Greeley agreed to offer space in his paper for presentation of the administration's point of view. Who would provide such a semiofficial response? Nicolay himself was glad to do it.

At key moments in the Lincoln administration, John Nicolay was almost always at the President's side. When Lincoln signed the Emancipation Proclamation on New Year's Day 1863, it was Nicolay who handed him the pen. Later that same year Nicolay accompanied the President on his trip to Gettysburg to dedicate the battlefield cemetery. After breakfast on the morning of November 19, Nicolay went to the upper room of the Wills House where the President had spent the night. He remained with Lincoln until the President was called down to take his place in the ceremonial procession to the cemetery. In their hour alone, they worked together in preparing the final draft of the President's Gettysburg Address. It is possible that Nicolay's role was purely secretarial, but it seems far more likely, given their close relationship, that the President wanted reactions and suggestions concerning the speech he was about to give.

Nicolay was also close at hand for Lincoln's most difficult moment in the White House. In 1862, Willie Lincoln, age 11 and his father's favorite, died unexpectedly after a brief illness. "At about five o'clock this afternoon," Nicolay wrote to his fiancée, "I was lying half asleep on the sofa in my office when his entrance roused me. 'Well, Nicolay,' he said, choking with emotion, 'my boy is gone—he is actually gone!' and, bursting into tears, turned and went into his own office."

Despite his close relationship with Lincoln and his constantly expanding duties, Nicolay's official status remained that of a lowly letter-copier. Although the post of "President's Private Secretary" had been established by law, its salary—$2,500 per annum—was considered ludicrously small, even by the standards of the time. To make matters worse, there were no adequate provisions for Nicolay's administrative expenses. The economies of the Republic had permitted no increase in the annual stationery appropriation since the days of John Adams, and it remained at $250. This meant that Nicolay and Hay had to buy out of their own pockets every pen and every sheet of anything but document paper they used during their four years in the White House.

Given the tiny salary, the impossible hours, and the small recognition associated with his job, it was only natural that Nicolay suffered occasional bouts of self-pity. In his letters to his fiancée he often seemed lonely, homesick, and restless. Even in the first busy months of his service he found Washington as boring as "an obsolete Almanac" and reported that his only diversions were "some comfortable dinners" and "quiet little orgies on whiskey and cheese in my room."

On Christmas Day 1861—his first Christmas in Washington—Nicolay complained that he and Hay were "moping the day away in our offices like two great owls in their holes." In an hour or two, they expected to leave the White House and trudge three blocks in the cold to Willard's Hotel for a meal, "without anything special to remind us that there are such things as Christmas dinners . . . calculated to make one forget the drudgeries and 'unholy' days of life."

As the casualties mounted in the Civil War and Washington filled up with a steady stream of dying and wounded soldiers, Nicolay's depression began to intensify. "This being where I can overlook the whole war and never be in it—always threatened with danger and never meeting it—constantly worked to death yet doing nothing, I assure you grows exceedingly irksome and I sometimes think even my philosophy will not save me." But he kept working and kept sending off the letters to Therena Bates, twice every week without fail. For him, the letters to Therena were the only antidote to "that sameness in everything that surrounds us here, that makes it almost impossible to get oneself interested in anything but that which somehow pertains to the war or to the troubles of the country."

Lincoln, of course, was subject to similar depressions and he often turned to Nicolay or Hay to find relief. During the darkest days of the war when he found it difficult to sleep, the President would look for a light under the door of the bedroom that his secretaries shared. Lincoln was fond of reading Shakespeare aloud, and would often keep the young men awake long past midnight, declaiming favorite passages from *Macbeth* or the history plays. One summer evening while reading the opening soliloquy from *Richard III,* he noticed that John Hay's eyes had begun to droop and that the young man was falling off to sleep. The President closed the book immediately and thoughtfully ordered his overworked aide to bed. On another occasion, Lincoln retired for the night with a volume of Thomas Hood's caricatures in his hands, but he found himself so amused at what he saw that he got up and walked down the long, silent White House hallways in search of companionship. When he entered the secretaries' bedroom he was, as John Hay wrote in his diary, "utterly unconscious that he, with his short shirt hanging above his long legs and setting out behind like the tail feathers of an enormous ostrich, was infinitely funnier than anything in the book he was laughing at. What a man it is! Occupied all day with matters of vast moment, deeply anxious about the fate of the greatest army in the world, with his own fame and future hanging on the events of the passing hour, he has such a wealth of simple bonhommie and good fellowship that he gets out of bed and perambulates the house in his shirt to find us that we may share with him the fun of one of poor Hood's queer little conceits."

Lincoln also shared other diversions with his aides: whenever possible, he pulled Nicolay away from his desk to enjoy the varied fare at Ford's or Grover's Theatre. On November 9, 1863, Nicolay and Hay joined the President in seeing the exciting young actor John Wilkes Booth as the star in a play called *The Marble Heart*. Lincoln's reaction was not recorded, but Hay confided to his diary that he found Booth's acting "rather tame than otherwise."

In terms of entertainment, Nicolay had his own special passion: he was a fanatic devotee of grand opera. In his Illinois days, he had sung first tenor in a community choir, taught himself to play the flute, and become an outspoken champion of "quality" music. Eventually, this enthusiasm led to an unpleasant confrontation with a disgruntled Cabinet officer. During the war years, the Marine Band gave regular concerts at the White House and Nicolay viewed these occasions as a means of refining the public's taste. At his urging, the band startled its listeners by introducing arrangements of operatic arias into its afternoon programs. This innovation was soon brought to the attention of Navy Secretary Gideon Welles, whose department was responsible for the funding and administration of the Marine Band. Welles immediately put an end to experiments with "effete" European fare, and ordered the band to play strictly martial and American music. Nicolay was deeply upset and went directly to Welles to protest. This was one facedown that Nicolay could never win: the gruff Navy Secretary, with a biblical beard hanging halfway down his chest, refused to be intimidated by a youthful White House aide. In his diary, Welles commented that Nicolay's "refined music entertained the few effeminate" but was "insipid to most of our fighting men, and inspired no hearty zeal or rugged purpose." Welles concluded that "martial music, and not operatic airs, are best adapted to all," and there the matter rested.

The incident reminds us that Nicolay, despite his heavy responsibilities and solemn exterior, was in many ways an overgrown adolescent. In the last months of the Civil War, whenever news came over the telegraph of Union victories, Nicolay and Hay would come screaming and dancing into the President's office, waving the dispatch overhead as if it had been an American flag. In discussing their chief, the two secretaries seldom used the terms "The President" or "Mr. Lincoln"—they preferred to identify him with secret pet names that they invented. In the playful letters the two men exchanged whenever Nicolay was away from Washington, they referred to Lincoln as "The Tycoon" or "The Ancient" or, in tones of awed respect, as "The American." Their code name for the First Lady was equally revealing of their attitude toward that part of the Lincoln family—to them, Mary Lincoln was generally "The Hellcat."

Relations had been strained from the very beginning. Mrs. Lincoln was inclined to resent the time and affection that the President lavished on his secretaries. The years in Washington were an ordeal for her in any event: with her Southern background and close relatives fighting for the Confederacy, she was frequently the object of public suspicion. Out of the depths of her insecurity, she tried to dazzle the capital with clothing and entertainments, and was constantly searching for new sources of money. Ultimately that search brought her into direct conflict with her husband's secretary.

Nicolay appears to have been the chief disbursing authority for the $20,000 annual budget allotted by Congress for running the White House. When Mrs. Lincoln economized on her domestic arrangements, dispensing with the services of one of the full-time stewards, she expected that the government money she had saved should go directly to her. From the perspective of the 1970's, after watching one American President diverting millions of taxpayer dollars for his personal gain, Mary Lincoln's suggestion seems to be a trivial matter indeed. But to Nicolay and Hay—both of whom prided themselves on flawless personal integrity—the idea was anathema. They turned Mrs. Lincoln down cold, and no tantrums or threats on her part could overcome their objections. In bitter fury she retaliated—forcing Nicolay and Hay to reimburse the government out of their meager secretarial salaries for the hay their horses consumed while quartered at White House stables. In general, she did what she could to make life difficult for the two young men. As John Hay reported to Nicolay in one of his jaunty letters, "the Hellcat is growing more hellcatical every day."

Matters came to a head near the beginning of 1864. Along with Mrs. Lincoln, Nicolay shared responsibility for formal White House social functions. It was his job to ensure that the entertainments were conducted with dignity and that all invitations had been issued correctly. With this assignment in mind, he was appalled to learn that Mary Lincoln had vindictively excluded Treasury Secretary Salmon P. Chase and his family from the invitation list for the Cabinet dinner of 1864. At the time, Chase was conspiring to deprive Lincoln of renomination by the Republican Party, and the touchy political situation made the proposed social snub all the more unthinkable. When the First Lady remained adamant in the face of Nicolay's protests, she left the secretary with only one choice. He referred the snub to "the Tycoon," who, after a short conference with his wife, ordered that Chase's name be restored to the list. "Whereat there arose such a rampage as the House hasn't seen for a year, and I am again taboo," Nicolay reported. In her rage, Mrs. Lincoln sought revenge by striking Nicolay himself from the list, at which point the secretary curtly refused to provide any further aid with her dinner preparations. Finding herself unable to administer the affair without him, she was forced to back down and beg forgiveness from the young man—an intense humiliation for such a proud woman. Thereafter, she worked implacably to persuade her husband to fire his trusted aide.

She was aided in her efforts by the Speaker of the House and other politicians who urged the President to replace the stiff-mannered Nicolay with some "inside guardian of affable address." As it happened, this pressure against him coincided with Nicolay's own growing weariness with his job. "It is a feeling of duty and not one of inclination that keeps me here," he confided to his fiancée. "It seems as if circumstances surrounding my position are getting worse every day,'' he reported to Therena. "I am beginning seriously to doubt my ability to endure it a great while longer.''

It is one mark of Lincoln's dependence on Nicolay that the President delayed so long before making a move. Finally in March 1865, shortly before his inauguration for a second term, Lincoln was informed by the Secretary of State that the Consulate in Paris had become vacant and that the position ought to be filled before the adjournment of Congress. Lincoln lost no time in sending up the name of John George Nicolay. The Senate confirmed the nomination without a dissenting vote on the same day it was received.

Nicolay appeared to be delighted with his new job. It would give him a chance to tour Europe for the first time. But most importantly, it would allow him to bring his engagement, at long last, to a successful conclusion. As he proudly wrote to Therena: "The salary is $5,000 per annum.'' To further soften the blow of Nicolay's dismissal from the White House, Lincoln named John Hay as Secretary to the Paris Legation—allowing the two friends to continue working together. Meanwhile, the new Secretary to the President was to be Noah Brooks, an amiable California newspaperman who had specifically endeared himself to Mrs. Lincoln by defending her in articles and editorials.

Both Lincoln and Nicolay continued to drag their feet about the final date of the secretary's departure—there were dozens of loose ends to tie up with the war approaching its conclusion. Nicolay also felt that he was entitled to a short vacation before resigning his position officially. With Lincoln's blessings he left for a brief cruise to Cuba, where he "delighted in the warm sunshine'' and relaxed his jangled nerves. On the return trip, Nicolay stopped to represent the White House at a ceremonial flag-raising at Fort Sumter, commemorating the Union recapture of that island stronghold. As his ship continued on its way north in the brisk spring weather, Nicolay looked forward to his return to Washington and a few more productive weeks at Lincoln's side. But as they sailed into Chesapeake Bay, a pilot came on board to help with the navigation and brought the first whisper of an alarming rumor: the President had been shot in Washington. At first, Nicolay refused to believe the news, writing it off as "one of the thousand groundless exaggerations which the war has brought forth during the past four years.'' At dawn the next day, as the little ship sailed past Point Lookout, he heard the mournful reports of the minute guns and saw the gray light falling on flags at half-mast: he knew then that the worst was true. He went ashore immediately in a special boat and found a Washington paper giving all the horrible details. Lincoln had been shot in Ford's Theatre, in a box which Nicolay himself had often shared. The assassination came on one of those few occasions in four and a half years when Nicolay was not at the President's side and his distance from the event only intensified his grief.

Back in Washington, he found the executive mansion as "dark and still as almost the grave itself. The silence and gloom and sorrow depicted on every face are as heavy and ominous with terror as if some greater calamity still hung in the air, and was about to crush and overwhelm everyone.'' Later, after the funeral, he felt "too depressed in spirits" to write to Therena because "words seemed inadequate to describe my own personal sorrow at the loss of such a friend as the President has been to me. . . . I think that I do not yet, and probably shall not for a long while realize what a change his death has wrought in my personal relations.'' He continued to fûnction as Secretary to the President—spending weeks arranging Lincoln's official papers, meeting with the new President, Andrew Johnson—but his personal life had been shattered. He even talked of further postponing his marriage to Therena but fortunately, while visiting her in Illinois before leaving for Paris, he was persuaded to tie the knot.

During his four years as Consul in Paris, Nicolay was obsessed with thoughts of Lincoln and dreamed of writing an epic biography that would glorify the fallen President. Nicolay and Hay had originally conceived this idea during their first year in the White House and planned to work on the project together. During their stay in Paris, however, the two friends were much too busy to begin work. Nicolay's time was taken up with the thousand trivial details of his job and in fighting frequent skirmishes against political enemies who wanted to remove him from his position. In 1869, with the beginning of the Grant administration, those efforts finally succeeded; Nicolay returned to the United States and began looking for a job.

At first he tried to make a living as a writer. He prepared a few newspaper and magazine articles on Parisian life, but the $10 per column which he was paid was hardly enough to feed his family. He wrote lyrical, sentimental poetry and sent some of it to *Atlantic* magazine for consideration. The editor of *Atlantic* was Nicolay's old nemesis, William Dean Howells—the man who had deprived him of the coveted job of writing Lincoln's campaign biography. After seeing the poems, Howells added insult to injury—he returned them to Nicolay without comment. In desperation, Nicolay wrote to his friend Senator James Harlan, asking that President Grant appoint him "Minister to Bogotá"—a minor diplomatic post which was quite a comedown for a man who had once stood at the center of power. In his letter requesting the job, there is a pleading tone that is almost pathetic. ''. . . the President could not make another such appointment which would strenghten him so much among Lincoln's friends,'' Nicolay insisted. "Neither will he forget, I hope, that my own hands carried to the Senate every military nomination of his from Brigadier to General.'' Despite this pointed reminder of past services, the post in Bogotá went to another man.

Nicolay's hungry years came to an end in December 1872, when he won appointment as Marshal of the United States Supreme Court. One of the reasons he was able to secure the job, as he explained to a correspondent, was that he knew personally six of the nine justices from his days as Lincoln's aide. His new post carried with it a modest salary, excellent social standing, a pleasant office in the Capitol, and very little work. Aside from a few hours a week spent on court-related clerical and ceremonial functions, Nicolay would be free to concentrate his efforts on the Lincoln biography that he and Hay had been planning. Nicolay labored every day in the second-floor study of the sturdy home he had bought in Washington, only a few blocks from the Capitol. The room was crammed with Lincoln mementos and dominated by a large photograph of the late President, sitting between his two secretaries. At the center of the study, Nicolay had placed his old desk—the same enormous desk he had used in the White House. He had been lucky enough to purchase it at one of those sales of "decayed furniture" that take place in Washington whenever some official decides to modernize his office. As Nicolay's daughter recalled, "This desk seemed to bring old days very close. . . . My father could almost see Mr. Lincoln's tall figure pause beside it for a moment as he crossed to his private office."

Hay watched with concern his partner's growing absorption in nostalgia and urged Nicolay to put his work in realistic perspective. "The war has gone by," Hay wrote. "It is twenty years ago. Our book is to be read by people who cannot remember anything about it. We must not show ourselves to the public in the attitudes of two old dotards fighting over again the politics of their youth."

Before their work was even finished, Nicolay and Hay signed a contract with *Century* magazine for its serial publication. The two authors received an advance of $50,000—an unprecedented sum at the time. Their chapters appeared, one by one, every week for a period of four years. Then in 1890 the complete work was released in ten deluxe volumes, totaling more than 4,700 pages. One might think that this literary event would have clearly established Nicolay's important role in the history of the Lincoln administration, but this was not the case. In the course of more than a million and a half words on Lincoln, Nicolay included only half a dozen brief mentions of himself. He had no doubt come to the conclusion that any emphasis on his own service could only detract from the glory of his idol.

Till the end of his life, Nicolay consecrated all his remaining energies to efforts to enshrine Lincoln's memory. With Hay, he edited a two-volume edition of Lincoln's *Collected Works,* and then began a one-volume condensation of their popular biography. Meanwhile, he suffered from eye trouble and recurrent ill health. At times his crippled vision made it necessary to remain in a darkened room for days on end. He eventually gave up all forms of reading that did not relate to Lincoln, went out into society very rarely, and conserved every ounce of strength for his work. After his gentle wife died in 1885, he lived alone with his only child, Helen, a sober, scholarly girl who aided her father in his self-appointed role as keeper of the Lincoln flame.

Nicolay contracted his final illness in the summer of 1901, at the age of 69. In September, John Hay came to see him for the last time. President McKinley had just been assassinated and Hay, who was serving as Secretary of State, wore a black arm band. Before he went up to his old friend, Helen Nicolay whispered to him that she had kept from her father the news of this latest tragic murder. Hay immediately offered to remove his arm band, but Helen told him it would not be necessary: Nicolay's eyesight had deteriorated to the point where he would not be able to notice. He died a week later and the new President, Theodore Roosevelt, sent White House flowers to the funeral.

It was always easy for Nicolay's detractors to dismiss him as "a routine mail clerk" whose only virtue in life was his fanatical devotion to Lincoln. Yet the record tells a different story. With few precedents to guide him, he carved out a major role for himself and began the long tradition of powerful White House aides. He may have been unpopular with various politicians and members of the press—many of whom he offended—but no one ever questioned his intelligence or his honor. Unfortunately, the same could not be said of his immediate successors.

CHAPTER TWO

SCOUNDRELS AND LOSERS

During the administrations of Andrew Johnson, U. S. Grant, and Rutherford B. Hayes, the White House staff entered a period of spectacular decline. The men who succeeded John Nicolay resembled the Sorcerer's Apprentice of the fable: they waved their arms and tried to influence events in the style Lincoln's aide had recently established, but lacked the deft touch of the master. Each of the three aides discussed in this chapter served his President badly. William Rogers failed because of sickly incompetence; Orville Babcock because of financial greed and a lust for personal power; the alcoholic Robert Johnson because he simply could not help himself. Babcock stands as one of the more remarkable personalities ever to serve in the White House and achieved the sort of absolute dominance within the executive mansion that other assistants have craved. The unsavory reputation of the Grant administration stands as an eloquent tribute to his efforts. In the cases of Johnson and Rogers, the miserable service they provided helped ensure that two decent Presidents would achieve only limited success. These tales, though less than inspiring, can serve an important purpose; they illustrate far more clearly than success stories the impact of individual aides on the course of history.

Robert Johnson:
The Wayward Son

On the cold, drizzly night of April 14, 1865, Vice-President Andrew Johnson went to bed early. Some friends had suggested that he come along with them to Ford's Theatre, where President Lincoln was due to make an appearance, but Johnson politely declined. The clean sheets on his hotel bed seemed warm and inviting on such a dreary night. He had been Vice-President for little more than a month; he occupied a modest, two-room suite at the Kirkwood while his family remained back home in Tennessee. On the evening of the 14th, Johnson fell immediately into a deep and comfortable sleep, and he was only half-conscious of the heavy pounding on his door that began around 10:30. At first he chose to ignore the noise and rolled over onto his side, but a husky voice from the hall called out, "Governor Johnson, if you are in the room, I must see you!" The Vice-President got up, lit the lamp at his bedside, stepped into a pair of trousers, and shuffled into his outer room.

He opened the door to Leonard Farwell, a former governor of Wisconsin and a close friend. Farwell was breathless, having run all the way from Ford's Theatre to the hotel, but he immediately gasped out his news: Lincoln had been shot in the head and lay near death. Johnson grasped Farwell's hand for a moment, then put his head on his friend's shoulder for support. The next morning, Andrew Johnson was sworn in as the seventeenth President of the United States.

From Nashville, Johnson's daughter wrote to him of the family's reaction. His aging, invalid wife was "almost deranged" with the fear that Johnson himself might soon be assassinated. Only one member of the family was oblivious to what had happened: Robert Johnson, the new President's oldest surviving son. At 31, Bob Johnson was already a hopeless alcoholic, and the news of Lincoln's death found him in his "usual condition." His disgusted sister reported that his most recent binge had left him totally insensible to the nation's calamity.

Within two months, Andrew Johnson brought his wayward son to Washington and installed him as Secretary to the President. The indulgent father hoped that White House responsibilities would sober and redeem the beloved boy; instead, Robert Johnson's incredible performance helped bring disgrace and disaster to his father's administration.

Historians are still puzzled as to why all three of Andrew Johnson's sons led such dissolute and self-destructive lives. Charles, the oldest, was also the first to fall prey to alcoholism. A licensed physician who served in the Union Army in the Civil War, he died by falling off his horse during a routine ride behind his own lines. Johnson's youngest son, Andrew Jr., also died young: he expired at 27, exhausted by problem drinking and failures in the newspaper business. Robert was the middle son and his father's favorite. His letters show that he worked hard to maintain that position. He sent his father detailed accounts of his older brother's drunken sprees and highlighted his own noble efforts to "help" the unfortunate Charles. "I done my best to keep him from going," reads one self-serving and scarcely believable example, "but go he would, and the only thing I could do was to watch him and keep him straight if possible—I failed in that. . . . I regret it very much, but it cannot be remedied now." Meanwhile, Robert maintained a careful silence about his own drinking problems, and instead filled his correspondence with gossip about politics—the consuming interest that he and his father shared.

In the 1850's, Andrew Johnson was the most powerful Democrat in Tennessee, having raised himself from illiterate tailor's apprentice at age 17 to governor of the state at age 45. When he went away to Washington in 1857 to serve in the U.S. Senate, his boys seemed to flounder without the guidance of their domineering parent. They all struggled to please him from afar, and Robert, for his part, began the study of law with his father's old friend, Sam Milligan. Within a month of winning admission to the bar, Robert announced his candidacy for the state legislature. His father's popularity assured his election, but this still left the problem of earning a living. A legislator's salary covered little more than personal expenses and Robert was far too careless and ambitious to supplement that income in the routine practice of law. Urged by his mother to try to settle down, the 25-year-old legislator decided to follow a well-worn path to financial security and set out in search of a wealthy wife. There was no shortage of candidates. "What do you think of my marrying Miss Childress, provided I can get her?" he wrote to his father, and went on to state the young lady's qualifications: "She is of good family and has property in her own right to the amount of at least 40,000 dollars." Apparently, his plans were frustrated when Miss Childress turned him down, for within two weeks he was busy with another project. "I will write to you in a few days in regard to my marrying," he promised his father. "What do you think of Miss Hattie Brown?" This attempt met with no more success than Robert's first, perhaps because reports of his drinking habits had preceded him. Yet the young man had no time for disappointment, for he was soon swept up in the excitement of election year 1860.

Senator Andrew Johnson was a favorite-son candidate for the Democratic Presidential nomination, and he asked Robert to attend the convention to represent his interests. Robert traveled with the Tennessee delegation to Charleston, South Carolina, and immediately began sending his father paranoid dispatches about alleged "betrayal" by longtime political allies. At the same time, Robert maintained a childish faith that the father he worshipped would, through some miracle, win the nomination. As he wrote to his father on the eve of the balloting: "I have an abiding faith and a presentiment that the convention will nominate you—I have never yet been deceived in any presentiment I have had and am as confident of the truth of the present one, as the Sun will sink behind the western hills this evening . . . 'mark it down'—the stars have said it.'' The events that followed proved that Robert's psychic powers were distinctly limited: his father never received more than 13 delegate votes on the floor of the convention, of a total of 202 needed for nomination.

Nevertheless, within a few months Andrew Johnson had emerged as a major national figure. When the Southern states withdrew from the Union following Lincoln's election as President, Johnson was the only Senator from a Confederate state who remained at his desk and continued to function as part of the U.S. Congress. He worked hard to prevent Tennessee's secession, and when he failed in that he gave full support to Union war efforts. As a result, the Johnsons who remained at home were branded as traitors by their Tennessee neighbors. Robert, who shared his father's views, delivered several "stirring speeches" against secession and eventually came to fear for his life. "If they had arrested me," he wrote to his father, "I have no doubt that they would have hung me . . . It is impossible to put on paper the scenes that have taken place in East Tennessee since you left." Eventually, the Johnson family escaped to Union-held territory, and Robert made his way to Washington. When he arrived, he immediately demanded an appointment as "Colonel of Volunteers," even though he had no prior military experience. The authorities were in no position to refuse his request: he was the son of Senator Andrew Johnson. Winning his commission proved so easy, in fact, that Robert eventually decided that the rank of colonel was beneath his dignity. He asked to be named a brigadier general instead and demanded a full brigade of cavalry to command. While badgering his father incessantly about this latest scheme, Robert became involved in a bitter squabble with another Tennessee colonel: each accused the other of "luring away recruits." Robert was arrested but quickly released through his political influence. Meanwhile, he was drinking heavily and occasionally absenting himself without official leave. Reports of Robert's behavior soon found their way to his father, and in letter after letter, Andrew Johnson pleaded with his son to straighten up and "be a man." In response, Robert assured his troubled parent that "the men, without exception, love and respect me, and will follow wherever I lead, and will have no other commander, and what I say for them to do—they will do, with cheerfulness, but will not submit to any other officer." Later, Robert's troops all signed a handwritten petition supporting his contention, urging him not to resign his command, and "fully and heartily endorsing" all his past conduct.

Shortly before the Battle of Chattanooga, with Union hopes hanging in the balance and his native state as the battleground, Robert was suddenly and inexplicably ready to give up his commission. His father had to plead with him to remain in the Army and try to sober up. It was a particularly difficult moment for Andrew Johnson, and he begged his unhappy child for some shred of evidence of "a determination to serve the country as a sober, upright and honorable man. Though you are my son, I feel I am not discharging the duty of a father who has devoted his whole life to the elevation of those he expected to leave behind him. . . . I would be willing this night to resign my existence into the hands of Him who gave it.'' On the very day of the battle, Robert wrote his response, promising to remain at his post and to make a new start in life. Andrew Johnson was "more than rejoiced that you had determined to reform your course and become a sober man.'' A year later, with the war nearing its close, Robert was still dreaming of grandeur and fighting a losing struggle against alcoholism. In desperation, he had devised a plan to "pull up stakes and go west.'' He wrote to his father: "Taking everything into consideration, after mature reflection, I believe I will resign and try my future in some of the new territories. Next Sunday is my birthday, and I have, in anticipation thereof, cast away forever my past conduct. . . . I will succeed. . . . The intoxicating bowl goes to my lips no more.'' Like most of Robert's noble plans, this latest resolution came to nothing.

With this background in mind, Andrew Johnson's decision to place his son in a sensitive White House position seems nothing short of incredible. It is all the more incredible when one considers that even before Robert's arrival, the new President had already been damaged by whispers about drunkenness in the White House. Historians now agree that Johnson himself was never a drinking man; to the best of our knowledge, he was seriously intoxicated only twice in his life. Unfortunately, one of those occasions was the day of his own inauguration as Vice-President —March 4, 1865. Having just recovered from an attack of typhoid, Johnson had asked to remain in Nashville and to take the oath of office at a later date, but Lincoln wanted him to come to the inauguration ceremonies to demonstrate national unity. When Johnson arrived in Washington he was weak from travel and while waiting to enter the overheated Senate chamber, he asked for a single glass of brandy to steady his nerves. After drinking it down quickly, he remained pale and shaky and asked for another glass. By the time he finally walked out to the podium, his face was red and puffy and he swayed visibly on his feet. He rambled on incoherently for several minutes while members of the distinguished audience whispered to one another "Stop him!'' and "What a shame!'' When it came time for the oath of office to be administered, Johnson had a difficult time repeating the words. His public humiliation could hardly have been more complete.

Within just five weeks, this Washington laughingstock had become President of the United States. Common sense dictated that Johnson should at all costs put an end to the false rumors about "Andy the Sot.'' Nevertheless, he called his alcoholic son to Washington and placed him squarely in the public eye.

It was an enormous risk and Johnson knew it, yet during Robert's first months in the White House he appears to have acquitted himself with honor. He handled much of the Presidential correspondence, carried his father's messages to the Congress and the federal departments, and stood beside the President during visiting hours, taking down notes on both trivial and important conversations. In general, his smiling, boyish demeanor seemed to offer a pleasant contrast to his father's grim intensity. One of the reasons for Robert's initial popularity with official Washington was that he did almost nothing to limit public access to his father; gone were the days when John G. Nicolay's cold and watchful eye worked to protect the President's time. Though this easygoing approach may have endeared Robert to White House callers, it did not serve the interests of efficient administration. As Secretary of the Navy Gideon Welles complained to his diary, the President was "overrun with visitors," and no one seemed willing to take action to slow the tide.

The first sign of serious trouble came at the New Year's reception for 1866—a disorderly and sloppily planned reception that was a far cry from the well-organized entertainments that had been run by John Nicolay in the White House. Immediately thereafter, Robert Johnson's drinking habits began to create a scandal. Senator Samuel Pomeroy of Kansas, one of the President's most bitter political foes, paid a visit to the White House one afternoon and claimed that he saw the President, Robert, and the President's son-in-law all sitting together as drunk as lords. Later, Pomeroy disavowed his previous story and claimed that Robert was the only one who was really drunk. Nonetheless, the gossip about the President was repeated as far west as St. Louis, and the public image of "Andy the Sot" gained new currency.

This talk was soon supplemented by whispers that the White House was serving as a center for prostitution and other forms of corruption. It is certainly true that Robert Johnson had a weakness for women of easy virtue and granted White House access to a number of unsavory characters. One such individual was Mrs. L. L. Cobb, a buxom woman with a questionable past who had gained an underground reputation as Washington's leading "pardon broker." Following the Civil War, many Southerners needed Presidential pardons in order to resume full civil and political rights, and Mrs. Cobb boasted that she could use her favored position with White House "friends" in order to obtain such pardons promptly. Lafayette C. Baker, the indomitable head of the National Protective Police (forerunner of the Secret Service) was determined to prove that Mrs. Cobb was acting illegally. Baker ordered one of his operatives to pose as a former Confederate in need of a pardon and sent him to Mrs. Cobb. The controversial lady then demanded a down payment of $50, in return for which she presented a written promise that she would deliver a signed pardon the next day. After only a 24-hour delay—because Mrs. Cobb claimed that the President was ill—she appeared with the pardon as promised and exchanged it for four more $50 bills.

This bit of enterprising undercover work led to Mrs. Cobb's arrest and the resulting publicity proved terribly damaging to the administration. The President's lenient policy toward the South had already provoked widespread criticism; the Cobb case made it seem that part of that policy had been motivated by venal considerations. Even after it was demonstrated that Mrs. Cobb's only White House connection had been Robert Johnson—and never the President himself —the entire administration remained tainted by the scandal. What made the situation all the more ironic was that Robert derived no financial benefit from his questionable transactions—he was selling Presidential pardons for nothing more than "personal favors" from the handsome Mrs. Cobb. Nor did he terminate this embarrassing relationship after the case burst into the headlines. One Illinois politician reported that "there is too much whiskey in the White House, and harlots go into the private secretary's office unannounced in broad daylight. Mrs. Cobb did that since the trial while a friend of mine was waiting for an audience . . . and she came out leaning on the arm of a drunken son of the President."

Clearly, this situation could not be allowed to continue. The President called for a secret consultation between his friend, Navy Secretary Gideon Welles, and a Washington physician named Dr. Norris in order to discuss Robert's problems. Dr. Norris, who had recently examined the young man, suggested that Robert had been "beguiled into intemperance after he became of age, through his generous qualities, goodness of heart, and friendly disposition." The good doctor, therefore, thought it "possible to reclaim him." Secretary Welles recorded in his diary that he himself had "very little expectation of such a result," but noted that in the past he had heard Robert talk about his own alcoholism "in a manner to touch my sympathy in his behalf." The doctor and the Navy Secretary agreed that the best solution for Robert would be a lengthy and relaxing ocean voyage aboard a U.S. Navy ship. It was no accident that this plan would also serve to remove Robert from the White House and from the public eye, and to give the President a chance to reorganize the staff before his political losses became irreversible. Welles held several meetings with Secretary of State William Seward before they came up with the idea that Robert's cruise would be an official voyage of inspection concerning the slave trade on the African coast. The fact that both the Secretary of State and the Secretary of the Navy spent many hours of their time developing a scheme to get him out of the country is the best indication of Robert's truly disastrous impact on the administration.

The unfortunate young man enthusiastically agreed to the plans for his trip, but on the morning when the captain of the ship came to call for him, Robert was not in the White House. He had "decamped—out on a spree," and as usual during his binges, he could not be found. Despite the weeks of careful planning, his ship was forced to sail without him. Several months later, Robert did go on a brief cruise to Liberia, but the experience did nothing to help his alcoholism, and he was soon back in the White House, plaguing his father's administration once again. Though he spent some time at home in Tennessee, he returned to the executive mansion near the end of his father's term and continued to work at his job during whatever lucid moments he enjoyed. He was never a powerful White House aide, but his very presence at the center of events prevented the emergence of the sort of effective, coordinated staff that might have saved his father from the series of blunders that led to his Impeachment.

Andrew Johnson left the White House in disgrace in 1869. His family returned to Tennessee, but the former President set out almost immediately to make a few appearances trying to vindicate his record. Robert, whose depressions and drunkenness had grown steadily more acute, remained behind in Greeneville, the little town in which he was born. There, just six weeks after his father left the Presidency, Robert died suddenly at the age of 35. In a touching letter, his ailing mother described the circumstances. "He was well and on the street at five o'clock," she wrote, "and at dusk, as the servant went as usual to light his lamp, she discovered that he was in a deep sleep. He was never aroused from it. All the physicians of the village were immediately called in, but alas! too late to do any good. He breathed his last at half-past eleven that night, without a single groan or struggle.

"I do not suppose he ever made an enemy in his life. He was certainly the most popular boy ever raised in this part of the country, and continued so after he became a man. Oh, if he could only have spoken a word to us! but he passed into the tomb, unconscious of all around him."

In the town of Greeneville, there was some talk that Robert had "died by his own hand," and eventually this speculation found its way into some of the later biographies of Andrew Johnson.

In reporting Robert's death, the newspapers generally emphasized his better qualities, in particular his four years of service in the Civil War. "He was a young man of fine abilities," declared the Nashville *Republican Banner*. "He had his faults and weaknesses, like other men, but he was ever generous and chivalrous, a true friend, an affectionate brother and son." Only the Chicago *Post* allowed partisan bitterness to set the tone for its gloating account. "The devil came for the old man, and not finding him, took the son."

Perhaps the most pathetic postscript to Robert's life came in a letter from his younger brother, Andrew Jr.—the last surviving son of the former President. "O my dear mother," young Andrew wrote in an unsteady hand, "I know how hard the blow is for me to bear, and how much harder it was for you. Mother, if this can be any comfort to you read this, I most solemnly swear never no never to let any kind of intoxicating liquors to pass my lips believe me mother this promise will never be broken."

Ten years later this last son was dead himself at the age of 27.

O. E. Babcock:
Orville The Incredible

On February 18, 1876, in a packed courtroom in St. Louis, the opening gavel sounded on what the newspapers billed as "the most important trial in our history." The defendant was General Orville Babcock, Private Secretary to President Ulysses S. Grant. Babcock was an extraordinary man, and he was charged with an extraordinary crime: according to the prosecution, a conspiracy with Babcock at its head had cheated the public treasury of more than $4 million. Even in today's terms this is an impressive total, but by the standards of 1876 the figure was absolutely mind-boggling. The defendant's friends, however, believed none of it. To them, Babcock was a dashing soldier and a public servant of spotless integrity—a political martyr whose only crime was his unfailing loyalty to President Grant. Whatever the final verdict of the jury in St. Louis, one point was not in contention: that Orville Babcock was the most powerful and controversial aide who had ever served in the White House to that time.

The road that took him to such unprecedented heights of unofficial power began auspiciously: he was born on Christmas Day 1835, the eighth of ten children of a prosperous Vermont farmer. Babcock's grandfather had fought with distinction in the Revolution, and his father served two terms in the Vermont legislature. This political connection helped young Babcock to win appointment to the United States Military Academy where he specialized in the difficult field of military engineering and graduated third in his class in May 1861. As it turned out, his timing was nearly perfect: the Civil War had begun less than three weeks before and promising young officers were very much in demand. By 1863 he had risen to the rank of lieutenant colonel and dazzled a succession of commanding officers. Young Babcock enjoyed the pomp associated with his position and cut an impressive figure in his immaculate blue uniform with the brightly polished gold braid. His contemporaries considered him unusually handsome and commented frequently on his ruddy complexion, wavy auburn hair, and perfect white teeth shown in flashing smiles. Adding to this strong physical presence was an unfailing air of self-confidence and goodfellowship which endeared him to officers and enlisted men alike.

In the spring of 1864, Babcock received another promotion and a new assignment that changed the course of his life. He was named one of the aides-de-camp to the new General in Chief of the Union Armies, U. S. Grant. Grant

39

was still something of an enigma to his troops and to the country at large. He was slovenly, introverted, and moody—far from the traditional mold of a military hero. In the dapper, talkative Babcock, the general saw a young man who was in many ways his opposite—a dashing officer accomplished in precisely those areas where Grant felt most deficient. Shared dangers on the battlefield solidified their friendship. On October 27, 1864, at the Battle of Hatcher's Run, Grant, as usual, insisted on riding directly to the front to watch the progress of his troops. Babcock accompanied him, riding a few yards behind. As the two men approached a bridge, an enemy shell came whistling down on them and exploded under the neck of Grant's horse. The animal reared and got its legs tangled in a coil of loose telegraph wire lying on the ground. With his horse struggling to free itself and enemy fire finding his range, Grant fought desperately to maintain his saddle. Betraying no sign of emotion, Babcock dismounted slowly, walked over to Grant, and calmly uncoiled the wire from the horse's leg. Little was said of the incident afterward, but it is entirely possible that Babcock had saved Grant's life. It was not the sort of occurrence that the general was likely to forget.

With the war over, Grant continued in his position as commander of the armies and Babcock remained a key member of his staff. The aide was now adorned with the rank of brevet brigadier general, and his ringing laughter and infectious high spirits became a fixture at the Grants' Washington household. For all practical purposes he was a member of the family; as Grant's son recalled, "we all knew and loved him." Babcock's ties to the Grant family were only strengthened by his decision to marry in November 1866. It was no accident that his handsome, 27-year-old bride hailed from the Grants' hometown of Galena, Illinois, and happened to be one of Mrs. Grant's closest personal friends.

If Babcock had serious thoughts of politics during this period, he managed to keep them well-concealed. He busied himself with routine Army matters and took a notably skeptical view of the Grant-for-President talk he heard all around him. Yet neither Babcock nor Grant himself was able to resist the massive wave of public sentiment that was sweeping the general toward the White House. When Grant was elected in 1868, Babcock kept his Army commission and was officially assigned to the staff of the new General-in-Chief—William Tecumseh Sherman. But all Washington understood that Babcock's real job was in the White House, as one of two Private Secretaries to the new President. The other secretary, Horace Porter, was another Army careerist from Grant's wartime staff, and the influential Senator Charles Sumner was soon grumbling against the "illegal military ring" in the executive mansion.

From the first days of the new administration, Babcock made the transition from the military to the political arena more smoothly than did his often bewildered chief. When Grant proved unable to persuade the distinguished New Yorker, Hamilton Fish, to serve in the Cabinet as Secretary of State, he dispatched Babcock as his emissary. The suave aide paid a hasty visit to the Fish home and proceeded to win over Mrs. Fish, who in turn convinced her husband. It was fortunate for the President that Babcock succeeded: the bumbling Grant had already sent the Fish nomination to the Senate. A few months later, the President was once again confused about his Cabinet. Unable to decide which of two men to name as Secretary of War, he brought his problem to Babcock. Without hesitation, Babcock recommended General William Belknap, and Grant hastily followed his advice. In the years that followed, the Secretary of War consulted Babcock frequently—at times seeking his approval for even minor expenditures within the War Department. This total dependence of a Cabinet member on an ambitious Presidential aide deeply disturbed Secretary of State Fish. "The truth is," he complained to his diary, "Babcock fancies himself President of the United States, and Belknap don't know better."

On occasion, Babcock deliberately misled the President in order to maximize his personal influence. When a State Department paper urging a cautious approach to Spain's troubles in Cuba was forwarded to the President, Babcock was anxious to discredit it: the young general favored a more risky, interventionist policy. With full knowledge that the document in question had actually been prepared by the Secretary of State, Babcock led Grant to believe that it had been written by a minor diplomat the President particularly disliked. Later, Secretary Fish suspected Babcock of additional trickery. According to Fish, it became a regular practice for Babcock to draft letters in Grant's name, present them for the President's approval, and then add unauthorized and controversial sentences after that approval had been granted. Fish also began to wonder why all press leaks from the White House invariably advanced Babcock's projects or worked to discredit his enemies.

Without doubt the most astonishing example of Babcock's drive for power concerned his performance in the great Santo Domingo fiasco. The entire incident grew out of a legitimate desire on the part of President Grant to secure use of Samaná Bay as a Caribbean coaling station for the U.S. Navy. In the summer of 1869, recalling Babcock's background as a first-rate military engineer, Grant dispatched his aide to Santo Domingo to investigate the feasibility of the project. Babcock's official instructions from the Secretary of State called for reports on the population, agriculture, minerals, trade, currency, and government of Santo Domingo—but he was granted no diplomatic authority whatever.

On the voyage south, Babcock enjoyed the company of a small group of Yankee businessmen with a special interest in the island republic. These dedicated entrepreneurs had bought up thousands of acres in Santo Domingo in the hope that the United States would someday annex the country. Under American control, the value of their land would increase spectacularly, ensuring a magnificent return on their investment. It is unclear precisely what these wily speculators offered Babock in return for his cooperation, but a letter from one of the leading speculators written at the height of the crisis told the President's aide: ". . . we want to interest you in a *material* way, in our Survey Company. . . . Will advise further with you about the Bank, and if anything is done you shall be *in*."

Another eager participant in the conspiracy against Santo Domingo's independence was none other than the "heroic" President of that island nation,
Buenaventura Báez. The rewards promised him by the American businessmen
went so far beyond the paltry sums he could steal from the national treasury that
he was only too ready to terminate Santo Domingo's national sovereignty. More
than a year before Babcock's visit, he had offered to "sell" his republic to the
United States in return for $2 million and the promise of American warships to
keep him in power. At that time, with Andrew Johnson in the White House, there
had been no takers in Washington, but Báez expected better from Grant.

No sooner had Babcock's ship docked on the island than elegant carriages
whisked him away, his business colleagues in tow, to the province of Azua,
where Báez had built an impressive vacation retreat. When the Americans arrived, an open-air, late-afternoon banquet awaited them. The rich tropical sunset
provided the perfect conclusion for the meal, and afterward the party broke up
into little groups enjoying cigars under the cool evening sky. At that point, Báez
and Babcock managed to slip away to an interior room for a long, private
conversation.

Babcock remained in Santo Domingo for six weeks after that, but he spent
little time investigating minerals and agriculture or exploring the engineering
possibilities of Samaná Bay. In fact, Babcock seldom ventured far from the
Presidential Palace: all his energies were concentrated in top-level negotiations
with Báez. From the very moment he set foot on the island, Babcock's audacity
had been breathtaking, and for the duration of his protracted stay he never
bothered to write to Grant to tell the President what was going on. Instead, he
returned to Washington on September 6 and presented the administration with a
fait accompli: a fully detailed protocol providing for American annexation of
Santo Domingo. Among other things, Babcock had committed the United States
to "remit forthwith" $100,000 in cash and $50,000 in arms, and to protect Báez
against possible intervention from Haiti.

Babcock was in high spirits on the day Grant presented the agreement to his
Cabinet. The smiling aide waited in the Cabinet Room, proudly exhibiting
specimen ores and other island products to the Cabinet members as they walked
in. When they treated him coldly, Babcock took offense and departed, but
Grant went ahead with the presentation. "Babcock has returned, as you see,"
he said, "and has brought a treaty of annexation. I suppose it is not formal, as
he had no diplomatic powers; but we can easily cure that."

Part of the proposed "cure" was to send Babcock on a second trip to Santo
Domingo. This time he was accompanied by a U.S. Naval force, of which he
was designated "supreme commander." One of the purposes of this expedition was to help "maintain order" during the plebiscite on annexation that had
been planned by Báez. This notable exercise in democracy went forward exactly as planned: the official vote totals were 15,169 casting ballots in favor of
annexation and 11 brave souls voting against.

Having ascertained "the will of the people" in Santo Domingo and secured an official treaty, Grant and Babcock pressed forward to seek the approval of the U.S. Senate. Here they ran into one massive roadblock: Senator Charles Sumner, chairman of the Foreign Relations Committee. Sumner was outraged by nearly every detail of the proposed annexation, but he was particularly incensed at the role of Babcock. In a thunderous Senate denunciation, Sumner attacked the President's favorite as a "young officer, inexperienced in life, ignorant of the world, untaught in the Spanish language, unversed in International Law . . . and unconscious of the Constitution of his country."

Nonetheless, Babcock continued to play a leading role in lobbying for approval of his treaty. Santo Domingo was a "paradise of opportunity," he told a group of businessmen. "It's unbelievable," Babcock insisted. "There's mines there that would make Golconda look cheap, and the soil's so rich things grow while you look at them." Before long, the administration was backing up these seductive fantasies with political muscle. Grant cracked the whip over wavering Senators, threatening retaliation against any Republicans who voted against the treaty. Key federal appointments were openly traded for Senate votes. The incumbent Attorney General, Rockwood Hoar, was summarily asked to resign to clear the way for a political deal involving his seat on the Cabinet.

Yet Grant and Babcock were not the only ones who could play political hardball over the Santo Domingo issue. After a speech in Chicago, Senator Sumner sharpened his attacks to include hints of official corruption at the highest levels. The Senator told a reporter that he had been informed by a reliable source that much of the coast of Santo Domingo was already staked off into lots clearly marked "Babcock" or "Báez," with one or two particularly choice pieces of real estate designated with the name "Grant." Sumner's story was every bit as fanciful as Babcock's account of fabulous gold mines, but it succeeded in getting its point across. In fact, Babcock became so irritated at the Senator's attacks that he indicated that "if he were not officially connected with the Executive he would subject Senator Sumner to physical violence." Considering the Senator's past, this was a particularly ugly threat: in 1856, Sumner had been permanently crippled in a vicious beating on the Senate floor by a pro-slavery hothead.

By the time the Santo Domingo treaty came up for Senate vote in June 1870, passions on both sides of the issue were at a boil. The final roll call—with 28 in favor of ratification and 28 opposed—was a disaster for the administration. Grant had fallen far short of the necessary two thirds, and the bitterness of this defeat left a lasting mark on his Presidency. The chief executive was now more inclined than ever to view everyone in Washington as either an implacable enemy, scheming constantly against the administration, or a loyal friend and supporter who could be trusted absolutely. Rather than destroying Grant's confidence in Babcock, the Santo Domingo adventure actually brought the two men closer. Grant continued to refer to his aide by the pet name "Bab" and was, according to one White House clerk, "as affectionate with him as so quiet a man could be."

Babcock took full advantage of the situation and manipulated the President's emotions as skillfully as a virtuoso musician handling his chosen instrument. With no higher authority than his title as "Private Secretary to the President," Babcock wrote to personal friends boldly offering key diplomatic appointments. He also seemed to exercise a veto power over appointments recommended by others. Secretary of State Fish wanted to name the poet James Russell Lowell as Minister to Russia, but confided to a friend that "I know not whether 'Bab' will allow it." The appointment did not go through.

Meanwhile, with whatever time he could spare from his backstairs intrigues, Babcock supervised the massive federal construction projects that characterized postwar Washington. Grant, more than any President before him, took a personal interest in the development of the capital city. Babcock, with his engineering background, seemed the perfect man to coordinate federal plans, and he was given the official title "Superintendent of Public Buildings and Grounds" to supplement his White House responsibilities. In this capacity, he personally directed the remodeling of the executive mansion and other projects, spending hundreds of thousands of taxpayer dollars. As construction moved forward, there were persistent rumors that through such devices as false measurements and exaggerated cost reports, some of the money entrusted to him had found its way into Babcock's pockets. Grant cheerfully ignored such charges and wrote them off as the work of jealous rivals.

By the beginning of Grant's second term, Babcock and his pretty wife had established themselves at the top of Washington's social pyramid. In countless receptions and drawing rooms, Babcock was the center of attention: he smiled at everyone, and his ruddy cheeks flushed with enthusiasm. He became particularly celebrated for the gorgeous bouquets he brought with him everywhere —with flowers freshly picked from the White House greenhouses Babcock had constructed at public expense. Jesse Grant, the President's son, recalled Babcock as "the most disinterestedly friendly person I have ever known. His was almost a passion for helpfulness . . . . He was never so happy as when exerting himself in behalf of his friends, and to Colonel Babcock every acquaintance was a friend." One such friendship involved William Crook, a minor clerk on the White House staff. Years after Babcock's fall from grace, Crook recalled the episode of a famous Washington lawyer who came into the White House secretarial offices and told everyone about a marvelous, newly discovered mine. Here was the chance of everyone's life to make some money—and all that was needed was a modest investment. Crook had no capital, but he was so anxious to share in the "sure thing" that he hinted to Babcock that he needed a loan. Babcock responded immediately by offering $1,000 in cash, secured only by Crook's friendly promise. This episode shows admirable generosity and consideration on the part of Babcock, but it also demonstrates something else: that despite his modest salary as an Army officer Babcock was equipped with an impressive supply of ready cash. While Horace Porter, his fellow officer and White House aide, could not afford the price of a carriage, the Babcocks were enjoying the best of capital society and freely lending money to their friends.

Where did the money come from? By the first months of 1876, the answer to that question was well known to any American who picked up a newspaper.

The public humiliation of the President's top aide was a long, painful process that began innocently enough—with the appointment of Benjamin Bristow as Secretary of the Treasury. Bristow was a Civil War hero of stubborn integrity whose selection had originally been intended as a sop to the complaining reformers in the Republican Party. Yet no sooner had he settled into office than Bristow began to realize that the charges of corruption were, if anything, understated. The new Treasury Secretary began a secret investigation of the Internal Revenue Service which slowly revealed the outlines of a gigantic conspiracy. The frauds appeared to center in the Internal Revenue office in St. Louis. The head of that office was a third-rate political hack named John McDonald, who had been appointed by Grant at Babcock's suggestion. McDonald's administrative district included the three centers of the American distilling industry—St. Louis, Chicago, and Milwaukee—and McDonald had quickly developed a cozy arrangement with the leading distillers. Under this plan, rather than paying their full excise taxes to the government, the businessmen would pay bribes to McDonald and his agents, who in turn would submit fraudulent reports to Washington. The whiskey producers could save hundreds of thousands of dollars in taxes, while McDonald and his confederates grew rich. The few honest distillers who at first resisted this plan were brought into line by IRS harassment and intimidation. This impressive network of corruption soon spread into several states and cheated the government of $4 million in less than two years.

Bristow was anxious to bring the conspirators to justice, but an unseen hand seemed to frustrate his efforts. Every time he dispatched secret investigators to St. Louis to seize incriminating evidence, the whiskey conspirators seemed to know in advance that the agents were coming and the evidence invariably disappeared. It was a frustrating pattern, repeated several times, and Bristow came to the conclusion that the Whiskey Ring had a representative at the very highest levels of the executive branch. Yet at first, not even Bristow dared suspect that this representative was the President's own right-hand man and indispensable aide—that gallant soldier, Orville E. Babcock.

Later evidence revealed the rich rewards Babcock received for his efforts; it was clear that his honor could not be purchased cheaply. Babcock had pocketed some $25,000 in cash payments from his coconspirators, much of it sent through the mails in envelopes without return addresses. On one particularly pleasant morning, the postman brought Babcock a box of fine cigars sent from St. Louis; wrapped around one of the cheroots near the bottom of the box was a $1,000 bill. There were other tokens of esteem from McDonald and his friends, including a huge diamond shirt stud which weighed nearly four carats and cost $2,400. When Babcock showed disappointment over a flaw he discovered in the stone, it was cheerfully replaced with a finer one. With such generosity in mind, it is hardly surprising that Babcock found time for several trips to St.

Louis to confer personally with McDonald. During these visits, Babcock must have been lonely for his wife and children, because McDonald consoled him regularly with exquisite wines, delicious meals, and other delights of the city. It was in this context that Babcock first made the acquaintance of a fabled courtesan, known locally as "The Sylph." McDonald's lyrical description can perhaps give some idea of the lady's charms:

> Her form was petite, and yet, withal a plumpness and development which made her a being whose tempting, luscious deliciousness was irresistible. Most beautiful of face, with eyes of deepest azure, in whose depths the sun beams seemed to gather, and the fires of love from flames of flickering constancy, seemed ever and anon to melt into love itself. Her hair was like threads of gold and silver blended, and when she loosed her locks they fell like the shimmer of sunlight, and quivered like the glamor the moon throws on the water. She was the essence of grace, distilled from the buds of perfection, and with a tongue on which the oil of vivacity and seduction never ceased running; she was, indeed, a sylph and syren, whose presence was like the flavor of the poppy mingled with the perfumes of Araby.

Babcock proved no more immune to such "tempting, luscious deliciousness" than one might expect, and in return for The Sylph's pleasing company, as well as the other favors which McDonald lavished on him, he served as the Washington pivotman for the Great Whiskey Ring. As usual, Babcock performed with skill and audacity and managed to deflect the President's suspicions from the principals in the conspiracy. When Bristow presented Grant with evidence of the Whiskey Ring, the President responded, "Well, Mr. Bristow, there is at least one honest man in St. Louis on whom we can rely—John McDonald. I know that because he is an intimate friend and confidential acquaintance of Babcock's."

In order to succeed in his investigation, the determined Treasury Secretary resorted to extraordinary measures. A special squad of Treasury investigators was handpicked for integrity, ability, and discretion. When these men met to discuss strategy, they did so in some city other than Washington—usually in New York. All communications were in a new cipher personally devised by Bristow. Eventually, these precautions paid off in a successful raid of midwestern distilleries. Enough evidence was seized to indict more than 250 individuals. Babcock was not among them, but Bristow did turn up a number of suspicious telegrams sent from Washington to McDonald and his coconspirators. These communiqués appeared to warn the leaders of the ring of impending investigations by Treasury agents. "Put your house in order. Your friends will visit you," read one dispatch. Later came word that, "I have succeeded. They will not go. I will write you." Most of these telegrams had been signed with the mysterious code name "Sylph." Playing a hunch, Bristow searched out the originals on file in the Washington telegraph office. The handwriting on those forms was unmistakably Babcock's.

Certain that he had at long last cornered his wily foe, Bristow presented his evidence at a Cabinet meeting. Grant immediately called Babcock into the room to provide an explanation. The fast-talking aide never denied that he had sent the telegrams, but insisted that they had no connection with the Whiskey Ring. According to Babcock, the secret correspondence actually concerned the efforts of a nefarious woman called "The Sylph" to blackmail the President. He and McDonald had been struggling heroically and effectively to block this attempt.

This explanation satisfied no one other than Grant, and Babcock knew he stood on shaky ground. Vacationing with Grant at the seashore resort of Long Branch, New Jersey, he did his best to save himself by manipulating the President's suspicious nature. According to Babcock, Bristow was an ambitious schemer who lusted after the Presidency and hoped to build his own reputation by disgracing Grant. To bolster this point, Babcock and his friends showed the President a letter in which one of Bristow's lieutenants resolved "to reach the bottom or top of the White House" in the course of his investigations. Months later, testimony before a Congressional committee showed that the words ". . . or top of the White House" had been inserted as a forgery into a perfectly innocuous sentence in order to provoke Grant's paranoia. Such methods may seem crude, but they had their effect. As the much-heralded "Whiskey Trials" convicted one conspirator after another, the President summarily dismissed one of the most aggressive and successful prosecutors as an "enemy of the administration." Grant also violated every standard of judicial propriety by meeting with a member of the St. Louis Grand Jury who reported to the President on the secret deliberations of the jury room. Time and again, it seemed impossible to keep secrets from Babcock's prying eyes. On one occasion, the Solicitor of the Treasury confidentially reported to the President that he had secured eyewitness evidence that $500 had been mailed from St. Louis to Babcock. Within an hour, Babcock knew of it and blithely informed the Solicitor that anything said to the President was as good as said to him.

When Babcock's indictment became inevitable, the elusive suspect suddenly changed gears in his efforts at self-preservation. Loudly proclaiming his innocence to anyone who would listen, he insisted that a special Army court of inquiry be convened to investigate the charges against him and to clear his "good name." Grant thought this a splendid idea and instantly appointed three generals known to be sympathetic to Babcock. The ploy might have worked except that the prosecutors properly refused to hand over their evidence to military authorities and forced the President's aide to play his last, desperate trump card. A few days after Babcock's formal indictment on charges of conspiracy to defraud the government, Grant issued a startling circular through his Attorney General. The document prohibited the St. Louis prosecutors from offering immunity to suspects who turned state's evidence. By denying the government attorneys one of the basic tools used in all conspiracy cases, Grant seriously crippled attempts to gather evidence.

As his trial opened in St. Louis, Babcock tried to put aside his fears. He had retained the finest defense lawyers available, including three former judges and a former Attorney General of the United States. The judge in the case was a personal friend of Grant's who hoped that generous treatment of Babcock might win him appointment to the Supreme Court. The Republican press loyally portrayed the defendant as a martyred hero, and ran touching human interest pieces about his pregnant wife and two brave children, praying tearfully for their father's acquittal.

From the first day of the trial, the defense strategy was clear-cut. Babcock's lawyers made no attempt to explain away the mountain of incriminating evidence, but instead sniped at technicalities to prevent that evidence from reaching the jury. Even so, the prosecution offered a combination of original documents and eyewitness testimony potent enough to convince all but the most biased observers.

In Washington, Grant called an emergency Cabinet meeting to discuss the progress of the trial. According to one of those present, the President seemed "worried and excited." He showed the Cabinet officers a series of telegrams from the defense attorneys warning that Babcock would be convicted unless the President appeared personally as a witness. While the Cabinet sat in astonished silence, another dispatch arrived and was handed to Grant. It declared that the most recent speech by the prosecution indicated an absolute necessity for the President's testimony. With his jaw set, Grant announced that he planned to board the next train for St. Louis, and that he wanted to take at least two members of the Cabinet with him. In short, the President of the United States was ready to rush halfway across the continent to appear as a defense witness in a criminal prosecution instituted by his own government!

As soon as they overcame their shock, the Cabinet officers convinced Grant that a personal appearance would be a mistake, but they could not dissuade him from giving a deposition in support of Babcock. To Grant's military mind, it was unthinkable to desert a comrade under fire.

The President gave his deposition in the White House on February 12, the process occupying more than five hours of his time. The Chief Justice himself had been called in to act as notary. When this testimony was rushed to St. Louis and read to the hushed courtroom, it proved the turning point in Babcock's trial. In his deposition, Grant swore time and again that he had never noted anything in his secretary's conduct or conversation which indicated a connection with the Ring, and that in view of their unusually close relationship the President would certainly have known if Babcock had been guilty. After this emphatic statement, a vote to convict Babcock would have been a vote to accuse Grant of either criminal complicity or incredible blindness.

The last day of the trial, Babcock looked as if he had spent a sleepless night. His florid complexion was faded, and his eyes had a dull, watery expression as if he had been weeping. At 3 P.M., as the exhausted defendant rested quietly in his chair, the jury returned to the courtroom after only the briefest deliberations.

When the "not guilty" verdict was announced, he jumped up, his face crimson, and went straight to the jurors. His eyes filled with tears, he shook hands with each member of the panel, thanking them profusely, and then, in a typically expansive gesture, shook hands with everyone else in the courtroom, including the members of the prosecution. As he stepped outside onto the cold, sunny street, the waiting crowd cheered him, then escorted him triumphantly to his hotel rooms. Telegrams of congratulations began to pour in from all over the country and even from the capitals of Europe. Brandy and champagne flowed freely all afternoon and evening. At about 9 P.M., Babcock stepped outside his hotel, mounted a carriage, and gave a half-hour speech to a crowd of 400 that had gathered to hear him. There was also a serenade by the band from the Government Arsenal, the biggest and best musical ensemble in St. Louis.

At the White House, Grant received the news with undisguised satisfaction. He immediately sent his son Fred to Mrs. Babcock with congratulations. Upon hearing of the acquittal, the good lady reacted in the appropriate Victorian fashion: she fainted, and remained in hysterics for several hours.

Most thoughtful observers were stunned and disgusted by the verdict, and even some Republican newspapers admitted that Babcock had been acquitted solely on the strength of Grant's testimony. Other Republican organs were more partisan in their exultation. The Chicago *Inter-Ocean,* for instance, ran an editorial which compared General Babcock, somewhat implausibly, to Jesus Christ: "All honor to the jurors who were able to banish prejudice and do exact justice! Crucify him, crucify him did not reach the jury room. All honor to the court." In this same spirit, a charitable subscription was organized to cover Babcock's legal expenses. More than $30,000 was raised from leading Republicans, including a future President of the United States—Chester A. Arthur. The single most substantial contributor, a former Secretary of the Navy, was honored for his $5,000 gift when Babcock's newborn son was named after him.

Yet even such political allies expected that Babcock would resign his post as Private Secretary to the President upon his return to Washington. His continued presence at the White House would be an embarrassment to Grant and to the entire Republican Party, which faced an uphill battle in the forthcoming Presidential elections.

On February 29, however, when the Secretary of State arrived at the White House, he was horrified to find Babcock at his usual desk just outside the President's office. After passing the aide in frosty silence, Fish went in to Grant and complained bitterly. Grant assured the Secretary that Babcock's departure was imminent and that he had been invited back to the White House only for a few days. At the same time, Babcock told his friends in the press that rumors about his resignation were unfounded.

On March 1, when Secretary Fish returned to the White House, Babcock was still there. This time the President told Fish that Babcock was expected to resign at any moment. In fact, Grant had delayed his meeting with Fish for half an hour while waiting for that resignation to arrive. The situation was both ludicrous and pathetic: the President of the United States simply did not have the heart to demand the departure of his cherished favorite.

The stalemate might have continued indefinitely if other events had not intervened. On March 2, with Babcock's position still ambiguous, all Washington was buzzing with a new scandal. This time the principal was Babcock's good friend, Secretary of War Belknap, who all but admitted having taken bribes in return for trading post privileges on Indian reservations. As the administration continued its internal collapse, it became clear even to the President that he could no longer afford Babcock's controversial presence. By March 5, the Private Secretary had packed the mementos from his office and been formally replaced by Grant's son, Ulysses. At the President's insistence, however, Babcock maintained his position as Superintendent of Public Buildings and Grounds.

Then on April 16, less than two months after his Whiskey Ring acquittal, Babcock was indicted on new charges as a participant in the bizarre "Safe Burglary" conspiracy. This case involved an episode from nearly two years before, in which the office of the U.S. Attorney in Washington had been burglarized and key evidence stolen from his safe. The missing documents, according to the prosecution, included evidence of Babcock's guilt in submitting false measurements for one of his public construction projects. The prosecution went on to charge Babcock and his cohorts with planting some of the stolen evidence on an anti-administration reformer in order to discredit the man and to blame him for the burglary. The entire plot was so complex and foolhardy that only a man of Babcock's fabled audacity could have attempted it. After a much-publicized Washington trial, Babcock once again slipped through to acquittal, but this time there were widespread charges of bribery and jury-tampering. As the New York *Tribune* wryly reported the verdict, "The friends and employees of the accused, including perhaps half the jury, could not, we are informed, conceal their astonishment and their joy."

At long last, even Grant seemed to be losing confidence in his former aide. According to one newspaper report, the President was ready to "throw him overboard." Apparently, Grant instructed Bristow to fire twelve clerks in the Treasury Department who had been appointed at the request of Babcock. Yet other moves by the President seemed to tell a different story. Nothing was done to remove Babcock from his post as Superintendent of Public Buildings and Grounds, despite questions from leading Republican Congressmen. Furthermore, Grant managed to appoint him to yet another responsible and comfortable engineering position, as Inspector of Lighthouses for the Fifth Federal District. The week before leaving the White House, the President also found time to write an unqualified letter of thanks to his controversial friend. "For faithful and efficient service as Private Secretary for more than six years of my two terms of office," Grant wrote, "he has my acknowledgments and thanks, and the assurance of my confidence in his integrity and great efficiency."

After 1877, Babcock concentrated that "great efficiency" on his duties as

Lighthouse Inspector. He was given charge of a large staff and seemed to enjoy his numerous inspection tours throughout the country. Establishing a comfortable home near his headquarters at Baltimore's Fortress Monroe, Babcock frequently entertained old friends from White House days. They found him as pleasant, high-spirited, and generous as ever. Though it was rumored that he benefited improperly from proceeds of his various legal defense funds, Babcock played a quiet, respectable role as a "leading citizen." He saw Grant very rarely, but their relations remained intimate and cordial. As Grant confessed in his last years, "I have made it the rule of my life to trust a man long after other people gave him up."

In 1884, Babcock was 48 years old and still serving as Inspector of Lighthouses. President Chester Arthur, that onetime contributor to the Babcock Defense Fund, had nominated him for a minor Army promotion and the appointment was pending in the Senate. Near the end of May, Babcock sailed for Florida to check on construction of a new lighthouse at Mosquito Inlet, in remote, unpopulated country south of Daytona Beach. This intriguing tropical expedition seemed a good chance for relaxation and adventure, and Babcock invited several of his personal friends to accompany him. From the time they left Baltimore this jolly party was plagued by high winds and bad weather. At Mosquito Inlet, Babcock refused to delay their cruise further by waiting an extra day for the tug he had requested to tow his two-masted schooner over a treacherous sand bar. In politics and on the battlefield, Babcock had never been afraid to take risks. Boldly boarding a little whaleboat that had pulled up beside his ship, he ordered its captain to steer through the heavy seas toward Mosquito Bar.

All went well until they reached the enormous, sweeping breakers that crested over the sandbar. The six-man crew gripped the oars while Babcock and his assistants huddled nervously in the stern. As they soared upward, then came crashing down, the steering oar broke and the captain was thrown into the sea. He regained the boat, but it had tipped to one side and was filling. Another breaker roared up from behind and hurled them all into the water. As Babcock and his companions struggled for the surface, they were struck by the bulk of the heaving boat. Moments later, the survivors shivered in silence on the beach as they watched Babcock's body come sweeping in to shore. When the storm cleared a steamer arrived to pick up the corpse.

For days, the papers were full of stories of his death, and even the Democratic press saw his end as somehow heroic. It might have been expected of the flamboyant Babcock that even in his demise he would make good newspaper copy. When Grant heard of the disaster, he was approaching the sad end of his own life. Dying of throat cancer, deeply in debt, he still managed to mourn his old friend. "General Babcock was a very able man," he told the press, "and a brave and good soldier."

Historians have been less generous in their appraisal. William B. Hesseltine wrote that Babcock "fished for gold in every stinking cesspool and served more than any other man to blacken the record of Grant's administration.'' The kindest words Allan Nevins could muster were that ''under Napoleon or Mussolini, who knew how to use an unscrupulous talent, he might have made a great name.'' For better or worse, Babcock was the first White House aide to receive massive publicity and to openly manipulate the President he served.

William K. Rogers:
The Honest Incompetent

In place of Babcock's corrupt brilliance, William Rogers offered the country the well-intentioned fumbling of an honest man hopelessly out of his depth. His position in the White House depended entirely on his touching intimacy with Rutherford B. Hayes—a relationship reminiscent in its sentimentality and intensity of the later celebrated friendship between Colonel House and Woodrow Wilson. That emotional dependence and the weak staff operation it engendered played an unheralded though important role in preventing Hayes, an intelligent and sensitive chief executive, from living up to his potential as President of the United States.

Before coming to the White House, William Rogers had failed in three different careers as a minister, lawyer, and real estate speculator. Born in Circleville, Ohio, in 1828, he won his Episcopal ordination at Kenyon College not far from his home. After only a few months on the pulpit, however, he discovered that his bookish personality was ill-suited to the constant human contact demanded of a working minister. Rogers also complained of ill health. All his life he suffered from severe digestive problems, variously diagnosed as "chronic dysentery" or "acute dyspepsia," and it may be that he was the first of numerous Presidential aides who suffered from what we know today as ulcers.

It remains a mystery why Rogers thought that a legal career would agree with his weak stomach more readily than his work in the ministry, but by the age of 24 he had studied law, been admitted to the bar, and moved to the bustling metropolis of Cincinnati. As a matter of course, he joined the Literary Club of Cincinnati where he made the acquaintance of Rutherford B. Hayes, a fellow Kenyon alumnus who was six years his senior. Hayes had already won some success as a practicing attorney and he agreed to take Rogers on as his assistant. The younger man offered his new boss unqualified adulation and loyalty which more than made up for his lack of legal skills. Rogers was described by one contemporary as "kind and gentle-spirited as a child" and by another as a man "of delicate and slender frame, as gentle and modest and confiding as a woman." Hayes responded well to these qualities and declared his new partner to be "in his own way, pretty near perfection." The frail

53

young bachelor soon became a constant guest in the Hayes home, where an infant son learned to address him as "Uncle Billy."

The happy partnership might have gone on indefinitely, but in 1856 Rogers' health began to deteriorate. His doctors ordered him to abandon his law practice and to move away from the city, at least temporarily. Reluctantly, Rogers headed west and found a pleasant refuge in the unspoiled north country of the Minnesota Territory. Though he was physically separated from Hayes, their friendship developed a new intensity through the mails. Many of Hayes's letters to Minnesota were later destroyed by Rogers' heirs because of "the intimate nature of the manuscripts." Yet one of the surviving documents gives us an idea of the tone of the correspondence. "I wish you were my brother," Hayes wrote, "so I shall have a *claim* upon your thoughts and affection. . . . I feel lonesome and lost without you. So now be a good brother to me, write often." Hayes even entertained the idea of moving to Minnesota if it turned out that his partner was forced to stay there permanently. "I feel almost as if I would have to follow you," he wrote.

A developing political career, however, kept Hayes in Cincinnati. After distinguished service in the Civil War he won election to the U.S. Congress. Rogers, of course, had been too sickly for military service; preoccupied with personal affairs, he was married at the height of the war. Several years passed before Congressman Hayes had the chance to visit Minnesota and meet the bride, but when he did he pronounced her "a noble woman." He wrote to Mrs. Hayes that Rogers and his wife "seemed as happy as any family I have seen in a long time." During thirty-one years of marriage the Rogers produced four talented children, the youngest of whom was christened "Rutherford Hayes Rogers" in tribute to his father's friend.

Rogers' luck in supporting his flourishing brood was mixed, at best. Though admitted to the bar in Dakota County, Minnesota, his halfhearted attempts at the practice of law met with little success. By the year 1870, he had confirmed his total dependence on Hayes when he turned to his old friend as a long-distance business investor in some real estate speculation to develop shops and businesses in the new city of Duluth. This new partnership gave Hayes an excuse for several trips to Minnesota, where he enjoyed summer outings in unexplored woods and thickets with Billy Rogers following along "where his health and strength permitted."

The Republican convention of 1876 offered an absorbing drama for connoisseurs of the great sport of politics. There were several leading candidates for the Presidential nomination—including Benjamin Bristow, who had won a national reputation (and the hatred of the Republican establishment) for his relentless prosecution of Babcock and the Whiskey Ring. After six deadlocked ballots, the party leaders turned to a compromise candidate with no visible enemies: the favorite-son governor of Ohio, Rutherford B. Hayes. In anticipation of just such a surprise, Hayes had sent for Rogers to share his moment of triumph. As he received news of the nomination, Hayes was briefly "un-manned" and turned to his old friend with tears in his eyes.

Rogers naturally wanted to play a role in the campaign that lay ahead, but Hayes seemed to have a difficult time thinking of tasks for him to perform. The candidate's best friend wound up spending most of the summer in Boston, worrying over the preparation of an official Hayes biography. Finally, in the fall, Hayes was ready to trust Rogers with a campaign mission of genuine importance. The party professionals had decided that $100,000 had to be raised immediately to swing the crucial state of Indiana. In an emergency move, Hayes sent Rogers to the East Coast to approach a series of major capitalists. Rogers proved no better at raising money for a political campaign than he was at generating capital for his own business enterprises: he returned to Hayes empty-handed.

This marked one of many setbacks suffered by the Hayes campaign. Democratic Presidential candidate, Samuel J. Tilden appeared to sweep to victory in November. His popular vote total placed him ahead of Hayes by 260,000. The wily Republican managers, however, refused to accept defeat and began contesting returns from three Southern states. Success in these challenges could win the Presidency for Hayes by the barest possible majority in the electoral college—185 to 184. For months, bitter debate raged in Congress while the final result hung in the balance. It is to Rogers' credit that he had nothing to do with the shady maneuvers on Hayes' behalf; he gave up hope and went home shortly after the election.

Hayes, however, continued to expect the best and tried to recruit a White House staff. He turned first to two experienced Ohio politicians but both men turned him down. The salary and prestige of White House service seemed beneath their dignity, and the well-publicized misdeeds of Orville Babcock had given a bad name to the post of private secretary. Billy Rogers, however, was in no position to pass up a job, and Hayes decided at the last minute that his old friend would be an acceptable choice. As an ordained minister and a man without contaminating political experience, no one could question his personal integrity.

When he arrived at the capital, Rogers received the traditional greeting Washington reserves for rank outsiders suddenly elevated to positions of power: he was socially snubbed and bitterly criticized. "It was unfortunate for Mr. Hayes that he felt obliged to appoint as his private secretary Mr. Rodgers (sic) of Minnesota," sniffed the nation's leading political reporter, Ben Perley Poore. Rogers did little to advance his own popularity with the press. In general, he treated reporters as if they were some lower form of life, and resolutely denied them the juicy tidbits and "inside information" that Orville Babcock had provided so graciously. Perhaps the best indication of the press attitude toward Rogers was that it took the New York *Times* two full years to spell his name correctly.

The Hayes administration was marked by bitter patronage battles between the President and Congressional leaders of his own party. The rage of these Republican potentates was only increased when they visited the White House and found that the President's top aide neither knew nor cared who they were. On countless occasions, a skillful intermediary might have helped smooth relations between the President and Congress, but Rogers' hero worship led him to treat even the mildest critics of Hayes as The Enemy. He soon became so unpopular with leading politicians that some of the duties performed by strong private secretaries in the past had to be taken over by the President's 22-year-old son, Webb. At all Cabinet meetings it was Webb Hayes, and not Rogers, who sat at the President's side taking notes and handling papers.

No matter how disappointing his performance, Rogers' position remained secure because of his continued intimacy with the President. Feeling totally isolated from the rest of Washington, Rogers found a home a block from the White House, and his children were the constant playmates of the youngest members of the First Family. Andrew Rogers, who was 5 years old, became a special favorite at the White House. Over the summer months Rogers and his wife frequently joined the Hayes family for relaxing cruises down the Potomac River to explore historical sites in Virginia. Hayes and Rogers also liked to unwind with long, rambling discussions about God, fate, and the afterlife. Hayes had a strong religious streak, but tended to be unconventional in his approach while Rogers, as a former clergyman, advanced the claims of traditional belief.

During the hectic, disorienting years of his Presidency, Hayes placed enormous value on Rogers' familiar company, childlike simplicity, and unquestioning loyalty. Occasionally, the President would consult him on some intraparty maneuver or ask his help in preparation of a veto message. But Rogers' chief function was to provide Hayes with moral support *after* a major decision had been reached. In one typical interchange, Hayes showed Rogers an already finished speech, prepared for delivery at a soldier's reunion. The aide responded with enthusiasm, assuring the President, "It is so good!" and then repeating his verdict with emphasis. Hayes seemed to appreciate such praise, even though he noted in his diary that Rogers "thinks well of almost anything I do."

As the President's term drew to a close, Rogers began to offer Hayes a distorted view of the prospects for reelection. Hayes had announced early in his Presidency that he intended to retire after four years, but Rogers seemed anxious to stay on in Washington. "It would be a long story to tell of the numbers who took an interest in the second term talk for you," he reported to Hayes. Unfortunately, that interest was not strong enough to prevent Hayes' retirement, and when the President returned to Ohio in 1881, Rogers decided to follow him. He settled in Columbus to practice law with a much younger man, abandoning his onetime home in Minnesota. He hoped that his reputation as a former Secretary to the President would bring him clients, but Rogers also invested much time and energy in efforts to revive his real estate projects in Duluth. Hayes was still a partner in these enterprises, but not even the sponsorship of a former President could assure Rogers' success. In a melancholy diary entry in 1887, the 65-year-old Hayes reported a visit from his old friend. "He is interested with me at Duluth," Hayes wrote. "Hence his visit . . . . He added two thousand dollars to the debts for which I am his surety." Hayes still saw Rogers as "a man of fine culture, noble sentiments, a true friend" but realized that he was "so unselfish and unsuspecting that his business ventures have generally been failures."

The two men saw each other for the last time when Hayes paid a visit to Rogers' Columbus home in the winter of 1892. The former President's last years had been saddened by the death of his wife, and the conversation soon turned to that favorite topic of old: the immortality of the soul. As evening descended and Hayes got up to go, Rogers dropped one last remark concerning his own confidence in a life after death. "Hold fast to that," Hayes said as he moved toward the door, "hold fast to that."

A few months later the former President was dead at 70; Rogers followed him to the grave in August of the same year. Friends of the onetime aide reported that he had been busy with his law practice up to the very day of his death, when struck by a sudden attack of angina pectoris. In tribute to Rogers, one small-town Ohio paper observed that "as private secretary to the President his responsibilities at least equaled, and his labors, not to mention the delicacy of his duties, much exceeded those of a cabinet officer." Nevertheless, "he studiously avoided public mention and was entirely content with the love of his family and the esteem of his friends."

Rogers proved so successful in this pursuit of obscurity that his obituary never appeared in the national press. He was one of the most passive and least ambitious men ever to serve in the White House and seemed decidedly out of place in a position of responsibility. As with Robert Johnson and Orville Babcock, his experience illustrates the risks a President takes when he allows nonrational personal factors to dominate his relationship with a top aide. As we shall see, many later Presidents, including Jimmy Carter, have unhappily ignored that lesson.

CHAPTER THREE

THE SILENT PARTNERS

The Presidents who occupied the White House from 1881 to 1897 left something less than an indelible impact on the national imagination. Thomas Wolfe eloquently described three of them—Garfield, Arthur, and Harrison—in his short story "Four Lost Men." They "had been living, real and actual people in all the passion, power and feeling of my father's youth. And for me they were the lost Americans: their gravelly vacant and bewhiskered faces mixed, melted and swam together in the sea-depths of a past intangible, immeasurable and unknowable as the buried city of Persepolis."

If these Presidents have vanished from our consciousness, then what of the aides who served them? Those assistants—Joseph Stanley Brown, Daniel Rollins, and Elijah Halford—are the real "Lost Men." Their stories nonetheless merit our attention and contain elements of courage, deceit, assassination, romance (with a President's daughter), ghostwriting, resourcefulness, self-sacrifice, illness, and religious faith.

The fourth White House aide discussed in this chapter—Grover Cleveland's longtime friend and confidant Daniel Lamont—may not exactly be a household name but has at least escaped the dismal obscurity that envelops the others. During his patron's second term, he became Secretary of War—one of the first Presidential assistants to use White House service as a stepping-stone to a position of visible power. In terms of political savvy, native intelligence, and administrative ability, Lamont had every advantage over his boss. Contemporaries agreed that without him Cleveland might not have been President and certainly could not have succeeded in the office.

What all four of these men had in common was a quiet but dedicated approach to their work. After the heroics of the Lincoln era and the blundering corruption of the Gilded Age, the White House staff had reached a point of stability and modest competence.

Joseph Stanley Brown:
Rookie of the Year

On the morning of July 2, 1881, President James A. Garfield sat down at breakfast with his chief aide to deliver a set of last-minute instructions. After four wearing months in the White House, the President was about to leave on his first vacation. He planned to attend his class reunion at Williams College, and then go on with his family for several days of outdoor relaxation in the beautiful Berkshires of Massachusetts. During his absence, the business of the White House would be left in the hands of his private secretary, Joseph Stanley Brown. It was a heavy responsibility for a boy of 22—a gangling, homely youth with no executive experience.

After breakfast, the young secretary went up to his second floor office and set to work. It was a Saturday, with Congress in the midst of its summer recess, and the crowds of office-seekers that had plagued the executive mansion during the first weeks of the new administration had now disappeared. Sitting at his desk, staring out at the radiant lawns and clear hot skies, Brown felt a sense of tranquility that was extremely rare for a White House aide. Then the door to his office opened suddenly and the President stepped in, followed by the Secretary of State. "Never have I seen two finer looking specimens of men," Brown later recalled. "They appeared, as they smilingly said their farewell, almost debonair or rather like two splendid college boys off for a joyous lark." The President's last admonition to his aide was, "Goodbye, my boy. . . . Keep a watchful eye on things and use the telegraph freely if necessary." With a gracious handshake he strode off down the stairs to his waiting carriage.

Brown returned to the routine paperwork on his desk, but half an hour later he was interrupted once again. One of the White House doormen, who normally would not have bothered the President's Private Secretary, came haltingly to his desk and whispered, "Mr. Secretary, there is a rumor that the President has been shot." After the briefest moment of shock, Brown dismissed the servant with a smile and a wave of the hand. "Nonsense!" he said. "The President has no enemies and the story cannot possibly be true." Yet hardly had the doorman left the room than an official messenger staggered to Brown's desk. "Oh, Mr. Secretary, it's true!" he cried. Garfield had been shot by a frustrated office-seeker while waiting for his train at the Washington station. "They are bringing the President to the White House now," the messenger warned.

Another man might have been paralyzed by shock, but Brown sprang immediately into action. A room had to be readied for the wounded man and doctors summoned. Washington police had to be called in to guard the White House. The War Department had to be put on alert. The press had to be handled and curious crowds kept away. The President's family, already away on vacation, had to be notified and comforted.

By the time the bleeding President arrived at the White House on a pile of mattresses loaded on the back of a wagon, his 22-year-old secretary had already taken firm command. From the second-floor window, Brown watched as Garfield was slowly carried to the South Portico on an improvised stretcher. As they bore the President carefully up the stairway, Brown stood to one side and looked down. The President's hand "feebly moved in recognition and around his lips hovered a wan smile." For Brown, "the temple had fallen, and the idols lay shattered." In the eighty days that followed, he faced one of the greatest challenges ever encountered by a White House aide. He came to this trial with less preparation, and from a more unlikely background, than any of the Presidential assistants who preceded him.

Brown's grandfather was a fugitive from English debtor's prison named Nathaniel Stanley. After arriving in Baltimore he wanted to change his name but was unable to come up with anything more imaginative than "James Brown." His male descendants kept the "Stanley" as a middle name. His grandson, Joseph Stanley Brown, was born in the slums of Washington, D.C., on August 19, 1858. His only education came at the Washington public schools. While still a teenager he managed to teach himself shorthand, and also the new and very unusual skill of "type-writing." These qualifications enabled him to secure a stenographic position at age 17 with John Wesley Powell, the scientist and explorer who was the founder of the U.S. Geological Survey. Powell was involved in frequent battles with Congress to win funding for his various projects, and one of his most dependable allies was the rising Congressman from Ohio, James A. Garfield. It was well known that Garfield was shorthanded for secretarial help, and as reward for the Congressman's loyal support, Powell offered him the part-time services of the energetic young stenographer, Mr. Brown.

On the December morning in 1878 when Brown walked into his office for the first time, Garfield saw an awkward adolescent, with a square, clumsy jaw, protruding ears, and wavy hair. "Well, young man," Garfield sighed, "what can I do for you?" Brown straightened up and answered in the best Horatio Alger fashion, "It's not what you can do for me, but what I can do for you, sir." What he proceeded to do that morning was to take down twenty-five letters with astonishing speed and accuracy. In the months that followed, working for the Congressman primarily in the evenings and on weekends, Brown managed to make himself indispensable to Garfield.

In the summer of 1880, Brown was as startled as the rest of the country when the deadlocked Republican convention turned to his boss as a dark horse Presidential nominee. Brown feared that this new prominence would drive a wedge in their friendly relations, but Garfield told him, "I need all my friends now. Please stand by, old man, and look after things as usual." As Brown recalled years later, "Events were certainly moving at an accelerating pace for me, and every day held a new thrill."

Garfield conducted his campaign from his home in Ohio, which was the usual practice for Presidential candidates in those days, and the young secretary happily moved into the attic. He shared this space with Garfield's two oldest sons and when additional guests arrived the three boys were driven into the barn. In every way, Brown came to function as a member of the family. On election day they all sent a round-robin letter to the two boys who were away at prep school, and the note included some friendly words from "Joe Brown." "Jolly feed," he reported, "canvas-backs, oysters, ham in champagne. Yum yum. Wish you were here."

On the whole, Brown's work during the campaign left little time for such diversions. The volume of mail was absolutely staggering and Garfield insisted on answering all of it. The New York *Times* reported that between the nomination and the inauguration more than 100,000 letters had been mailed from the tiny village post office near Garfield's home. As Brown recalled, "It was drudgery, but for an impressionable youth there was great exhilaration in this game of national politics."

After that game was won, and Garfield had eked out a razor-thin victory in November, the demands on his secretary temporarily relaxed. Brown spent a joyous Christmas with the Garfields, complete with "family councils in the evenings before the winter fires, when every aspect of the future was discussed from White House decorations to Cabinets." According to Brown, Garfield made it a practice to try out controversial suggestions on the family dog. Soon the secretary had taken the place of this honorable canine, "but always with the privilege of barking back."

One of Garfield's most perplexing problems involved the choice of a White House staff. "I am more at a loss to find just the man for Private Secretary than for any place I should have to fill," he wrote to a friend. In correspondence with his predecessor, Rutherford B. Hayes, Garfield showed a pointed awareness of the shortcomings of past Secretaries to the President. "I know there were many heart-burnings . . . growing out of Grant's course on that subject," he wrote, while tactfully ignoring the heartburnings that grew out of Hayes' selection of the inept William Rogers.

Garfield's first choice as Private Secretary was John Hay, the brilliant writer, politician, and diplomat who had worked with Lincoln and Nicolay some twenty years before. Much to Garfield's disappointment, Hay had no interest in returning to the White House. He politely declined the job offer, claiming that the post required "a stronger heart and a more obedient nervous system than I can hope to boast.'' As he warned the President-elect, ''the contact with the greed and selfishness of office-seekers and bull-dozing Congressmen is unspeakably repulsive.''

As the President-elect pondered alternatives to Hay, the press was full of rumors and suggestions. Two of Garfield's longtime personal friends seemed interested in the job, but the President-elect was unwilling to appoint them. He was concerned about charges of ''cronyism,'' especially after the experience of his immediate predecessors. As inauguration day approached, Garfield decided to put off his decision indefinitely, and thereafter, through sheer force of inertia, Joseph Stanley Brown drifted toward the top White House post. No formal announcement was made, but as Brown continued to play a larger and larger role in the preparations for the new administration, it became common knowledge that he would continue at the President's right hand.

On the stormy night before the inauguration, Brown was up till dawn making copies of the President's address. In the morning, with the Washington streets piled high with snow, he delivered the text to the national news bureaus. After returning to his room at 8 A.M., he ate breakfast and then crawled into bed, utterly exhausted. He slept till four in the afternoon, and by that time the ceremonies were over and he was anxious to join the new President in the White House. When he arrived at the gate of the executive mansion, however, he was paralyzed by the sight of the cool imposing columns and massive doors of the center of national power. He must have wondered whether he belonged there after all, as he tried to determine what he would say to the guards and the servants in order to gain access to the President. Yet no sooner had Brown's foot touched the bottom stair than ''the miraculous happened'': the main door flew open and a black doorman boomed out, in the most respectful and ingratiating tones, ''This way, Mr. Secretary.'' William Rogers, outgoing Secretary to the President, was waiting upstairs to greet his successor.

Some of the permanent White House clerks were less gracious in welcoming Brown; one of them described him, rather contemptuously, as ''the new and *very young* private secretary.'' Though he was a political nonentity who had won his job largely through default, Brown acted swiftly and decisively to establish his authority. His first move in the White House was an unequivocal order to servants and clerks that all individuals—and even visiting cards—must go first to Brown before being sent to the President. Brown accurately weighed his own assets for the job. ''I knew Washington life, had no illusions, some courage, a fair sense of humor, and intense loyalty to my chief.'' He also understood that his paramount duty as chief White House aide was ''the protection of the President from the public—and I might add, his friends. . . .''

During the first weeks of the Garfield administration, this was no easy task. For Brown, ''each day saw the milling of a hungry mob of job hunters working overtime. I understood what it meant to be thrown into a den of wild beasts as were the ancient martyrs.'' One typical incident involved the postmistress from Fort Worth, Texas. When informed by the Postmaster General that her chances for reappointment were slim, she broke all rules of procedure and went straight to the White House. As she told her story to Brown, she gradually became more and more emotional until she burst into a fit of hysterical weeping. The thirty or forty other petitioners who were also waiting in the secretary's office looked on with interest as Brown struggled to take the situation in hand. "The only thing to be done," he recalled, "was to place her firmly but gently in an easy chair commanding a view of the beautiful grounds with its early spring flowers and whistling blackbirds, and admonish her to regain composure." Later, "the dear lady made other and less tearful calls . . . and the Postmaster General in the end proved to be kind."

By the end of May, business at the White House had begun to settle onto a more even keel, but the strain of those first three months had taken its toll on Brown. Living in the White House in the same second-story bedroom Nicolay and Hay had shared, he found it impossible to escape from the constant demands of his work. Mrs. Garfield became concerned for his health, and at her suggestion the President agreed to send his exhausted aide on a vacation. Six million dollars in government bonds had to be delivered personally to London, and Brown was assigned that undemanding task. Despite minor irritations on his trip, he was grateful for the "bracer." His absence also made the President more conscious than ever before of the value of his young aide, "I miss Brown (who is today in mid-ocean)," Garfield confided to his diary, "for his anticipating thoughtfulness in reference to office work." Two days later, the President repeated the theme. "The crowd of callers was very great. I miss Brown whose tact saved me from many people. . . ."

When Brown returned to the White House on the evening of July 1, Garfield was delighted to see him. The President could now leave for the Massachusetts vacation he had been anticipating, secure in the knowledge that his aide would be on hand to run the White House. "You have had your holiday," he told Brown, "now I am going to have mine." The next day—July 2, 1881—Garfield was cut down by an assassin's bullet.

Twentieth-century medical practices could probably have saved his life and even by the standards of the time he seemed to have a good chance for recovery. For more that ten weeks he lay immobilized and occasionally delirious, hovering between life and death. During the crisis, Vice-President Chester Arthur found himself in a particularly difficult position since Garfield's assailant had noisily proclaimed himself a member of Arthur's faction in the Republican Party. With a real threat of executive chaos, the only government officer willing to take responsibility for White House administrative decisions was the President's young and inexperienced secretary.*

Brown's courageous and unfailingly competent response to the challenges of those difficult months won him the respect of all Washington insiders. Under

* Since 1967, the Twenty-fifth Amendment to the Constitution has provided for the temporary succession of the Vice-President in cases of Presidential incapacity such as Garfield's.

Brown's direction, the White House was transformed into a temporary hospital to give the wounded President every chance for recovery. All those who sought to enter the building were now required to show an official pass, signed personally by Brown. In order to keep the public fully appraised of the President's dramatic fight for life, Brown developed a new and more businesslike relationship with the press corps. He released regular bulletins every morning, afternoon, and evening. It was out of the question to trouble the wounded President with the avalanche of mail that descended on the White House, but Brown knew that Garfield would want the letters to be answered. In order to handle letters and other documents, Brown ordered the construction of a special stamp with a replica of Garfield's signature. It was the first time that such a stamp was used in the White House.

As if these labors were not enough, Brown accepted additional burdens with the President's family. He showed special concern for Garfield's only daughter, Mollie—a lovely, sensitive girl of 14. Just four weeks after the shooting, Brown found time to accompany Mollie and the younger children on a summer outing to Mount Vernon designed to lift their spirits. Mollie reported in her diary that "the weather was just perfect & we all rushed around generally. Poor Mr. Brown," who was no doubt thoroughly exhausted from his White House ordeal, "had to lie down for a little while because he felt the motion of the boat and it made him ill."

For Brown, the worst moment of that bitter summer came one night when Mrs. Garfield summoned him.

> Waiting a moment until control of her voice was assured, she said, "Will you tell me just what *you* think the chances are for the General's recovery?" One look in the anguished face of that wonderful woman and I threw truthfulness to the winds, and lied and lied as convincingly and consolingly as I could. As soon as decency permitted I excused myself, but once beyond the door all restraint gave way and I was an utterly shattered and broken secretary. The whole period was one prolonged, hideous nightmare . . . .

The Washington heat became intolerable in early September and Garfield himself requested a move to the seashore. The doctors okayed the plan, and the President was painstakingly transported to the resort town of Elberon, New Jersey. Brown naturally accompanied him. At first, the change of scenery seemed to lift Garfield's spirits, but then his condition took a sudden turn for the worse. On the night of September 19, Brown retired early, leaving word with the servants that he should be called if necessary.

> Towards midnight there came the fateful tap on my door. I can still hear the long solemn roll of the sea on the shore as I did on that night of inky darkness, when I walked from my cottage to his bedside. The family and physicians were present, and the scene was tragic and harrowing beyond words to describe. Gradually the

gasping breath came at longer and longer intervals, and in a few minutes the venerable Dr. Hamilton stepped to the bedside and gently and tenderly composed the features of the heroic soul he had learned to love.

For Brown the agony was not yet over. It was deemed essential that some member of the official household be present at the formal autopsy. In order to spare the Garfield family, it was Brown who volunteered.

After the funeral and the final farewells to the President, Mollie Garfield wrote:

> It has been a long time since I wrote in my diary, & I feel like a different girl now. We all thought darling Papa was on the sure road to recovery, but we were all mistaken. . . . I had almost forgotten to speak of one person, who has been a great help and comfort to Mamma, through all of this, and this is Mr. Brown. For so young a fellow, he certainly has done *well*. Even on that awful 2nd of July, when everything and everybody were in such confusion, by the time we reached Washington all was in running order, every man knew just what he had to do, & there were no questions, 'What must I do & where shall I go?' Mr. Brown had arranged everything. And so it was from the time Papa was hurt till now. I will say for Mr. Brown, that he has as much good common sense as any older man with a great deal of experience.

Apparently the new President, Chester A. Arthur, agreed with her. He asked Brown to stay on at the White House, and for three months the weary secretary helped the new administration put itself in order. Arthur wanted Brown to remain at his job permanently but the young man declined. His energy had been totally drained and he felt an overriding commitment to the Garfield family.

At the request of Mrs. Garfield he devoted the next two years to sorting and arranging the late President's papers. None other than John Nicolay, hard at work on his own Lincoln biography, had written to Mrs. Garfield urging her to appoint one of the President's most intimate associates to attend to that task. Brown was the obvious choice and was given responsibility for the twenty-nine huge packing crates filled with Garfield's papers. These treasures were stored by Brown in a specially constructed fireproof chamber not far from his bedroom, complete with the most up-to-date security alarm.

While Brown remained in Washington the Garfields returned to Ohio and Mollie, for one, came to feel the separation more keenly than she had expected. On October 29, 1882, she reported in her diary: "Last week nearly every day I had a fit of the dumps. I don't know but the main reason is I miss Mr. Brown so much." In the pain and confusion following the assassination, she had found herself powerfully drawn to the man who took her father's place as a source of strength. A month before her sixteenth birthday she confessed, "I believe I am in love. . . . I don't believe I will ever in my life love any man as I do Mr. Brown—and it can't be merely like . . . and it isn't infatuation, for when I first knew Mr. Brown I didn't like him at all. Maybe Mr. Brown has a vague, very vague idea about me. But that, I can't tell.''

Mrs. Garfield watched her daughter's growing infatuation with concern. Despite his services to the family and to the country, Brown hardly seemed a suitable choice as romantic hero for a young girl. He was plain and poor, with no education and hazy prospects. Mrs. Garfield was deeply attached to the young man, but accepting him as a son-in-law was a different matter. Nevertheless, in the event that Mollie persisted in her feelings it seemed best to prepare Brown as far as possible. In 1885 he was sent off to Yale at Mrs. Garfield's expense, where he pursued the study of geology. His interest in the subject grew out of his two years as secretary to Major Powell of the U.S. Geological Survey, and Brown proved to be a gifted scholar.

By the time she was 20, the handsome Mollie Garfield was recognized as one of the most marriageable women in the country and rumors about her future began to fill the press. When Mrs. Garfield whisked Mollie away to England in the fall of 1887, the newspapers reported that she did so in order to take the girl's mind off Joseph Brown. Though he refused to discuss the matter with reporters out of consideration for the Garfields, Brown soon found himself cast as the hero in just the sort of romantic and melodramatic spectacle that the nineteenth century loved. He was seen as the poor young man of "pluck and principle," hoping that true love would conquer social barriers and allow him to marry the daughter of his former boss. Eventually, Mrs. Garfield decided to give in to public opinion and the wishes of "the young folks." She told the press that "gossips have presumed to put Mr. Brown in a false position . . . . Instead of opposing the suit of Mr. Brown I have welcomed it. I know how manly he is and how worthy of every confidence." Brown met the Garfields at the dock upon their return from Europe and was allowed to present Mollie with a ring. To forestall wagging tongues, Mollie openly admitted "it is a small stone, but a *very* good one."

Only one obstacle remained in the path of true romance: it seemed to Mrs. Garfield quite out of the question that a President's daughter should marry anyone with the unspeakably prosaic name of Joe Brown. She suggested to Brown that since his grandfather's real name had been Nathaniel Stanley, and since Stanley had been the traditional middle name of all males in his family anyway, he should legally change his name to Joseph Stanley-Brown. The young man agreed, and the wedding announcements featured the first public appearance of his elegant new name.

The ceremony was held at the Garfield home in Mentor, Ohio, a few weeks after Stanley-Brown received his degree from Yale. Details of the scene enchanted readers of society pages everywhere. Joseph asked Mollie not to wear a veil because it looked "unnatural," and after their vows the newlyweds went in to supper through a curtain woven entirely of daisies.

As a honeymoon, the Stanley-Browns sailed to Europe, where Joseph studied geology at Heidelberg. Back in the United States, he went to work for the U.S. Geological Survey, then left government service for a series of middle-level business positions. In 1899 he met E. H. Harriman, the famous railroad tycoon, who invited the onetime Presidential aide to become assistant secretary of the Union Pacific. Later he entered a major New York banking house as director of its railroad properties. He eventually became a full partner in the firm and grew conspicuously wealthy. In 1929, at age 70, he sold out his share of the business just a few short months before the stock market crash. The uncanny luck that had aided him from the beginning stayed with him to the very end. He lived to see the professional success and social prominence of all three of his children: after all, these well-to-do offspring were the grandchildren of a President of the United States. During the last years of his life, Stanley-Brown spent much of his time in the fashionable California community of Pasadena, where he had purchased a winter home. He died there at age 83 in November 1941; Mollie survived him by six years.

At the time of his death, Stanley-Brown was hardly a conspicuous figure: his small New York *Times* obituary appeared next to the death notice of "ANDREW J. KENNY, 71, QUEENS SEWER CHIEF." To his friends and acquaintances he was the comfortable and conventional businessman Joseph Stanley-Brown—they would never have recognized young Joe Brown, the scrappy, hardworking assistant to the President of the United States.

Brown's stay at the White House had lasted less than a year; it was only a small part of his long life and distinguished career. He was never tempted to return to politics, and near the end he must have looked back on his experience with Garfield as an out-of-place boyish adventure. Yet it was more than that. At a moment of national crisis, a youth of 22 performed invaluable service to his country and added new dignity to the traditions of White House service. For that above all, Brown deserves to be remembered.

Daniel G. Rollins:
The New York Connection

Never before had the members of Congress looked forward to the President's annual message with such an odd combination of curiosity and dread. Everyone in Washington knew that Chester Arthur, who had come to office at the death of Garfield, was woefully unprepared for the responsibilities of the Presidency. The only public office he had ever held was Collector of the Port of New York. He had been a faithful cog in New York's Republican machine for some twenty years until the national leaders attempted to please that machine by giving Arthur the "harmless" slot of Vice-President on the ticket of 1880. When Garfield died in September 1881, even Arthur's closest associates were horrified at the prospects for the nation. "Chet Arthur, President of the United States!" one of them exclaimed. "Good God!"

As the Clerk of the House read the President's words on December 6, the members of Congress listened with "an air of interest not often attained of late years in reading productions of this sort." Many of them had expected the worst from the new President, but Arthur's lengthy message demonstrated an impressive grasp of the issues facing the nation. His language was forceful, often elegant, and he managed to strike just the right tone of dignity and responsibility. The next day the entire nation seemed to breathe a sigh of relief. The headline in the New York *Times* announced "THE PRESIDENT'S MESSAGE: AN ABLE REVIEW OF NATIONAL CONCERNS," while the *Tribune* seemed stunned at the fact that Arthur's state paper "was quite up to the average of such compositions." *Harper's Weekly* reported that "the message has impressed the country very favorably, and . . . has won for Arthur a regard and confidence which we trust will be retained throughout his administration."

It is doubtful that the public reaction would have been as favorable as it was if the nation had known the truth about Arthur's message—that every word of it had been written by another man. Moreover, the real author of the document was neither a member of the President's official staff nor even a resident of the national capital. He was a working politician in New York City, whose decisive but well-concealed role in the Arthur administration marks a unique chapter in the history of Presidential assistants.

The name of Arthur's long-distance advisor was Daniel G. Rollins. He was born in Great Falls, New Hampshire, in 1842 to a family of eleven children. The Rollins clan had long before established itself as one of the state's leading families: Daniel's father was a respected probate judge and one of his cousins became a U.S. Senator.

In school the young man proved himself a prodigy. He enrolled at Dartmouth at age 14, yet graduated as salutatorian of his class. He was one of the youngest graduates in Dartmouth history, and at 18 he was ready for Harvard Law School.

Rollins began his legal career in 1863 in Portland, Maine, where he also played a role in the local Republican organization. Three years later his political connections won him an appointment as Assistant U.S. Attorney in New York, and Rollins moved to the city permanently. He earned a reputation as a brilliant public prosecutor, particularly gifted at demolishing defense witnesses under cross-examination, and "his name soon became a terror to offenders awaiting trial." The press often commented on his extreme popularity with his fellow lawyers. "His well knit, neatly dressed little figure with his fine massive head was one of the most familiar and one of the most agreeable sights at the bar," said the New York *World*. A lifelong bachelor and a self-proclaimed "man's man," Rollins was compared to a "banty-rooster" with a sharp Roman nose, curly black hair, and a bushy mustache. He naturally traveled in New York's most elite social circles, including the fashionable (and staunchly Republican) Union League Club.

Another member of that club was Chet Arthur, the tall, portly, side-whiskered "gentleman boss" of the New York Customs House. In addition to common interests in fine wines and Republican politics, he and Rollins shared a strong tie as loyal sons of Psi Upsilon fraternity. For Rollins at Dartmouth and Arthur at Schenectady's Union College, membership in Psi Upsilon had been an important adolescent experience, and both men maintained a lifelong interest in fraternity affairs. As President, in fact, Arthur hosted a special dinner for Psi Upsilon in the White House, and on another occasion sent a telegram to the fraternity's convention in which he urged "his brethren" to "sing for my sake the old refrain:

> Then till the sands of life are run
> We'll sing to thee Psi Upsilon
> Long live Psi Upsilon! Psi Upsilon!"

The friendship between the two fraternity brothers blossomed quickly. Rollins frequently abandoned his lonely suite of rooms at 80 Madison Avenue to enjoy the lively hospitality of the Arthur home at 123 Lexington. Despite protests from Arthur's long-suffering wife, Chet and his friends dearly loved the evenings they spent together drinking, talking politics, and smoking cigars till the small hours of the morning.

Rollins became New York's District Attorney in 1881, the same year Chet Arthur became Vice-President. Despite the pressures of his job, he naturally found time to stand by his friend during the difficult period while Garfield battled for his life. Rollins and two other comrades were with Arthur on the night of September 19 when a messenger boy arrived at 11:30 with news of the President's death. Within minutes, telegraphic dispatches confirmed the first report. Rollins rushed out to find a judge to administer the oath of office and stood close at hand while Chester Arthur was sworn in as the twenty-first President of the United States.

The new President delayed two months before moving into the White House and spent a long time trying to organize his staff. Having never before lived in the capital city, he found himself surrounded by men he did not know or trust. Eventually, he developed personal confidence in Joseph Stanley Brown, but then Brown insisted on leaving the White House. To fill Brown's place as Private Secretary, Arthur selected a former aide from his Customs House days—an amiable young man named Fred Phillips. Phillips responded to the demands of his job with the dignity and restraint of a true gentleman: according to one of the clerks at the executive mansion, Phillips "usually got to the office about 10 or 11 o'clock and left early in the afternoon." During more than three years in the White House, Phillips' most celebrated accomplishment was shooting an alligator at close range while accompanying the President on a hunting trip to Florida.

Given this vacuum on his Washington staff, it was inevitable that Arthur would turn to his old friend in New York for aid and guidance. In particular, the President understood that a successful message to Congress was crucial to establishing his credibility as chief executive. Rollins, supplied with reports and recommendations from Cabinet members, began working on the speech weeks in advance in an atmosphere of total secrecy. In a letter from New York on November 12, he complained of ill health and apologized to Arthur for the slow pace of his work. In the same letter, Rollins seemed obsessively concerned that no one learn the details of his working relationship with the President. He scrawled the word "Private" in large letters across the top of the document and in the body of the note demanded: "Please tell me how I can address you so that the letter will truly be opened by nobody but yourself." This request strongly suggests the existence of additional pieces of intimate correspondence between Rollins and Arthur, but such letters have never been found. Rollins' precautions were so effective, in fact, that his authorship of Arthur's key speeches remained a well-kept secret until 1925. In that year C. M. Hendley, one of the second-level White House secretaries, revealed in a transcribed interview that Rollins wrote not only Arthur's first Congressional message in 1881, but all of his subsequent annual messages as well. Hendley recalled that Rollins used to come to Washington regularly to advise the President and put finishing touches on crucial state papers. On one occasion, Hendley was one of the secretaries assigned to work with Rollins, copying the words that would later be released in the name of the President.

Despite his continued residence in New York, Rollins found numerous opportunities to work with the President. In addition to his regular visits to

Washington, the two men frequently vacationed together. After Mrs. Arthur died of pneumonia in 1880, the President delighted more than ever in Rollins' hearty bachelor companionship. In the summer of 1882 they cruised together along the coast of New England and the next year Rollins accompanied the President on a much-publicized trip to Yellowstone Park.

In 1884, Arthur made a halfhearted attempt to win the Republican nomination for a Presidential term in his own right. Rollins, who had recently been elevated to a minor judicial position in New York, was prevented from assisting Arthur in an overtly political manner, but he remained on hand as the President's confidant. Arthur seemed almost relieved when the Republican convention nominated another man: that decision freed him to return to New York and the gracious, easygoing life that he loved.

In retirement, Arthur's activities were limited by deteriorating health. For several years he had been suffering from Bright's disease—a wasting kidney ailment—and a year and a half after leaving the White House the former President died at age 56. Rollins waited at the bedside during Arthur's last hours of consciousness and acted as one of the executors of Arthur's estate.

After his friend's death, Rollins pursued his career with less spectacular success than he had enjoyed as the favorite of a U.S. President. In 1887 he lost a race for the New York State Supreme Court, then entered private practice and devoted his energies to advancing the interests of a series of corporate clients. In 1897, while enjoying a summer vacation at his family's "old homestead" in New Hampshire, he died peacefully at the age of 55. The newspaper obituaries were extravagant in praise of the legal and judicial abilities of this brilliant, busy little man—but they never mentioned his participation in the administration of Chester Arthur.

Even today, Rollins' role remains totally unrecognized and perhaps that is the way he would have wanted it. Certainly, the acute shortage of documentary evidence is no accident. We know that most of Arthur's personal and official papers were willfully destroyed, though the circumstances of that destruction remain a mystery. One of the ex-President's close friends, Oscar Masten, guessed privately that Rollins, as executor of the Arthur estate, was the responsible party. As recently as 1970, Arthur's 99-year-old son-in-law advanced another story: that the former President, lying on his deathbed, ordered a functionary to fill three large garbage cans with papers and then burn their contents.

Whatever the true circumstances, many details of the Arthur-Rollins relationship will never be known. From our modern perspective, for instance, it is hard to understand why Rollins never took a full-time position on Arthur's Presidential staff. In 1881, however, the move from New York District Attorney to Presidential assistant would have been an unthinkable step down. Insiders might recognize the importance of a President's chief aide, but the public's understanding lagged far behind. It remained for the next administration—that of Grover Cleveland and Daniel Lamont—to take a series of giant strides in winning institutional respectability for the position of Presidential aide.

Daniel S. Lamont:
The Assistant President

On election night 1884, Daniel Lamont chewed nervously at the edges of his brush mustache as he watched the returns come in. The other members of Grover Cleveland's inner circle began celebrating prematurely, but Lamont knew better. He was Governor Cleveland's private secretary, and during the months of the Presidential campaign he had been closer to the nuts and bolts of the Democratic operation than anyone else. He knew the situation in every state, and on election night he manned a special telegraphic command post in the New York governor's mansion. In the next room, Cleveland sat back beaming and received the congratulations of his cronies, but for his quiet, bald-headed secretary the real battle was only beginning.

In the late hours of the evening a young man appeared at the gates of the governor's mansion with an urgent message. The stranger was unwilling to give his name or divulge the nature of his mission to anyone other than Cleveland or Lamont. The guards would have kept him outside all night if a lower-level aide hadn't overheard the confrontation and offered to escort the young man upstairs. Behind closed doors the stranger revealed to Lamont that he was an operator in the local telegraph office. In the course of his work that evening he had noticed a startling and secret dispatch going out over the wire. The Republican managers in New York City were ordering their upstate operatives to "go slow" in counting the votes—to delay official tallies as long as possible and wait for further instructions. With Republicans in control of fifty of the sixty county election boards in the state, this would give them enough time to tamper with local returns and throw the state to the Republican candidate, James G. Blaine. Lamont knew that the race was unbelievably close all across the country, and a Blaine victory in New York would assure him the White House. Quickly thanking the young man—whose name has been lost to history—Lamont snapped into action.

For weeks in advance of the election, he had worried about the accuracy and honesty of the vote count—after all, "The Fraud of '76" was still a painful memory. In that election eight years before, the Democrat, Samuel J. Tilden, had won an apparent victory only to be denied the Presidency by postelectoral manipulation. In order to avoid a similar disaster, Lamont had arranged for a loyal Democrat to monitor the vote tabulations at each of the 2,000 polling places in New York State. Now, with his worst nightmares about to come true, he proposed to use this little army to protect Grover Cleveland's vulnerable victory. He prepared telegrams to each of his monitors, sending out a clear and urgent message: make sure that the count in your district is completed swiftly and that the returns are filed by noon tomorrow according to provisions of the election law. Lamont worked alone except for the assistance of one weary staff member, and this man received some heavy teasing from the Presidential candidate. "The work is all over!" Cleveland called out from the midst of the continuing celebration. "Shouting time is here. Come in and shout." Fortunately for the Democratic cause, Lamont and his friend refused the invitation and continued toiling till dawn. Questions came in from across the state about proper procedures in tabulating the votes, and Lamont calmly answered them all. As the sun came up over the stone hulk of the state capitol, Lamont dragged himself from his desk and walked out to buy a morning paper. Unofficial returns in the press awarded Cleveland New York State—and the election—by the hairbreadth margin of 1,200 votes. Yet any illusion that the fight was over was quickly dispelled that afternoon by a succinct telegram from the Republican nominee. "Claim everything!" Blaine ordered his troops, and the party faithfully proceeded to do just that. The outcome of the election remained in doubt for more than a week as the politicians scrambled over recounts and challenges in half a dozen states. As the tension mounted, supporters of the two candidates took to the streets in noisy demonstrations for their favorites. Grover Cleveland chose to ignore the turmoil and refused to take command of the situation. Concerning one set of top-secret calculations on the continuing vote count in New York, Lamont admitted that Cleveland "doesn't know anything about these figures. I haven't dared show them to him. I don't know what he would do, but I know very well what I want to do." What Lamont wanted to do was to call a special session of the Democratic State Committee and authorize untold thousands of dollars for the hiring of 300 election lawyers—five for each country—to ensure the honesty of Republican officials. He also handled the press and public, issuing constant affirmations of Democratic confidence. "We have won this fight, and by the living God we'll hold it!" he declared, in the strongest language this soft-spoken man was ever heard to use.

At long last, ten days after the election, even the most die-hard Republicans were ready to concede defeat. The final count in New York showed

563,154 votes for Cleveland
562,005 for Blaine.

In the closest Presidential election in American history, a switch of just 575 ballots would have changed the outcome. As the Democratic managers began to breathe more easily, they got together one evening for a post-mortem and some choice cigars. There was no question for any of them that Lamont's efforts had made the difference in securing Cleveland's victory. At the very least, his foresight and determination in the post-election struggle had spared the nation a damaging and unresolved electoral crisis. In light of his role in Cleveland's triumph, Lamont's unprecedented importance in the administration that followed is somewhat easier to understand.

This extraordinary man was born on February 9, 1851, in Cortland County in central New York State. His ancestors were hard-working Scottish farmers who could trace their lineage back to the year 1250. Lamont's father earned his living as a country merchant and young Daniel spent long hours working in the family store. In rural America of that era such general stores were often centers for political discussion and activity, and by age 16 Daniel had developed a lively interest in the Democratic Party. At 17, Daniel went away to Union College in Schenectady. From the beginning, Lamont found it difficult to concentrate on his studies. His letters to a friend back home are full of descriptions of fishing expeditions—angling was one of his lifelong passions—and sophisticated comments about local electoral contests. Lamont participated in state senatorial and assemblymanic campaigns in Schenectady—an unusual step for a college boy in the 1860's. When his candidates triumphed, Lamont wrote home that "my chances for a good position at Albany are excellent." Sure enough, he managed an introduction to Governor John T. Hoffman, who was so impressed with the precocious politico that he wanted to incorporate Lamont into the party apparatus. Dropping out of school at age 19, Daniel accepted appointment as deputy clerk of the New York Assembly. "I am the youngest person that has occupied a like position in some time," he proudly announced in one of his letters. "My salary will range from 7 to $10 per day—so you can see I hope to at least pay my way, while the experience will be worth something to me."

Almost immediately, it was worth a seat as delegate to the state Democratic convention—even though Lamont was still below voting age. At the convention, and through much of his subsequent career, he distinguished himself by his absolute loyalty to his party's leaders. After reaching age 21, Lamont returned home and ran for county clerk and then assemblyman. In both cases he made an honorable showing in a "red hot Republican district" but lost by a few hundred votes. In future years he received many offers to run for public office but was never tempted again. He always preferred the subtle pleasures of behind-the-scenes power to the risk and confusion of personal campaigning.

Through the 1870's, Lamont worked at a series of quiet party jobs, moving up steadily in the Democratic hierarchy. He served as clerk to the Democratic Central Committee, then as chief clerk in the New York Department of State. Lamont was widely praised for his "astonishing facility for keeping his mouth shut"—an admirable quality in a politician. "If it be true that 'speech is silver but silence is golden,'" one powerful Congressman observed, "then Lamont was a bonanza gold-mine." Reform-minded Governor Samuel J. Tilden took full advantage of this Democratic treasure, and advanced Lamont as one of his key friends and advisors. When Tilden ran for President in 1876, Lamont helped coordinate that campaign and watched in desperation as the Republican candidate, Rutherford B. Hayes, "stole" the election. In 1878, Lamont took a job as a reporter for the Albany *Argus*—a newspaper published by Daniel Manning, boss of Albany County and chairman of the statewide Democratic Party. Much of the day-to-day administration of the paper was left to Lamont, and the ambitious young man eventually acquired a financial interest in the journal.

In 1882, Lamont's boss Dan Manning helped engineer the election of Grover Cleveland as governor of New York. Cleveland's one year as mayor of Buffalo had won him a reputation for rugged integrity, but he knew next to nothing about state politics and administration. A burly, bull-necked bachelor who found it difficult to accept advice, he stubbornly resisted the idea of appointing a private secretary. As governor-elect he wanted to do all his work himself, but a few weeks before inauguration the press of mail and administrative duties began to overwhelm him. He notified Daniel Manning that he needed help, and the state chairman knew just the man for the job. Manning quickly gave Lamont a leave of absence from his duties on the *Argus* and sent him off to Buffalo to assist Grover Cleveland.

For Lamont, the new situation was full of possibilities. With the Presidential election less than two years away, the Democrats suffered from a shortage of attractive candidates. As the governor-elect of the nation's largest state, Cleveland was mentioned as a Presidential possibility before he even took his oath of office. Whether his star would continue to rise, or whether he would be shunted aside as one more exploded hope, would be determined by his performance in the first few months as governor. Because of Cleveland's inexperience, that performance depended to an unusual extent on the competence and energy of his aides.

Cleveland was lucky to find Lamont and he knew it. "Lamont is a wonderful man," he told a friend. "I never saw his like. He has no friends to gratify and no enemies to punish." Cleveland appointed Lamont as his permanent aide and gave him the position of "military secretary," complete with the honorary rank of colonel. It was one of the ironies of Lamont's career that this most unmilitary little man should be known for the rest of his life as Colonel Lamont.

A man less subtle and flexible would have found Grover Cleveland impossible to handle. Lamont soon learned that the only way to work with the man was to employ what one capital reporter euphemistically described as "indirection." A good example of Lamont's slick technique came early in the term when the governor planned to appoint a man to state office whom the secretary knew to be totally unworthy. Rather than bringing his objections directly to Cleveland's attention, Lamont enlisted the aid of the lieutenant governor in a confidential scheme to block the appointment. One morning while Cleveland and Lamont were working side by side at their desks the lieutenant governor walked in according to plan. After a brief greeting to Cleveland, he went up to the governor's secretary and began a casual conversation about Lamont's "old friend," the controversial appointee. The lieutenant governor had heard that the man had been visiting Albany recently and wondered whether he had been sober at the time. At this point Cleveland, who had returned to his paperwork, set down his pen and began eavesdropping on the conversation that was, after all, being staged for his benefit. After the little skit was finished, Cleveland's opinion had been changed and another man received the appointment.

Lamont's attempts at manipulating the governor were seldom so complex, but careful calculation remained a consistent theme in their relationship. In private, Lamont once spoke of the need to keep "The Big One" from "jumping the track." Lamont's influence in Albany was so pervasive that one reporter awarded him the private nickname "The Other Governor."

Certainly, Cleveland's trust in his clever aide seemed to be absolute. When he went away on a brief hunting and fishing vacation, he left Lamont in charge of the governor's office and also, to an extent, in charge of the governor himself. "I wish you would tell me how long I can stay here," he wrote to Lamont from his mountain retreat.

On a normal working day the two men toiled together for ten hours or more, often leaving the office past midnight. These hours may have made sense for the bachelor Cleveland, who had few interests outside his work, but Lamont had a family to consider. In 1874 he had married Julia Kinney, a childhood friend from his native village, and they soon had three daughters. Mrs. Lamont stoically resigned herself to her husband's impossible schedule and devoted her time to "doing what was best for his career." This meant cultivating a special friendship with Cleveland, and she became one of the governor's favorites.

By 1884, Lamont had done such a good job in establishing Cleveland's reputation as a capable governor that "Grover the Good" won his party's nomination for the Presidency. The campaign that followed was "practically managed" by Lamont, according to the New York *Tribune,* "although others had the name of having conducted it." Lamont proved himself a master of detail and also displayed impressive gifts as a political image-maker. For Cleveland, the key phrase in the campaign was the famous declaration, "A public office is a public trust." The phrase was repeated endlessly by Democratic orators, discussed time and again in the newspapers, and even today appears in high school history texts as a quote attributed to Cleveland. The fact is that Cleveland never spoke those words or claimed them as his own, even though he expressed similar sentiments on several occasions. The source for the candidate's most celebrated aphorism was a heading from a Democratic campaign pamphlet—a pamphlet prepared by Daniel Lamont.

After the dust had settled on the bitterly contested election, and on Lamont's successful efforts to prevent vote fraud, it was widely assumed that "the Colonel" would serve as Cleveland's White House secretary. The only one who wasn't sure about this arrangement was Lamont himself. He was exhausted from the electoral ordeal and wanted more time to spend with his family. He also found a number of business possibilities in New York more attractive than the office of Private Secretary to the President. Cleveland, however, was absolutely adamant about his need for Lamont and they argued the matter for weeks. At one point, another member of the staff was visiting the executive office and casually mentioned the rumors about Lamont's going on to Washington.

"I don't know about that," Lamont replied. "My interests lie here in New York."

Cleveland suddenly swung around in his chair and grunted, "You're going to Washington with me. If you don't go, I won't. That's all."

Lamont smiled "a hopeless sort of smile" but did not reply. A few weeks later he was on the train to the national capital.

Lamont's record in Washington shows that Cleveland was wise in insisting on his friend's continued service. The teamwork of the two men, their joint approach to every detail of executive business and their seeming ability to read each other's minds, deeply impressed contemporary observers. Early in the term reporters dubbed Lamont "The Assistant President": he was the first person in American history to be regularly hailed by that title. By the end of Cleveland's first term, the New York *Times* was describing him as the most successful Presidential aide since the days of Lincoln and Nicolay and raving about Lamont's "universal popularity."

Even members of Congress joined the chorus of praise. Representative Champ Clark, who later became Speaker of the House, felt Lamont was entitled

> . . . to one benediction from the Sermon on the Mount: "Blessed are the peacemakers." In politics . . . that was his chief business; and certainly since that famous utterance no man needed a peacemaker on his staff more than Mr. Cleveland. He had no equal in provoking men to wrath and Lamont no rival in applying poultices and administering soothing syrup. As an emollient for soreheads and sore-headed politicians he excelled slippery elm or anything else in the *materia medica*.

The secret of Lamont's success was his ability as a sympathetic listener. When an irate politician arrived in the secretary's White House office, Lamont tilted back in his chair, fixed the visitor with his smiling and attentive eyes, and sat quietly until the man was finished. An enormous mustache covered Lamont's mouth, obscuring his expression and leading some observers to describe him as "inscrutable." By the middle of Cleveland's first term, Lamont's characteristic silence became so well known that it served as the subject for an anonymous poet pretending to be Cleveland's voice in a Republican campaign pamphlet:

> And this explains why we are never wont
>   To trust to any save our friend Lamont . . .
> Dan knows our inner life, and so discreet
>   Is he, the world imagines us a Cato;

Our sottish, unchaste life would prove a treat
   To scandal-mongers seeking toothsome data;
But all who try to pump good Daniel meet
   The silence of a most discreet potato.

The mention of Cleveland's "sottish, unchaste life" alluded to the President's habit of enjoying an occasional drink in the White House. Public suspicions were first aroused by reports that Cleveland and Lamont would sit down to dinner in a glum mood, and then emerge an hour later full of smiling good fellowship and jollity. Eventually the awful truth came out: both the President and his secretary relished brandy and soda or straight whiskey with their meal. It would never do for a respectable journal to report such an abomination directly, so the New York *Tribune* adopted the euphemism "mince pie" as a code word for whiskey. "Have another quarter of mince pie with me," it reported the President urging Lamont after a particularly frustrating day, "and we'll eat forgetfulness to the issue."

After dinner, no doubt invigorated by their indulgence, the two men invariably returned to work. They toiled even longer hours than they had at Albany, and it was not uncommon to see lights in their offices burning past two in the morning.

Daily visits by Lamont's children played an important part in White House life, providing Cleveland with some of his rare breaks from official routine. Often in midmorning the President walked with the two little girls down to the fountain on the south grounds to feed the goldfish. He found their company so delightful that in April 1885 he asked all of the Lamonts to come live with him in the White House. "I am sure we can arrange matters in quite a nice way," he wrote, and promised that "Mrs. Lamont could boss the job in the internal arrangements." The Lamonts eventually turned down his invitation but tried to spend as much time as possible in Cleveland's company.

In the long run, temporary visits from old friends could not satisfy the President's deepest needs. For several years he had entertained the idea of marrying Frances Folsom, the beautiful daughter of his onetime law partner. Since her father's death in 1875, Cleveland had served as guardian to the girl and ten years later, shortly after her graduation from college, President Cleveland formally proposed marriage. The resulting engagement remained a closely guarded state secret. As Cleveland complained to his sister about his plans, "I can't talk to anyone about them except the Colonel." When the press finally discovered the sensational news that the President was planning to end his bachelor state, Miss Folsom happened to be out of the country. Cleveland worried about the way the reporters would pounce on her when she returned from Europe, and so dispatched Lamont to rescue the maiden. As soon as the ship docked, Lamont whisked the bride and her mother aboard a special vessel waiting in the bay, conveyed them successfully to a hotel, then returned to Washington to report to the President and help with the wedding arrangements. The next few weeks in the White House were even more hectic than usual, as national attention focused on the great event. Poet Eugene Field, best known for his children's verses, turned his talents to a series of "White House Ballads." One of them, "The Tying of the Tie," described the bachelor awkwardness of "Sir Grover" as he tried, unsuccessfully, to knot a wedding cravat on his thick neck. At the last moment he was saved by the plucky "Sir Daniel," who mounted a chair and did the job in short order.

Even for professional jesters, it was hard to exaggerate Lamont's importance in the preparations. Once the President and his bride "Frank" (for Frances) had escaped to their honeymoon retreat in Deer Park, Maryland, Cleveland immediately wrote his secretary: "Frank and I have been talking a good deal today about the wedding and in recalling the details of the affair we have run against you so often that I think we are both willing to admit that if it hadn't been for 'poor Colonel Lamont' (as Frank calls you when she recounts all you had to do) we shouldn't have been married at all." Believe it or not, Cleveland went on to urge the Lamonts to join the bridal pair on their honeymoon. "You have had so much to do with all that concerned our marriage that we should be glad to have you the first to see us in our new relations."

The publicity surrounding the wedding substantially increased the President's popularity, but it by no means assured him of reelection. The Republicans united behind a bland former Senator from Indiana named Benjamin Harrison, while the Democrats were plagued by poor organization and lackluster campaign leadership. Lamont provided no small share of what brains were actually used in the canvass, but his continuing White House responsibilities precluded the sort of comprehensive role he had played four years before.

As the campaign heated up, some Republican propagandists turned their fire on the Cleveland-Lamont relationship; for the first time since the fall of Orville Babcock, the personality of a White House assistant became a matter of public controversy. In a Republican booklet called "The Imaginary Conversations of 'His Excellency' and Dan," Cleveland was portrayed as a bumbling pawn in the hands of the secretive, devious Lamont. In one of these conversations, entitled "Getting Ready for Emergencies," the two men look ahead to their gloomy prospects in the upcoming elections:

> HIS EXCELLENCY: Dan, it is possible, of course, that something may occur to cause me to—ah—change my residence after the 4th of March, 1889, but if not, you will understand that your present position is open to you as long as you wish to keep it.
>
> DAN: I am greatly obliged to you, your Excellency.
>
> HIS EXCELLENCY: Yet, if something unforeseen should happen—and if you should conclude to take the governorship of New York at any time—why, in that case you—you would want a—a private sec—
>
> DAN (with emotion): I understand, my dear friend. You shall have the place, Grover, if anything happens.
>
> HIS EXCELLENCY (relieved): Thank you, Dan.

This skit was only a campaign fantasy, but there was also serious speculation that Lamont might seek the New York governorship. Most Democrats agreed he would make an excellent candidate, but after Cleveland lost his bid for reelection Lamont resolved to turn away from politics. He had ignored his own interests far too long while serving Cleveland, and now he proposed to build financial security for his family. As Secretary to the President, he had developed a friendship with Navy Secretary William C. Whitney. Whitney was a New York millionaire with heavy interests in the city's developing transit industry. After the Democrats were turned out of the White House, Whitney put Lamont to work consolidating all the existing streetcar lines into the new Metropolitan Traction Company. Within four years the former White House aide managed to build a personal fortune and establish a reputation as one of the best financial managers in New York.

During Benjamin Harrison's Presidency, Cleveland spent much of his time in his cottage on Cape Cod. Though he enjoyed the presence of his wife and infant children, his letters to Lamont are one long, lonely plea for additional companionship. "And now I want to write to you upon a more important subject than any other that will find a place in this epistle, and that is the matter of your proposed visit here," he wrote in July 1890. "Our house is much larger than the one we had last year. . . . I believe we could make you quite comfortable." A year later the former President was still trying to lure his old friend into a visit. "I know it is not always easy to break away from family and other pleasant surroundings to make visits, but I hope it is not necessary to tell you how delighted we would be to see you here. . . . There is no politics in the atmosphere of this place, and we can promise you that you will not be annoyed at all with the anxiety of anyone here on political subjects or movements. The trout season closes Sept. 1 but I believe we can find good bass fishing."

Lamont usually declined these invitations: his business enterprises demanded nearly all of his time. He worked so hard, in fact, that he became seriously ill and his doctors ordered a long trip abroad. Before his departure Cleveland wrote him, saying, "A great many friends will miss you, but none of them I believe as much as I, for though I don't see you so very often I kind of feel safer when you are in the country." There could hardly be a more direct statement of Cleveland's dependence.

In 1892 the former President decided to make another run for the White House and Lamont naturally took charge of the campaign. When Cleveland swept to a surprisingly easy victory—thereby becoming the only President ever elected to nonconsecutive terms—he wanted Lamont to return with him to the White House as private secretary. The rising corporate executive, however, had little desire to resume his old job. As one of his friends tactfully informed Cleveland, "there is such a thing in politics as promotion," and Lamont would consider nothing below a Cabinet post. Since Cleveland could hardly conceive of another term as President without Lamont's support in Washington, his old friend was duly appointed Secretary of War. Lamont's only prior connection to the military was tenuous indeed: his purely honorary title of colonel. As one

Congressman wryly observed, "No able-bodied man in America looked less like a son of Mars or a disciple of Bellona than Mr. Secretary Lamont."

Fortunately, the nation was at peace during the years Lamont presided over the War Department and he enjoyed enough free time to resume his role as Assistant President. The New York *World* claimed that Lamont's real title should have been "Secretary of Politics and Expediency" rather than Secretary of War. He was constantly at the President's side and the most powerful men in the country sought his ear as a means of reaching Cleveland. When steel baron Andrew Carnegie wanted to communicate his views on the Venezuelan boundary dispute, he contacted not the Secretary of State but Secretary of War Lamont. "If you think worth while," he wrote, "I should like the Great Chief to know of this idea." Even the Vice-President of the United States felt that he had to go through Lamont in order to win favorable treatment from Cleveland. "The few recommendations I have made for appointments have met with so little favor that I am reluctant to call attention to the request again," wrote Vice-President Adlai Stevenson, founder of the Illinois political dynasty. "I can say to you truly that you are the only gentleman connected with the administration to whom I would make mention of this matter." Lamont's influence over every branch of government was presumed to be so great that whenever he went to New York a crowd of some thirty office-seekers would board the same train in hopes of "buttonholing" him along the way.

One of the reasons for Lamont's continued dominance in the second Cleveland administration was the absence of serious rivals for the President's favor. Two weeks before the inauguration, Cleveland plaintively wondered "why there are not, within the circle of my life, more Lamonts. . . ." Certainly the new Secretary to the President, Henry Thurber, did little to fill the chief executive's needs. Thurber was a well-connected and well-intentioned socialite with no political ability, and much of the power normally associated with the President's secretary passed to Lamont. Enjoying unprecedented influence in the government and the special prestige of his Cabinet post, the years as Secretary of War were happy ones for Lamont. For the rest of the country, however, those years marked a time of suffering and hardship.

Two months after Cleveland's inauguration the stock market collapsed and plunged the nation into the worst depression it had experienced up to that time. Nearly 20 per cent of the work force was unemployed and many of the laborers who managed to keep their jobs were forced to accept drastic cuts in pay. The situation inevitably exploded in a series of bitter labor struggles. The most famous of these was the Pullman Strike, which disrupted rail traffic across the country. Rather than negotiate with their starving employees, the railroad operators turned to Washington with the request that federal troops be used to break the strike. To his credit, Lamont was one of the few Cabinet members who opposed government intervention. His advice was based on purely political rather than moral or humanitarian grounds: he feared that the use of the U.S. Army would offend Democratic politicians in Illinois. When pressure from the business community mounted, Lamont's reservations disappeared and he faithfully administered Cleveland's decision to send in the troops. The result was widespread rioting and bloodshed in a strike that previously had been characterized by its peaceable restraint. During the height of the crisis, Cleveland hardly slept and Lamont took up temporary residence in the White House in order to be close to his chief.

Throughout the years of the Depression, Lamont showed greater concern for the profits of major businessmen than for wages of American workers. While Congress debated tariff schedules in 1894, he spent most of his time trying to influence the outcome while taking his instructions directly from Wall Street. Lamont's onetime business partner, the powerful tycoon and former Navy Secretary William C. Whitney, sent the Secretary of War regular memos with requests for favorable governmental treatment. Lamont faithfully advanced his friend's interests and managed to serve himself in the process. Using Whitney's tips on the stock market and his own inside information, Lamont made a series of profitable investments and occasionally shared his knowledge with his friends. One clerk in the federal land office recalled, "Dan Lamont told me to buy, and said to hold on until a certain price was reached." Following this advice, the young man realized a profit of $34,000 on an initial investment of $5,000.

The success of such speculation and the recovery of the entire economy might have been seriously undermined if the public had known the truth about the President's health. On May 5, 1893, Cleveland noticed a rough spot on the roof of his mouth. An examination by the White House physician revealed a cancerous growth the size of a quarter. An immediate operation was imperative or the President's life might be endangered. After consultation with Lamont, Cleveland feared that news accounts of his illness might send the already faltering stock market into a totally disastrous tailspin. In this situation, Lamont's well-known propensity for "keeping his mouth shut" proved an invaluable asset. He was the only Cabinet member taken into the President's confidence, and he handled all preparations for the top-secret operation. There was even discussion between Lamont and the operating physician on developing a cipher code for their letters "in case anything unfortunate happens." In order to avoid suspicious reporters, the surgery was performed while the President was "on vacation" aboard a private yacht cruising down New York's East River. Most of Cleveland's upper left jaw, part of his palate, two teeth, and some diseased bone tissue were surgically removed. After the operation the ship took the President directly to his summer home on Cape Cod, where Lamont told the press that Cleveland was tired from his duties and needed time alone. Later, when rumors began to circulate about a serious illness, the resourceful Lamont assured a press conference that it was "only a bad case of dentistry." This same story about the routine removal of two decayed teeth also served to explain Cleveland's slight difficulty in adjusting to the artificial jaw of vulcanized rubber which had been fitted into his mouth. In order to protect the President's secret, bold-faced lies were occasionally necessary. In New York, Lamont told reporters that "stories of an operation are absolutely untrue and without a particle of foundation" and suggested that such rumors "ought to subject the authors to criminal prosecution." As it turned out, the President's operation proved a complete success. Cancer never reappeared and Cleveland lived on for fifteen years. It wasn't until 1917, long after the death of all the principals, that the public learned the truth for the first time. Lamont had successfully engineered one of the most remarkable cover-ups in White House history.

After his surgery the President's reliance on Lamont became more intense than ever before. In a letter from his vacation home in 1894, the President wrote, "I want to see you very much indeed. . . . I am sure that our cool air would do you good. There is a matter I ought to act on within the next week, concerning which I feel that if possible I must have your advice." On another occasion, after once more requesting advice, the President of the United States added a plaintive note. "Can you not write me a letter?" he begged.

When Cleveland left the White House in 1897, the nation's economy had not yet revived and the President was despised by much of the country. He retired to a quiet colonial house in Princeton, New Jersey, while Lamont returned to New York to resume his business career. In short order, Lamont won appointment as vice-president of the Northern Pacific Railroad and as a director on the boards of more than a dozen other corporations. The former Secretary of War made thorough use of the government contacts acquired during his years in Washington though his longtime loyalty to the Democratic Party fell by the wayside as he became a major tycoon. In 1900, Lamont negotiated directly with Republican boss Mark Hanna to arrange a $50,000 contribution from one of Lamont's corporations to the GOP campaign fund.

Lamont's success in business brought him a fortune reckoned in the millions and a rustic estate, Altamont, in New York's scenic Dutchess County. When he managed to get away from his affairs in the city, he enjoyed life as a country squire. Lamont personally supervised an extensive remodeling of his old mansion, and showed a strong interest in every tree and garden on his property. There was also time for his family: Lamont's letters show the care he took in selecting just the right books, dogs, ponies, and other gifts for his daughters.

In 1901, J. P. Morgan and other leading lights of Wall Street relied on Lamont in organizing the Northern Securities Company, a promising rail monopoly covering much of the American West. Unfortunately for Lamont and his friends, the new President, Theodore Roosevelt, was outraged by the plan and chose Northern Securities as the first major target for his celebrated "trust-busting" policy. The government attacked the proposed company in court as a "combination in restraint of trade" and no amount of wire-pulling by Lamont could dissuade Roosevelt from his course. The Supreme Court finally decided the case in the government's favor in 1904.

There is little doubt that the years of litigation and strain associated with the Northern Securities controversy contributed to Lamont's death at age 54. On

July 23, 1905, he was relaxing with his family at his country estate. He went for a drive with his wife in the afternoon and appeared to be in good health and fine spirits. At dinner the Lamonts entertained several guests and around nine o'clock, just as the meal was ending, the host complained that he felt ill and went up to his room. He collapsed before reaching his bed and a doctor who was among the dinner guests could do nothing to revive him. Lamont died at 9:15, the victim of an apparent heart attack.

The first person summoned by the bereaved family was Grover Cleveland. One of Lamont's daughters sent off a simple message: "Father died tonight. Come at once." Upon hearing the news, Cleveland's immediate reaction was, "No death outside the circle of my own family could have affected me more." The former President did what he could to comfort the mourners and six months later he was surprised to find that his "traditional" Christmas gift from Lamont, a box of fine cigars, arrived as usual. Mrs. Lamont had thoughtfully sent them on. Cleveland told her he was "especially touched because this kind of remembrance of me was precisely such as had come to me from another name deeply engraven upon the most sacred tablets of my memory."

Cleveland was not alone in mourning his old friend: the newspapers made much of Lamont's death and his photograph, rimmed with black, appeared on front pages everywhere. In death as in life he achieved stature and prominence undreamt of by previous Presidential aides. Lamont was, as Representative Champ Clark remembered him, "the nonpareil of private secretaries. . . . He accomplished more with less friction than many of the men who stuck their legs beneath the presidential mahogany."

A recollection of William C. Hudson, an Albany reporter and good friend to both Lamont and Cleveland, best sums up the position of "Silent Dan" in the White House. In 1885, shortly after Cleveland's inauguration, Hudson came down from New York to visit the executive mansion. Hudson wanted to speak with Lamont, but word came from the office that the all-powerful aide was too busy to see him. Disappointed in his desire to chat with Cleveland's secretary, Hudson had to settle for second best: he was shown in directly to see the President of the United States.

Elijah Halford:
A Good Strong Methodist

As the new White House secretary trudged upstairs to his office, Captain Densmore, the chief doorkeeper, looked on disapprovingly. The captain, a large, fine-looking man, noted the frail physique and sallow face of the 46-year-old newcomer and commented to his assistant, "He'll not last a week." The secretary, Elijah Halford, overheard the remark and remembered it when he attended Captain Densmore's funeral before the end of the term. Thirty years later, in his published reminiscences, Halford was still gloating over the incident. In the midst of the self-serving narrative, he did his best to conceal the fact that Captain Densmore's prediction had almost come true. During his first year of White House service, Halford proved the first, but by no means the last Presidential aide to break under the strain of his official responsibilities.

Elijah Walker Halford was born in Nottingham, England, in 1843. His early career showed strong similarities to that of Lincoln's secretary John Nicolay. Both men were brought to the United States by their parents at age 5. In both cases, the fathers died before the sons reached maturity (Halford was 12), and the young men were left to fend for themselves in the rural Midwest. Halford worked as a grocer's helper, a hired hand on a farm, and eventually, like Nicolay, secured a job as a printer's devil on a small-town newspaper. He applied himself diligently to his work for the Hamilton (Ohio) *Intelligencer,* and in his spare time developed an enthusiasm for politics. In 1856 he was swept up in the Presidential campaign of John C. Frémont, "The Great Pathfinder." Young Halford enlisted in a group called "The Junior Pathfinders," donned the official Frémont hat and cape, and marched in numerous torchlight parades for his candidate. Three decades later, as Secretary to the President, Halford had the opportunity to present his onetime hero with an honorary pension that had been specially voted by Congress.

On the eve of the Civil War, Halford's newspaper career took him to the rising city of Indianapolis. He secured a job as a journeyman printer for *The Journal* where, after wartime service as an Army clerk, he ultimately rose to the august position of editor in chief. In that capacity he met Benjamin Harrison, one of the city's leading citizens and the scion of a distinguished political family. The two men discovered they had much in common. Not only were they both transplants from southwestern Ohio, but they also shared a passionate interest in religion. Harrison was an elder in the Presbyterian Church and superintendent of an Indianapolis Sunday School, while Halford was a devout Methodist who often spoke from the pulpit. Both men struck their contemporaries as cold and self-righteous, and their harsh judgments of the rest of humanity naturally drew them together. Harrison praised Halford as "a thoroughgoing example of a self-made man. All that he is, he has become through his own persevering efforts." Halford, for his part, saw Harrison as "a wholesome Christian" and "a natural aristocrat."

When Harrison prepared to enter statewide politics Halford stood at his elbow, using the pages of *The Journal* to support two unsuccessful tries for the governorship. When Harrison won election to the U.S. Senate in 1880, he rewarded Halford with appointment as clerk to the subcommittee on Indian affairs. The position gave the Hoosier journalist some Washington experience, but before the end of the term Halford returned to Indianapolis, where he continued to serve Harrison's interests. Early in 1888, *The Journal* became the first paper in the country to suggest Harrison as Presidential material.

When the Republican convention convened in Chicago, Harrison was still a dark horse and the local papers refused to mention his name or to reprint his statements. To overcome this obstacle, the resourceful Halford arranged for special trains to run from Indianapolis to Chicago carrying bundles of *Journals* for the delegates' breakfast trays each morning. Halford also played a role as a member of the convention's Platform and Resolutions Committee, making sure that all party planks harmonized with the ideas of the Man from Indiana. Halford's careful preparations finally paid off on the eighth convention ballot when Benjamin Harrison won the Republican Presidential nomination. The hardworking editor could not resist a sense of personal accomplishment, and neither could his wife. Mrs. Halford happened to be sitting on the platform of the convention hall at the time of the climatic ballot. When the roll call ended she suddenly rose in her seat and began singing a church hymn at the top of her voice. All eyes focused on her and soon the crowd on the floor and in the galleries joined in the song—a mighty chorus of satisfied Republicans praising God for the nomination of Benjamin Harrison.

The general election provided the Halfords with further evidence of Divine Providence when Harrison lost to Cleveland in the popular tally but managed to eke out a victory in the electoral college. That victory brought the Indiana editor to the White House as the President's private secretary and forced him to confront one of the hot political issues of the era. Civil Service Reform stirred deep emotions in those days, as good government crusaders insisted that federal jobs should be awarded on the basis of merit rather than on political considerations. In some of his preelection *Journal* editorials, Halford seemed to agree with them, but when he helped the President replace thousands of Democrats with suitably loyal Republicans he conveniently reversed his position. In the process, he also managed to look out for his personal interests—engineering the appointment of his brother-in-law as postmaster in Champaign, Illinois.

One of the most colorful descriptions of Benjamin Harrison as President was provided by a young reformer named Theodore Roosevelt, who saw the leader of his own party as a "cold-blooded, narrow-minded, obstinate, timid old psalm-singing Indianapolis politician." "Dad" Halford was the sort of private secretary you would expect for a chief executive answering to this description. He cut a somber figure in the White House with his long face, drooping mustache, and close-cropped gray hair. According to newspaper accounts he invariably dressed in either "a sober grey or else a solemn black." His religious bent was well known. Secretary of War Redfield Proctor used to say, "Halford and I are good strong Methodists. Halford is good, and I am strong." To the President, Halford was "Lige" (short for Elijah) or occasionally "Brother Halford."

As with many of his predecessors, the secretary shared both work and relaxation with his boss. On every pleasant afternoon the President took a long walk of three to four miles, and Halford generally accompanied him. These refreshing outings gave the President the chance to discuss White House business with his secretary. Some days, to vary the routine, the two friends would drive in a dark-green landau to Virginia or Maryland. When it rained they remained indoors and played billiards.

Despite such diversions, Halford suffered intensely under the pressure of his first year as secretary. The insatiable demands of office-seekers left him frustrated and exhausted. Though the press was sympathetic to Halford as a former newspaperman, the Baltimore *Sun* couldn't help noting his increasingly "wretched health." Then, on October 4, 1889, came the climax: Secretary Halford collapsed at his desk in the White House, throwing the executive offices into chaos. Halford's condition was so serious that he could not be moved, and after two days he underwent long and painful surgery in a room of the executive mansion. None of the press accounts mention the specific nature of Halford's illness, and in the secretary's memoirs the episode is completely ignored. Certainly the sketchy information provided to the public reflected a desire on Halford's part to cover up his illness. President Harrison was deeply worried about his aide and allowed Mrs. Halford to move into the White House so she could be near her immobilized husband. Fortunately, Halford's surgery was reported "a complete success" and after three weeks the secretary was back on his feet. Halford was determined to stay at his job, but the draining public receptions which had been temporarily curtailed during his absence had to be cut back on a permanent basis. Since the early days of the White House it had been common practice to allow several hours a week for curious citizens to come in and shake hands with their President. At Halford's direction this practice was eliminated, thereby lifting an irritating weight from the shoulders of the President and his staff, but also denying them those regular "public opinion baths'' that Abraham Lincoln found so useful. As Halford proudly declared, "Seeing the President is not now so simple and unceremonious a 'Stampede' as it once was.''

After the flow of visitors had been checked, Halford still had to endure the demands placed upon him by members of the First Family. The President's three grandchildren lived in the White House and one of them, known to everyone as "Baby McKee," was a particular terror. Given free run of the executive mansion, he crawled happily from room to room like a fat little crab. More than once Halford was startled in the midst of a meeting with the President to feel a warm, pudgy arm suddenly embracing his leg. One day during a conference Baby McKee slipped into the secretary's office without attracting notice and soon a roll of important state papers had disappeared from Halford's desk. The secretary began a frantic search while the President waited. As Halford pulled back the window draperies and found Baby McKee, the unhappy aide could not withhold a cry: the infant was merrily stirring the contents of a huge spittoon with the precious roll. As Grandpa sent the child off to his nurse, it was Halford's job to clean the slimy brown stains from the documents.

For Halford, such minor irritations were followed by a major loss. His wife died in 1891 from the respiratory ailments that had been troubling her for years. The President was on a speaking tour in Georgia when he heard the news, and regretted that he was unable to drop his commitments and rush back to the capital. Mrs. Halford's death was unhappily typical of the Harrison years. This brief administration, undistinguished by stirring issues or major accomplishments, was strangely marked by a series of personal tragedies. Treasury Secretary William Windom died in office and Navy Secretary Benjamin Tracy, a close friend of the President, barely escaped with his life from a fire in which his wife and daughter perished. The loss of Secretary of State James Blaine's two grown sons broke that gentleman in mind and body and left him an invalid for much of the term. At one point, Harrison and Halford struggled to handle the work of four different Cabinet officers who were incapacitated. The crowning blow came during Harrison's last year in office, when his own wife's health began to deteriorate. The President spent several hours every day at her bedside and forced Halford to take on a larger share of the day-to-day executive business. Fortunately, the secretary's health proved equal to the challenge, but there was also a Presidential campaign to handle. First came the difficult convention battle to assure Harrison's renomination—an effort which Halford personally supervised—and then the general election contest against the President's old rival, Grover Cleveland. With his wife critically ill, Harrison refused to campaign personally. Halford tried to take up some of the slack, traveling to the Midwest to make speeches for his boss, but he was not particularly effective as a stump orator. On October 25, 1892, the First Lady died in the White House. Two weeks later the President lost the election to Cleveland and the Harrison administration drew to its melancholy close.

The loss of the White House left Elijah Halford at loose ends. After his four draining years as Secretary to the President he had little desire to return to the pressures and excitement of newspaper work in Indiana. His wife was dead and his daughter had married, so at age 50 he faced the future alone. He wanted comfort, security, and companionship, and during his last weeks in the White House, Benjamin Harrison moved to provide it for him. The lame-duck President appointed his aide as a paymaster in the U.S. Army with the rank of major. During the Civil War, Halford had served in a similar capacity and the detailed, disciplined administrative work seemed to agree with him. After 1893 he remained in the Army for fourteen years. He served as paymaster for troops going to Cuba in the Spanish-American War, and later his duties took him to the Philippines.

During occasional breaks from military service, Major Halford also found time for political chores. Six weeks before the Republican convention in 1896, he acted as Harrison's spokesman in taking the former President out of the running for another term. The next year, when the Republicans returned to power under William McKinley, Halford spent several days in the White House as a "volunteer assistant." He helped McKinley's staff in handling the crowds of visitors and setting up a system of organization, but when the Army called him back to active duty the new President made no move to keep Halford on hand.

With an army pension providing his basic needs, Halford devoted his old age to religious and charitable pursuits. He was chairman of the Methodist Laymen's Missionary Movement and a member of the International Committee of the Young Men's Christian Association. In 1919 he wrote a long series of articles for *Leslie's Illustrated Weekly* recalling his White House years as a pleasant and productive period and extolling Harrison's "stainless administration." Halford offered few revelations about his late friend and colleague, but did assure the world that "dogs instinctively recognized him as a friend. He seldom passed dogs or unattended children without a kindly smile and friendly nod." Halford survived till age 95. He spent the last thirteen years of his life in complete obscurity, living in New York with his grandson, a member of the medical faculty at Columbia University.

As a Presidential aide he was in many respects the last of his kind. A faithful servant to a thoroughly passive President, Halford had an obsession with trivial details that future aides could not afford. On the whole, his successors chose to follow the more activist, ambitious lead that had been established by Daniel Lamont, as the White House staff moved into a demanding new era.

CHAPTER FOUR

THE EFFICIENCY EXPERTS

Throughout the nineteenth century, Presidential aides had conducted their affairs in the homey, unbuttoned atmosphere of a country store. During the administration of William McKinley, the cult of efficiency and "sound business principles" finally arrived at the White House.

The resulting changes were both stylistic and structural. The ranking executive aide, known since Buchanan's days as "President's Private Secretary," received the far more impressive and official-sounding designation of "Secretary to the President." Congress also authorized a significant raise in salary to the respectable level of $6,000 a year. Needless to say, the workload increased accordingly. McKinley became the first chief executive to decree that every letter to the President "written in a respectful spirit" deserves an answer. To handle such responsibilities, the White House staff swelled to twenty-seven individuals, including secretaries, messengers, ushers, typists, and clerks of various grades. The annual appropriation to support this substantial establishment reached $44,340—nearly four times what it had been under Grant.

The men who held the top White House job under these altered circumstances were all typical of the "scientific businessman" ideal so widely admired in their era. Clean-cut, hard-headed, practical, and energetic, they played an important part in the development of the modern Presidency. As Teddy Roosevelt discovered, much to his delight, a more effective staff meant a more powerful chief executive. With proper support from his aides, the President could finish more work and handle more responsibilities than ever before, while still finding time to bellow at the world with bull moose ferocity.

George B. Cortelyou:
The Humanized Machine

In *H.M.S. Pinafore,* Sir Joseph Porter describes his spectacular rise:

> As office boy I made such a mark
> That they gave me the post of a junior clerk.
> I served the writs with a smile so bland
> And I copied all the letters in a big round hand—
> I copied all the letters in a hand so free
> That now I am the ruler of the Queen's Navy!

Gilbert and Sullivan may have aimed their satire at targets far from Washington, D.C., but the career of a real American nearly fit the description. Using his skills at shorthand and dictation, a resourceful clerk named George B. Cortelyou rose from lowly government stenographer to a position in the Cabinet in less than ten years. By age 46, he was considered a leading prospect for the Presidency itself. His story, as one Washington correspondent observed, showed "a meteoric progress without parallel in the history of the Republic."

The secret of Cortelyou's success was his absolute and flawless self-mastery. His friend and patron William McKinley reported with admiration that "Cortelyou never loses his head." Even his enemies agreed that this was a man who seldom—if ever—made mistakes. As *Living Age* magazine observed, "his unruffled competency, thoroughness, and discretion took on something of the unerringness of a humanized machine."

That machine first went into operation on July 26, 1862. Cortelyou was the son of a Brooklyn businessman of French Huguenot ancestry. The founder of the family in the New World was Captain Jacques Cortelyou, who made the first official map of New Amsterdam in 1657. For generations, the Cortelyous were successful New York merchants, but by the time George was born they were richer in family pride than they were in material possessions. The young man had to win his own way in the world, and attended Brooklyn public schools, Long Island's Hempstead Institute, and the State Normal School at Westfield, Massachusetts. His literature teacher at the latter institution recalled that "Mr. Cortelyou's school work was not so brilliantly done as it often was by exceptionally bright students; but he possessed far greater thoroughness and accuracy." This conscientious young man dreamed of going to Harvard, but his plans never materialized. Instead, he enrolled at the New England Conservatory of Music and studied piano. Years later he could still delight (and astonish) his friends with accurate renditions of Mozart, Beethoven, and Schubert. As a profession, however, music seemed far too insecure for a young man without independent means.

Returning to New York, Cortelyou devoted himself to the study of stenography—an eminently practical field. The system of modern business shorthand had only recently been developed and Cortelyou achieved such mastery of the skill that he was soon teaching it to others. When he won employment at $5 a day as "stenographer and typewriter" for the New York Customs Service, he was able to marry his longtime sweetheart. Lily Morris was the daughter of Cortelyou's former principal at the Hempstead Institute, and he had known her since he was 15. A plain, plump homebody, she looked forward to a modest middle-class life with her new husband and could hardly have anticipated the dazzling career that lay ahead.

At age 29, Cortelyou landed a position as confidential stenographer to the Surveyor of the Port of New York and began to build a reputation for efficiency among the city's Republican politicos. Within four months, he had an attractive offer to go to Washington as private secretary to the Fourth Assistant Postmaster General. As Cortelyou commented in later years, "To men in every walk of life, stenography has been the handmaid of Opportunity, helping them in coming along."

After arriving in the nation's capital, Cortelyou impressed his superiors with his personal appearance as well as his secretarial skills. His thin frame, spectacles, and ramrod straight bearing reminded his colleagues of a "minister or college professor" rather than a humble clerk. His grooming was also exceptional for a man of his station. "Observe his serious attire, never creased by any hand save the tailor's," suggested one capital reporter, "his spotless and perfectly starched linen; the unclouded lustre of his shoes; the symmetrical precision of his cravat; the correct immovable perch of his eyeglasses; the glossy smoothness of his near-black hair, always brushed straight back from his forehead, and from New Year's Day till Christmas never showing a wisp misplaced." Was it any wonder that this earnest young man attracted favorable attention from the leading officials in the Post Office Department? When the Democrats under Grover Cleveland swept back into office in 1892, Cortelyou was asked to remain at his job despite his Republican affiliation.

One afternoon at a Cabinet meeting President Cleveland remarked that he needed an expert stenographer and asked the members of the Cabinet to find him a suitable man from among their employees. The Postmaster General spoke up immediately. "I believe I have in my department the very man you want," he said. "He's a handsome young fellow, as smart as lightning, as methodical as a machine, and, above everything, *a gentleman.*"

In summarizing Cortelyou's qualifications, the Postmaster General may have revealed more than he intended. The government bureaus were full of grubby, competent clerks but Cortelyou seemed something out of the ordinary—a gentleman, a man of breeding. In the course of his career, Cortelyou neatly combined two separate and somewhat contradictory American ideals. On the one hand he could pose as a restrained, disinterested aristocrat who served the public from a sense of noblesse oblige; at the same time he was also a hard-driving self-made man who used extraordinary talents to shoulder his way upward. The unique combination gave his drive for success its cutting edge.

After Cortelyou was transferred to duty at the White House, President Cleveland took a liking to him almost immediately. On the third occasion they worked together, Cortelyou solemnly confessed that he was a Republican and wondered if the Democratic President really wanted him to continue in such a delicate position. Cleveland, somewhat annoyed at being interrupted from the dictation at hand, turned sharply and replied, "I don't care a damn about your politics. All I want is somebody who is honest and competent to do my work." Within three months, Cortelyou had been promoted to executive clerk at the White House. Though Cleveland continued to rely on War Secretary Daniel Lamont as his principal advisor, Cortelyou spent more and more time with the President and won respect as Cleveland's personal stenographer. He also increased his usefulness by taking a legal course at night and winning a law degree from Georgetown University.

In 1897, when William McKinley took over the White House, Cleveland made a point of personally recommending Cortelyou. McKinley agreed to keep the stenographer on the staff and placed him under the command of John Addison Porter, the new White House secretary. Porter was a wealthy Yale-educated newspaper publisher and Connecticut state legislator who had provided key support for McKinley in the Presidential campaign. After the election, Porter wanted a diplomatic post as his reward, but McKinley offered him the White House job instead. Judging from his subsequent record, Porter would have done better as a diplomat. In the White House he developed a reputation as "the social secretary"—a man preoccupied with receptions, gala dinners, and an inflated sense of his own importance. Porter's pre-White House career had been more distinguished than that of any previous secretary, and he wanted to enlarge the prestige of his job accordingly. The change in his official title from "President's Private Secretary" to "Secretary to the President" made Porter particularly proud. He added further legitimacy to his post by commissioning a series of framed portraits of his predecessors. The likenesses decorated the secretary's office and Porter took considerable pride in them—though the smiling face of the well-known rascal, Orville Babcock, was conspicuous in its absence. When the McKinley administration passed from the scene these portraits were removed and forgotten, but some of Porter's other innovations showed more lasting results. The White House staff was permanently expanded as a result of Porter's personal pleas to Congressmen. In his letters the secretary bid for sympathy by reporting that he and his colleagues often worked past midnight. By the end of McKinley's first term the clerical staff had more than doubled.

These reenforcements, however, could not rescue Secretary Porter from his own ineptitude. Plagued by ill health, an uncontrollable temper, and a vain pompous manner that offended nearly everyone, the distinguished Mr. Porter continued to flounder in his job. Preoccupied with the prestige of his office, he gladly let its considerable power pass to the hands of others. It soon became common knowledge in the capital that the most influential White House aide was not Porter but the soft-spoken young man with the stern good looks —George B. Cortelyou. While Porter fussed over social arrangements or went home to Connecticut on one of his frequent leaves-of-absence, Cortelyou took authority on his own initiative and began making himself indispensable to the President. Personal chemistry with McKinley played a key role in his rise. The President, a homespun Ohioan, vastly preferred Cortelyou's brisk, no-nonsense attitude to Addison Porter's stuffy pretensions. Mrs. McKinley developed a similar fondness for the young stenographer, who helped to fill a painful gap in her domestic life. During the early years of their marriage, the McKinleys lost two infant daughters and remained childless for the rest of their lives. Ida McKinley never fully recovered from the death of her children and she became an invalid, subject to frequent epileptic seizures. Cortelyou displayed an extraordinary sensitivity to her situation. One summer evening he even instructed the weary President to go to his wife, leaving the remaining paperwork for another day. McKinley admitted he "was glad of that, for he was afraid Mrs. McKinley might be waiting for him." Eventually, Mrs. McKinley came to feel so comfortable with Cortelyou that she spent some evenings knitting in a corner of the Cabinet Room while her husband and his aide quietly reviewed state papers. Whenever the McKinleys traveled, Cortelyou accompanied them. At train stations and hotels he helped the President in pushing Mrs. McKinley's wheel chair. On vacation evenings he often entertained them by playing the piano—a worthy use of his earlier musical training. In a quiet, undemonstrative way the First Lady accepted him as the son she never had.

All the while Cortelyou faced the growing demands of a family of his own. His wife bore him two sons and two daughters, and they lived in a modest home three blocks northeast of the Capitol. Their neighborhood was invariably described in press accounts as "unfashionable," but on his modest salary Cortelyou could hardly afford better. During the busy Washington social season he made it his policy to turn down all invitations. He wanted to be home with his children as much as possible, but he also considered it essential to make himself available to the President at all hours.

For the Cortelyou children the most treasured occasions were visits to the White House to see their father at work. On one such visit the two boys, Bruce and Win, were sitting with their mother in the Red Room, chatting with Mrs. McKinley, when the President suddenly walked in. McKinley always wore a

pink carnation in his lapel and it was his habit to present the boutonnieres as
mementos to children who called at the White House. Seeing the two little
Cortelyous in a state of happy agitation, he handed his carnation to the older
boy, Bruce. Then he selected another flower from a vase for Win, but before
presenting it he wore it for a few moments in his buttonhole so that Bruce
would not be able to lord it over his little brother. Half a century later, Bruce
Cortelyou recalled that incident as his first lesson in the true meaning of tact.

It was this same consideration and delicacy of feeling, so characteristic of
McKinley, that kept the President from speaking frankly to Addison Porter.
McKinley had supplanted his secretary in all important functions and hoped the
man would resign. During the time of crisis leading to the Spanish-American
War, it became more clear than ever before that Porter was irrelevant in shaping policy and that Cortelyou was the President's real right-hand man. With
mail pouring into the White House in unprecedented volume, Cortelyou prepared daily analyses of what the public was saying. He also digested press
accounts and editorial opinions for the President, and so became a crucial advisor on issues of war and peace. In these hectic days, Cortelyou learned to
revere McKinley for his patient endurance of every sort of strain. One day
when the administration was bitterly attacked on the floor of Congress, Cortelyou went in to leave some messages with the President. As he turned to go,
he noted the pale, careworn face behind the desk and for several moments he
hesitated just beyond the door. He wanted to find some words of support or
affection he could offer his chief. Finally, Cortelyou went back in and stood
rigidly and awkwardly before the desk. "Mr. President," he began, "I want to
say to you that in these busy days we hope you will feel no hesitation in calling
upon any of us outside at any hour of the day or night for anything we can do."
The statement was no revelation, since the overburdened staff had been toiling
ceaselessly for the last several months. But McKinley understood Cortelyou's
words for what they were intended to be—a pledge of love and personal devotion. "Mr. Cortelyou, I know you will," the President sighed. "I know you
will, and I appreciate it."

McKinley's war ordeal ended quickly with the surprisingly easy American
victory. The President signed the official peace protocols with Spain in a quiet
ceremony from which newsmen and photographers were excluded. The occasion was considered so private that the Secretary of State was the only Cabinet
member in attendance. Yet by special invitation, George Cortelyou was there at
the historic moment—standing by the side of his triumphant chief.

In April 1900, Addison Porter finally resigned his position because of ill
health. The doctors diagnosed his condition as "overt mental strain." Eight
months later he was dead at 44, but the persistent press of business allowed no
time for mourning in the White House. After Porter's departure, Cortelyou
assumed in title the position he had held in fact for several years. *Harper's*
magazine reported that the new Secretary to the President soon saw to it that
the White House was "better organized than any private business—surely a

striking innovation in the government service.'' Cortelyou's accomplishment was all the more impressive in light of the enormous increase in Presidential business as America entered the twentieth century. During McKinley's first term alone, the executive offices had to dispose of some 400,000 pieces of mail. Cortelyou personally reviewed nearly all of these letters, leaving brief shorthand instructions in the upper-left corners. The letters then went to lower-level clerks who wrote out appropriate responses using a comprehensive ''precedent index'' prepared by Cortelyou. The President himself saw less than one percent of the mail addressed to him, and most replies went out over Cortelyou's name. The secretary's signature was used so frequently, in fact, that Cortelyou ordered a special stamp with a facsimile of his handwriting. A few years before it had been considered a daring innovation when a stamp was made with President Garfield's signature, but now even the secretary was too busy to sign all the letters himself.

For Cortelyou, another area of major responsibility was the organization of the President's daily schedule. Every morning when McKinley sat down at his desk he found a neat, typewritten sheet headed ''The President's Engagements'' set out in front of him. This gave the complete minute-by-minute program for the day. Beside the name of each visitor to be seen or every piece of business to be transacted, Cortelyou provided confidential notes to guide the President. When questions of national policy required immediate attention, McKinley found additional papers awaiting him in which Cortelyou coolly formulated the essential questions and politely requested Presidential decisions.

Somehow, in the midst of his various duties, Cortelyou still found time to devise an entirely new approach to the job of White House press relations. In previous administrations, reporters gathered the news through haphazard, informal conversations with executive personnel. Gross inaccuracy was often the result. Under Cortelyou, the role of an official White House press spokesman developed for the first time. The secretary personally prepared written statements describing the President's policies and decisions and then distributed them to the gentlemen of the presss. Cortelyou also saw to it that a skilled White House stenographer was present whenever the President spoke in public. With astonishing speed, verbatim transcripts were prepared and duly handed to reporters in order to reduce the danger of misquotation. Eventually, Cortelyou began supplementing Presidential transcripts and policy statements with skillfully packaged ''human interest items'' which the press corps hungrily snapped up. Washington journalists were so delighted with these innovations that they didn't seem to notice that White House news was being managed as never before.

The love affair between Cortelyou and the press bore fruit in a nearly unanimous chorus of public praise for the secretary. *The Independent* magazine reported that ''in all that we have known about Cortelyou we have never known him to blunder over anything,'' while *Living Age* described him as ''one of those Americans who make the business of government seem ludicrously easy." What impressed reporters most was the secretary's legendary self-possession in face of the impossible demands of his job. According to an article in *World's Work* magazine, "he saw every man, woman and child who entered the President's office and knew what they came for and what they got. He read every message that came and went by wire, post or messenger and kept the whole great game in his head as a player at chess does." Later in the same article the author "had not the slightest doubt in the world" that if Cortelyou were at his desk and the report came to him that the President had fallen from the top of the Washington Monument "he would with mechanical calmness order the proper person to send an ambulance."

The President's physical safety was, in fact, one of Cortelyou's special concerns. After a series of political assassinations in Europe, Cortelyou began to worry that some maniac might take a shot at McKinley. One night the secretary went around testing the White House window locks; he found several that failed to work and ordered them immediately repaired. Periodically, Cortelyou dispatched members of his staff to check on the easygoing Secret Service guards and the results were sometimes troubling. On one occasion, Cortelyou's deputy found the second-story guard asleep on a lounge in one of the bedrooms. After watching him in that condition for twenty minutes, the man was awakened in the presence of his superiors. After that, Cortelyou's icy stare helped keep Secret Service men on their toes.

In September 1901, Cortelyou's concern for security led him to question part of the President's plans for a visit to the Pan American Exposition in Buffalo. The schedule called for a massive public reception at "The Temple of Music" in which McKinley would shake hands in the midst of thousands of people. Acting on his own authority, Cortelyou twice removed the reception from the program, but both times the President insisted on restoring it. When Cortelyou continued to argue against the public handshaking, McKinley exclaimed, "I have no enemies . . . No one would wish to hurt me."

Overruled by the President once and for all, Cortelyou took out his frustration in telegrams to Buffalo, ordering city officials to take extraordinary precautions. Though his instructions were followed to the letter, he remained tense and anxious on the day of the President's appearance. Cortelyou stood, as always, at the President's side as the crowd of greeters poured in through the doors at the far side of the building. They formed a single file, under the watchful eyes of security guards, and hurried forward to shake the President's hand. Only five or six minutes after the reception began, Cortelyou sent word to the guards that he would soon raise his hand as a signal that the doors should be closed; too many people had already been admitted. As the secretary prepared to give his signal, and Bach organ music throbbed under the shuffling of the crowd, the President's hand was knocked aside and a man lunged forward. A handkerchief wrapped around his right fist concealed a revolver, and two quick shots struck the President in the stomach. With a look of absolute astonishment on his face, McKinley collapsed into Cortelyou's arms. The aide helped the wounded man to find a chair. Meanwhile, guards fell on the assailant, wrestled him to the ground, and began pummeling him with their fists. The President, watching the furious action, managed to murmur, "Don't let them hurt him."

Once the first hushed shock had passed, the crowd began to panic. A stampede toward the doorways was punctuated by hysterical screams. The chair where McKinley sat was like the eye of a tornado. A few men huddled around him fanning his face with their hats. Cortelyou bent close, while the President fumbled pathetically at the wound in his belly. His hand was bloody as he raised it to Cortelyou's shoulder. "My wife," he whispered, "be careful, Cortelyou, how you tell her—oh, be careful!"

Within minutes help arrived and the President was carried to a nearby home. Doctors appeared at the scene, but stood aside and waited for orders. Cortelyou came over and stared at them with the look of a man who was assuming command. "Gentlemen," he said, "I do not know one of you." The secretary was quickly assured by those present that these were the best surgeons in the city. "Well," Cortelyou snapped back, "go ahead and operate."

"Now?" the doctors asked.

"Certainly now," the secretary insisted. "Is it not better to do it at once?" Several months later, Cortelyou was asked how he had managed to preserve his extraordinary calm amidst the confusion. "There was nothing else to do," he replied simply. "If a man had lost his head he would have been of no use."

For eight days, McKinley struggled for his life while Cortelyou quietly took charge of the federal government. At his direction, executive business proceeded as usual. According to *Harper's* magazine, he became "the acting President of the United States, performing all the duties of that office. . . . Constitutionally there was no inter-regnum, but if the actual conditions could be recorded Mr. Cortelyou's name might well appear between those of President McKinley and President Roosevelt."

The transfer of federal power to Theodore Roosevelt was certainly one of the smoothest in the nation's history. Cortelyou took it upon himself to school the new President in the day-to-day business of the White House and found TR to be a remarkably quick study. As their relationship developed, Roosevelt put aside any notion of replacing Cortelyou with an aide from his personal staff. A passionate advocate of "the strenuous life," Roosevelt admired the secretary's inexhaustible energy and his ability to toil twelve to sixteen hours a day. The cautious, level-headed aide served as a particularly effective balance to the excitable President—and Roosevelt knew it. He also knew that Cortelyou was an invaluable bridge to conservative elements in the financial community and Republican Party who looked somewhat askance at the Roughrider in the White House. When they appeared together in public, Roosevelt lost no opportunity to extol Cortelyou's virtues, holding him up as a sterling representative of the ethic of hard work and public service. One afternoon, on a sudden impulse, the President went even further. Two reporters had come to the White House to ask about the controversy surrounding the Secretary of the Interior. In the middle of the conversation, Roosevelt's face lit up, as he turned on his heel and shouted out in his piercing falsetto, "Cortelyou, step here a moment!"

Drawing the secretary and the two reporters into a confidential huddle, the President intoned, "Whenever a vacancy shall occur in the cabinet it is my purpose to appoint Mr. Cortelyou if he will accept, and I want that distinctly understood." Cortelyou offered his bland smile and without another word went back to his desk.

In September 1902, Cortelyou and the President traveled to Pittsfield, Massachusetts, where Roosevelt met with the governor and delivered an address. After the speech they were riding through the streets of town in an open, horse-drawn carriage when a trolley came careening toward them on a collision course. In the split second before impact, Cortelyou's mind flooded with horrible memories of McKinley's death; the secretary bent forward and shielded President Roosevelt with his own body. As the speeding streetcar rammed into the side of the carriage, a Secret Service man beside the driver was killed instantly. The other members of the party were thrown thirty feet onto the pavement. Cortelyou jumped up immediately and ran to the President, who was lying by the side of the road insisting he was not hurt. Roosevelt's leg was in fact badly injured, but he quickly noted that Cortelyou's wounds seemed even worse. The secretary was bleeding profusely from his neck and shoulder, and Roosevelt took out his handkerchief and tried to staunch the wound. The moment help arrived for his aide, Roosevelt angrily limped toward the unscathed trolley motorman. "Who has charge of this car?" he demanded. "I have," the frightened man replied. Shaking his fist, Roosevelt bellowed, "This is the most damnable outrage I ever knew!" The hapless motorman went to jail for eighteen months, while Cortelyou and the President returned to Washington to nurse their wounds. The entire experience forged a new link in their relationship. To Theodore Roosevelt, with his well-developed warrior complex, coolness in the face of physical danger was the highest test of a man—a test which Cortelyou had passed admirably. Standing side by side, the two comrades had sustained honorable wounds while facing the enemy—even though that enemy was only a speeding trolley.

After Cortelyou's injuries had healed, and after he had served Roosevelt for a year and a half as White House secretary, the President made good on his earlier promise to elevate his aide to the Cabinet. On February 16, 1903, Cortelyou assumed the post of Secretary of Commerce and Labor—the first man in American history to hold that title. The creation of this new department had been one of Roosevelt's pet projects and he wanted a man of extraordinary ability to organize its operations. In stepping down as Secretary to the President, Cortelyou no doubt sacrificed some of his behind-the-scenes power, but his new position offered compensating advantages. For one thing, his salary was raised to $8,000 a year, from the modest $6,000 he had received for his White House labors.

Within sixteen months, the new department was running so smoothly that Roosevelt felt free to shift Cortelyou to another special assignment. He persuaded the Cabinet officer to accept the chairmanship of the Republican National Committee, and with it responsibility for Roosevelt's reelection drive in 1904. It may have been an odd assignment for a man never before involved in electoral politics, but Cortelyou performed with his usual effectiveness. He demonstrated particular finesse in the fine art of fund-raising, winning huge contributions from many of the same corporations he had recently regulated as Secretary of Commerce and Labor. This practice produced outraged howls from the Democrats, who attempted to coin a new word—"Cortelyouism"—to denote the use of political muscle to squeeze contributions from big business. Yet such charges bothered Cortelyou very little, and they seemed to trouble the electorate even less: Roosevelt won in a landslide, and his campaign manager was rewarded with another Cabinet position in the new administration.

This time Cortelyou took over the Post Office Department, the same branch of government in which he had begun his Washington career as a lowly clerk some thirteen years before. Under his administration, the postal deficit was reduced to its lowest point in years and dependability was raised to a new standard. In 1907, Cortelyou switched to his third Cabinet post and the most important assignment of them all. Assuming control of the Treasury Department, he pursued a resourceful, activist policy that helped minimize the effects of the financial panic of 1907.

As Secretary of the Treasury, Cortelyou emerged as a major contender for the Republican Presidential nomination in 1908. He had headed three federal departments with conspicuous success, and surely no man in the country understood the workings of the White House better than he did. There is no doubt that Cortelyou was interested in the Presidency, but his delicate position within the Cabinet precluded active campaigning.

The major factor in settling the nomination was the endorsement of President Roosevelt, who was retiring at the height of his popularity. Years later, in a conversation with one of his business associates, Cortelyou recalled an eventful afternoon visit to Roosevelt's gracious Long Island home. While the two men were secluded in the study, the President quietly announced that he had looked over the field and decided that Cortelyou should be the Republican standard-bearer. The unflappable aide replied that on principle he opposed the idea of a President picking his own successor, but that he was pleased with Roosevelt's decision all the same. Naturally, Cortelyou went home that evening "walking in the clouds."

Though the description of the meeting seems vivid enough, our only evidence that it actually took place comes from Cortelyou's memory many years after the fact. Other material strongly suggests that Roosevelt always placed other names well above Cortelyou's on his list of Presidential possibilities. Nonetheless, the Treasury Secretary felt perfectly confident in the belief that he had received a binding promise from the President. Then without warning, at the close of a formal Cabinet meeting, Roosevelt called to his side William Howard Taft, the Secretary of War. Cortelyou watched as Roosevelt threw his arm around the shoulders of the big man and proclaimed, "I want you to meet the next President of the United States, William Howard Taft." The President never explained his apparent change of heart, nor did Cortelyou choose to raise the matter with him. It may have been that the President, despite his respect for Cortelyou, preferred a successor who was more distinctly a Roosevelt protégé. No matter how long they worked together, Roosevelt could hardly forget that Cortelyou's most important political patron had been McKinley, and that his personal loyalty to the martyred President could never be replaced.

Unable to secure employment as President of the United States, Cortelyou gratefully accepted a job as president of the nation's largest utility. Under Cortelyou's leadership, Consolidated Gas eventually developed into the mammoth Consolidated Edison Corporation. Raw statistics tell much of the story: when he began his job the firm employed 10,448 workers, but by the time he retired, twenty-eight years later, the rolls had swelled to 45,821. At the same time, the value of the company had risen 306 percent, from $243 million to $990 million.

At age 73, Cortelyou retired from this prosperous enterprise. In addition to his revenues on various investments, he received a pension of $30,000 a year—five times as much as he had been paid for toiling night and day as White House secretary. Cortelyou died of a heart attack in July 1940 at his beautiful Long Island estate, Harbor Lights. He was 78.

Looking back at his career, the conclusion is inescapable that Cortelyou was one of the most remarkable administrators of his generation. It is hard to define exactly what qualities constitute executive genius, but there is no question that Cortelyou had them. He brought organization, clarity, and logic to government departments notorious for their inefficiency. Ike Hoover, who worked as an usher in the White House for forty-two years, believed that Cortelyou was the most effective aide ever to serve an American President, and today that still seems a reasonable judgment.

Reservations about Cortelyou all centered on his icy, methodical intensity and his apparent lack of personal foibles. A 1903 article by Henry MacFarland was typical of the tone adopted by many capital reporters. It is only with extreme reluctance that the writer admits that Cortelyou "is human, he gets weary, doubtless he makes mistakes, although I never heard of any sufficiently important to be remembered."

William Loeb Jr.:
The King of the Secretaries

On the afternoon following his inaugural ceremonies in 1899, the new governor of New York shattered tradition by storming directly to his office and getting down to work. Inauguration day had always been reserved for polite festivities, but Theodore Roosevelt could not abide senseless delay. He roared through a series of meetings with department heads, pacing the room and bellowing instructions. Meanwhile, four stenographers waited in terrified silence in the adjoining office. They had already heard from one of their colleagues, a shorthand expert who had accompanied Roosevelt in his campaign, that "Teddy was a terror to take." With his frantic energy and staccato delivery, Roosevelt presented a nearly impossible challenge to anyone assigned to transcribe his words. When the afternoon's conferences concluded, the moment arrived that the secretaries had been dreading: the governor appeared briefly at the door to his inner office and shouted, "Send me in a good stenographer!" No one moved and no one spoke until chunky, round-faced William Loeb, a part-time member of the secretarial force, stood up quietly and went in to Roosevelt. His timid colleagues breathed a sigh of relief at Loeb's foolhardy voluntarism; even behind closed doors they could hear TR's piercing, high-pitched voice rattling the walls in a fury of nonstop dictation. It was several hours before Loeb emerged from his ordeal. He appeared to be unscathed and what's more, the governor seemed pleased with his performance. The next morning, as Roosevelt arrived and flung open the doors to his chambers, he immediately demanded "that same stenographer I had yesterday."

So began a relationship that changed the lives of both men. To Loeb, Roosevelt became "the best friend I have or ever expect to have" while TR, near the end of his Presidency, publicly described Loeb as "the man who has been closest to me politically."

On the face of it, they seemed an oddly matched pair—Roosevelt, the self-confident Manhattan patrician who was part of America's very highest society; and Loeb, the obscure plugger from the wrong side of the tracks who was so ashamed of his background that he did his best to obscure it. The evidence strongly suggests that Loeb was Jewish, and certainly most of his contemporaries made that assumption. One of the rumors that made the rounds in New York City for years was that Loeb had been denied admission into the Union

League Club because of his Semitic heritage and that Theodore Roosevelt eventually resigned his own membership in protest. It hardly mattered that Loeb as a young man had joined the Episcopal Church, that his only child was baptized an Episcopalian, and that when he died Loeb received an Episcopal funeral. In the eyes of a bigot a Jew remains a Jew. Years after Loeb's death his son, a prominent New Hampshire newspaper publisher, was still answering anti-Semitic slurs: on one occasion he did so by printing a huge front-page copy of his own baptismal certificate, featuring Theodore Roosevelt's name as godfather. Such a response, of course, accepts the basic premise of the anti-Semite—that Jewish heritage is somehow a disgrace that must be denied at all costs. Despite this attitude on the part of the Loeb family, the prestigious *Encyclopaedia Judaica* lists William Loeb's service in the White House as an important advance for American Jews.

It is difficult to determine the precise details of the Loeb family's religious history since the three Jewish congregations in Albany, their hometown, do not retain membership records from the nineteenth century. We do know, however, that William Loeb's father was born in Baden, Germany, and came to the United States in 1850; his mother, Louise Meyer, was an immigrant from the Alsace-Lorraine. The elder Loeb worked as a small-time merchant and a barber, but seemed to fail at everything. William Jr. was born in 1866 in the family's rundown Albany home, the first of seven children. He attended public schools until age 12, when he had to go to work in order to help his family. In his first job he served as a messenger boy for Western Union, delivering press dispatches to the local newspapers. One of those papers was the Albany *Argus,* whose night editor at the time was Daniel Lamont, future "Assistant President" to Grover Cleveland. On long, slow evenings, Lamont liked to relax for a few moments with the well-mannered messenger boy. "Billy" Loeb would sit down beside the editor's big mahogany desk, while Lamont tilted back his chair and smiled behind his walrus mustache. After several months, Lamont developed a fatherly interest in the boy, and one night he observed, "You like to read. You ought to be in school." He then startled the young messenger with a generous and unsolicited proposal: Lamont would lend Billy enough money so the youth could prepare himself as a lawyer. Loeb's pride prevented him from accepting such charity, but Lamont's kindness was not forgotten. Twenty-five years later, as Secretary to President Theodore Roosevelt, William Loeb invited his old friend to the White House. As Lamont stepped into the office and settled himself in the chair beside Loeb's desk, he laughingly observed how the old pattern of Albany days had been exactly reversed.

Though he could never afford a legal education on his own, Billy Loeb did manage to save enough money to attend Miss Walters Secretarial School, where he mastered stenography. He went on to a quick series of secretarial jobs until he discovered that the most desirable positions in Albany invariably went to young men who had political clout. With single-minded determination he set about making the connections he needed, joining the Republican organization in his ward and involving himself in the day-to-day business of the party. His loyal service paid off when he won appointment as stenographer of the New York State Assembly. Additional political plums soon followed, including the part-time position in the governor's office that led to his fateful contact with TR.

Years later, in explaining his relationship with William Loeb, Roosevelt recalled, "When I was Governor of New York I was just as erratic about hours as I am here, and when I was seized with a desire to work Loeb was the only stenographer or secretary whom I could find after office hours, and it is the same now." In other words, Loeb was the one willing to sacrifice all personal privacy in order to satisfy his boss. At the time he met Roosevelt, Loeb was 32 years old—a rootless single man at the margins of the middle class, ignoring whispers about his Jewish background, juggling a quick series of part-time jobs. When TR asked him to drop his other positions and to become a full-time gubernatorial aide—with a generous salary supplement to be paid from the governor's own pocket—Loeb happily agreed. Roosevelt provided his life with the focus it lacked. TR was the colorful hero of the Spanish-American War, a combative, electric personality who turned even routine political scraps into holy crusades. Service to such a master allowed Loeb to combine his drive for material advancement with a sense of righteousness and purpose. Loeb was only eight years younger than the youthful governor, and the father-and-son pattern that applied to other politicians and their aides was never a factor in this relationship. Instead, Loeb wanted to *be* Roosevelt, to live vicariously through his dynamic chief. A pudgy gumdrop of a man with round, liquid brown eyes and thinning black hair, Loeb did his best to remake himself in Roosevelt's image. He chose pince-nez spectacles identical to Roosevelt's, cultivated a thoroughly Rooseveltian brush mustache, and even wore his hair in TR's close-cropped style. In dealing with visitors in the governor's office, Loeb overcame his native reserve and tried to reproduce TR's brisk, hearty manner. Loeb's outside interests also began to show the indelible influence of his employer. Since Roosevelt was a Harvard man noted for his literary taste, stenographer Loeb, a high school dropout, soon acquired an impressive collection of Carlyle, Dickens, and Macaulay. While TR, the great outdoorsman, preached the virtues of the strenuous life, his flabby aide took up horseback riding and actually became quite good at it. Another man might have grown uncomfortable with such slavish devotion from a member of his staff but to an egotist of Roosevelt's dimensions, imitation seemed indeed the sincerest form of flattery.

In 1900, New York's Republican boss Tom Platt decided to "kick Roosevelt upstairs" by nominating the uncontrollable governor for the Vice-Presidency. Roosevelt had little enthusiasm for the office, but he found himself powerless to resist the tidal wave of public support that quickly formed behind his candidacy. During the campaign, Loeb traveled with TR and attended the inauguration ceremonies in March 1901. By that time, Loeb had already been named as "Stenographer to the Vice-President"—filling the only staff position allotted to the nation's second-highest officer. In taking the job, he suffered a sharp cut in pay but comforted himself with the thought that he would have plenty of free time. The duties of the Vice-Presidency seemed so utterly inconsequential that Loeb and Roosevelt hatched fanciful schemes for filling their idle hours. Shortly before the inauguration, TR suggested that they enroll together in one of Washington's law schools and complete the legal training that they both lacked. Not only would they have a bully time as celebrity schoolboys, but they would prepare themselves for a return to private life. Since the Vice-Presidency invariably proved a political dead end, they would return to New York once the term was over and hang up the shingle of "Roosevelt and Loeb, Attorneys at Law."

The two men might have begun their studies in the fall semester if tragedy had not intervened. The assassination of William McKinley made Theodore Roosevelt the twenty-sixth President of the United States and thrust Loeb into a position of national importance. Many observers believed that he would become the new Secretary to the President, but Roosevelt asked George B. Cortelyou to stay on in that post in order to stress the continuity of national leadership. Loeb was given the title "Assistant Secretary to the President" and expected to work closely with Cortelyou. The division of authority between the two men was never precisely defined, but in general Cortelyou maintained administrative control of the White House while Loeb concerned himself with Roosevelt's personal and political affairs. It was Loeb, for instance, who began meeting with party chieftains from around the country in order to lay the groundwork for TR's nomination for a Presidential term in his own right in 1904.

By the first months of 1902, the assistant secretary felt secure enough in his new White House job to welcome the additional burdens of marriage. His bride was Catherine Dorr, 26, whose father ran a tavern back home in Albany. Like Loeb himself, she was the child of German immigrants and an accomplished stenographer. Avoiding both church and synagogue, they were wed in Albany City Hall, with the city clerk doing the honors. Immediately afterward they returned to the capital, eventually settling into a comfortable home on Q Street in northwest Washington. In the back of the house was a flower garden, on which Loeb lavished much attention, and a stable for a horse or two. In addition to his wife and his horses, Loeb also acquired a pair of dogs—a mongrel hound and an Airedale—and became inordinately fond of them. Loeb was 36 at the time of his marriage, and fathered only one child: William Loeb Jr., who was born in 1905. This son grew up to achieve his own sort of fame as the outspoken, right-wing publisher of a string of newspapers in New England and Nevada. The younger William Loeb has remained a lively, controversial figure through the 1970's.

Whatever free time Loeb enjoyed after his work and his family was generally devoted to the Freemasons. He had joined the Masonic Order in Albany and served for a time as master of his lodge. He had a complete collection of Masonic manuals in his home and finally rose to the rank of thirty-third degree Mason. While Roosevelt was Vice-President, Loeb helped persuade him to enroll in a Masonic lodge, but TR never shared his aide's enthusiasm. For Loeb, Freemasonry helped fill the void left by the absence of any durable religious identification. At the end of his life, he left a generous bequest to the order—though he modestly insisted that the exact amount never be revealed.

With Loeb and Cortelyou working side by side in the White House, Roosevelt enjoyed the services of a powerhouse staff that would have been the envy of any executive. The slick teamwork of the two secretaries contributed immeasurably to Roosevelt's success in his first years as President, but it was only a matter of time before Loeb tired of his secondary staff role. He began urging the President to name Cortelyou to a Cabinet position—a promotion which Cortelyou himself heartily desired. Working together for this common goal, the two aides achieved their customary success. Cortelyou's appointment as the new Secretary of Commerce and Labor in February 1903 left William Loeb in undisputed charge of the White House staff.

As Secretary to the President, he kept the same office he had shared with Cortelyou and simply moved his desk to a more commanding position in the room. Adjoining Loeb's office on the other side was a large executive workroom, where a quiet army of clerks and stenographers toiled away at all hours. Now and again, one of these drones popped into the main office to seek Loeb's instructions. The Secretary to the President wasted little time on such occasions, snapping out his orders with an air of impatient authority. This plump, broad-shouldered little man in the gentlemanly clothes that always seemed a bit too large for him projected a sense of command so unmistakable that one reporter observed: "You could tell at a glance he was the king of secretaries."

Throughout his kingdom, this monarch insisted on spare and businesslike surroundings. No longer did the colorful portraits of previous Presidential secretaries decorate the walls as they had during the McKinley years. In their place, Loeb permitted only a framed replica of the great seal of the United States and one stuffed armadillo, standing like a melancholy sentinel in a corner of the room. No one seemed to know how or why the animal came to be there, but it remained as an object of curiosity and humor. Loeb's desk was an unadorned mahogany affair with a row of reference books lining the outer edge and papers stacked in orderly piles. Of central importance on the desktop was the telephone, still a relatively recent addition to the White House establishment. During the Roosevelt administration, phone service remained primitive and unreliable and extension lines had not yet been invented. One central receiver served the entire executive mansion and it is significant that Roosevelt placed it on Loeb's desk and not his own. The secretary received all incoming calls and summarized their contents for the President. If return calls were necessary, Loeb placed them in the President's behalf so that Roosevelt himself never had to speak on the phone. TR, who felt somewhat uncomfortable with the troublesome long-distance talking machine, gladly delegated to Loeb even the most delicate high-level conversations.

In day-to-day dealings with White House visitors, the new secretary played a similar role. He proved so protective of the President's time that he earned the nickname "Stonewall" Loeb. In place of Cortelyou's smooth, mechanical efficiency, he offered a reception that was gruff and bristling with energy. One afternoon a New York publishing executive came to see the President about a hitch in the postal service that affected his business. Within two minutes, Loeb had grasped the situation and announced, "It won't be necessary to see the President." Before the startled executive could raise an objection, Loeb had reached for the phone and rung up one of the top officials in the Post Office Department. With a curt, ten-word order, he solved the problem at hand, then hung up the receiver, and rose to show his guest to the door. The visiting publisher could hardly believe it: Americans were not yet accustomed to the idea that a Presidential aide could bully at will even the highest-ranking federal officials.

Not all White House callers came away so pleased with their reception. In 1905 a young woman arrived who demanded to see the President at once. Judging from her dress, bearing, and handsome appearance, a White House doorman described her to Loeb as a lady of distinction. When she pranced in to the secretary's office, Loeb said he was anxious to help her, but that she must declare her business before she could see the President. In a state of breathless agitation, the glamorous visitor related a tale about the Pittsburgh postmaster illegally opening her mail and demanded that the man be dismissed. Loeb calmly replied that this was a matter for the Postmaster General, and not the President. At this, the lady began to break down completely, crying bitterly, shouting her protests, and slowly opening the large handbag under her arm. There, resting on top of its contents, was a pearl-handled revolver. Loeb jumped up and grabbed the gun as the lady reached for it herself. Within moments, the Secret Service had arrived on the scene and hustled the screaming, struggling intruder into custody.

Such incidents, along with the recent memory of McKinley's assassination, led Loeb to an obsessive concern for the President's safety. TR naturally chafed at the idea that Secret Service men must follow him on all his hikes, gallops, hunts, or auto rides, and began inventing schemes to evade his dour escorts. He took a small boy's delight in thwarting the protective arrangements so carefully arranged by Loeb. The situation deteriorated to the point where Loeb could stand it no longer. One afternoon he confronted the President with an ultimatum: either Roosevelt would put up with the Secret Service and accept Loeb's decisions on all matters of safety, or the secretary would resign his post immediately and storm out of the White House. The President's response was unconditional surrender. "Billy," he said without hesitation, "you are perfectly right and you shall not hear another word of complaint from me."

Showdowns of this sort were very much the exception in the Loeb-Roosevelt relationship. The President was not the sort of man who patiently absorbed the advice of his colleagues; for the most part, Loeb tried to influence his chief through informal comments thrown out during the course of their work. Their most fruitful interchanges often came late at night, while Loeb took the President's dictation. Though dozens of crack stenographers served on the White House staff, Loeb still had no rival in the accurate transcription of the President's words. When TR intervened between labor and management in the big coal strike of 1902, Loeb sat at his side and took notes during the marathon negotiations. Frequently, the aide could be seen leaning over and whispering advice into Roosevelt's ear. The other participants agreed that these whispered conferences had a visible impact on the course of the negotiations.

On many occasions, Loeb's advice saved TR from costly blunders. Left to his own devices, Roosevelt could be an impetuous man whose enthusiasm overcame his good sense. His affection for the Catholic Cardinal of Baltimore, for instance, led him to draft a letter to the Pope urging that the favored prelate receive an important assignment then pending in the United States. When Loeb got wind of the plan he was horrified. Not only would Catholics be outraged at Roosevelt's shameless interference in Vatican affairs, but Protestant fundamentalists would charge that the President had been tainted by a "Papist plot." After a few minutes of listening to Loeb's strenuous objections, Roosevelt reluctantly backed down and left his Holiness the Pope to conduct church affairs without the assistance of the President of the United States.

On those occasions when Loeb's careful vigilance failed to keep Roosevelt from stumbling over the edge, the secretary was at least on hand to cushion the fall. Loeb cheerfully accepted the blame for dozens of little White House mistakes, even when the President himself was obviously responsible. Thomas Lipton, the famous British merchant and yachtsman, was once denied an invitation to the White House since TR made no secret of his distaste for the man. The incident provoked a storm of international protest and a minor crisis in Anglo-American relations. At the height of the controversy, Loeb bravely stepped forward and told the press it was all his fault. Loeb's scapegoat role was even more transparent a few months later after TR's enthusiasm for his favorite horses provoked a short-lived scandal. In submitting his executive budget, Roosevelt requested $60,000 for maintenance of the White House itself, while $90,000 would go to maintenance and improvement of the adjoining stables. Congress and the press naturally howled in outrage, and Loeb offered an unconvincing explanation of how it had been his personal error that had attached undue importance to the President's mounts.

Most embarrassing of all was Roosevelt's scheme to dress White House attachés in formal, braided livery like servants in a European royal household. Oddly enough, history repeated itself seventy years later when President Nixon hatched a similar plan for the White House guards. In both cases, the public response was the same: indignation, derision, and plenty of laughter at Presi-

dential pretensions. After withdrawing the controversial uniforms, even so insecure an individual as Richard Nixon managed to make jokes about his own
mistake. President Roosevelt, however, reverted to habit and dispatched Loeb
to claim public responsibility for the error. It hardly mattered that knowledgeable observers only scoffed at such pretense; Loeb's role as whipping boy allowed the larger public to go on thinking of TR as a flawless hero who never
stumbled. Even more importantly, Loeb's martyrdom permitted the President to
continue seeing himself in those same terms. This was one of the reasons Loeb
was so indispensable to the President—psychologically as well as politically.
The secretary himself never complained about the abuse he was forced to accept. "That was all my fault," he told a reporter about another Presidential
misstep. "Just put the blame on me. That's what I'm here for, and I am perfectly willing to stand for it."

Every once in a great while the careful Loeb deserved the blame he received.
Such was the case with the great Reformed Spelling Crusade, a quixotic and
ill-fated drive in which Loeb encouraged the President every step of the way.
For years, Roosevelt had been interested in proposals to make written English
more logical and more phonetic. A group called the Spelling Reform Association recommended a series of moderate changes for this purpose, such as sub-
stituting "dropt" for "dropped," "thru" for "through," and "thoroly" for
"thoroughly." As President, Roosevelt assumed he had the power to change
the English language through executive fiat. He ordered the government printer
to adopt the suggested reforms on all official documents. What's more, he
promised the leader of the Reform Association that "Mr. Loeb, himself an
advanced spelling reformer, will hereafter see that the President, in his correspondence, spells the way you say he ought to."

Needless to say, Roosevelt's latest fad provoked unbounded hilarity in the
nation's press. Elaborate and fanciful forecasts were made of the future spelling
in Presidential papers. Whole columns were written using purely phonetic
spelling which bore no relation to Roosevelt's modest reforms. Secretary of
State John Hay teasingly signed a note to the President, "Jon Hä." Roosevelt
laughed along with his critics at most of this nonsense, but when Congress
began serious debate on the subject it was no longer a laughing matter. Congressional leaders attacked Roosevelt's well-intentioned initiative as a dictato-
rial attempt to undermine the American way of life. Time-honored spelling in-
consistencies were staunchly defended along with motherhood and the flag. In
the face of mounting criticism, Roosevelt finally revoked his order to the public
printer and surrendered to Congress. Loeb, however, refused to give up so
easily. This "advanced spelling reformer" could not believe that so obvious
and sensible an improvement in written English could be overruled by mis-
guided public sentiment. For months, he continued to insist on the new spelling
for all of the President's correspondence.

A fitting finale for the entire episode came in September 1907, as Roosevelt
stood on the deck of the Presidential yacht and watched a naval review off

Oyster Bay. Alongside the stately warships chugged a modest craft bearing reporters and decorated with a hand-lettered sign. As the ship approached him, Roosevelt saw that its sign read "Pres Bot." The President waved his hat and roared with delight. "Reformed spelling!" he bellowed across the water. "A most delicate compliment! A most delicate compliment!"

Unfortunately, TR's brushes with the press were not always so congenial. Roosevelt particularly resented it when journalists managed to pry loose confidential information from the White House or the federal departments. On occasion, Roosevelt would speak his mind at a closed-door Cabinet meeting only to find a transcript of his remarks on the front page of the papers the next morning. Responsibility for plugging such irritating leaks naturally fell to William Loeb, and the ubiquitous secretary repeatedly wrote Cabinet heads: "The President says it looks as if there is a leak in the Department and he would like to be advised how the information got out." Such letters, along with the threatening circulars Loeb eventually devised, offered a vent for his frustrations but no practical results. In the end, Loeb proved just as ineffective in stopping high-level leaks as the other White House "plumbers" who have grappled with the problem over the years.

The secretary did get results, however, with some of his direct pressure on reporters to give the administration the kind of coverage it wanted. Like Cortelyou before him, he handled every detail of Presidential press relations, but Loeb was far more aggressive than his predecessor in his dealings with reporters. He employed what might be described as a carrot-and-stick approach. If a journalist wrote about the administration in a manner Loeb considered "fair," then that reporter was rewarded with the full cooperation of the White House. The secretary made himself available day and night for questions and conversation, and it was not unusual for reporters to call him at home as late as one in the morning. If, on the other hand, a newsman proved consistently unfriendly to the administration, he was swiftly banished into outer darkness. For such malcontents, Loeb not only denied access to the President, but tried to cut off all news sources in the federal departments. "Let me talk to you about this man," he once urged Secretary of War William Howard Taft about a particularly hostile reporter who had requested an interview. "I wouldn't have anything to do with him," Loeb concluded and naturally enough, Secretary Taft had nothing to do with him.

Loeb's special fury was reserved for newsmen who cast aspersions on the President's character. In November 1904 the Boston *Herald* gave prominent space to an account of the Roosevelt children torturing a turkey that had been sent to the White House as a Thanksgiving gift. According to this story, the President's sons released the bird from its cage shortly before the holiday, then chased it around the lawn and plucked at its feathers until the poor animal collapsed. The President, it was alleged, stood by and laughed uproariously at the entire spectacle. Not content to report the "facts" of the episode, the *Herald* went on to editorialize against TR for his callousness and cruelty.

Upon reading these charges for the first time, Loeb immediately declared that there was "not one word of truth" in the *Herald*'s story. The turkey in question, he explained, was alive and well and living at Oyster Bay. Far from torturing the beast, the Roosevelts admired its beauty so greatly that they had decided to spare its life and shipped it to the barnyard of their Long Island estate. Loeb urged reporters who wished to verify his story to interview the bird in its new home. The real turkey in this case, the secretary insisted, was the Boston *Herald,* which had issued "a long series of similar falsehoods, usually malicious and always deliberate." This record called for retaliatory action. "Until further notice," Loeb ordered all employees of the executive branch, "the departments will exclude the individuals responsible for this series of misstatements from all facilities for information." So sweeping and effective was his decree that even the federal weather bureau in Boston denied the *Herald* access to its daily predictions until the paper agreed to retract its story.

Loeb's concern for favorable press led him to supervise personally all of TR's trips to the hinterlands. Post office dedications, political tours, and "inspection visits" of dams, parks, and construction sites could all be manipulated for public relations purposes. Loeb soon learned that sympathetic publicity could even be gained from Roosevelt's frequent vacations in the great outdoors. During one hunting expedition in Mississippi, the President generously refused to shoot a bear cub because it was too small. The incident produced an orgy of favorable comment as well as a new phrase—"Teddy Bear"—for the national vocabulary. In addition to arranging every detail of TR's travel plans, Loeb invariably accompanied his chief on all the longer trips. While Roosevelt tramped through the woods in search of elk or mountain lion, Loeb set himself up in a hotel room in the nearest town and attended to the business of the Presidency. He received hundreds of telegrams, many of them in code, asking for the President's attention. Most of these messages Loeb answered on his own, without bothering The Great White Hunter. At times, the secretary was forced to interrupt his work in order to help keep Roosevelt entertained. During a junket to Florida, TR persuaded his secretary to drop all business one afternoon and sail out to an unspoiled island off St. Augustine. Though the weather was chilly and grim, Roosevelt insisted on diving into the surf the moment they arrived. As the President thrashed through the waves and yelled for companionship, Loeb dutifully but briefly immersed himself, freezing his limbs to the point of numbness.

Loeb accepted such discomfort as one of the hazards of his job; traveling with the President had conditioned him to occasional indignities. At the conclusion of one glorious hunting party in Louisiana, TR and his comrades decided to celebrate their success by feasting on the carcasses they had brought back to camp. Loeb was invited to join them, but when he arrived at the campfire banquet he learned that the main course consisted of two enormous grizzly bears. Though Loeb's appetite for bear meat was well under control, he dared not offend the President. When the jubilant Roosevelt handed him a heaping, greasy plate of this hunter's delight, the secretary chewed away respectfully and tried hard to smile.

Fortunately for Loeb, Roosevelt usually proved far more attentive to the feelings of his aide. In public settings he showed every mark of respect for his secretary and tried to be a true friend as well as a gracious boss. Since Loeb was so clearly TR's social inferior, these little signs of esteem took on added importance. At Cabinet meetings, the President sometimes addressed the department heads informally or casually, but his secretary was always "*Mr.* Loeb"—with an emphasis on the "mister." At formal White House dinners, Loeb always occupied a place of honor, seated at one end of the long banquet table. Roosevelt explained that he placed Loeb there because he considered his aide to be cohost for all social functions.

In a sense, this position accurately reflected Loeb's intimacy with the entire Roosevelt household. He enjoyed an especially warm friendship with Mrs. Roosevelt, who considered him a good influence on her emotional husband. The New York *Times* reported that Mrs. Roosevelt was in reality Loeb's "strong-hold" in the White House, and that she often enlisted his aid in "bringing the President around" on matters that concerned her. Loeb proved so useful an ally in these palace intrigues that the First Lady began holding him up as a model to her children. In many instances, excessive praise by a parent can ensure a child's resentment, but for the younger Roosevelts it proved difficult not to like their pudgy, vaguely comical "Uncle Billy." After all, he labored day and night at the White House and seemed an indispensable adjunct to their hero-father. Loeb treated the children with sober respect, and his attitude was never patronizing. At times, he would interrupt pressing business to see to their special needs, such as arranging transport to the White House of a favorite pony. His patient service won Loeb the ultimate compliment: the children permitted him to attend their White House birthday parties. He was the only adult in the world, aside from their parents and one favorite aunt, who ever attained that distinction. In return, the secretary lavished Christmas gifts on all the Roosevelt children, and for years after leaving the White House he continued that tradition. Even in 1918, when the Roosevelt boys served in the U.S. Army in distant outposts around the world, Loeb sent his customary offerings for their Christmas stockings.

During the White House years, his responsibilities as financial manager of the Roosevelt clan occasionally forced Loeb to play a stern role with the children. When the two oldest boys went away to Groton and then to Harvard, Loeb supervised their bank accounts and saw that they always had the funds they needed. If one of them made an error in handling money, it was Loeb who provided the corrective. Theodore Roosevelt Jr. made just such a mistake during his first few months on his own, and Loeb solemnly proclaimed that a "bank account is not elastic and only good for the amount deposited—which means you have overdrawn your fourteen dollars." Kermit Roosevelt, the President's second son, became particularly dependent on Loeb's avuncular attentions. From the White House, the secretary sent books and research materials to help the boy with his battles as a member of his prep school debate team. After graduation, when Kermit enrolled at Harvard, Loeb even went up to Boston for a day to help him get settled.

The First Family's reliance on the versatile Mr. Loeb extended to every area of daily life. He served all the Roosevelts as a financial manager, inspecting all the bills that came into the White House and preparing the checks to pay them. This same meticulous eye for monetary detail led to Loeb's best-publicized triumph as a White House aide. In 1904, when an old friend from Albany days visited Loeb and warned him of possible frauds against the government by major sugar importers, Loeb took his suspicions to the President. At first, TR showed little interest in the matter, but after several conversations he agreed to authorize an undercover investigation. Loeb personally supervised the search for evidence, reaching into the Treasury Department for personnel. For nearly three years his efforts were frustrated. It was not until November 1907 that the secret investigation finally went public with charges that the "Sugar Trust" had rigged its scales in New York harbor in order to cheat the government of import duties. Amid spectacular headlines and universal applause for Roosevelt, a series of criminal cases went to trial. Convictions were returned on March 5, 1909—the day after TR left office. In his autobiography, the former President gave Loeb nearly exclusive credit for the timely exposure of the sugar frauds.

This courtroom spectacle of corporate vice brought to bay by government virtue added luster to the last months of an administration already enormously popular. For Roosevelt, the main question was whether the worshipful electorate would actually allow him to step down. After winning a full term of his own in 1904, he had announced that he would not seek reelection, but by 1908 the Republican Party was swept by a "Draft Roosevelt" movement. The President could not decide how to respond. On the one hand, he was only 50 years old and far too vigorous to settle for a quiet retirement. On the other hand, he had promised the public he would not run again and he feared that breaking that promise, and shattering the tradition against third terms, would compromise his standing with the people. TR continually reminded the press that he was not a candidate, but at the same time refused to endorse anyone else, thereby leaving room for further speculation. A definitive decision had to be made but no one was bold enough to try to force Roosevelt's hand—no one, that is, except William Loeb.

One morning shortly after he arrived at his desk, Loeb gave orders not to be disturbed and went in to the President. He shut the door to the inner office, sat down with his chief, and told him, in no uncertain terms, that he must make up his mind about the forthcoming campaign. If he continued to hesitate, the pressure to run for another term would become irresistible. The only way TR could avoid renomination was to announce his endorsement of someone else and then do everything possible to build up that chosen candidate.

Listening to Loeb's arguments, TR sighed and nodded his agreement. As

Roosevelt had once commented to a member of his Cabinet, "Loeb's judgment in politics is that of an expert." After several more conversations that same day, the President was ready to follow his aide's advice and throw full support to the candidacy of Secretary of War William Howard Taft.

No sooner had the decision been made than Loeb began working to secure the nomination for Taft. He took time off from his White House duties to meet with local party leaders and line up pledges of convention support. By the time Taft was nominated and elected, Loeb's political activity had become so conspicuous that nearly everyone in Washington expected him to win appointment as Republican national chairman. Taft, who wanted to escape from the shadow of Roosevelt's domination, quickly denied the rumors, but still faced the problem of what to do with Loeb. For a while there was talk that Loeb would follow Cortelyou's example and move from the White House to a major Cabinet post. Roosevelt himself seemed to favor this plan, but Taft bridled at the suggestion. Though he respected Loeb, he felt somewhat uncomfortable with the White House secretary's aggressive, pugnacious demeanor.

A suitable niche was finally found just a few weeks before the inauguration. Roosevelt wrote to Taft suggesting Loeb's appointment as Collector of the Port of New York, and this time Taft agreed. The collectorship was a choice patronage plum which commanded an enormous staff and a comfortable $12,000 salary. In offering the job, Taft went to great lengths to be gracious. "There is not any man in the United States," he wrote to Loeb, "to whom I feel more grateful and for whom I have more pleasure in doing the right thing than you."

After Loeb's ten whirlwind years with Roosevelt, the New York collectorship could not help being an anticlimax. Nevertheless, Loeb resolved to make the most of his opportunity. With characteristic energy, and his usual flare for publicity, Loeb set out to "clean up the customs mess." His previous experience in exposing the sugar frauds gave him some valuable insights for the job. As collector, he enforced the law vigorously and impartially, cracking down on prominent socialites as well as low-life smugglers. By the end of his four years in office, Loeb had saved the government hundreds of thousands of dollars and won the respect of even his most skeptical critics. Twenty-two years after he left the post, an oversized portrait of Loeb was hung permanently in the office of the collector to commemorate his distinguished service.

Loeb's most difficult decisions as collector involved his role in national politics rather than official duties at the Customs House. By 1910, while TR was still away on an extended world tour, the relationship between the former President and his chosen successor had already begun to sour. The Taft-Roosevelt split, inflamed by differences over policies and personalities, left William Loeb in an extremely awkward position. He felt intense personal loyalty to Roosevelt at the same time that he was a federal appointee officially responsible to President Taft. Loeb's first difficulty arose in June 1910, when Roosevelt asked him to make arrangements for the former President's triumphal return from abroad. TR cabled from Europe that any public celebrations must be on a "big scale" or not at all. Following these instructions, Loeb helped plan a huge jamboree at Madison Square Garden and made arrangements for all craft in New York harbor to sound their whistles in salute to the returning hero. When President Taft expressed interest in coming to New York to participate in the festivities, it was Loeb's delicate task to dissuade him. "It will be a T.R. day," the collector wrote, "and there will be no other note sounded."

As the breach between Taft and TR grew more serious over the summer, some Republican managers looked to Loeb as the key to preserving party unity. If only Loeb would return to his old post as White House secretary then all would be well. Taft had proven himself woefully inept as a politician, but with Loeb's experience, prestige, and finesse the administration could still be saved. Most importantly, Loeb's return to the White House would blunt the growing antagonism of Theodore Roosevelt. For his part, Loeb seemed willing to give up the collectorship and play the role of peacemaker in Washington, but the initiative would have to come from Taft. Unfortunately, the President's stubborn pride forced him to reject Loeb and turn instead to a series of second- and third-rate aides who led his administration into still deeper trouble.

When Roosevelt began talking seriously of challenging the President's renomination in 1912, the Taft administration was all but doomed. Loeb, among others, pleaded with Roosevelt not to become a candidate. "The only course for you," Loeb told him, "is to stay quietly at Sagamore Hill and mind your own business. By the time 1916 comes around the whole Republican Party will be yelling their heads off wanting you to be their candidate." This was excellent advice but Roosevelt, like an old war-horse scenting battle, seemed constitutionally incapable of heeding it. He plunged forward with his ill-fated candidacy and left his former secretary in a state of anguish. In February 1912, Loeb dutifully offered his services as manager of TR's campaign. The former President declined, citing Loeb's own best interests in his explanation. Since Loeb was not well-to-do, Roosevelt insisted, he could hardly afford to give up his position in the Taft administration.

Through the spring of 1912, Roosevelt and Taft slugged it out in the Republican primaries, while William Loeb looked on helplessly. Despite TR's success in most of these contests, the Republican convention ratified the choice of the conservative "Old Guard" and nominated Taft. TR, in a fury, stormed out of the party and took his followers with him. Running as a "Bull Moose" Progressive in November, Roosevelt outpolled Taft, but by shattering the Republican Party assured victory to the Democratic candidate, Woodrow Wilson.

As the Democrats took over in Washington, Loeb resigned the collectorship and accepted a top-level business position in New York. Oscar Straus, a friend and former Cabinet officer in the Roosevelt administration, arranged Loeb's appointment as a manager of the Guggenheim metallurgical and financial empire. It seems ironic that after a lifetime of denying Jewish affiliation, Loeb should take his place in a well-known Jewish enterprise which served as a prime target of anti-Semitism. Apparently, the salary the Guggenheims offered

Loeb helped him to ignore his old insecurities. He also proved ready to withstand attacks that were political in nature. *The Nation,* a leading progressive journal, lamented the spectacle of "Mr. Roosevelt's pupil and right-hand man, his trusty and well-beloved personal aide in the White House, passing directly from the service of the people to the service of the arch-enemy of the people. . . . One does not know whether to laugh or to weep. . . ."

Such condemnations did nothing to spoil the friendship between Roosevelt and Loeb. With his newfound financial security, Loeb purchased a five-acre shorefront estate, Waterleigh, which adjoined TR's property at Sagamore Hill. As new neighbors in this idyllic Long Island setting, the two friends became more intimate than ever. Loeb spent every spare moment in the company of his former chief, sharing horseback rides, swimming, or endless, rambling conversations on politics and history.

This interlude lasted only five years, before TR died suddenly at age 60 in 1919. For Loeb, the loss could hardly have been more devastating: the vital center had been removed from his life. At the funeral, he was asked to serve as an usher, along with members of the Roosevelt family. In the midst of the proceedings, there was a bustle in the church, and all heads turned to see the bulky, top-hatted figure of former President Taft, arriving unexpectedly. He was pushed to the front where the ushers were standing, and Loeb stepped up to meet him. He must have looked on Taft with cold eyes, remembering past affronts and injuries, for he took the former President and placed him in an obscure pew behind the family's servants. After Loeb abandoned him there, Archie Roosevelt, one of TR's sons, came up and tried to correct the situation. He offered Taft his hand and said, "You're a dear personal friend and you must come up further." He placed Taft in a more suitable position, behind the Vice-President of the United States and just ahead of the Congressional delegation.

With Roosevelt gone, Loeb abandoned any lingering interest in politics and concentrated on his business career. Following the path of Joseph Stanley-Brown, Daniel Lamont, and George Cortelyou, he went from devoted service as an underpaid White House aide to enormous wealth as a Wall Street tycoon. He became a director of numerous corporations, including Pacific Tin, Connecticut Light and Power (where he worked alongside his old colleague Cortelyou), Angola Mines, Congo Mines, Yukon Gold Company, and the Reo Motor Car Company. He also served as president of the Albany Southern Railroad and vice-president of American Mining and Smelting. Considering these credits, it is hardly surprising that in 1930, Loeb qualified for a highly publicized list of "The Fifty-Nine Rulers of America."

Despite his spectacular financial success, Loeb continued to look back on his years with Roosevelt as the most important time of his life. He was cofounder and president of the Roosevelt Memorial Association and devoted much of his time and money to its activities. Every year on TR's birthday Loeb led a small group of the President's onetime associates to lay a wreath on the hillside grave at Oyster Bay. After standing in silence for a few moments in the chill October haze, the loyalists retired to the North Room of Sagamore Hill. Here, surrounded by the stuffed heads and preserved skins of TR's hunting expeditions, they built a roaring fire, read aloud from the writings of their hero, and shared stories of the old days. At sunset, the members of this aging inner circle dispersed to their various homes or executive offices and struggled, for another year, to connect the drab but comfortable present with their memories of a glorious past.

Loeb lived on until September 1937 when, within a month of his 71st birthday, he contracted pneumonia. He died in a hospital bed after an illness of twelve days, with his wife and his only child standing at his side. Though he had suffered serious reverses during the Depression, Loeb still left an estate valued at $256,405.

His obituaries made no mention of the fact, but Loeb's years in the White House marked the high-water mark for the job of Secretary to the President. Like Lamont and Cortelyou before him, he did virtually everything for his boss, combining the modern-day functions of a Chief of Staff, appointments secretary, legislative liaison, personal stenographer, press secretary, political counselor, and intimate advisor. As the Presidency continued to expand, it became increasingly clear that no one man could continue to perform all these functions, and it is a tribute to Loeb's abilities that the concentration of roles lasted through the Roosevelt administration. When Taft's aides tried to duplicate the accomplishment, the result was disaster.

Charles Dyer Norton:
The Empire Builder

It is one of the ironies of White House service that the more effectively an aide does his job the harder it is to trace his personal impact on history. The most successful assistants work smoothly and unobtrusively. They merge purpose and personality so completely with the Presidents they serve that it is impossible to separate their accomplishments from the achievements of their employers. A blundering or corrupt assistant, on the other hand, can change events in a visible and dramatic way. It is easy to follow his trail because of the wreckage he leaves behind.

One such aid was Charles Dyer Norton, the arrogant, ambitious Secretary to President William Howard Taft. Norton was neither a thoroughgoing scoundrel like Orville Babcock nor a hopeless bumbler like William K. Rogers, and yet his negative impact was more decisive than that of any of his predecessors.

Norton was born in Oshkosh, Wisconsin, on March 12, 1871, the son of a Congregationalist minister. At age 14, young Charlie went to work for the Northwestern Life Insurance Company in Milwaukee. To the sale and preparation of insurance policies, this boy businessman brought the same fervor that his father devoted to the word of God. By the time he was 18, Charlie had saved enough money to pay for his college tuition. He enrolled at Amherst, his father's alma mater, and graduated in 1893. Immediately thereafter he took a job with *Scribner's* magazine in New York but soon found himself bored with the undignified drudgery of lower-level journalism. The romance of business was in his blood, and after a year and a half with *Scribner's* he returned to his old association with Northwestern Mutual. As part of the firm's busy Chicago office, his rise was swift and dramatic. Norton had the gifts of a born salesman, with his strikingly handsome face, superabundance of nervous energy, and boundless confidence in his own abilities. He also had the good sense to marry well, wedding Katherine McKim Garrison in 1897. She was the daughter of a distinguished Hudson River family, a laughing, bright-eyed beauty who managed to charm everyone with her sense of humor. What's more, she was the favorite niece of Oswald Garrison Villard, the wealthy publisher of the New York *Post*. At the time of the wedding, Villard took an immediate liking to Charlie Norton and later praised him as "one of the most attractive and brilliant young men of his day."

It was only a matter of time before this rising star left his mark on the Chicago business community. In 1899 he launched his own insurance firm and enjoyed spectacular success from the beginning. Active in civic affairs, Norton made it his special mission in life to devise a comprehensive "scientific" plan for Chicago's future development. As president of the Merchant's Club, he organized a committee of aggressive young businessmen to achieve this goal. For more than four years, they worked closely with Daniel H. Burnham, the visionary architect and urban planner who had designed the Chicago World's Fair of the previous decade. The result of their labors was finally presented to the public amid great fanfare in 1909. In many ways this grandiose "Plan of Chicago" was typical of Norton. It called for a building program of imperial proportions, including sweeping boulevards, a system of parks and forest preserves, graceful plazas, a beautifully developed lakefront, and an advanced ring of highways surrounding the central city. Practical and political considerations played only a secondary role in the grand design, but it nonetheless represented a milestone in the history of city planning.

In the spring of 1909 one of Norton's colleagues from the committee that developed the plan, a genial, white-haired businessman named Franklin MacVeagh, won appointment as Secretary of the Treasury in the new Taft administration. Before leaving Chicago, MacVeagh pleaded with Norton to come along to the Treasury Department and to accept the post of First Assistant Secretary. Norton agreed at the last minute and won much praise for his decision. As he freely informed the press, he was sacrificing a $50,000 a year insurance business for a government salary of $4,500. The money meant little to him, he said, when compared to the chance for public service.

In his new post, Norton personally took charge of the fiscal bureaus and managed to save the government some $2 million. Such feats of organization were bound to catch the President's eye, especially when that President was suffering from acute problems with his White House staff.

William Howard Taft was an enormous, affable chap with a sandy-brown walrus mustache, ruddy complexion, and twinkling blue eyes. His six-foot, 310-pound frame was guided by a brilliant mind, though he had no taste, and little talent, for politics. He had not wanted the Presidency, but a combination of his wife's driving ambition and the urging of his friend Theodore Roosevelt had pushed him to the foreground. His chief ambition in life was to serve on the U.S. Supreme Court—a goal he finally realized eight years after leaving the White House. Even more than most Presidents, Taft needed a White House assistant who was aggressive, competent, and politically savvy. Yet instead of the strong figure his situation demanded, Taft was saddled with a timid, meticulous little man named Fred W. Carpenter.

Carpenter had been Taft's faithful secretary for over ten years, following his boss around the world on several occasions. He was efficient enough in a purely clerical sense, but the substantive demands of the top staff position were clearly over his head. Carpenter's problem was so obvious that even a clerk in the White House mailroom, one Ira T. Smith, was able to spot it. "He always wanted to please the President," Smith observed, "and thus was ineffective in trying to correct the situation that had arisen." The New York *Times* described Carpenter's predicament in more colorful language: "When the President scowled at him he trembled, and when the President scolded, he wilted with terror. When Mrs. Taft expressed disapproval of things in general or in particular, Carpenter's teeth chattered."

Though Carpenter's troubles amused many Washington observers, they were no laughing matter to the Taft inner circle. A number of the President's senior advisors—in particular his older brother and financial backer Charles P. Taft—told the chief executive in no uncertain terms that Carpenter had become an administrative liability. Taft, however, did not have the heart to replace his longtime aide until another position could be found for him. Finally, in May 1910, Fred Carpenter was rewarded for his trials with appointment as American Minister to Morocco. In that capacity, the newspapers surmised, he could sip his lemonade "in the midst of barbarians, sandhills, and bandits," far from the more savage realities of Washington politics.

In selecting a replacement as Secretary to the President, the advisors urged Taft to find a "live wire" who could "put the pieces together again and bring some order into the White House routine."[With his reputation for efficiency and dynamism, Charles Dyer Norton seemed a perfect choice. Taft actually had his eye on Norton even before he made the decision to remove Carpenter. In the spring of 1910 the President asked the young Chicagoan to accompany him on a tour of the Midwest. On the train between St. Louis and Cincinnati they ate breakfast together and wound up talking for several hours. Norton touched just the right chord with the President when he made a contemptuous reference to Theodore Roosevelt. The first strains had already begun to appear in the relationship between Taft and TR, and the President was pleased to see that Norton did not share the worshipful attitude toward Roosevelt that infected most Americans. Captain Archie Butt, Taft's friend and military attaché, reported at the time that "the President has taken the greatest fancy to Norton and talks most freely to him, far more than he would to some of his cabinet."

On June 6, 1910, Captain Butt reported: "There was a buzz of excitement about the White House today. The new secretary, Charles D. Norton, was sworn in and promptly began to attend to his duties in a masterful and able way. I believe that the President has found the right man for the place." Visitors to the executive mansion in those pleasant days of early June all seemed to share Butt's optimism. Even battle-scarred veterans of the Washington press corps were at first dazzled by Norton's self-confidence and physical magnetism. As he approached middle age, the new secretary maintained the boyish good looks of a college athlete. His high cheekbones, sensitive mouth, wavy hair, and deep piercing eyes left an indelible impression. He was tall, slim, graceful, and always dressed at the peak of elegance. The President himself delivered the opinion that his aide "lacked only one thing to make him perfect, and that was humor. He has not a scintilla of it."

A sense of humor would have been particularly useful in light of Norton's lofty ambitions. As Secretary to the President, he planned to reorganize the federal bureaucracy and to change the fundamental nature of his job. According to Norton's dream, a permanent, professional White House staff would provide the government with the continuity it had always lacked. These career officials would be above politics, serving continuously from one administration to another. By adopting this system the U.S. government could function as efficiently as a large corporation: the White House staff would resemble the company's administrative officers, while elected officials played the role of a board of directors.

Norton's plans for an independent White House establishment showed an obvious contempt for the democratic process. The administration's critics charged that he was motivated by a lust for power and the desire to build a personal empire within the executive branch. Congress, nonetheless, considered his proposals and on one point, at least, gave Norton his way. Insisting that salaries had to be increased in order to attract a "better class" of Presidential assistants, Norton secured raises for the four top members of the White House staff. For his own position, Norton asked that the salary be increased from $6,000 to $10,000 a year. The Senate approved the idea, but a budget-conscious House of Representatives forced Norton to settle for $7,500.

In dealing with Congress, Norton accepted such compromises, but his attitude toward his own White House colleagues was rude and inflexible. In one of his first initiatives, he assembled the executive employees to inform them that he wanted "men with brains and a college background" for all staff positions. His obvious implication was that the current crop of clerks held neither credential.

"He was the first modern efficiency expert I had ever seen in action," lamented mail clerk Ira Smith, "and I'm afraid that my reaction was to wish for a return of the catch-as-catch-can days of the gay nineties." In one typical move, Norton attempted to speed up the work of the White House mail room by presenting Smith with ten specially designed rubber stamps for forwarding letters to the various departments. Unfortunately, the dates on the stamps had to be changed every day with a pair of tweezers. Smith found it "so much quicker to write the name of the department on each letter" that he refused to use Norton's new equipment. This little episode might stand as an epitaph for the secretary's entire efficiency crusade. Norton failed to understand that a truly gifted administrator must take into account the ideas and feelings of his subordinates. Before long, the whole staff came to resent his delusions of grandeur.

Norton did nothing to help his cause with his high-handed treatment of Taft's favorite stenographer, Wendell Mischler. Unable to tolerate the idea that anyone else on the staff might enjoy a personal relationship with the President,

Norton decided that Mischler should be fired. One afternoon he sat down with the clerk, calmly dictated a letter of resignation, and then ordered the stenographer to sign it. Mischler refused and tried to see the President, but Norton had left orders that he was not to be admitted. For two weeks the embattled clerk remained in a state of limbo until he managed to explain his cause to A. I. Vorhys, a personal friend and Republican national committeeman from Ohio. After offering "a few choice bits of profanity," Vorhys commanded Mischler to "come with me." They marched together toward Taft's inner office, but as Norton saw them coming he jumped up to block the door. Vorhys roughly shoved him aside and burst in on the President. He stated the situation as briefly as possible, and then asked, "Is this your wish, Mr. President?"

Taft blinked back at him in disbelief and replied, "Why, Mischler is the last man I would want to see go!" Needless to say, the stenographer retained his post at the White House while Norton was forced to swallow his humiliation.

Despite such incidents, the energetic new secretary enjoyed a position as the President's undisputed favorite. In the presence of reporters, Taft jocosely referred to Norton as "the Under-President" and "my alter ego." At times, such signs of affection led Norton to take unwarranted liberties with his chief. While traveling with Taft, Norton once strolled unannounced into the President's railroad car, threw himself onto the sofa, and stretched out to make himself comfortable. The President, who remained formally seated, raised his eyebrows noticeably while the Secret Service men in the room looked on in astonishment. Norton talked for several minutes from his reclining position before he became sensitive to the uneasiness around him. "Mr. President," he innocently inquired, "you don't mind my resting here?"

"Guess you are pretty tired," Taft grunted, but at that point Norton could take the hint. He carefully straightened up before continuing his conversation.

Norton's gestures of disrespect were not always limited to symbolic questions of protocol. On one occasion, he openly criticized the President in the presence of a prominent Congressman. This Illinois Representative had been urging Taft to "boldly attack" former President Roosevelt and to seize unequivocal command of the Republican Party.

"Not yet, old man," Taft responded, patting the Congressman on the arm. "That is not my method."

"It may be well to try a new method," sneered Norton. He then turned to the Congressman and added, "It is what I have been advising him."

For most Presidents, such a patronizing remark from a White House assistant would have constituted an unforgivable offense. The easygoing Taft, however, simply tried to brush it off. "My methods are the best for me," he mumbled defensively. The President also contrived to ignore Norton's habit of quite literally winking at his White House colleagues from behind Taft's back. Captain Archie Butt interpreted these knowing glances as Norton's attempt to show off to the staff how well he "handled" the President.

It was part of Norton's strategy for President-handling to let Taft out of his sight as little as possible. Over the summer months the chief executive went horseback riding every afternoon and Norton naturally insisted on coming along. Never mind the fact that he had no skill as a rider and admitted that he was "afraid as death of a horse"; borrowing a mount from the Secretary of War, the President's "alter ego" resolved to master the equestrian arts. He brought to such leisure time pursuits the same nervous intensity with which he approached his work.

In one form of relaxation, at least, Norton's cool, unsmiling countenance worked as an advantage. During a visit to New York, the President and his party sat down to a friendly game of poker at the home of Henry Clay Frick, the head of U.S. Steel. The chandeliers in that fabulous Fifth Avenue mansion burned until the small hours of the morning, by which time Charles D. Norton emerged as the big winner. Archie Butt supposed that "to his dying day he will be telling people how he fleeced the President of the United States."

If only Norton had played politics as skillfully as he played poker, the Taft administration might have been spared disaster. The secretary was a political bungler of the worst kind—a novice who was totally unaware of his own limitations. Archie Butt discerned "that he is greatly impressed by the most trivial discussions in politics at present and interpolates over the simplest statements of fact, 'That's very important.'" One night at the White House he sat through dinner with a Texas politician who discussed in detail the pros and cons of his possible race for the governorship. After listening intently to the mealtime conversation, Norton filled a temporary silence by offering his considered opinion: "That was all very interesting, wasn't it?"

In Norton, such laughable naiveté was incongruously wedded to a love of palace intrigue. For months he clumsily schemed against the Secretary of the Interior until he finally secured his resignation. Norton also worked for the downfall of Treasury Secretary Franklin MacVeagh, the old friend from Chicago who had brought him to Washington in the first place. Rumor had it that Norton was becoming frustrated with his job as Secretary to the President and that he coveted MacVeagh's place in the Cabinet. Even Ike Hoover, a White House usher, began to notice Norton's attitude toward MacVeagh. "He certainly has it in for him," he said, "and spends his time when with the President mocking the Secretary of the Treasury."

Norton failed in his drive to dislodge MacVeagh, but some of his other plots brought dramatic and disastrous results. The most famous of these was the "Patronage Letter," a woefully inept political ploy conceived and executed without the President's approval. The purpose of the letter was to mend fences with Republican "insurgents" who had become disenchanted with the Taft administration. Norton began by admitting in writing what the dissidents had suspected all along—that the administration manipulated federal patronage to undermine its opponents within the party. The letter went on to promise that this practice would be discontinued in the interest of Republican unity. As if to claim personal credit for this enlightened departure, Norton attached his own name to this curious document.

When the patronage letter appeared in newspapers across the country it enraged, rather than appeased, Taft's opponents. With a single stroke, Norton made the administration appear both foolish and unscrupulous. The New York *Times* called the letter "an astonishing confession" while one of the President's longtime defenders considered it "the most serious mistake which has been made during the administration."

As criticism mounted, Norton attempted to deny responsibility for the fiasco. At first he claimed that the letter had not been intended for publication and "crept into print through a mistake." This explanation ignored the fact that the secretary's office had prepared dozens of copies of the statement and that Norton had personally handed them out to his favorite reporters. Though Taft never formally disowned his aide's blunder, he told one close friend that had he seen the letter before its release "he never would have let it go out in that form."

As the storm clouds darkened over the White House, the First Lady, a sharp-tongued semi-invalid, became concerned over Norton's baleful influence on the President. "Will," she said irritably one morning at breakfast, "you approve everything—everything Mr. Norton brings to you. . . ."

"Well, my dear," her husband smiled back, "if I approve everything, you disapprove everything, so we can even up on the world at any rate."

"It is no laughing matter," Mrs. Taft insisted. "I don't approve of letting people run your business for you."

"I don't either, my dear, but if you will notice, I usually have my way in the long run."

"No you don't," she maintained. "You think you do, but you don't."

In this particular domestic quarrel, history has proven the First Lady correct. The confidential record of Taft's split with TR shows that the President's good intentions were frustrated by the maneuvers of his chief aide. Taft himself wanted nothing so much as peace with his predecessor. His political survival demanded it, and all his instincts urged him in that direction. Norton, however, harbored an abiding hatred for the former President and did what he could to drive a wedge between Taft and Roosevelt. At one point, he smugly declared to the head of the Secret Service that he planned to "eliminate Colonel Roosevelt as a factor in national politics." Norton recognized that the activist, highly personalized Presidency TR represented ran directly counter to any schemes for an entrenched White House establishment. Norton also distrusted Roosevelt's notion that big business must submit to government regulation. Hostility to the former President soon became an obsession and began to guide all of Norton's decisions. "He sees Roosevelt everywhere," Archie Butt reported, "and the President no sooner gets quieted down than Norton repeats more gossip and gets him all upset again."

The secretary also carried his anti-Roosevelt campaign to leading members of Congress. A Senator once came to Taft and said that he had heard from Norton that "the President feared some sinister action from Mr. Roosevelt." Taft seemed genuinely perplexed by this report. "You must have misunderstood Norton," he said, "for it is *he* who thought Roosevelt was inimical to me, and he has harped on it so much that I feared he knew something which he did not wish to divulge to me."

One detail which Norton most certainly "did not wish to divulge" was the extent of his meddling in New York State politics. Working closely with Vice-President James ("Sunny Jim") Sherman and other archconservatives, Norton decided to humiliate Roosevelt at the New York Republican convention. The former President wanted to deliver the keynote speech at the party gathering in his home state, but his enemies plotted to deny him that honor. When Archie Butt warned that Norton's participation would inevitably implicate the President in this anti-Roosevelt plot, the secretary naively promised that "the President is out of it. We have seen to that. His record is clean." The press nevertheless described the showdown in New York as an open struggle between Taft and TR. When the anti-Roosevelt forces won a temporary advantage, Norton dropped his claims of Presidential noninvolvement and declared it a "great victory for the administration." To celebrate, he went for a ride in the Presidential touring car with Taft and Archie Butt.

"Have you seen the newspapers this afternoon?" the President inquired. "They have defeated Theodore."

Norton let out a low, self-satisfied chuckle and Taft soon joined him with his hearty laughter. "We have got him," Norton declared, "we have got him—as sure as peas we've got him!"

Archie Butt did not know what to make of this display. A Georgia gentleman and career Army officer, he had served in the White House under Roosevelt as well as Taft and felt loyalty to both men. Riding along in the President's open car as the afternoon faded into evening, Butt wondered whether Taft and Norton "realized what they were saying or doing."

As Butt feared, Theodore Roosevelt refused to surrender without a fight. He took his cause to the floor of the New York state convention, where the delegates elected him temporary chairman and confounded the plans of his enemies. This dramatic turnaround encouraged those elements in the party who wanted TR to mount a direct challenge to Taft in 1912. When the press began speculating about a third term for Roosevelt, the need for some form of accommodation became so obvious that even Norton could no longer ignore it. In cooperation with Roosevelt's friend Lloyd Griscom, he arranged for the two Republican leaders to come together in a "summit meeting" at New Haven, Connecticut.

On the stormy afternoon of September 19, 1910, TR arrived several hours late at the private residence where the President awaited him. Despite the tension in the air, Roosevelt reported that "Taft and Norton were more than cordial and made a point of being as pleasant as possible." To break the ice, TR told stories and the President laughed aloud, but Archie Butt felt that "it was all strained.'' During the course of the meeting, Roosevelt could barely conceal his distaste for Norton. Whenever the secretary began a sentence, TR ignored him and continued speaking. Friends of the former President observed that this was his characteristic behavior ''when he wished to show contempt.''

The much-heralded encounter in New Haven settled none of the basic issues between Taft and TR and the President told reporters after Roosevelt's departure ''not to take the meeting too seriously.'' The entire episode might have been quickly forgotten had it not been followed by another one of Norton's disastrous blunders. On the train out of New Haven, the secretary could not resist the temptation of offering reporters his own description of what had occurred. According to Norton, TR had begged the President to meet with him because Roosevelt needed administration help with his political battles in New York State. In addition to its obvious distortion of the facts, this account seemed deliberately designed to insult Colonel Roosevelt. When TR learned of Norton's statement, he immediately denied that version of events and accused the secretary, and by implication the President of the United States, of duplicity and betrayal. His words were so strong that the correspondent who brought Taft the text of TR's statement waited in silence for the President's response. At first the broad, ruddy face showed a look of alarm, but then Taft forced himself to laugh. Archie Butt, who witnessed the scene, found it an unnatural laughter, ''full of concern, as when one whistles in a graveyard.'' Before their face-to-face encounter in New Haven, a slim chance had remained that Taft and Roosevelt might be reconciled; Norton's act of bad faith following the meeting had buried that chance, once and for all.

As gray autumn days replaced the last warmth of summer, a mood of deep depression settled on the White House. ''Norton looks like a death's head himself,'' Archie Butt reported, ''and well he might, for in every paper and from every side he hears condemnation of his chief when he knows that it is he and no one else who has brought the trouble about.'' The clerks in the office, who hated Norton from the beginning, now rejoiced at his disgrace. They chuckled among themselves and punched one another in the ribs whenever the grim secretary passed them by. Mrs. Taft seemed relieved that the aide had at last fallen from grace. ''Will said the other evening that Mr. Norton was very fresh,'' she told a friend, ''so I think he sees through him now, but it may be too late.''

While the capital buzzed with rumors of his imminent departure, Norton clung tenaciously to his job. Cabinet members continued to complain that ''the President won't let us say a word against Norton'' and an eerie atmosphere of plot and counterplot prevailed at the White House. Charles D. Hilles, a promising public servant who had taken over Norton's old job as Assistant Secretary of the Treasury, felt that he could not talk to the President in the executive offices without Norton's eavesdropping on every word. In order to conduct a confidential conversation, Hilles made special arrangements to meet Taft for a walk at twilight and soon found himself mentioned prominently as Norton's possible successor.

Senator Murray Crane called at the executive mansion and also seemed obsessed with secrecy. A few months before, he had been described in the press as "the chief political adviser of Mr. Norton," but as he huddled with Archie Butt in the darkened recesses of the White House basement he thoroughly disowned his former protégé. It was impossible to talk with the President, Crane whispered, as long as Norton remained at his post. According to the Massachusetts Senator, Norton had single-handedly separated the President "from almost every friend he ever had in public life and had almost made him hateful in the eyes of the House and Senate." How many White House aides in history could boast so decisive an impact?

On the morning of January 18, 1911, John Hays Hammond, head of the National League of Republican Clubs and one of Taft's closest friends, came to see the President. For weeks, reporters, Congressmen, and members of the Cabinet had all been urging him to make this call. As Hammond sat down with Taft, he reminisced about the old days, when he had predicted that his friend would one day occupy the White House. "I asked you then to make me a promise," he recalled. "With all our admiration for President Roosevelt, we agreed that he often acted impulsively without seeking advice from his friends or without making sure information was not being kept from him. I asked you to promise me that, when you were in the White House, I should always have the privilege of telling you anything that concerned your welfare, however disagreeable it might be. You shook hands on that, didn't you? Now I've come to tell you about Norton."

The President listened attentively. Two days later Norton submitted his resignation.

Though the secretary departed without a formal farewell to the White House staff, the lower-level clerks were unwilling to let him off so easily. A number of them found out exactly when he was leaving the office for the last time and gathered in silence near the door. They stared at Norton as he walked out and then burst into a jubilant and well-rehearsed hymn of praise.

The new Secretary to the President was, as expected, Charles Dewey Hilles. An easygoing politico and professional social worker, he offered a dramatic contrast to Norton. Hilles' first priority in the White House was to try to patch up the quarrel with Theodore Roosevelt, but he found it impossible to undo the damage Norton had left behind. A competent if colorless administrator, Hilles went on to supervise Taft's reelection campaign in 1912, in which the hapless President carried only two states and finished third behind Wilson and TR.

Norton's experience in Washington damaged Taft's career, but it did nothing to dim the secretary's own prospects in the business world. After leaving the White House, he accepted a job as vice-president of First National Bank in New York, one of the nation's three largest financial institutions. On his first day at work he found his desk covered with flowers and telegrams of congratulations—a far cry from the brickbats he had been receiving in the White House.

Though Norton stayed far away from politics for the rest of his life, he devoted much of his time to other forms of public service. During World War I, President Wilson appointed him one of the seven members of the Red Cross War Council. In this capacity, Norton crossed swords with his onetime employer, William Howard Taft. The former President urged that the Red Cross treat German wounded alongside our own troops. Norton, who had never been known for his forgiving attitude toward those he considered his enemies, strongly disagreed. "We do not propose to be tried for treason," he shrilled, "to lend aid and comfort to our enemies. We intend to attend to our own *American* Red Cross affairs."

After the war Norton took up a new cause: leading a group of prominent executives who wanted to create a long-range plan for the development of New York City. Having won universal acclaim with his Plan for Chicago some thirteen years before, Norton's dreams for New York were even more ambitious. To research the new project he went to Europe in the summer of 1922, meeting with architects and planners in half a dozen countries. He loved every detail of the work, but the strain and excitement of travel left him exhausted. A few weeks after his return to New York he became seriously ill. Norton was only 53, but a lifetime of tension and overwork had ruined his health. He died March 6, 1923, at his home on East 66th Street. The mourners at the funeral included his wife, his three children, and major figures from the New York financial community.

Norton's eulogists emphasized his record of business leadership and community service, barely touching upon his unhappy interlude in the White House. His term as Secretary to the President lasted less than a year, and it was only natural that his friends would try to forget it. As the New York *Times* observed, "the position of Secretary to the President shrunk several sizes under the Taft administration."

Mail clerk Ira Smith, who certainly had the viewpoint of an insider, saw Norton's months in Washington as "a turning point in the evolution of the White House staff"—completing the transformation begun under McKinley. Smith summarized the change in the memoirs he wrote years later:

> The small, intimate group that had previously gathered devotedly around the President and had considered itself on familiar terms with him was never completely restored. This was not entirely a result of Norton's operations, although they delineated the change. The fact was that the office of the Presidency was becoming too big and too busy to permit the continuance of the old set-up. Somewhere in Taft's administration the one-big-family atmosphere faded out, and when Woodrow Wilson became President, the times had changed and we were in for a busy office that had little chance for byplay, gossip, or an occasional game of craps in the basement.

The loss of camaraderie among the staff left the White House a far lonelier place for future Presidents. It is not surprising that the next man in line turned to a friendly outsider as his most important personal aide.

CHAPTER FIVE

A SINGULAR FRIENDSHIP

Edward M. House:
The "Dear, Dear Friend"

The two friends always found it difficult to say goodbye.

In the winter of 1915 one of them left Washington on a delicate diplomatic mission to Europe. His comrade, the President of the United States, went along to the railroad station. As they waited together the President's eyes grew moist. "Your unselfish friendship has meant much to me," Woodrow Wilson said, and heaped praises on this "most trusted friend."

At that point the President's companion, a gentle little man named Edward House, made a declaration of his own. "I have tried all my life to find someone with whom I could work out the things I have so deeply at heart," he sighed. "I had begun to despair, believing my life would be more or less a failure, when you came into it, giving me the opportunity for which I had been longing."

The next day House continued his thoughts in a letter to the President: "My! How I hated to leave you last night. Around you is centered most of the interest I have left in life and my greatest joy is to serve you. Your words of affection at parting touched me so deeply that I could not tell you then, and perhaps never can tell you, just how I feel."

Within twenty-four hours he felt the need to write Wilson once again: "Goodbye, dear friend, and may God sustain you in all your noble undertakings. . . . You are the bravest, wisest leader, the gentlest and most gallant gentleman and the truest friend in all the world."

This is hardly the blunt, businesslike tone one would expect from two leading politicians. It is, to put it baldly, the language of love.

Unconsciously at least, Edward House recognized the deep sexual resonance in his interaction with Woodrow Wilson. His honeyed words contained an edge of calculation and the President remained chronically vulnerable to them. The evidence strongly suggests that the two men never consummated their affection: Sigmund Freud himself wrote about the friendship without finding indications of a physical relationship. Nevertheless, the intensity of Wilson's attraction to his top advisor so far transcended the conventional bounds of friendship that it can be understood only as a consuming and ultimately self-destructive passion. If House and Wilson had been private citizens the course of their intimacy might have been important only to them. But they lived their lives at the very

137

center of world power and their curious connection changed the fate of millions.

Edward Mandell House was born in Houston on July 26, 1858. His father, Thomas William House, was an English immigrant who settled in Texas while it was still under Mexican rule. A baker by trade, the elder House prospered as a dealer in candy, dry goods, and cotton. By the time of the Civil War, he was acknowledged as one of the three wealthiest men in Houston. He owned an up-to-date store, a fleet of merchant ships, and a half-dozen major plantations.

After marrying the daughter of a prominent jurist, House lived out the dream of every red-blooded Texan: he sired seven children, all of them boys. Edward Mandell, the youngest, was named after a Jewish merchant in Houston who was a friend and business associate of his father. When Edward entered politics years later, his opponents whispered that his middle name indicated the ''taint'' of Jewish blood. Unlike his predecessor William Loeb, House never concerned himself with anti-Semites and as a result the baseless rumors continued even after his death.

Eddie House grew up in the rough and occasionally violent atmosphere of the Texas frontier. According to his own recollections, he spent many hours of his childhood practicing the quick draw in front of a mirror. All the House children owned real pistols and used them constantly in their play. They also enjoyed slingshots called ''Nigger shooters'' with which they tormented the black fieldhands who worked the family's plantations.

As the youngest of seven sons, Eddie had a difficult time holding his own in this world of brute strength and combat. When he was 12 his mother died of tuberculosis, leaving him vulnerable and alone. In the same year, House suffered an accident that changed the course of his life. While playing recklessly on a swing, the rope snapped and sent him hurtling to the ground. His head struck a carriage wheel and for several weeks he ''hovered between life and death.'' As soon as he recovered, ''malaria fastened upon me, and I have never been strong since.'' Poor health became a way of life. He slept in a bed whose head was raised five inches to facilitate his breathing. Hot weather made him ill and every summer he vacationed in New England or Europe. His energies were limited and his appearance was frail.

These developments solidified the personality traits which came with his position as the baby of the family. In dealing with those around him, Edward relied on quiet manipulation rather than strength. One of his schoolmates recalled that he won attention by playing the role of peacemaker in their dormitory. House used to deliberately provoke quarrels between his friends so that he could later step in and help them make up.

For a year, House attended a boys' academy in Bath, England, but for the most part his education took place at prep schools in Texas and Virginia. At 17 he attempted to enter Yale, but failed the entrance examination. The college administration suggested that he enroll at Hopkins Grammar School in New

Haven in order to prepare for a second try at Yale. Instead of concentrating on his studies House spent most of the next two years dreaming about politics. His best friend was Oliver Morton Jr., the son of a prominent Republican Senator from Indiana. House visited Washington several times as Morton's guest and on one occasion met President Grant and most of the Cabinet. These experiences led him to the conclusion that "two or three men in the Senate and two or three in the House and the President ran the government. The others were figureheads."

Such information did not help him with his Yale examinations; in 1877, House failed again. This time his father gave up on Yale and enrolled Edward at Cornell. The young man enjoyed the social aspects of college life, but remained stubbornly untouched by the slightest curiosity about books or ideas. When he became an advisor to the President at age 54, House found it necessary to furnish his New York apartment with an impressive library, though observant visitors noted that the expensively bound volumes remained fresh and unopened.

In 1879, T. W. House suffered a severe stroke and his youngest son promptly dropped out of Cornell to return to Texas. When the old man died a few weeks later, Edward settled down in Houston to manage his share of his father's estate. This inheritance was substantial enough to provide House with an income of more than $25,000 a year for the rest of his life and House soon added to his wealth with a series of successful business ventures of his own.

At age 23, this young Texas aristocrat took a bride. It is significant that in the unpublished "Reminiscences" in which he devoted page after page to his friendship with Woodrow Wilson, he dispensed with his marriage in a single sentence. "I married Loulie Hunter, Hunter Texas, on August 4, 1881 and travelled Europe for a year." This was his only mention of the woman with whom he shared fifty-seven years of his life. From other sources we know that Loulie House was a devout Presbyterian and an accomplished hostess who loved to wear "diamond ornaments" in public. *Collier's* magazine described her as "a beautiful type of the Southern woman." She used to call House "her lamb" and took inordinate pride in his accomplishments, while making few demands for herself or their two daughters.

Politics was House's consuming interest and he devoted more and more time to it as he grew older. In 1885 he relocated his family in a rambling home in the hills of Austin. The move brought him within a few blocks of the state capitol and the center of Texas political life. House began to entertain on a lavish scale, and the leading figures of the state Democratic Party became regular guests at his home. In the 1890's, House became particularly friendly with James S. Hogg, the fiery, controversial governor of the state. An outspoken champion of "the little people," Hogg won the enmity of the vested interests by his fight to regulate the Southern Pacific Railroad. He also won an enduring footnote in American history by whimsically naming his two daughters Ima and Ura Hogg. When he ran for reelection in 1892, the major corporations and all the daily newspapers in the state opposed him. Edward House took up his cause because Hogg's populist idealism appealed to him and because, as the only wealthy businessman in Hogg's corner, he could easily dominate the campaign.

Acting as chairman of an unofficial campaign committee, House ignored the regular party structure and rigorously shunned publicity. He put together an effective grass roots organization and quietly prepared for a "battle royal" on election day. When Hogg won an upset victory, House emerged as the dominant wizard of Texas politics. The governor wanted to reward his friend with a major appointment, but House refused everything. The only tribute he accepted was a purely honorary commission as lieutenant colonel on the governor's staff. His friends began to use the title, and soon the occasional mentions of "Ed House" in the press gave way to the more respectful "Colonel House." Though he claimed to be indifferent to the honor, the title stuck with him for the rest of his life. At one point he bought the uniform that was officially appropriate to his rank, but after looking at its heavy epaulettes and gold braid he could not bring himself to wear it.

In the decade that followed, House consolidated his position as behind-the-scenes boss of the Texas Democrats. He selected three subsequent gubernatorial candidates and managed to secure their election. Describing his role as "playing with politicians," House enjoyed every minute of it. Many times his protégés offered him positions of visible power, but he always preferred to remain in the background and to act the part of a gentleman reformer. William Allen White attributed to him "an almost Oriental modesty, a Chinese self-effacement. . . . He is never servile, but always serving."

His colleagues sometimes felt that House lacked ambition, but the Colonel strongly disagreed with them. "My ambition has been so great that it has never seemed to me worthwhile to strive to satisfy it. . . . If someone had offered me the Presidency on a silver charger, like the head of John the Baptist, probably I would have accepted the fit. But I was too well aware of the realities of politics to indulge in such speculations."

Those realities dictated that a small, frail man with a receding chin and a weak voice would not make an effective candidate; such a man must exert his influence on individuals rather than attempting to sway a crowd. When meeting people in an intimate setting, House usually made a favorable impression. His features included oversized ears, prominent Mongolian cheekbones, and a trim mustache. To Charles Seymour, the president of Yale, "the face was that of an Eastern philosopher who had discovered the answer to the riddle of life, no emotional disturbance at any time touching his voice or the lines around his eyes and mouth." Others saw his face as a mask that deliberately concealed his true feelings; they found the blank look in his feline blue eyes to be "singularly disconcerting." House never raised his whispery voice and seemed incapable of laughing aloud, though he occasionally let himself go in a low half-chuckle. His tact and discretion were legendary. Woodrow Wilson admiringly compared him to a fox.

By the year 1910, this quietly ambitious man had grown thoroughly bored with Texas politics and turned his attention to the national scene. With the Republicans split by the Taft-Roosevelt feud, the Democrats stood an excellent chance of capturing the White House for the first time in sixteen years. House resolved to attach himself to a promising candidate and he carefully considered the field. His first choice was Mayor William J. Gaynor of New York City, the colorful reformer who had made a name for himself by defying Tammany Hall. House traveled to New York to meet with Gaynor, and after a pleasant dinner with the mayor decided that he was indeed Presidential timber. Returning to Texas, House arranged for the state legislature to invite Gaynor to address a special joint session in order to build his prestige in the Southwest. When the mayor inexplicably refused this offer, House took it as a personal affront. "I wiped Gaynor from my political slate," he wrote, "for I saw he was impossible."

While House looked around for a candidate to replace Gaynor, many of his Texas friends urged him to support a political newcomer named Woodrow Wilson. A former history professor and president of Princeton, this recently elected governor of New Jersey held strong appeal for a public weary of conventional candidates.

In his memoirs, Colonel House shamelessly exaggerated his role in Wilson's preconvention campaign. "I decided to do what I could to further Governor Wilson's fortunes," he wrote. "I spoke to all my political friends and following, and lined them up one after another. This was in the winter of 1910–1911." This claim is unsupported by facts; during the period in question, House remained lukewarm, at best, in his attitude toward Wilson. "Wilson does not altogether satisfy me as a candidate," he wrote to a former Texas governor, suggesting that "some man not now mentioned may yet get the nomination and that would please me best of all."

By the time House joined Wilson's campaign, the Presidential bandwagon was already rolling. The candidate nonetheless recognized the Colonel as the most influential Democrat in the Lone Star State and treated him with unusual respect. When House paid one of his periodic visits to New York, the Governor asked permission to come up from Trenton to meet him. House must have been flattered and their appointment was scheduled for four in the afternoon of November 24, at the Colonel's suite at the Hotel Gotham.

That first meeting proved a fateful one for both men. The moment Wilson appeared a magical and rapturous atmosphere settled on the room. "We knew each other for congenial souls at the very beginning," House later recalled. "We agreed about everything. That was a wonderful talk. The hours flew away. . . ." Their conversation might have continued into the night except for the other appointments on Wilson's schedule. As the meeting ended, they spoke up simultaneously, each man asking when the other would be free again. Laughing over their mutual enthusiasm, they arranged an evening a few days later "when Governor Wilson should come and have dinner with me."

This second encounter, once again in the privacy of the Colonel's suite, proved even more satisfying than the first. This time the two men had the chance to talk at great length and their conversation covered "everything." "We found ourselves in such complete sympathy, in so many ways," House remembered, "that we soon learned to know what the other was thinking without either having expressed himself."

"Governor," House exclaimed, "isn't it strange that two men, who never knew each other before, should think so much alike?"

"My dear fellow," Wilson replied, "we have known each other all our lives."

This sentimental tone ran through all of the Colonel's direct contacts with Wilson, though in private House took a more cynical view of the relationship. "He is not the biggest man I have ever met," House wrote to his brother-in-law, "but he is one of the pleasantest and I would rather play with him than any prospective candidate I have seen. . . . It is just such a chance as I have always wanted for never before have I found both the man and the opportunity." In a letter to one of his Texas protégés three days after meeting Wilson, House expressed confidence in his ability to manipulate this newfound friend. "The more I see of Governor Wilson the better I like him," he wrote, "and I think he is going to be a man one can advise with some degree of satisfaction."

When the Democrats gathered in Baltimore for their national convention, they nominated Wilson on the forty-sixth ballot and moved the Colonel's dream of power a giant step closer to reality. Though he had played only a minor role in the preconvention battle, House plunged into the center of activity for the fall campaign. Wilson's campaign manager, William McCombs, recalled that the Texan "was around headquarters every afternoon, trying to meet everybody." House held no official title in the organization but his intimate friendship with the candidate gave him wide-ranging authority. One afternoon, McCombs came to the governor for a private conversation only to find House and Wilson seated side by side. Instead of leaving the room to allow the campaign manager to speak confidentially with his candidate, House "sat silently, in a bowed position, his hands crossed over his chest." He never took his eyes off Wilson and with "servile alacrity" nodded at the candidate's every word. To McCombs, "his manner was nothing more or less than that of a dignified flunky."

Flunky or not, this was the sort of relationship Wilson wanted. Even after his election to the nation's highest office he remained painfully insecure and no one understood his emotional needs better than House. "I never argue with the President when we disagree," House admitted. Whenever Wilson came to him for suggestions on drafts of his speeches, it was the Colonel's policy "to nearly always praise at first, in order to strengthen the President's confidence in himself which, strangely enough, is often lacking." In order to take full advantage of this insecurity, House flattered his friend in the most lavish possible terms. "You are so much more efficient than any public man with whom I have heretofore been in touch that the others seem mere tyros," he once wrote. On other occasions he assured Wilson that "no man has ever deserved better of his country" or told him that "the part you are destined to play in this world tragedy is the noblest part that has ever come to a son of man." Another man might have been embarrassed by such effusions, but Wilson soaked them up as hungrily as a crackpot messiah. "I do not put it too strongly," House purred, "when I say you are the one hope left to this torn and distracted world. Without your leadership, God alone knows how long we will wander in the darkness."

House knew what he was doing with all this extravagant praise. Years later he admitted in an interview that all that had been necessary to persuade Wilson to pursue a certain course of action was to assure the President of a glorious place in history. A glance at the Colonel's diary from the White House years suggests that he used this tactic frequently, deliberately, and with a minimum of sincerity. When the President responded to the Pope's peace proposals of 1917, House told Wilson, "you have again written a declaration of human liberty. . . . You are blazing a new path, and the world must follow or be lost again in the meshes of unrighteous intrigue. . . . I believe your reply to the Pope is the most remarkable document ever written." In the privacy of his diary, however, House grumbled that "I should have written somewhat differently myself. . . ." He also claimed credit for all positive elements in the President's statement, pointing out that Wilson "has covered all the points I asked him to embrace, and has left out all the dangerous points to which I called his attention."

Wilson never suspected the Colonel's insincerity because the words of fatuous flattery were what he needed to hear. As the son of an overbearing Presbyterian minister, Wilson grew up with a morbid sense of guilt and an abiding fear of his own unworthiness. Convinced that the outside world judged him as harshly as he judged himself, he could relax only in an atmosphere of uncritical and unwavering adulation. Many observers noted that the President seemed most comfortable when surrounded by admiring females. He was never "a man's man," as Edmund Starling, his Secret Service companion pointed out, and the only male "whose company he seemed to relish was Colonel E. M. House." House provided him with the acceptance and devotion of the most attentive wife or lover. "You are the only one in the world to whom I can open my mind freely," he told the Colonel, "and it does me good to say even foolish things and get them out of my system."

This sense of comfort was based on Wilson's knowledge that the Colonel was in no sense a potential competitor. "What I like about House," he told the Secretary of the Navy, "is that he is the most self-effacing man that ever lived. . . . He wants nothing for himself. His only desire is to serve those of us charged with guiding the administration." House carefully nurtured the idea of his modesty and self-sacrifice. He once wrote the President: "That my entire life is devoted to your interests, I believe you know and I never cease from trying to serve you.'' He insisted time and again that he cared nothing for power and publicity and was motivated purely by his affection for Wilson. ''I do not think you can ever know, my great and good friend,'' he wrote during the President's first weeks in office, ''how much I appreciate your kindness to me. . . . My faith in you is as great as my love for you—more than that I cannot say.'' When the two friends were apart, House assured Wilson, ''I think of you every day.''

In writing about this unusual relationship, Sigmund Freud suggested that the President unconsciously identified with Colonel House. As a child, Wilson had been sickly, frail, dreamy, soft-spoken, and hopelessly overawed by his ''masterful'' father. The President saw these same traits in House and seized the chance to recreate his boyhood pattern. This time Wilson himself played the role of dominant parent, but treated House with the love and indulgence which his father had always denied him. To Wilson, House was a part of himself—a shadow of his forgotten childhood. ''Mr. House is my second personality,'' the President said. ''He is my independent self. His thoughts and mine are one.'' In later years, House suggested that ''perhaps Wilson liked me because talking to me was like arguing with himself.''

In the period between the election and the inauguration, House seemed surprised that Wilson wished to be so intimate a friend. The President-elect prepared for his term of office by paying a half-dozen overnight visits to the small apartment the Colonel rented on Manhattan's 35th Street. Before his distinguished guest arrived, House sent his wife and servants packing to his daughter's apartment uptown so he could treat his patron to a night of perfect privacy. Dinner was carefully prepared in advance. During their first evening together, House took his guest to a Broadway performance of *Peg O' My Heart*. After the theater they returned to the apartment for milk, sandwiches, and rambling conversation until after midnight. The next morning, House arose at eight to prepare Wilson's breakfast. He had learned in advance to serve up the President-elect's favorite fare—a bowl of cereal and two raw eggs with a few drops of lemon juice squeezed into them. To pass the day, the two friends took a tourist boat to Ellis Island and later strolled through the Metropolitan Museum of Art.

In addition to the time they gave to relaxation, Wilson and House began laying plans for the new administration. The President-elect wanted his friend to serve in the Cabinet and offered him any post he desired other than Secretary of State. House graciously declined, noting in his diary that he preferred advising the President on matters in general to confining his activities to a single department of government. Honors such as Cabinet titles he left to lesser mortals, including two of his former cronies from the Texas Democratic Party. House suggested their names as part of the list of major appointees which he prepared at Wilson's request. In shaping his administration, Wilson followed the Colonel's recommendations for seven of the ten Cabinet departments.

At least as important as the men he pressed upon the President were the ideas

House planted in Wilson's mind. A few weeks before the inauguration, the Colonel gave his friend a curious novel by an anonymous author and urged him to read it. The book, *Philip Dru, Administrator,* told the story of an idealistic West Point graduate who leads an armed revolt against the reactionary government in Washington. Philip Dru wipes out the federal forces in one enormous battle and enters the capital as a conqueror. He suspends constitutional government, proclaims himself "Administrator of the Republic," and leads the country to a period of unparalleled social progress. Corruption is curbed in both government and business while workingmen are given a greater share of the wealth they produce. The currency is reformed, a graduated income tax is instituted, and a new, up-to-date constitution is adopted. After several years of inspired leadership, the great dictator steps down in order to restore democratic government. With his reforms complete and the applause of his countrymen ringing in his ears, Dru sails off to Europe with his sweetheart to organize a "League of Nations" that will ensure world peace for all eternity.

We do not know whether Wilson realized that the unnamed author of this visionary hodgepodge was none other than Colonel House. The Colonel had completed the book in absolute secrecy at the height of the Presidential campaign, indulging his personal fantasies at the same time he advanced his political ideas. Commenting on *Philip Dru* to one of his Texas friends, he showed how deeply he identified with his hero. "I am sending you the book of which I spoke," House wrote. ". . . It was written by a man I know. . . . My friend—whose name is not to be mentioned—told me . . . that Philip was all that he himself would like to be but was not." Dru was robust, handsome, charismatic—and military dictator of the United States.

House took every precaution to hide his connection with this alarming novel. The publisher composed all letters to the Colonel on his own typewriter to prevent even his personal secretary from discovering the author's identity. The critical response to *Philip Dru* showed that House's concern for anonymity was entirely justified. The New York *Times* found the writer "quite incapable of producing a character or sustaining a plot." Walter Lippmann sneered that "the imagination is that of a romantic boy of 14 who dreams of what he would do if he had supreme power and nobody objected. . . . He shows what a splendid democracy a real autocrat could establish."

Publication of *Philip Dru* in the last months of 1912 produced widespread speculation as to the identity of its author. Many newsmen suggested that the novel was the work of that well-known egomaniac, Theodore Roosevelt; others supposed that William Jennings Bryan was the guilty party. The guessing game intensified over the years as the book's influence on the Wilson administration became increasingly obvious. "All that book has said should be comes about," observed the Secretary of the Interior. "The President comes to 'Philip Dru' in the end." Finally, five years after publication, an enterprising bookseller put two and two together. Noting that "so many of the ideas expressed in *Philip Dru, Administrator* have become laws of this Republic, and so many of his ideas have been discussed as becoming laws,'' he suggested that the novelist must be the President's closest advisor. ''Is Colonel E. M. House of Texas the author?'' he concluded. ''If not, who is?''

House never responded to this clever deduction. He had no desire to remind the President that some of the key items in Wilson's legislative program —including the much-praised Federal Reserve Act—had been borrowed from the pages of the Colonel's book. ''It was invariably my intention with the President . . . to make him think that ideas he derived from me were his own,'' House said. ''In the nature of things I had thought more on many subjects than had the President, and I had had opportunities to discuss them more widely than he. But no man honestly likes to have other men steer his conclusions. We are all a little vain on that score. Most human beings are too much guided by personal vanity in what they do. It happens that I am not. It does not matter to me who gets the credit for an idea I have imparted.''

By avoiding reporters, House not only reassured Wilson as to his selfless devotion but built up a national reputation as an all-powerful man of mystery. House won far more publicity with his quiet and confidential mode of operation than he would have with the most blatant self-advertisement. His only concern was that the frequent speculation about his behind-the-scenes influence might begin to offend the President. In 1916, Mark Sullivan wrote in *Collier's* that the administration would have been equally successful if House had been the chief executive and Wilson the advisor. The Colonel noted the article in his diary and commented, ''these are the things I fear most.''

House need not have worried—Wilson found that the Colonel's prominence served an important purpose. Since everyone in the country knew of House's intimacy with the President, the Colonel handled thousands of people who would otherwise have troubled his chief. Dividing his time between Washington, New York, Texas, Europe, and his summer home on Cape Cod, he met with businessmen, office-seekers, inventors, Congressmen, Cabinet members, foreign ambassadors, and even justices of the Supreme Court. House processed an astonishing variety of personal and political matters, dealing effectively with every branch of the federal establishment. He became, in the phrase of historian John Morton Blum, ''the government's ex-officio Prime Minister.''

Whenever the Colonel happened to be in Washington, he showed up at Cabinet meetings and greeted the members as they came in. Usually he had something to say to each of them and his brief comments carried great weight. When vacancies occurred in lower-level positions, the Cabinet chiefs regularly asked House to suggest replacements; by following his recommendations they could be sure of pleasing the President. Nothing seemed too small for the Colonel's supervision: the Secretary of the Interior once asked his permission before accepting an honorary degree from a major university. In dealing with the Cabinet, House understood that he filled a vacuum that had been left by Wilson. ''The President lacks executive ability,'' he wrote in his diary, ''and does not get the best results from his Cabinet or those around him. . . . No one can see him to explain matters or get his advice. Therefore they come to me and I have to do it at long range. . . ."

House even acted as an occasional intermediary between Wilson and the White House staff. Whenever a cook wanted a raise or a clerk proposed a change in daily routine, the matter came to the Colonel's attention. The President's personal physician once noted that Wilson suffered attacks of indigestion whenever his secretary, Joe Tumulty, discussed business at the dinner table. Instead of taking the issue directly to Tumulty or mentioning the observation to his Presidential patient, the doctor went to House. Within hours, the Colonel tactfully settled the matter with the secretary and the executive digestion immediately improved.

For the most part, House enjoyed a smooth working relationship with Tumulty, a plucky, genial Irishman who had served Wilson since his days as governor of New Jersey. Under different circumstances, this capable young man might have proven himself an outstanding Secretary to the President, but the House-Wilson partnership undermined Tumulty's importance. The secretary handled the press and coordinated the President's schedule, but the whole world knew that House was the man to see if you wanted results at the White House.

House, in fact, assumed some of the general functions that had been performed in previous years by White House secretaries. "The President and I transact a great deal of business in a very short time," the Colonel reported in his diary. "He seldom or never argues with me after I have told him that I have looked into a matter and reached a conclusion. He signs letters, documents, and papers without question." Though he held no official position and drew no government salary, House saw nothing incongruous in his enormous executive power. "I wish I could always be here," he wrote, "to do those things for the President and give him time to devote himself to the larger problems which confront the country. . . ." The slightly patronizing tone is reminiscent of latter-day aide H. R. Haldeman, who wanted to protect President Nixon from all "trivial" concerns so he could devote himself exclusively to the "big questions." In more candid moments, the Colonel recognized the personal advantages in this arrangement. "He does not realize," House exulted in 1918, "that there is but little of importance that goes to him, either directly or indirectly, that I have not either passed upon beforehand or at least know about. It may be well that this should be so."

Perhaps the most remarkable aspect of the Colonel's position was the fact that he maintained it while spending most of his time away from the White House. Complaining constantly that the Washington climate imperiled his health, House avoided the capital as much as possible. This policy served a political, as well as a medical purpose: by strategically manipulating his absences, House deepened the President's sense of dependence. Wilson often pleaded for visits from his friend and looked forward to the Colonel's Washington arrivals with boyish anticipation. He usually went out to meet House at the railroad station and arranged his schedule so they could be together constantly. In the middle of one of these visits the Colonel took suddenly ill, thereby spoiling the elaborate plans the President had made. House wanted to return to New York or enter a hospital in Washington but Wilson wouldn't hear of it. The President kept his friend a virtual prisoner in the White House, providing doctors, medicine, and nurses at government expense and personally supervising the sickroom activities.

Whenever the two men separated they maintained an intense and highly personal correspondence. House wanted to protect the privacy of these letters and worked out a complex system to circumvent the mail clerks and secretaries of the White House staff. The Colonel addressed his letters not to the President but to the veteran White House usher Ike Hoover. Inside these packets he placed sealed envelopes which Hoover was ordered to deliver personally—and confidentially—to the President. In responding to these letters, Wilson banged out replies on his own portable typewriter, making no carbon copies so that his words would remain an absolute secret.

Even without written correspondence Wilson felt that a mystical, telepathic bond kept him connected to House. For even the most critical diplomatic missions the President refused to give his friend specific instructions, believing that the Colonel's thoughts and purposes would always be identical to his own. "You need no instructions," he said, "your mind echoes mine."

This heightened sensitivity to each other played a role in even their most casual interaction. Occasionally, the two friends went for outings in the countryside near Washington. They once spent a night together in a rustic lodge, talking till 12:30 before preparing for sleep. As the Colonel crawled into bed, Wilson "came into my room to see that everything was properly arranged." The next morning, the President's concern for his friend took an even more concrete form. "He arose a half-hour earlier than was necessary, merely to give me the uninterrupted use of our common bathroom. This illustrates, I think, as well as anything I could mention, his consideration for others and the simplicity of the man."

The Colonel's small apartment in New York City remained the most congenial setting for their intimacy. Before each of Wilson's visits, House moved his wife uptown, barred his front door, and disconnected his telephone. Thanks to these elaborate precautions, he could offer Wilson the blessed choice between going to bed at an early hour or enjoying an evening of uninterrupted fireside conversation. "The matter of entertaining a President within such confined quarters as our little apartment is not an easy undertaking," House admitted. "However, the confusion will cease the moment the President arrives. . . . When he is once here, everything appears as peaceful as if there were no such things as noise and confusion in the world."

These visits became even more important to Wilson in the summer of 1914 after the death of his wife Ellen. "I have never seen a man more dependent on a woman's companionship," the Colonel observed and did what he could to lift the President's spirits. Like all who knew Wilson, House realized it was only a matter of time before the President took a second wife. Sure enough, after less than a year of mourning, he proposed marriage to Edith Bolling Galt, a buxom, well-bred Virginia widow. This romance appalled his political advisors, who feared that a wedding so soon after the death of his first wife might jeopardize the President's chances for reelection in 1916. Leading Democrats wanted House to dissuade Wilson from his precipitous course, but the Colonel knew better than to interfere with the ways of love. While his diary registered a growing irritation at Mrs. Galt's claims on the President, House showed her every superficial courtesy and encouraged the President's nuptial plans. He helped select a wedding date, and even went to Tiffany's on Wilson's behalf to pick out engagement and wedding rings. He also provided Mrs. Galt with unsolicited advice on the best way to "help" the man she was about to marry. The future First Lady listened respectfully, but began to resent the Colonel's intrusion in her most intimate affairs.

After the wedding, House focused his attention on plans for the President's reelection battle. The administration faced an uphill struggle against the resurgent and reunited Republicans, and Wilson wanted House to take over as Democratic national chairman. The Colonel refused, citing his usual excuse of poor health, but nonetheless installed his son-in-law as party treasurer and managed to dominate the campaign organization. He confidently predicted victory, but also made special plans in case of defeat. House suggested to the President that in the event Charles Evans Hughes, the elegant, bearded Republican candidate, won the November elections, Wilson should immediately appoint Hughes Secretary of State. Then Wilson and his Vice-President would both resign, making the Secretary of State the new President under the laws of White House succession that applied at the time. This extraordinary plan would allow Hughes to take over the government at a critical moment in international diplomacy without the awkward four-month interval between election and inauguration day. Wilson secretly agreed to the Colonel's scheme, and on election night it looked as if he would be called upon to put it into effect. Early returns indicated a Republican sweep, and it was not until two days later that the final count gave Wilson an extremely narrow margin of victory. After the fact, House smugly declared, "I believe I can truthfully say that I have not worried a moment."

On the evening of the inauguration, House watched the festivities with the Wilsons. "The family generally were at the main windows. The President and Mrs. Wilson sat by a side window, curtained off, and asked me to join them. The President was holding Mrs. Wilson's hand and leaning with his face against hers." Whatever his mixed feelings about Wilson's wife, House was pleased to be part of this charmed circle. "We talked quietly of the happenings of the day and I spoke of my joy that we three, rather than the Hughes family, were looking at the fireworks from the White House windows."

At ten o'clock the President went up to his study while Mrs. Wilson remained downstairs to talk to House. She suggested to him that during Wilson's second term he should accept the post of Ambassador to Great Britain. From her point of view the move made perfect sense; with her chief competitor tied up on the other side of the Atlantic, Edith Wilson would exercise an uncontested hold on the President's affections. House, on the other hand, had no desire to give up the position he had so painstakingly built up over the last four years. Why should he take on a London diplomatic post when he already enjoyed overall supervision of American foreign policy?

The Colonel's remarkable role in international affairs began early in Wilson's first term, when the clouds of war gathered over Europe. As he considered the situation, House longed to apply his gifts as a charmer and manipulator in a last-minute attempt to avert disaster. With Wilson's blessing, he traveled to the continent in the spring of 1914 on a mission he called "The Great Adventure." He aimed to hammer out a series of compromises on the issues dividing the major powers. Though he carried no formal commission from his government, the crowned heads of Europe honored him as a personal representative of the American President. "The life I am leading," he exulted in his diary, "transcends in interest and excitement any romance." Kaiser Wilhelm of Germany, who particularly enjoyed the Colonel's company, recalled years later that House's mission "almost prevented the World War." While the Colonel patiently pursued his peace initiatives in London, a Serbian fanatic shot the Austrian Archduke in the town of Sarajevo and triggered a chain of events that led inexorably toward war.

The American public viewed the ensuing slaughter with horror and disdain, wanting no part of it. Propagandists who claimed that the war represented the elemental struggle between freedom and tyranny could hardly be credited. Russia, surely the most autocratic state in Europe, fought alongside the supposedly freedom-loving Allies and one of the officially announced Allied war aims specified the seizure of new territory for the Czar. On the other side, it must be remembered that the Germany of Kaiser Wilhelm bore only a superficial resemblance to the nightmare Germany of Adolf Hitler. In 1914 the Germans enjoyed a well-established constitutional government, lively political parties, and the most advanced social welfare policies in the world. The nation's only "crime" in the prewar period was its desire to catch up to Britain and France in building an empire of overseas possessions. At the beginning of the war, in fact, a substantial body of American opinion favored U.S. support for the German cause. Many other Americans strongly backed the Allies, but the overwhelming majority distrusted both sides and favored a policy of strictest neutrality and noninvolvement. That was precisely the policy that Woodrow Wilson promised the people. When he won reelection in 1916, he ran on the slogan "He Kept Us Out of War."

Within six weeks of his second inauguration, this "Peace President" ordered American boys to join the bloodbath and persuaded a divided nation to accept his decision. "Why did the Americans declare war upon Germany?" asks the English historian Andrew MacPhail. "Their territory was not infringed; no treaty was broken; their sovereignty was not challenged; no enemies appeared on the horizon, still less upon their land borders or upon their coasts. There was no cause for fear, no reason for panic, none, in short, of those inescapable forces that impelled Germany, France, England, Russia, and Belgium into the last refuge for nations desiring to endure." The only way to follow America's crooked and confusing road to war is to consider the internal politics of the Wilson administration. At the center of that politics, of course, stood Colonel E. M. House.

From the firing of the first guns in Europe, House was a committed partisan of the Allied cause. His father had been born a British subject and House himself had spent a year of his boyhood as a student in the English city of Bath. Though he worked for peace before the war began, once the killing commenced he did everything he could to force the United States into battle. Walter Lippmann described him as "the protagonist of what might be called the British imperialist view." He became "the honest broker between Wilson, who longed for peace without entanglement, and the people on both sides of the Atlantic who had set themselves to draw the U.S. into the war."

House knew he could never succeed with Wilson if he revealed his true intentions. Instead, he followed a policy he had stated revealingly in *Philip Dru*. "If we would convince and convert," Philip tells his soulmate Gloria, "we must veil our thought and curb our enthusiasm, so that those we would influence will think us reasonable." When advising the President, House talked only of world peace. He encouraged Wilson in his attempts to mediate the conflict, but rejoiced in his diary when the British rejected these offers. "I feel they are determined to make a complete job of it while they are in it," he wrote, "and I also feel in my heart that it is best for Germany, best for Europe, and best for the world to have the issue settled for all time to come." Nothing less than the complete destruction of Germany would satisfy him as he reverted to the dreams of glory and conquest he had expressed in *Philip Dru*. When the President hesitated, House worried that "we had lost our opportunity to break with Germany. . . ." This was a strange point of view in an administration publicly committed to keeping the peace. "I am surprised at the attitude he takes," the Colonel complained when Wilson seemed to take his own pledges seriously. "He evidently will go to great lengths to avoid war."

House, meanwhile, went to great lengths in the opposite direction. The key issue in American foreign policy was "Freedom of the Seas," or the right of neutral shipping to deliver goods to the belligerents. During the war that right was menaced by both the British and the Germans, who initiated blockades against one another. With their superior surface fleet, the British stopped American ships bound for German ports, while German submarines threatened cargo destined for England. Despite the essential symmetry in the situation, House made sure that German and English provocations were treated very differently. After a series of incidents with the British Navy, the State Department prepared an emphatic and angry note of protest to His Majesty's government.

House intercepted the note in the President's office and took it with him to a top-secret meeting with the British ambassador. The diplomat read the document in horror and told House it would end all chance for Anglo-American cooperation. This was a development that House refused to tolerate, and he sat down with the ambassador to compose an acceptable substitute for the State Department communiqué. The result was an inoffensive memorandum that contained a general discussion of the issues but no direct protest. Owing to his influence with Wilson, House saw to it that this was the version dispatched to London while the solemn, well-considered State Department draft disappeared into the government files. In effect, the Colonel had arranged matters so that a British ambassador dictated American foreign policy.

If House had displayed similar flexibility and consideration in dealing with the German leadership, world peace might have been concluded in 1915. In February of that year, James Gerard, U.S. Ambassador to Berlin, cabled Wilson that an historic opportunity had arrived. Top officials in the Kaiser's government wanted the American President to offer a concrete proposal for peace, and if that plan seemed reasonable they were ready to stop the killing. "Success is dependent on immediate action," Gerard insisted. "It is my belief that if you seize the present opportunity you will be the instrument of bringing about the greatest peace which has ever been signed, but it will be fatal to hesitate or wait a moment."

Wilson seemed perplexed by this urgent telegram and ordered the ambassador to refer everything to House. The Colonel was in London at the time, enjoying an elegant round of dinners and receptions with British leaders. In the midst of his friendly discussions, House showed little interest in the news from Berlin. As the Colonel hesitated, Gerard saw the chance for a truce slipping from his grasp, and he desperately wired London: "Germany will make no peace proposals, but I am sure if a reasonable peace is proposed now (a matter of days, even hours) it would be accepted."

In his response, House found it necessary to reassert his personal authority. "The President has just repeated to me your cablegram to him, and says he has asked you to communicate with me in the future. . . ." He then dealt a remarkably casual death blow to the ambassador's hopes. "As far as I can see, there is no prospect now of my getting to Berlin soon, so I take it, we will have to let the matter drift until another period of deadlock ensues."

It was no surprise when Secretary of State William Jennings Bryan, finding his pacifist policies undermined at the highest levels, submitted his resignation. It had been clear for some time that Colonel House carried more clout than the entire State Department. All major ambassadors—including Gerard in Berlin—owed their appointments to the Colonel and felt an abiding sense of loyalty to him. Foreign governments learned to take their business to House rather than working through the official channels. When Robert Lansing took over as the new Secretary of State, Wilson gave him only a few hours of his time, and then ordered Lansing to drop everything and travel 350 miles to the

Colonel's vacation home on Cape Cod. There, House would brief him on the duties of his office. "Should I," House asked the President, tell Lansing "the whole story" of "my European work?" "No, not fully," answered Wilson, "but enough to get him to work in harmony with us."

This famous harmony between the two friends depended on certain shared blind spots in their perception of the world. In May 1915, a German U-boat sank the *Lusitania,* a British liner carrying a cargo of munitions along with 1,000 passengers. One hundred fourteen Americans perished, and House hoped that the incident would lead to war. Two days after the sinking, he urged the President to send an ultimatum to Berlin. "If war follows," he wrote, "it will not be a new war but an endeavor to end more speedily an old one." Something in the Colonel's mind left him blind to the fact that it *would* be a new war for the United States and for the American soldiers who were supposed to sacrifice their lives.

House proved similarly obtuse in his relationships with British representatives, refusing to recognize that English and American interests were not identical. With the British ambassador in Washington, House developed a private code which he never revealed to Wilson or anyone else. His meetings with this English diplomat were often shrouded in secrecy, featuring complex arrangements to elude reporters and spies. Once they conferred for hours in a dark alley beside Penn Station, huddled inside the Colonel's parked limousine with the shades drawn and a chauffeur standing guard. Such cloak-and-dagger tactics make sense when one considers the Colonel's distressing habit of sharing state secrets with his English friends. In the study of his Manhattan apartment he regularly received Sir William Wiseman, head of British intelligence in America, and handed him classified State Department documents. During his frequent visits to Europe, House provided Sir Edward Grey, British Foreign Secretary, with copies of the most confidential and sensitive government papers.

The personal friendship that flourished between House and Grey eventually bore fruit in a remarkable plan to force American participation in the war. In the fall of 1915, House proposed to the President that he call a humanitarian peace conference and summon all the belligerents. With the nations of the world assembled, Wilson would advance an American peace proposal while preparing to back up its terms with military force. All nations who accepted the U.S. plan would receive the support of American arms against any nations who dared reject it. To make sure that this grandiose scheme produced the desired effect, House would secretly consult the Allies and secure their approval in advance. He further proposed that Wilson's peace terms coincide with the announced Allied war aims. With these precautions, Wilson's humanitarian gesture would produce either an outright German surrender or a U.S. commitment on the side of the Allies. The charade of an international peace conference would prepare the American people for the sacrifices ahead while convincing them of the idealism and impartiality of their leaders.

The Colonel's devious plan may have fooled even Woodrow Wilson, who was seduced once again by the role of world deliverer. With the President's approval, House worked out a memorandum with Sir Edward Grey incorporating the key elements of the proposal. Even the Colonel's admiring biographers have had trouble explaining this document, in which our hero secretly commits the United States to war without a moment's consultation of Congress, the State Department, or the people.

Much to House's chagrin, his plan fell through because the British rejected it. His Majesty's ministers disliked the idea of a peace conference that would limit them to their moderate publicly-stated goals in the struggle against Germany. America seemed headed for war in any event and the British preferred U.S. support without preconditions. They assumed it would be only a few months, at most, before House persuaded the President to take the final step.

The British were right, of course. House never presented Wilson with a single dramatic choice between war and peace, but instead worked step by step to erode the official policy of neutrality. In the end the United States had committed itself so deeply to the Allied cause that a formal entry into the war was all but inevitable. U.S. banks and arms makers had advanced Britain and France billions of dollars in credit and an Allied defeat would have seriously damaged the American economy. When the Germans resumed their temporarily suspended campaign of submarine warfare in 1917, the President could no longer resist the bellicose urgings of his chief advisor. One day late in March, Wilson sat down at his portable typewriter and made notes for a war message to Congress. He showed House a sketch of his ideas and the Colonel wryly observed "that most of them were suggestions I have made from time to time." They worked together to bring the speech to its final form. "It is needless to say that no address he has yet made pleases me more than this one," House declared.

Other Americans were less pleased with the President's message. Fifty-six members of Congress voted against the declaration of war and Senator George Norris accused the President of betraying his principles for the sake of Wall Street. Wilson himself confessed to a newspaper correspondent that he had never been as uncertain about anything in his life as he was about the decision to enter the war. On the evening of April 2, when Wilson rode back from the Capitol after delivering his speech to a joint session of Congress, crowds lined the streets and cheered. "My message today was a message of death for our young men," the President whispered to Tumulty. "How strange it seems to applaud that."

House had little patience with his friend's doubts. "Wilson did not have a true conception of the path he was blazing," the Colonel complained in his diary. On the night of the war message, he joined the President, Mrs. Wilson, and Wilson's youngest daughter in the Oval Room where they "talked it over as families are prone to do after some eventful occasion. . . . I could see that the President was relieved that the tension was over and the die cast," House wrote. "I knew this would happen."

For the Colonel, the war remained a simple question of good and evil long after its tragic consequences had become clear to the rest of the world. As late as the 1930's, he insisted that his behind-the-scenes campaign for American involvement had been "the greatest achievement of his life." The Colonel's friend and authorized biographer A. H. Smith judged that to House, "more than to any other one individual, must be attributed responsibility for our ultimate participation in the war." The Colonel's bitterest enemies could say no worse.

Having pushed the President into a war, House naturally helped his friend in defining the goals of the conflict. The Colonel's interest in the subject was practical rather than ideological: he felt that a high-minded statement of war aims would strengthen the Allied will to win while undermining the morale of the Germans. Wilson agreed with this general approach, and the two men sat down in the President's study to hammer out the celebrated Fourteen Points. These included such worthy goals as open diplomacy, self-determination for all peoples, freedom of the seas, disarmament, and equality of trade. The final and most important of the Fourteen Points called for the establishment of an international body to enforce the peace, or League of Nations.

It would be stretching a point to suggest that the idea of the League originated with House. Thoughtful statesmen in many countries had been discussing similar schemes for years. There can be little doubt, however, that it was House who planted the concept with Wilson. In *Philip Dru, Administrator* the Colonel's fictional hero capped his career by creating an international political and military union; House believed that the war gave Wilson a chance to duplicate that achievement in real life. A permanent member of the White House staff recalled that even before the United States entered the fighting the League of Nations plan had become "Colonel House's pocket piece." He raised the subject with the President at every opportunity and assembled, at Wilson's suggestion, a group of academic experts to prepare a constitution for the proposed world body. The resulting draft of the Covenant of the League of Nations bore the Colonel's strong personal imprint. It won Wilson's approval with only minor changes; of House's 23 proposed articles, 18 were accepted as part of the final plan.

With the fresh American troops tipping the military balance in Europe the war raced to its conclusion. In the fall of 1918 the Germans asked for a truce, giving House the chance to put his dreams for peace into practice. He sailed for Europe with the responsibility for representing his government on the Supreme War Council that worked out the details of the armistice. The New York *Times* reported that "never in history has any foreigner come to Europe and found greater acceptance or wielded more power."

House enjoyed his role so thoroughly that he did not want to share it with anyone—not even the President of the United States. Wilson planned to come to Paris once the formal peace conference opened, but House advised him to stay at home. "I had discovered a great advantage diplomatically in appearing as an agent who had behind him a distant patron," he wrote. "I could deal in a friendly but firm way with the Allied chiefs just because I could refer back to my own chief; and I could threaten politely. . . . But if Wilson came to Paris, he would at once have abandoned the strong position inherent in isolation . . . and subjected himself to constant and intense personal pressure.''

The President learned just how intense that pressure could be when he disregarded the Colonel's advice and sailed for France. Wilson wanted to preside over a humane and generous peace, according to the principles of the Fourteen Points, but his idealism ran into determined opposition from the British and the French. The European powers had suffered heavily in the war and they wanted territory, reparations, and political advantages in return for their sacrifices. To Wilson, such goals seemed selfish and shortsighted. He remained convinced that imposing a harsh peace on Germany would only sow the seeds for future war.

Whatever his gifts as an orator and public figure, Wilson lacked finesse as a negotiator. As the conference progressed, he found himself outmaneuvered at every turn, and the first serious strains developed in his relationship with Colonel House. The Colonel, after all, had led him into war with the promise that the peace that followed would be perfect and pristine. When events in Paris pointed to a very different sort of settlement, the President began to blame House.

He also resented the Colonel's increasingly cozy relationship with the European leaders. By the time Wilson arrived on the scene, House had been dealing with the Allies for months. He had visited Europe on several occasions during the war and developed a series of personal friendships. At the peace conference, the Colonel's importance for the first time derived as much from his contact with others as it did from his intimacy with Wilson—a threatening situation for the President's delicate ego. What's more, the Allied representatives obviously preferred House's practical approach to Wilson's incessant moralizing. "If we could only deal with House," sighed Britain's Lord Balfour, "we would have nothing to worry about." Following an angry disagreement with Wilson, British Prime Minister David Lloyd George once hurried over to the Hotel Crillon to confer with Colonel House. While they were locked in private conversation in the Colonel's suite, Wilson came in unexpectedly, also to talk with House. Seeing Lloyd George in the room he excused himself icily and walked out.

Such irritations seriously compromised the Colonel's hold on his patron. On May 30, 1919, House lamented in his diary that "for the moment, he is practically out from under my influence." House explained this turn of events by blaming Mrs. Wilson. "He and I had no opportunity for long intimate talks as in the old days. When he was free he was naturally captured for automobile rides by Mrs. Wilson. . . . He no longer depended on me as during the months following the first Mrs. Wilson's death. He was enchanted by the second Mrs. Wilson and became constantly more dependent upon her.''

It is certainly true that the relationship between Wilson's wife and his best friend had been competitive from the beginning. On several occasions, Mrs. Wilson tried to warn her husband of the Colonel's role as a sycophant. "It seems to me that it is impossible for two persons to always think alike," she ventured, "and while I like Colonel House immensely, I find him absolutely colourless and a 'yes, yes' man." Later, she labeled the Colonel "a perfect jellyfish" but Wilson defended him. "God made jellyfish," the President laughed, "so, as Shakespeare said about a man, therefore let him pass, and don't be too hard on House." When she dared to accuse House of disloyalty, the President delivered his sharpest reprimand. "I would as soon doubt your loyalty as his," he declared.

Wilson's attitude started to change during the Versailles Conferences when his wife found evidence to support her charges. She carefully clipped a series of articles from the American press that praised House extravagantly at Wilson's expense. Some of the papers called House "the brains of the Peace Commission" and claimed that the only constructive work of the conference had been performed when the President was ill and House took charge. The First Lady suggested that these articles had been deliberately planted by the Colonel and those close to him, in particular his arrogant, abrasive son-in-law, Gordon Auchincloss. At House's request, Auchincloss had come along to Paris as an attaché of the Advisory Commission. He developed an unfortunate habit of referring to the President as "little Woody" in disparaging remarks that invariably found their way back to Wilson. In the presence of several leaders of the Democratic Party who visited the negotiations, Auchincloss bragged that "Kings, Prime Ministers and plenipotentiaries come to the Colonel to get the dope and then we have to tell Woody what to say to them." These remarks caused Wilson anguish precisely because they cut so close to the truth.

House made the situation worse when he ignored the President's feelings in efforts to advance his son-in-law's career. Several times he suggested to Wilson that Auchincloss take notes at the summit meetings of "The Big Four." Wilson turned down this request so many times that he ultimately lost patience. "House, when I want Auchincloss present, I will let you know," he snapped. "Please do not mention this again."

This unpleasant little incident fed Wilson's growing paranoia. As the conference moved to its climax he banned not only Auchincloss but House and all other Americans from attending the meetings of the Big Four. While European leaders received support from batteries of aides and secretaries, Wilson showed up utterly alone. The British suggested that House at least receive daily minutes of these meetings so the U.S. delegation could remain abreast of major developments, but Wilson vetoed the idea. He insisted that no American other than himself be allowed to review the proceedings.

This bizarre situation stemmed at least in part from Wilson's shame at the course of the negotiations. He needed to prove to the world that the war had indeed been a holy crusade, but the proceedings in Paris suggested a shabby, old-fashioned struggle for power. In his frustration, he felt a growing sense of guilt at having sent so many thousands of young Americans to their deaths. Wilson held fast to the details of the League of Nations Covenant with neurotic inflexibility, but gave in to the Europeans on point after point concerning the treatment of Germany.

The President's main problem, as the peace conference concluded its work, was how to persuade the Republican majority in the U.S. Senate to accept his diplomatic handiwork. House had worried over the situation for months in advance. Before the conference even began, he had suggested that Wilson appoint at least one Republican Congressman as a member of the peace commission. The President rejected the idea, insisting that if "justice" prevailed public pressure would force the Senate to ratify the treaty regardless of political considerations.

On the day after the formal signing, House talked with Wilson and urged him once more to meet the Senate in a conciliatory spirit.

"House," the President replied, "I have found one can never get anything in this life that is worthwhile without fighting for it."

House disagreed, reminding Wilson that the Anglo-Saxon tradition was built on compromise. The two old friends continued to argue, then terminated the conversation without resolving their differences. Later that evening, Wilson left for home, anxious to plunge forward in the ratification fight with the Senate. House remained in Paris to settle some details of the treaty's implementation. In a somewhat strained gesture of friendship, House accompanied the President to the railroad station to say goodbye. This was their last farewell; the two men never saw each other again.

The final collapse of their friendship owed more to circumstances than to conscious choice. To the end of his life, House insisted, "My separation from Wilson was not a break. It was caused by the illness of each of us, that drove a wedge between us." The Colonel claimed that if they had been able to talk face to face even once during this difficult period, their old intimacy would have been restored.

Whether or not House was correct in this assumption, it is clear that Wilson needed him as never before. Without the Colonel's support and guidance, the President simply fell apart during the political struggle over the treaty's ratification. As the debate began, the situation seemed far from impossible. The Senate actually looked with favor on the general concept of a League of Nations, though many Senators questioned the specific details of Wilson's scheme. In order to win the support of a majority, Wilson would have to reassure the "Mild Reservationists" and agree to some minor changes in the League Covenant. The President, however, would not hear of compromise. He had negotiated for months at Paris and now felt sick of negotiating. He announced that he would not alter a single word of the covenant and warned that "anyone who opposes me in that, I'll crush."

To rally support for his position, Wilson left Washington on a cross-country speaking tour. In city after city he railed against his Congressional opponents and presented his cause as a moral absolute. By the time he reached the Western states, his intimates feared that he was on the verge of a nervous breakdown. Utterly exhausted, the President endured severe headaches, sweated profusely, but still refused to slacken his pace. After midnight on September 25, while his special train sped through Colorado, Wilson finally collapsed. The remainder of his trip was canceled, but relief came too late to save his health. Four days after his return to Washington, the ailing President suffered a massive stroke. The left side of his body was paralyzed and his mind was seriously impaired. Admiral Cary Grayson, Wilson's personal physician, declared the President "a very sick man" and then worked with Mrs. Wilson to conceal the full gravity of his condition. Only Grayson, the First Lady, and Tumulty, the faithful secretary, were admitted to the sickroom. Lying there in isolation and semidarkness, Wilson's state bordered on delirium. His memory often lapsed, and he suffered periodic and uncontrollable fits of weeping.

Like the rest of the world outside the executive mansion, Colonel House had no idea how sick the President really was. Nonetheless, reports of his friend's "nervous exhaustion" concerned him and he sent numerous letters and cables to the White House. None of these messages ever reached the President. Mrs. Wilson made it her policy to keep from her husband "unimportant or distressing news" and she automatically classified all communications from Colonel House under this heading. Some of the Colonel's letters to the President were opened for the first time thirty-three years after their composition, when Wilson's correspondence was deposited in the Library of Congress.

Hearing nothing from House, the President became convinced that his friend had failed him. Why had the Colonel not rushed to his side in the hour of need? Mrs. Wilson may have been right all along—House was a traitor. Like a rejected lover, Wilson transformed the deep affection he had once felt into an equally powerful bitterness. As White House usher Ike Hoover described his state, "he was unreasonable, unnatural, simply impossible. . . . His feelings about Colonel House became an obsession. He could see no good in him at all. Encouraged by those around him, his obsession apparently turned to hatred. Yet he talked of him incessantly." Not even her husband's torment could persuade Mrs. Wilson to reveal the Colonel's letters; she must have taken a perverse satisfaction in the total victory over her onetime rival. "To think that the man for whom I have done everything, to whom I told my inmost thoughts, should betray me!" the President wailed, and then gave way to one of his crying spells. "What a blow it is! It is harder than death!"

The situation was tragic enough from a personal standpoint, but political repercussions gave it an added dimension. While Wilson raved and wept in the White House, the U.S. Senate continued to debate his treaty. By this time, the Senators had divided into three camps: the "Irreconcilables" who opposed any sort of U.S. involvement in the League of Nations; the "Mild Reservationists" who favored the treaty with minor changes; and the pro-Wilson Democrats who accepted the treaty as written. If the Wilsonians and the Mild Reservationists combined forces, they had more than enough votes to ensure American participation in the League. The problem was that Wilson, through his wife and others close to him, insisted that no treaty at all was better than a treaty with the Senate's reservations. If the moderates succeeded in modifying the treaty's details, Wilson would instruct his followers to vote against the final product. In a showdown, he would destroy his creation with his own hands.

When House finally returned from Paris, without authorization from the President, he watched developments with horror. After all the mistakes and disappointments of the war and the peace conference, he believed that the administration still had a chance to salvage something of value. If the United States entered the League of Nations, that newborn international agency might prove strong enough to prevent future wars. The future of mankind required that the Colonel somehow reach the President and persuade him to abandon his insane and self-destructive course.

House poured out his advice in a cogent and closely argued letter. He warned the President that his historical reputation hung in the balance and urged him to accept the treaty changes demanded by the Senate. To make sure that his message penetrated the wall of silence surrounding the chief executive, House gave it to his friend the Attorney General, who personally placed it in Mrs. Wilson's hands. As the days ticked by toward a final Senate vote, House waited for a response, but none arrived. He did not know if Wilson ever received the letter, but he resolved to try one last time to save the treaty.

No one understood the President's psychology better than House. He knew that pride and the fear of displaying weakness had forced Wilson into his confrontation course with the Senate. If a secret compromise could be worked out that would save the President from public embarrassment and give the appearance of victory over his foes, perhaps he would quietly change his mind. At the last moment before the showdown, House contacted Henry Cabot Lodge, Wilson's chief Senate adversary. Through one of his colleagues from the peace conference, House asked Lodge to write down his minimum demands for "reservations" to the treaty. If the President privately agreed to those reservations, would the Senator accept this unofficial compromise and allow the treaty to pass as it was written? Lodge tentatively agreed and spelled out the terms he required in less than one hundred words of signed statements. The substance of these changes was surprisingly minor, and House felt exhilarated at the chance for a breakthrough. He ordered his friend to take the documents to the President. They were breathlessly deposited at the White House—and never heard of again. In later years, House guessed that the First Lady personally destroyed the papers. In any event, Lodge's conciliatory gesture did not even receive the courtesy of a reply. On March 19, 1920, the Versailles Treaty went down to defeat on the floor of the Senate. In the galleries, some seasoned Washington observers actually wept.

Despite the utter failure of his leadership and the collapse of his personal health, Wilson nursed the pathetic hope that the Democrats might nominate him for a third term. He wanted the chance to vindicate his policies and waited expectantly at the White House for word from the national convention, but no one even placed his name in nomination. This rejection of the President was not enough to save the Democrats; the people were so disgusted with Wilson's record that they elected Republican Warren Harding by one of the greatest landslides in history. Wilson retired to a quiet home on Washington's S Street, where he lived out the remaining three years of his life in bitter isolation.

In 1921, Colonel House visited Washington at the invitation of President Harding and decided to call on Wilson to try to work out their differences. He went to the house on S Street, handed his card to the butler, and waited in the parlor. Within a few moments the servant returned with the news that the crippled former President, who seldom left the premises, was officially "not in." Wilson also refused to answer any of the Colonel's written communications —even when those letters began to pierce the shield that had been set up by Mrs. Wilson. "Don't mention House to me any more," he said to one of his friends who urged him to write to the Colonel. "The door is closed."

That door remained closed even after Wilson's death in 1924. When House heard the sad news he prepared to go down to Washington for the funeral. Before his departure Bernard Baruch, who had become one of Wilson's most important confidants in his final years, called House on the telephone. He told the Colonel in no uncertain terms that he "was not expected, there was no place for him at the service, and it might save embarrassment if he did not come down." The night after the former President was buried, House braved a rainstorm to attend public memorial services at Madison Square Garden. He was a lonely and inconspicuous figure, huddled in his raincoat and mourning quietly near the back of the massive crowd.

In the years that followed, the Colonel continued to offer a steady stream of advice and gossip to anyone who would listen. In the study of his New York apartment, he received an average of twenty people a day. "I have been close to the center of things, although few people suspect," he insisted. "No important foreigner has come to America without talking to me. . . . All the ambassadors have reported to me frequently. My hand has been on things." These attentions naturally pleased him, but could not satisfy his unabated craving for power. While in his seventies, House plotted to attach himself to a Presidential candidate and return to a position of influence. The man he chose for this purpose was a New York patrician named Franklin Roosevelt. The Colonel had been friendly with FDR's parents for some forty years and when Roosevelt became governor of New York in 1928, House saw his chance. He encouraged FDR to make a race for the Presidency, advised him on foreign policy, and helped win him the support of other aging relics of the Wilson era. During the campaign of 1932, House employed his familiar strategy of flattering the candidate wherever possible. "You know, Governor," he chirped, "some of your speeches are so good that they sound almost like Wilson's." It was the highest praise House could muster.

When Roosevelt won the election, the Colonel gleefully looked forward to once more running the country from behind the scenes. "I daresay certain people don't want the President to listen to me," he told a reporter, "but I'm sure I can influence him. He trusts me, and so does his mother. I've known him since he was a mere boy." Roosevelt listened politely to the old man's advice, but never took him seriously. The new President was surrounded by his own circle of energetic and youthful aides, who had no use for the fatuous codger they all called "Colonel Mouse." Eventually, House had to admit even to himself that his hopes for a comeback would never be realized. "He has been very nice to me," he said of Roosevelt, "although it was not worth my while advising him."

During the last years of his life, the Colonel spent much of his time trying to secure his place in history. He arranged his letters, diaries, and "intimate papers," selectively releasing to the public those items that portrayed him in a positive light. By the cozy fireside of his Manhattan study, he cultivated the friendship of college presidents and professors of history and arranged for the presentation of his papers as a special collection to Yale University. Under his supervision a series of biographies and articles appeared, all describing House as a selfless public servant and a statesman of international standing.

House died in New York in 1938. After a lifetime of complaining about his frail health, he survived to the honorable old age of 79. Up to the very end, he cheerfully gave out interviews about his friendship with Wilson and after his death the campaign of historical public relations continued to pay off. No Presidential aide or advisor has received more attention or won higher praise than Colonel House. Many accounts of the Wilson era are highly unbalanced in the Colonel's favor, stressing House's intelligence and discretion while playing down his devious tactics, insincerity, and contempt for democratic process.

In the end, House could disclaim any part in Wilson's more disastrous decisions because he held no official position in the administration. If the President made a mistake, the Colonel need only shrug his shoulders and record in his diary that Wilson had ignored his advice. There was never a question of resigning in protest, since House had nothing to resign. The Colonel loved power, but he always shunned responsibility.

His relationship with Woodrow Wilson has no parallel in our history. He was the only major aide whose standing with the President rested on deliberate manipulation at the deepest and most personal level. In order to achieve noble goals and a new world order, he knowingly preyed on the vulnerabilities of his friend. During the peacemaking process, House tried to save Wilson by advancing irrefutable rational arguments about the treaty and the league, but the Colonel's position of influence had never been based on rational considerations. Once Wilson's intense personal affection had begun to go sour, the whole world felt the tragic consequences.

CHAPTER SIX

DUBIOUS COMPANY

"This pitch doth defile; so doth the company thou keepest," warned Shakespeare in Henry IV, Part I. *Our Presidents of the 1920's, none of them titans even under the best of circumstances, ignored this advice and defiled themselves with some highly dubious company. Harding picked as his top aide a next-door neighbor from Marion, Ohio, whose chief qualifications for the job involved his skill at various sports and a solicitous concern for the President's love life. Coolidge selected a former Congressman who had been forced out of electoral politics on charges of patronage abuse. Hoover relied on a private detective with a special gift for turning up embarrassing tidbits about political opponents of "the Great Engineer." Once established in the White House, this redoubtable gumshoe, Lawrence Richey, concentrated his efforts on such important public services as compiling "black lists" of the administration's enemies and in general providing Washington with a foretaste of the Watergate mentality.*

The only laudable achievement from this particular group of aides came from C. Bascom Slemp, the wily politico who helped Calvin Coolidge do a reasonably convincing impersonation of a President of the United States. Slemp, as they say in Washington, "knew where all the bodies were buried," and this knowledge proved invaluable when Silent Cal, a New England hayseed with no national experience, found himself suddenly thrust into the Presidency upon the death of his predecessor.

George B. Christian:
The Boy Next Door

After the excitement of the Wilson era, America settled back to "normalcy" under the leadership of Warren G. Harding. Behind the scenes at the White House, the subtle maneuvers of Colonel House gave way to the commonplace clumsiness and corruption of George Busby Christian. Where House negotiated with world leaders and made life and death decisions affecting millions, Christian's proudest accomplishment was the concealment of the President's mistress from the prying eyes of the First Lady and the public.

Christian, was born near Marion, Ohio, in 1873. His father, Colonel George Christian Sr., was a blustery, hard-drinking Civil War veteran, militia officer, newspaper publisher, and businessman. The younger George attended local schools and the Pennsylvania Military College in Chester, Pennsylvania, where he received a degree in civil engineering. Returning to Marion, he went to work in a rock-crushing operation owned by his father. Under the colonel's approving eye, young Christian eventually rose to the exalted post of general sales manager of the White Sulphur Stone Company.

This is hardly the professional background one would expect of a Presidential aide, and if Christian had grown up any place on earth other than Mount Vernon Avenue in Marion, Ohio, his chances of serving in the White House would have remained as remote as his chances of reaching the moon. In 1891, however, a young man named Warren Harding moved with his bride to the new frame house next door to the Christians. Harding had already established himself as a family friend several years before. "When he was a 24-year-old editor of the Marion *Star*," Christian wrote, "I was a school boy in knickerbockers. One of my earliest recollections of Mr. Harding goes back to the nights when he frequently came over to 'our house' for a friendly game of Parchesi with my father."

The Christian home and the Harding home were separated only by a lawn and George thought "it would require a surveyor to find the dividing line." On languid summer afternoons the two families ate together in the shade of the Hardings' buckeye trees. Colonel Christian was one of the leading Democrats of Marion County and had once owned a rival newspaper, but he began to ally himself with his Republican neighbor in local political skirmishes. Harding explained this situation in the pages of the *Star* by admitting that he and the colonel were "sufficiently intimate friends to break a bottle of sarsaparilla water or nervine together occasionally. . . ." Nearly everyone in the town of 6,000 could understand the joke—the two men were well known for their enjoyment of beverages more potent than sarsaparilla.

When Harding ran for the State Senate in 1898, Colonel Christian was one of his most enthusiastic supporters. George Jr. also played a role in the campaign. "I was at the Court House in 1898," he recalled, "when, after an exceedingly close contest, he was nominated for his first political office, that of Ohio State Senator, by a majority of one vote. I ran all the way from the Marion County Court House to the office of the *Star,* where I breathlessly informed him of his nomination."

In the years that followed, George watched in awe as his good-natured neighbor from Mount Vernon Avenue moved from state senator to lieutenant governor to Republican nominee for governor of Ohio. Hoping to emulate his hero, George tried for a political career of his own. His father secured him a job as secretary to the Ohio Democratic Committee and later as a reading clerk at a Democratic national convention. At age 28, young Christian ran for the Ohio legislature but found himself crushed in a Republican landslide. Throughout his long association with Harding, Christian never formally attempted to switch his party allegiance. He remained a registered Democrat, even while serving a Republican President of the United States.

With his political ambitions stymied, George returned to the dreary routine of the sand and gravel business. His home life followed a pattern familiar for that place and time. He married Stella Farrar, the daughter of a modestly successful businessman in nearby Mansfield. The Christians had two sons: Warren—named after Harding—who became a career Army officer; and John, who worked in a bank. The marriage lasted till Christian's death though gossips in Marion and later in Washington reported that George had a sharp eye for the ladies.

In 1914, Harding won election to the U.S. Senate, and with it the opportunity to hire a private secretary on the government payroll. George Christian seemed a natural choice, especially since his father, the colonel, had done so much to promote Harding's candidacy. Before taking office, the Senator-elect asked his new secretary to accompany him on an "inspection tour" of Hawaii and California—financed by a Congressional expense account. Christian happily complied.

During his first year in Washington, George lived with the Hardings in their large brick house on Wyoming Avenue. Part of his job was keeping the Senator entertained, and they began each day by playing Ping-Pong at 6 A.M. In the evenings they usually left the Capitol early for a few sets of tennis before dinner. To Christian, the kindly, easygoing Harding seemed an ideal boss. The Senator loved to shake hands and make speeches—"bloviating" he called it —but had little interest in the day-to-day details of legislative business.

Harding's casual attitude left Christian with plenty of time to dream of a glorious future. As early as 1916, George was one of a handful of visionaries and fanatics who actually believed that the Senator from Ohio could one day become President. Another member of this devoted band was Harry Micajah Daugherty, a veteran politico and former chairman of the Ohio Republican Party. Daugherty, who later became Attorney General and figured prominently in the Teapot Dome scandal, conspired with Christian to push Harding forward, whether or not the Senator wished to cooperate. "Now I think we should without Harding knowing it canvass and keep in touch with the big field," Daugherty wrote to the secretary. Christian scrupulously followed this advice and encouraged Republicans across the country who showed an interest in Harding's candidacy.

The story of the deadlocked convention of 1920 and the "smoke-filled room" at the Blackstone Hotel that decided on Harding as a compromise candidate has become one of the country's enduring political legends. As word came down from on high and the delegates dutifully shifted their support to Harding, Christian stood on the platform in the convention hall nervously tabulating the votes. The moment his man won the necessary two thirds, he ran "with all possible speed" up to the National Committee offices where Harding was waiting. The breathless emissary naturally recalled his earlier footrace to notify Harding of his nomination for state senate, some twenty-two years before. As Christian arrived and pumped Harding's meaty hand, those gathered around waited for the first historic words the nominee would utter. The Senator's response was pure Harding: "Let's go," he declared.

When Harding swept the election and announced that Christian would be Secretary to the President, the appointment won general applause from the press. Wire service reports noted the similarity between the two Marion neighbors: "The secretary . . . is the small pea shelled out of the end of the same pod; as devoid of angles or guile as a buckeye, as pleasant as a lozenge, intelligent, alert, receptive. . . ." Christian's physical appearance added to his appeal; like Harding, he was a powerfully built six-footer, but with narrow hips and long, rangy arms in place of the candidate's massive torso. Christian's wiry black hair and flashing eyes made him look younger than his 47 years while a lantern jaw and craggy, overhanging eyebrows gave his face an air of nobility and determination. Colonel Bob Gates, a self-proclaimed expert on the White House staff, said of Christian, "He is the finest fellow to go fishing with that I ever knew. Great fishermen are invariably good men."

Despite his skill as an angler, Christian brought severe limitations to his job. The situation with the White House mail offers a case in point. Since the time of Nicolay, Secretaries to the President had been shouldering this onerous burden for their chiefs and routinely responded to all but the most important correspondence. Christian, however, worshipped Harding and felt unsure of himself, and so shared with the President an unprecedented number of cards, letters, and telegrams. Harding, for instance, carried on a running correspondence with a number of people who wanted him to give up tobacco. To a crackpot who wished to turn the White House into a bird sanctuary, Harding replied with thanks, asking the inventor to postpone his project "for the present." The President often toiled late at night to answer such juvenile or lunatic correspondence. One evening, Nicholas Murray Butler, president of Columbia University, went into the President's private office to find Harding groaning behind a huge stack of letters. Butler asked if he could look at some of the items on the desk, and after he saw their triviality declared it ridiculous for the chief executive to waste his time in answering them. "I suppose so," Harding sighed, "but I am not fit for this office and should never have been here."

It took months before Christian began asserting himself and relieving the President. As he expanded his authority, his good intentions occasionally carried him too far. The secretary noticed, for instance, that Harding felt an acute dislike for Samuel Gompers, president of the American Federation of Labor. Christian therefore decided that all messages from Gompers would be intercepted at the lower levels and never shown to the President. In effect, crank letters could get through to Harding, but letters from the country's most powerful labor leader could not.

Christian showed similarly poor judgment in handling the flow of visitors to the White House. The records of the executive mansion show that during Harding's two years and five months as President more than 250,000 people came into the office and shook his hand. Christian admitted that "friends have frequently come to me and were very frank in expressing their impressions that these receptions were an imposition on the President, and that I should take steps to relieve him of this burden." The secretary refused to take action, however, since Harding himself had not requested it and seemed to enjoy "meeting with the people."

While the President of the United States shook hands with innumerable girl scout troops and football teams, more important matters went unattended. When asked to make a decision about complex new tax legislation, Harding did not know where to turn. "Somewhere there must be a book that tells all about it, where I could go to straighten it out in my mind," he wailed. "But I don't know where the book is, and maybe I couldn't read it if I found it! There must be a man in the country somewhere who could weigh both sides and know the truth. Probably he is in some college or other. But I don't know where to find him."

It was Christian's job to provide the President with the men and information he needed, but he feared the presence in the White House of the nation's "best minds" would inevitably diminish his own importance. Christian jealously guarded his position and worked to undermine anyone who threatened his special relationship with the President.

One such threat came from Judson Welliver, a respected, Cornell-educated journalist who had been hired during the campaign to help Harding prepare speeches. After the inauguration he joined the Presidential staff as the first full-time speechwriter in the history of the White House. Welliver brought to his job a knowledge of national issues and world affairs that neither Harding nor Christian could match, and the President listened to his advice. Christian resented the situation, and managed to isolate the speechwriter from the rest of the Harding inner circle. Without allies in the White House, Welliver could never threaten Christian's dominant position.

In addition to their shared responsibilities in the office, Christian generally accompanied his chief in the fanatic pursuit of relaxation. Harding played golf at least twice a week, usually at the private course of his friend Ned McLean, an alcoholic millionaire who owned the Washington *Post*. Senators, Cabinet members, and visiting dignitaries often joined Harding and Christian in the Presidential foursome. On the links, Harding played "as if his life depended on every shot." He made bets with everyone, and at times wagered against himself on each hole. Colonel Starling of the Secret Service brought up the rear, keeping the accounts. At the conclusion of nine holes, a servant would bring out bottles of liquor and the players enjoyed illegal highballs while Starling added up the bets.

Even more than he enjoyed golf, the President loved to play poker. Games were held twice a week in the White House library. The regular players included Christian, Ned McLean, Attorney General Daugherty, and a few other members of the Cabinet and Congress. The First Lady, known to Harding as "the Duchess," often watched and mixed drinks but did not play. Secretary of State Charles Evans Hughes and Secretary of Commerce Herbert Hoover were invited to play one evening, but declined to participate. They were not asked again.

Alice Roosevelt Longworth, TR's sharp-tongued daughter, witnessed one of these sessions of the "Poker Cabinet" and recorded that "trays with bottles containing every imaginable brand of whiskey stood about" and that there was "a general atmosphere of waistcoat unbuttoned, feet on the desk, and spittoons alongside." Christian enjoyed these games as much as his boss, and occasionally slipped out of the White House to play on his own. One evening when Harding was supposed to be asleep, the secretary attended a poker party at the hotel suite of Doc Sawyer, Mrs. Harding's personal physician. Play was already hot and heavy when the door burst open without a knock, and there stood the President. "You fellows can't sneak off and have a party without me," he said, looking hurt. "I'm here for the evening." It never troubled Harding or his cronies that their whiskey-soaked entertainments violated the law. As a Senator, Harding had voted for the Eighteenth Amendment to ban the sale and manufacture of alcoholic beverages, but as President he expected his staff to make "special arrangements" with a Washington bootlegger.

Some of the President's other indulgences warranted more serious attention from his secretary. Shortly after the inauguration, a letter arrived in the White House that caught the attention of mail clerk Ira Smith. In a spidery, uncertain feminine hand the writer insisted that Harding "keep his promise" and acknowledge responsibility for his illegitimate daughter. The letter bore a New York postmark and the signature "Nan Britton."

Smith's instincts told him this was something more than an ordinary crank letter and he let it cool on his desk for a few days. Finally, he decided to show the document to George Christian. The secretary "got a bit white around the lips" as he read the message.

"My God!" he exclaimed. "If the President finds out we opened this he will fire both of us!"

Christian hesitated only a moment before ripping the letter into long strips, then tearing them once across for good measure. He deposited the remains in a wastebasket and returned to his desk without a word. When a second and third letter arrived from the same source, they received similar treatment.

Despite Christian's efforts to destroy evidence, the facts of the President's relationship with Nan Britton are now well known to historians. Harding's thirty-one years of childless marriage to Florence Kling brought him little joy. The Duchess was a bespectacled, hatchet-faced harridan five years older than her husband. In Marion she patiently helped her "Wurr'n" with his newspaper business, but became increasingly bitter and sickly as his career advanced. For ten years, Harding found relief and satisfaction in his affair with Carrie Phillips, the wife of one of his hometown friends. But when Harding refused to divorce the Duchess—largely for political reasons—Carrie went to Europe for three years and left him to the misery and frustration of his marriage.

At this vulnerable time in his life he took notice of Nan Britton, the precocious daughter of a Marion physician. Infatuated with Harding since age 13, she used to dally at the *Star* offices to gaze at her hero. At first, Harding viewed her crush with kindly indulgence—Nan was a pretty girl with hypnotic gray eyes, curly blonde hair, and a plump, provocative figure. When she left Marion at age 17, they exchanged a series of admiring letters and three years later, as a working girl in New York, Nan wrote to Harding to ask for a job. Her old friend, then a U.S. Senator, suggested that they meet in New York to discuss the matter. That first evening she confessed her adolescent love for him as they sat together in the lobby of his lower Broadway hotel. Later, he took her up to his room.

In the months that followed, Harding found Nan a job, sent her money on a regular basis, and visited her frequently in New York. At times he brought her to Washington and they made love after hours in the Senate Office Building. There, on a couch in Harding's private chambers, she conceived a child. Believing himself sterile, Harding made no arrangements for contraception and Nan noted later that "the Senate offices do not provide preventive facilities for use in such emergencies."

Harding never saw his infant daughter, but continued to look forward to his sessions with Nan. After he became President, a discreet and accommodating Secret Service agent named James Sloan made most of the necessary arrangements. On several occasions, Sloan even managed to slip Nan into the White House where she met with the President in a coat closet in his private office. With the First Lady increasingly suspicious of her husband, this cozy hideaway was the only place the two lovers could "share kisses in safety."

Despite all precautions, the Duchess once came close to surprising the couple in the act. Walter Ferguson, another Secret Service man who had been drawn into the conspiracy, met Nan one afternoon at Union Station. Unfortunately, her train was late and by the time they got to the White House Harding was furious. Timing was all important and any change in schedule raised unforeseen dangers.

After a few angry words, the President dispatched Ferguson to the back door outside his office while he and Nan retired to the closet. Not five minutes later the frowning Duchess, apparently tipped off by someone, confronted Ferguson and told him to step aside. The guard replied that it was a strict Secret Service rule that no one could enter through that door. So the Duchess marched around to the front entrance, where George Christian's desk stood in an anteroom. The secretary, suspecting what was afoot, stalled as best he could and tried to make small talk.

Meanwhile, as soon as Mrs. Harding left him, Ferguson dashed into the President's office and pounded on the closet door. He then hustled Nan out of the building in the nick of time. Though the Duchess tramped from room to room in search of her suspected rival, she found no one.

George Christian certainly played a part in the President's romantic adventures, but the nature of his role has never been precisely determined. In the memoirs she published after Harding's death, Nan Britton failed to implicate Christian directly in her intrigues. She probably feared a libel suit from the retired secretary—or else hoped for his cooperation in her continued efforts to extort money from Harding's family. Nevertheless, a strong chain of circumstantial evidence links Christian to the very center of the President's affair. Back in Marion, Nan was well known to young George and his family. As a flirtatious little girl, she used to persuade old Colonel Christian to take her to the drugstore for ice cream sodas. When she became Harding's mistress, the Senator appears to have relied on his secretary to find her a job. The position she accepted was at U.S. Steel Corporation, as assistant to C. L. Close—a man known only superficially to Harding but a longtime family friend of the Christians. James Sloan, the Secret Service man who acted as the President's most frequent and reliable go-between in relations with his blonde lover, also enjoyed a special connection with Christian. According to Nan Britton, Sloan had frequent and "intimate contacts" with the head of the White House staff. Most intriguing of all is the pseudonym Nan used in her overnight hotel visits with Harding. In one register after another in cities across the country, she signed her name "Miss E. N. Christian" or "Elizabeth N. Christian." Harding had suggested the alias the first night they spent together, saying, "It would be a 'good joke' to use his secretary's name.'' This casual comment does not explain the name's repeated use over a period of several years. Nor does it explain the fact that on the birth certificate for Harding's illegitimate daughter the baby girl bears the name "Elizabeth Ann Christian."

Though the inner details of these arrangements will never be known, it seems likely that Harding's "good joke" had a practical purpose. In the event of discovery, blackmail, or other disaster, the use of Christian's name might help protect his chief from exposure. In one way or another, the faithful secretary could take responsibility for explaining embarrassing details. Since Christian and Harding most often traveled together and bore a certain physical resemblance, the aide could even claim that he, and not Harding, was the one who spent those nights in Nan's hotel rooms.

The most astonishing aspect of Harding's amours—and of the other indiscretions of his administration—was the fact that the public knew so little of what was going on. When the President died suddenly in the middle of his term, the people mourned him as a great and upright leader who handled his office with dignity and competence. This positive image was a monument to slick public relations—and George Christian deserves much of the credit. In this one respect, he performed his job splendidly, cultivating reporters and establishing himself with the press as the most popular White House secretary since Cortelyou.

In 1923, Christian accompanied Harding on his last journey, the heavily publicized "Voyage of Understanding" to the West Coast and Alaska. It was not a happy trip for the President or his party. Though physically and emotionally exhausted, Harding could not unwind. Secretary of Commerce Herbert Hoover recalled in his memoirs that on the sea voyage from Tacoma to Alaska the President insisted on playing bridge, "beginning every day immediately after breakfast and continuing except for mealtime until midnight. There were only four other bridge players in the party and we soon set up shifts so that one at a time had some relief. For some reason I developed a distaste for bridge on this journey and never played it again."

In Seattle, on the way back from Alaska, Harding suffered what was probably a heart attack, but misdiagnosed as ptomaine poisoning. The party continued to San Francisco, where the ailing President checked into the Palace Hotel. Confined to his room, he sent Christian to Los Angeles to deliver a scheduled speech in his place. After completing this errand, Christian was in Glendale, California, when news of his friend's death reached him. According to the New York *Times,* "he stood with bowed head as he received it. He was visibly affected and for fully five minutes did not speak, but stood still, his hat in his hand, his eyes on the ground." When he regained his composure, Christian said, "I have lost the best friend I ever had, and so has every American."

In the weeks that followed, during elaborate funeral ceremonies in Washington and Ohio, Christian stood always at Mrs. Harding's side. Whenever she appeared in public she leaned on his strong arm. In private, he helped her sort through Harding's papers and cooperated in burning a large number of documents she considered unseemly.

At the request of the new President, Calvin Coolidge, Christian stayed on for several weeks at the White House to ensure a smooth transition of power. When he finally resigned, Coolidge sent him a warm letter of thanks, and within six months provided a more tangible reward. At that time, the President named Harding's protégé to the Federal Trade Commission. The job carried with it a $10,000 a year salary, $2,500 more than he had earned as secretary.

Though Christian's friends praised him as a public servant of "honesty and ability," his nomination soon ran into trouble in the Senate. With Congressional investigations turning up evidence of massive wrongdoing in the Harding administration, anyone so closely associated with the late President automatically came under suspicion. At first, Democrats charged that Christian had speculated in Sinclair Oil Stock, benefiting from inside knowledge gained at the White House. The former secretary indignantly replied that "I never owned a dollar's worth of any kind of stock in my life." The initial charges against him were soon dropped, only to be replaced by more substantive allegations. His opponents claimed that Christian had negotiated the sale of the Marion *Star* at a grossly inflated price, allowing the President to reap a windfall profit of questionable propriety. Then Houston Thompson, chairman of the Federal Trade Commission, swore to the Senate Commerce Committee that Christian had once called him into the White House and pressured him to drop a complaint against a Hollywood film company. The firm in question had contributed generously to a number of Republican campaigns. Christian admitted that the incident took place, but denied any wrongdoing. He insisted that his conversation with the FTC chairman involved only "innocent questions" rather than any attempt at unethical arm-twisting.

As opposition to Christian's nomination intensified, further reports began to circulate through the capital. The secretary—along with dozens of Harding's other aides and cronies—had been an occasional visitor at the notorious "Little Green House." In this K Street establishment, lobbyists and bootleggers offered whiskey, call girls, and other favors to their friends in government. Senator Robert ("Fighting Bob") La Follette, the flamboyant Progressive from Wisconsin, pledged himself to defeat Christian's appointment at all costs. If the former secretary failed to withdraw his name, La Follette announced his intention "to go into intimate details of matters of a personal nature."

Three days before Christian was scheduled to appear before the Commerce Committee and submit to cross-examination from Fighting Bob, he asked President Coolidge to withdraw his nomination. In a letter to the President, Christian continued to deny wrongdoing but recognized the political realities of the situation. Senator La Follette exulted in his victory and never presented the "intimate details of matters of a personal nature." We can only guess at what the Senator had in mind.

After his public battering during the confirmation fight, Christian retired to private life. He fell back on connections made through the Republican Party and secured a job with the Wanamaker Department Store chain. Once again he became an executive secretary—this time, to millionaire merchant Rodman Wanamaker. Later, Christian worked as an assistant to the vice chairman of the Merchant Fleet Corporation and as a lower-level executive in the Distillers and Brewers Corporation of America. He lived to the age of 78, but never attained the conspicuous sort of business success that other Presidential aides achieved after leaving the White House.

As secretary of the Harding Memorial Association, Christian did what he could to salvage his friend's reputation. Occasionally he wrote articles about his days in the White House and tried to rebut Harding's critics. "The accurate historian," he declared, "will rank Warren G. Harding as one of the really great Presidents of the United States of America. No other historical verdict will be possible. . . ." Despite Christian's brave words, seventy leading historians polled by Arthur Schlesinger in 1962 did find it possible to reach a different verdict. In rating the Presidents according to greatness, they placed Harding's name at the absolute bottom of the list.

In the last years before his death in 1951, Christian began to lose his eyesight. He became a pathetic figure on the Washington scene, largely confined to his home at 2734 Courtland Place. President Truman felt sorry for him and occasionally invited him back to the White House for ceremonies or social events.

At one of these occasions, Christian ran into his old friend, White House mail clerk Ira Smith. Though totally blind at this point, the old man immediately recognized Smith's voice.

"Remember, Ira," the former secretary sighed, "when we tore up the President's letters?"

"I remember," Smith replied. "You tore up the first one."

"Yes, I did," Christian said, letting his face crease into a beaming smile. "Good thing, too."

C. Bascom Slemp:
The Wire-Puller

Never before in the history of the White House had the appointment of a President's secretary created such a stir. The Democratic National Committee blasted the choice of C. Bascom Slemp as "an endorsement of office jobbery in politics." The NAACP protested to President Coolidge that "twelve million Negroes feel that they have received a slap in the face." A New York politician named Franklin Roosevelt challenged Coolidge to explain his choice of a man known for "shaking down federal officeholders," while Senator Robert La Follette declared that "there is no man in politics who does not know of Slemp's venality." For two days in a row, the New York *World* ran editorials under the headline, "Why Mr. Slemp is a Blunder." To summarize the arguments, the newspaper's editor offered a bit of doggerel:

> In picking Slemp, I think, Cal's bump
> Of acumen has taken a Slump.

After the new secretary's first year in the White House, however, it became clear that Cal's acumen had not deserted him at all. Despite Mr. Slemp's controversial past and comical name, he achieved precisely the results the President wanted, and restored power and prestige to the secretary's office.

Campbell Bascom Slemp was born September 4, 1870, in Turkey Cove, Virginia. This obscure hamlet in the southwestern corner of the state had more in common with Dogpatch than with the genteel, tidewater Virginia of popular imagination. The Slemp family traced its origins to Germany, but had lived in the mountains for more than a century. Over the years they produced so many offspring that their unusual name became familiar through the region.

Bascom's father, Campbell Slemp, was a prosperous farmer who served as a Confederate colonel in the Civil War. During the 1870's he began speculating in real estate and involved himself in local politics. In most of Virginia, as in the rest of the South, the Democratic Party faced little opposition. In the Slemps' home region, however, mountaineers occasionally asserted their independence by voting Republican. Very few blacks lived in the southwestern counties so the racial agitation that kept Democrats in power elsewhere had little impact. In 1879, Colonel Slemp won election as a Republican to the

Virginia legislature and went on to three terms in the U.S. Congress during the first decade of the twentieth century. His son Bascom helped him at every stage in his political career, serving as his page in the Virginia House of Delegates and then, after studying mathematics at Virginia Military Institute and law at the University of Virginia, as his campaign manager. The newspapers dubbed the elder Slemp "The Black Eagle of the Cumberland" while his son, known as the brains in the family operation, became "The Sage of Turkey Cove." In 1905, after his father's reelection to Congress, he took over as chairman of the Virginia Republican Party and maintained his dominance in the state GOP for the next twenty-seven years.

When "The Black Eagle of the Cumberland" died suddenly in the middle of a third term, his well-respected son was the obvious candidate to succeed him. This began Bascom's long career in Congress—he was reelected seven times. On many occasions, the Democrats attempted to "redeem" his district from Republican control, but "The Sage of Turkey Cove" always outmaneuvered them. His personal wealth played a major role in Slemp's campaigns—starting from the comfortable base provided by his father he parlayed investments in coal and timber into a business empire worth several million dollars. In the election of 1910, when Democrats mounted a particularly fierce challenge to Slemp, the Congressman and his supporters offered as much as $80 per vote to citizens who cast Republican ballots.

Slemp established a respectable record in the House of Representatives, but he did not exactly qualify as a farsighted statesman: 55 per cent of the bills he sponsored dealt with private pension claims from citizens in his district. His major accomplishments during fourteen years in the House were the construction of a coal mine rescue station near his home and a bill awarding $100,000 to his alma matter, VMI, to compensate for damage sustained during the Civil War.

Far more important than his activities on the floor of Congress was Slemp's role as a dispenser of federal patronage. During the first decades of this century, Democratic control of the "Solid South" was so absolute that few Republicans could be elected to office below the Mason-Dixon line. Nevertheless, the skeletal GOP organizations controlled thousands of postmasterships and other federal offices in the Southern states whenever a Republican occupied the White House. As one of his party's few Southern Congressmen, Slemp regularly advised Presidents on Dixie Republicans worthy of appointment. He also played a major part in national nominating conventions. Though Republican Presidential nominees had no chance of carrying Southern states, delegates from those states often voted as a bloc and determined who would win the nomination. Every four years at convention time, Slemp relished his position as one of the party's kingmakers.

Slemp's consuming passion for politics left him with little energy for a personal life. In official biographies he invariably listed his status as "bachelor," though he was in fact married for a time. In 1911 the 41-year-old Congressman wed Loberta Barton, a Louisiana socialite. Less than three years later she sued for divorce and their marriage ended quietly in an obscure Virginia courtroom. It is not surprising that Slemp would try to suppress information about the entire experience—for political, if not for personal reasons. During most of his years in Washington, Slemp's closest companion was his spinster sister Janie. They lived together for years and whenever the Congressman entertained she acted as his official hostess.

Slemp might have continued for the rest of his life as a member of Congress and a Republican wheeler-dealer if, in 1921, a patronage scandal had not exploded in his face. In that year, Congressional Republicans attempted to unseat a Virginia Democrat because of suspected vote fraud in his district. The Representative in question, Thomas Harrison, counterattacked by leveling charges at Slemp. He read into the *Congressional Record* conclusive evidence that Slemp had been selling federal offices in return for campaign contributions. This was a familiar practice in both political parties, but few Congressmen were as high-handed or obvious as Slemp in their efforts to extract money from potential appointees. Bascom's accusers even displayed endorsed $100 checks made out directly to Slemp. In his defense, the Virginian could only plead ignorance and insist that the funds he collected were used for legitimate campaign purposes. A few months after these revelations, Slemp announced his retirement from Congress. He declared that his decision was purely personal and had nothing to do with the scandal. Returning to the practice of law, he maintained his seat on the Republican National Committee and watched for new opportunities.

Slemp did not have long to wait. In August 1923, Warren Harding died during his tour of the Western states and thrust Vice-President Calvin Coolidge into the White House. One of the new chief executive's first and most important tasks was to find a replacement for George Christian as Secretary to the President. Coolidge summoned his party's Congressional leaders to the White House and asked their advice. They stressed that the Republican convention was less than ten months away and that Coolidge faced a difficult time nailing down the Presidential nomination. The progressive wing of the party, under the leadership of California's self-righteous curmudgeon Hiram Johnson, promised a ferocious fight in the primaries. To turn back these barbarians, the inexperienced Coolidge needed a seasoned politico as his top aide. The Speaker of the House suggested Slemp's name—surely, few men in the country knew more about the inner workings of Republican conventions. The former Congressman could also help the new President in his tricky relations with Capitol Hill. The appointment of Slemp made perfect sense—except for the fact that Bascom had just been driven from public life in disgrace. The President's advisors, however, brushed aside this "minor" objection and even converted it into an argument in Slemp's favor. How many successful politicians would interrupt their careers for a President who might be turned from office within a few months?

Slemp, on the other hand, could easily be persuaded to give up the joys of law practice at Big Stone Gap and take his chances in the White House.

The new President announced the appointment on August 14, provoking angry protests from press and public. Coolidge, who had been in office less than two weeks, seemed genuinely stunned by the response. He had expected commendation for selecting a stranger with national experience rather than turning to a personal friend or trusted stenographer as had other Presidents. He began to worry that the outraged moralists were right in their judgment of Slemp. One afternoon he called the new secretary into his office and cautioned him against unseemly political maneuvers. Under the circumstances, this gratuitous warning could have been seen as an insult, but Slemp refused to take offense. He quietly promised to observe all proprieties and handle his office discreetly. The President smiled, with his thin lips pressed together beneath the long pointed nose, and agreed to say nothing more on the subject. Slemp had previously humbled himself with another sweeping promise. As a precondition of White House service, Coolidge insisted that his secretary take no notes, copy no papers, and write no "intimate memoirs." He may have been new to the Presidency, but Silent Cal had an instinctive understanding of the value of secrecy behind the scenes.

After the initial burst of criticism, observers in the press began to find humor in the President's appointment of Slemp. Coolidge was a parsimonious New Englander who took pride in the fact that his rent was never more than $35 a month, while his new secretary was a multimillionaire. The New York *Times* suggested that certain similarities between the two men might lead to difficulties in the White House. "Mr. Slemp is only slightly less reticent than Calvin Coolidge," the newspaper declared. "One can imagine each of them waiting for the other to speak. There should be long eloquent silences."

Despite his natural reserve, Slemp, unlike Silent Cal, could be a gracious conversationalist. The Washington *Star* found him "mild mannered, gentle of speech, polished, and well-educated." His tall trim frame and long face with its crown of silver hair helped him cut an elegant figure in Washington society. His eyes were his most extraordinary feature—huge, inky black discs behind slightly drooping lids. Journalists often commented on his "masklike countenance" and "Oriental inscrutability," using precisely the same terms applied in previous decades to White House advisors Daniel Lamont and Edward M. House. A cool, emotionless appearance offered a natural advantage for any Presidential aide.

To prove himself to his wary chief, Slemp set out to clean up the administrative chaos left behind by Harding and Christian. The clutter on the President's desk gave some indication of the sorry state of affairs: Harding had allowed huge stacks of paper to accumulate with hundreds of items awaiting his attention. Slemp determined that in the new administration most of this incoming business could be handled at the lower levels. Unlike his predecessor, George

Christian, Slemp's ability to make decisions for himself was not impaired by an attitude of hero worship toward his boss. The secretary was actually two years older than Coolidge and his political contacts were far more extensive. He saw the President as a partner, not a demigod. Coolidge encouraged this attitude and welcomed his aide's aggressive moves to assume White House authority. "One rule of action more important than all others," the President said, "consists in never doing anything that someone else can do for you."

Within a few months, the New York *Times* reported that "the custom is growing of calling not to see Coolidge, but Slemp." According to capital rumors, the secretary could magically solve any problem—political, legislative, or administrative. So many different officials waited in line to call on C. Bascom Slemp that Washington wags suggested his name should be written out as "See Bascom Slemp." The *Times* solemnly pronounced that "not within memory of this generation in Washington has there been so responsible, tactful, and approachable a secretary to the President . . . ."

Thanks to Slemp, Coolidge faced fewer demands on his time than any other twentieth-century President. Silent Cal had good reason to take it easy: both of his immediate predecessors had collapsed under the strain of office. After Wilson's paralyzing stroke and Harding's death in the middle of his term, the public naturally worried that the Presidency was a man-killing job. Slemp wanted to deflate that myth and he felt personally responsible for protecting the President's health. "President Coolidge trains for the work of his office as a prize fighter trains for a fight," the secretary announced. "He has his breakfast at 7, his lunch at 1, and his dinner at 7. He takes exercise regularly in the morning and late in the afternoon, and he retires early." Coolidge, in fact, was notorious for leaving even the most important social gatherings so that he would be sound asleep by ten o'clock. To make the President's burdens even lighter, Slemp rearranged the schedule so that Coolidge had every afternoon to himself. No appointments were permitted after lunch, so the President was free to read a report, sit at his desk and stare out at the lawn, or, as he did most often, take a nap. Slemp proudly reported that Coolidge gained eight pounds while in office.

Another of the secretary's significant innovations was the institution of in-depth Presidential briefings. To fill gaps in Coolidge's background, Slemp assembled experts from across the country. Intensive discussions were held in the early days of the administration on each of the major national issues. The fact that Coolidge made little use of this information in his passive and uneventful Presidency can hardly be blamed on Slemp. As the secretary discreetly put it, the President was "not so much an originator of public policy as a policy administrator." Nevertheless, Slemp did what he could to lend a sense of drama to Coolidge's quiet leadership. In 1924 he arranged for the first radio broadcast of a State of the Union address, and the President's crisp Vermont twang made a good impression. Slemp ensured the largest possible listening audience for this event, and after the speech he wrote to some political friends in the mountains of Tennessee asking for a report on the local reaction. One of them replied, "There wasn't no reaction. Everybody liked it."

Subtly but effectively, Slemp maneuvered the President into a commanding position in the forthcoming struggle for the Republican nomination. Senator Hiram Johnson continued to press his quest, but Slemp's masterful use of patronage and publicity made the Californian's cause seem more and more a long shot. The death blow came in South Dakota. Johnson counted this progressive state as a sure thing and most of the President's political managers did not even want to contest it. Slemp, however, felt confident that Coolidge could capture the South Dakota delegation and the secretary personally took charge of the organizing efforts in the state. The result was a stunning two-to-one Coolidge victory, which shattered the morale and momentum of the opposition's forces. As Coolidge swept on toward the nomination, one typical press account hailed his secretary as "a master of political legerdemain, a conjuror, clairvoyant, wizard, sorcerer, who can do all manner of tricks and pull all manner of mystifying magic and transcendental deviltry. Slemp knows all the ropes, all the wires, all the wireless, all the wiles, all the artful dodges and card sharping of which the science of politics is cognizant."

Certain Democrats believed that Slemp knew too many tricks for his own good. The Senate's Walsh Committee, while investigating the Teapot Dome bribery scandals, suggested that the secretary had taken part in an attempted cover-up. Their evidence was skimpy and entirely circumstantial: Bascom had traveled to Florida and talked to a key witness a few days before the man met with Senate investigators. Yet in the carnival atmosphere created by previous revelations, even this minor coincidence generated major suspicions. Newspapers ran sensational stories linking Coolidge, through Slemp, directly to Teapot Dome. The Senate investigating committee encouraged the publicity and called Slemp as a major witness.

The secretary did not want to testify—his name had already been tarnished by the charges of patronage manipulation and he feared that this new embarrassment would ruin his career. Up to the last moment, he expected that Coolidge would intervene, invoke "executive privilege," and rescue him from an unnecessary ordeal. Silent Cal did nothing of the kind. He still felt uncertain of Slemp's integrity and refused to say anything, either publicly or privately, in support of his embattled aide.

The night before his committee appearance, Slemp could not sleep. He got out of bed at 6 A.M., feeling so nauseated that he had to call a doctor. He was in no condition to face the Senators, but he did not attempt to postpone his testimony. He knew that talk of his illness would be interpreted by the public as a sign of weakness and guilt.

Accompanied by his physician, Slemp arrived at the Senate Office Building at 10:30. The excitement in the hearing room was intense—it resembled the public interest surrounding the appearance of a later Presidential aide, Bob Haldeman, before another Senate investigating committee some fifty years later. As Slemp tried to push his way up to the witness table, his path was barred by a crowd of standing spectators. Bascom asked a uniformed guard, "What are all these people doing here?"

"Oh," was the reply, "the President's secretary is going to testify about the big oil scandal, and they are waiting to hear him."

When Senator Thomas Walsh banged his gavel to call the meeting to order, Slemp began to settle down. Democrats who hoped that he would drag the White House into the scandal were sorely disappointed; the veteran wire-puller, as the Washington *Star* reported, was "no slouch at Congressional investigations." He responded to tough questioning with long, rambling answers that included details about his golf game, the Florida weather, and personal friendships. He gave an impression of befuddled innocence and left the Senators without a scrap of new information. After the committee dismissed Slemp in frustration, the press announced that Coolidge and his aide had both been "cleared" of wrongdoing.

Despite his successful performance before the Walsh Committee, Slemp's personal reputation remained somewhat shady. Inevitably, he became an issue in the fall campaign. Senator Robert La Follette, running as a third-party candidate for President, tried to dramatize the situation. "There he sits today, in the White House," he thundered against Slemp, "closer to the President than any other living man, separated only by a swinging door. In all the history of the United States no man with such a record as that of Slemp has ever been selected by a President to act as his confidential advisor and official representative." A Democratic pamphlet circulated throughout New York State informed voters of the "confidential" record of Mr. Slemp and concluded with a question: "Do you approve of the President of the United States *rewarding* this man with high office?"

In the face of these attacks, Coolidge pushed Slemp into the background of the campaign and turned to Republican national chairman William Butler for most of the crucial decisions. Despite his diminished role, the secretary continued to perform valuable political services for his chief. His handling of the issue of the Ku Klux Klan offers a good example of his method of operation. Blacks hated Slemp because of his involvement with a "lily-white" Republican organization in Virginia, but on the national level the secretary knew the Klan was a liability. When John W. Davis, the Democratic nominee, asked Coolidge to join him in denouncing the Klan, Slemp devised an ingenious means of straddling the question. In September he wrote to a New York editor that the President was "not in sympathy with the aim and purpose" of the Ku Kluxers. Columnist David Lawrence called that letter "the smartest piece of politics I ever knew anybody to put over." According to Lawrence, enemies of the Klan rejoiced at the position taken by the President's secretary. At the same time, those who favored the Invisible Empire could say to themselves, "Well, the President didn't sign it. It was only his secretary."

Such tactics helped bring Coolidge a landslide victory in November and

Slemp expected an appropriate reward. He had signed on as secretary primarily to help the President win nomination and election. Now that the campaign was over he wanted a Cabinet appointment, perhaps as Postmaster General. Coolidge could not oblige him: the scandals of the Harding administration were too fresh in the public mind for the President to take into his Cabinet a man with so questionable a reputation. Slemp felt cheated and decided to resign after the inauguration. The secretary's job held little appeal for him when his path to advancement was clearly blocked.

The President accepted his aide's decision with regret and gave Slemp a formal farewell dinner in the White House. During their months of collaboration Coolidge's suspicions of Slemp had given way to respect, but the President's stiff and standoffish nature prevented genuine friendship. To succeed Bascom as secretary, Coolidge picked Everett Sanders, another former Congressman. This genial, bespectacled Hoosier quietly followed the routine established during Slemp's eighteen eventful months in office.

After leaving the White House, Slemp joined a prestigious Washington law firm. He maintained control of the Virginia Republican Party and continued to represent his state on the Republican National Committee. In 1928 he urged Coolidge to run for reelection, but when the President took himself out of the race Slemp promptly switched his support to Commerce Secretary Herbert Hoover. As usual, the Virginian's candidate prevailed at the national convention and went on to victory in the fall. Once again, Slemp's name was mentioned prominently as a possible Cabinet appointee and once again, he was passed over. After this new disappointment, Slemp gradually withdrew from active involvement in politics. By 1932 he had turned over leadership of the Virginia GOP to his local rivals. His timing was absolutely perfect: within a few months, FDR came to power and ushered in lean years for Republicans everywhere.

In retirement, Slemp kept up a lively correspondence with Calvin Coolidge and was an occasional guest at the ex-President's Massachusetts home. These casual and nostalgic contacts encouraged an affection between the two men that had never been present during their work together in the White House. Following the Roosevelt landslide in 1932, Coolidge wrote to his former aide, "I am glad that you and I are not in politics during these terrible times. I retired at the right time and am more and more thankful every day, but because I do not want to be in politics is no reason why I do not want to see my old friends. If I could have them about me as they were in Washington, my satisfaction in life would be complete." Six days after composing this letter, Coolidge died of a heart attack. Slemp never had a chance to pay the final visit that he had planned.

In old age, the Sage of Turkey Cove spent much of his time gathering artifacts for a proposed museum on the history of southwestern Virginia. He became obsessed with the project and left a generous bequest for the museum's construction after his death. The aging bachelor also sought more personal means of preserving his name, asking distant kinsmen or even poor mountaineers in his home county to christen their sons "Campbell Bascom" in his honor.

Slemp died in 1943, a month before his seventy-third birthday. The interment at the family cemetery at Turkey Cove was sparsely attended—his days of political power had been long forgotten. Today, if history books mention Slemp at all, they usually do so as a footnote demonstrating the corruption of the Republican Party in the South. The administration of Calvin Coolidge is seldom held up as an example of executive greatness, so Slemp's substantial contributions as Secretary to the President are easy to ignore. Yet placed within its historical context, Slemp's solid competence looks very good indeed. He followed a series of major advisors (Norton, House, and Christian) who, whatever their talents and promise, performed services of dubious value. Slemp, despite the embarrassments in his background, abused neither the trust of his chief nor the powers of his office. Unfortunately, the same cannot be said for the top aide in the succeeding administration, whose clandestine activities would have brought a blush to even the most cynical veteran of Watergate.

Lawrence Richey:
The Confidential Snooper

For years, Richard Nixon's apologists have attempted to excuse his abuses of power by citing the misdeeds of previous administrations. The Watergate White House, according to this argument, only extended practices begun under Franklin Roosevelt, John Kennedy, and Lyndon Johnson. The most striking precedent for Nixon's excesses can be found, however, not in the record of recent Democratic incumbents, but in the long ago Presidency of Herbert Hoover. As early as 1929, a White House aide spied on the opposition party, blackmailed a troublesome Senator, dispatched private detectives to plug press leaks, and compiled "black lists" of administration enemies.

Hoover is hardly the man one would suspect of dirty tricks. His reputation is that of a well-meaning but stubborn idealist who was blamed unfairly for the Great Depression. A generously financed research institution at Stanford University encourages favorable biographies. Historians stress Hoover's personal integrity and seldom mention the name of Lawrence Richey, a mysterious and even sinister figure who served as his principal aide for forty-two years. In a sense this obscurity is a tribute to Richey's success. Ministering to his employer's paranoia and attending to chores of questionable propriety, he always maintained the strictest secrecy.

Lawrence Richey was born in Harrisburg, Pennsylvania, in 1885. His family background, like so much else about him, remains obscure. His name at birth was either Ricci or Rizzi. In later years he insisted that he was only "part Italian," though contemporary reporters believed he was the son of immigrants.

Richey's career as an investigator began at age 13. He used to play baseball on a vacant lot adjoining the suspected hideout of a band of counterfeiters. One afternoon, U.S. Secret Service agents persuaded the boy to "accidentally" throw a ball through a window and return that night to break into the building. He managed to crawl inside and open the front door to the federal agents who proceeded to seize the evidence they needed.

In the years that followed, the Secret Service made frequent use of this plucky youngster and by the time he was 16 he had been hired as a full-time government operative. He began traveling around the country in pursuit of counterfeiters, often exposing himself to physical danger and occasionally making arrests at the point of a gun. When he was 21 his Secret Service superiors assigned him to the special detail protecting President Theodore Roosevelt at his home in Oyster Bay. TR took a special liking to the burly young body-guard, but not even the magnetic personality of the Roughrider President could keep Richey in government service when he saw the chance for a lucrative private career.

Following the example of several Secret Service colleagues, Richey set him-self up as a freelance investigator. He took on a number of unusual jobs, such as researching political corruption for a well-known muckraking journal called *Everybody's Magazine*. For a time he went to Alaska to manage a gold mine, but the enterprise proved a disappointment and he returned to the field he knew best. His private detective agency eventually landed contracts with some of the largest insurance firms in the country.

Richey was 32 years old and his business was prospering when he met Her-bert Hoover for the first time. That meeting was arranged by Mark Requa, a California mining tycoon and friend of both men. Hoover, who was serving as America's World War I food administrator, had mentioned to Requa his need for a "confidential snooper" to keep watch on the bureaucracy under his com-mand. A self-made millionaire who served the government without pay, Hoover could not abide the idea that corruption or inefficiency might taint his operations. He was an engineer by profession and put a premium on precise and detailed information. The only way he could feel comfortable in the untidy, unprincipled world of politics and government was to hire someone to spy on his subordinates.

Richey fit Hoover's needs perfectly, and following their first fifteen minutes of conversation the two men formed a lasting partnership. William Hard, Hoover's favorite Washington reporter, observed twelve years later that after the initial contact "there has not been a minute . . . that has not seen each in the total unreserved trust of the other." Richey gave up his private agency and began traveling around the world, serving as the eyes and ears of "The Great Engineer." His top-secret investigative reports allowed his employer to see the inner workings of federal agencies, political parties, and even foreign governments.

When Hoover became Secretary of Commerce in 1921, Richey assumed the title "Assistant to the Secretary." Newsmen knew him as the number two man at the Commerce Department, though his name never appeared on official payrolls. Hoover preferred to pay his friend out of his own pocket, and he rewarded him far more handsomely than government scale would have permit-ted. Richey's services were well worth the money, since he handled the department's Congressional relations in addition to continuing his investigative activities. Hoover sent his aide scurrying up to Capitol Hill whenever he wanted action from the legislators. If a Congressman proved intransigent, Richey could play political hardball. As one reporter delicately put it, he "showed the erring statesmen wherein they were wrong. Particularly, he pointed out the desirability of having a great and powerful department in a friendly frame of mind toward requests from constituents.''

One of his most significant maneuvers involved the selection of a new head for the Justice Department's Bureau of Investigation—the agency later known as the FBI. Attorney General Harlan F. Stone consulted Secretary Hoover on the decision, and Hoover asked advice from Richey in deference to his experience as a working detective. It was Richey who first suggested the name of John Edgar Hoover (no relation to the future President), an ambitious young functionary in the lower levels of the Department of Justice. The Attorney General followed Richey's recommendation, and for some fifty years the people of the United States lived with the consequences of that appointment.

Like J. Edgar Hoover, Lawrence Richey battled his enemies with ruthless intensity and believed that a worthy cause justified even the most questionable means. For Richey, Herbert Hoover's Presidential ambitions qualified as such a cause. In 1920, when Hoover's name was first mentioned as a candidate for national office, his opponents circulated rumors that he had once considered renouncing his American citizenship to accept a British title. These charges contained just enough substance that they might have caused Hoover some slight embarrassment, so Richey promptly journeyed to England to ''clarify'' the issue. While there, he reportedly ''took care of sundry files and records.'' In his autobiography, Hoover admits that Richey played a similar role during the Presidential campaign of 1928. When the Great Engineer emerged as the leading Republican contender, Democrats claimed that he had been convicted in a British court twenty-six years earlier for defrauding a Chinese national in a business transaction. Another candidate might have ignored such a charge, but Hoover, as reporter Charlie Michelson observed, ''was the thinnest skinned politician I have ever encountered.'' As Hoover tells it, some of his ''friends'' dispatched Richey to Europe, and the aide duly secured ''a written statement from almost every party to this old lawsuit, and every living lawyer on both sides connected with it. All these statements indignantly denied that there was the remotest truth in these libels and spoke most handsomely of me.''

Richey, however, did not content himself with answering criticism of his boss after it appeared—at times, he tried to cut off that criticism at its source. Pennsylvania's Senator James A. Reed was so bitterly opposed to Hoover's nomination in 1928 that he announced plans for a nationwide speaking tour to denounce the Commerce Secretary. Before Reed took the stump, Richey prepared a ''comprehensive precautionary counter blast,'' dealing with the Senator's whole past ''including his early peccadilloes in Sunday school.'' *The American Mercury* sneered that ''such a job is precisely to Mr. Richey's taste and always calls out the best that is in him.'' There is no doubt that he performed his task effectively: the Senator canceled his tour and Hoover went on to win the nomination and election without difficulty.

As Herbert Hoover took over the Presidency the nation looked to him for a bright new day of efficiency in government. Workmen bustled about the White

House during the first weeks of the administration, remodeling offices and knocking down walls to make a large new lobby and pressroom. The up-to-date lobby, with its white columns and severe stone benches, seemed to Drew Pearson "much after the order of those in the latest hospitals, chaste and not too comfortable." The amber-tinted walls of the pressroom held solemnly autographed likenesses of Harding, Coolidge, C. Bascom Slemp, and "other departed immortals." Reporters rejoiced that they now had room for several card games at once, but they were not entirely comfortable in their new surroundings. Because of the fresh yellow carpeting they felt constrained to get up from their game tables and cross the room to spittoons rather than using the bare floor as in days of old.

The physical improvements in the White House reflected significant changes in the organization of the President's staff. Since the administration of James Buchanan, when Congress first authorized the office of Private Secretary to the President, chief executives relied on this one, undisputed major domo of the White House operation. When Hoover came to office he suggested that three coequal secretaries divide the swelling workload; he wanted to bring government into line with the most advanced business ideas of efficiency and specialization. With his reputation for organizational genius he had little difficulty in persuading Congress to go along with the idea. Each of the three new secretaries commanded a relatively generous salary of $10,000 a year—a hefty raise above Slemp's $7,500 and a far cry from John Nicolay's paltry $2,500. They also enjoyed a number of special privileges, including the exclusive use of a sleek Pierce-Arrow touring car.

The best-publicized member of Hoover's new "secretariat" was George Akerson, a former newsman of Norwegian descent. A congenial backslapper with a broad pink face, Akerson enjoyed playing the piano, entertaining the ladies at Washington parties, and motoring around the capital in the new secretarial limousine. He was the first major aide in White House history whose full-time job was handling reporters. Because of this specialization, Akerson became known as the President's "Press Secretary" and the title has remained a fixture in Washington to this day. Like Richey, Akerson had worked with Hoover at the Commerce Department before coming to the White House. He wanted the world to believe he was the President's top aide and indispensable right-hand man, but he was no match for Richey. In the rivalry between the two men, the Press Secretary suffered such frequent embarrassment that he resigned before the end of the President's term to take a $25,000 a year job in the motion picture industry.

The second member of the secretarial trio was Walter Newton, a five-term Congressman from Minnesota who gave up a safe seat in the House of Representatives to join the President's staff. A back country orator with loose-fitting clothes, unshined shoes, and a booming voice, he was supposed to handle political and patronage affairs for the administration. Because of his Capitol Hill experience, he saw himself as the anointed successor to C. Bascom

Slemp, but Newton clearly lacked Slemp's discretion and finesse. His blunders caused great amusement to the Washington press corps and helped alienate Hoover from Congress during the darkest months of economic crisis. Originally, Newton hoped that his White House service would prepare him for a U.S. Senate race in 1930, but the Great Depression and the low public standing of the administration put an end to his political plans.

The third secretary was Richey, whose duties were at once the most far-reaching and the most difficult to define. When reporters asked him to describe his activities, he generally murmured, "Mr. Akerson will tell you what I do" and disappeared into the background. His office was a tidy, out-of-the way retreat seldom visited by reporters. Unlike Akerson and Newton, he had no desire to impress the public with his importance; he concerned himself with power, not publicity. Richey was a short stocky man who wore his black hair brushed back in pompadour fashion. His grooming was careful and modest, with a particular emphasis on gray business suits. Occasionally, he showed traces of a mysterious limp—presumably a reminder of one of his youthful adventures as a detective. *The New Republic* saw him as "an inscrutable son of Italy" with blunt features, poker face, and cold, dark eyes.

Officially, Richey was White House office manager, responsible for the President's correspondence and scheduling, but in reality he involved himself in every phase of the executive operation. Akerson and Newton resented his intrusion in their affairs and distrusted his propensity for spying. It was said that Richey placed dozens of federal officials under his surveillance—including at one time both his secretarial rivals. He wanted to make sure that everyone was "doing the job" for Hoover, but his efforts only added to the confusion created by the President's novel division of authority. Visitors who came to the White House on business never knew which of the secretaries to see. In an atmosphere of insecurity and competition, duplication of effort was the rule rather than the exception. Despite Hoover's reputation as a great administrator, the White House staff seemed notably less efficient than it had been under Coolidge.

During the internal struggles at the White House, Richey's key advantage was his personal relationship with the President. He had known Hoover far longer than the other secretaries. For the introverted chief executive, Richey's quiet, undemanding company was the next best thing to being alone. Hoover seldom relaxed, but when he did Richey was at his side. Every morning at exactly 7:30, the President dutifully played medicine ball—his only source of exercise. The participants would heave a weighted leather sphere back and forth over a ten-foot net. The general idea was to win points by forcing the opponents to drop the ball. Richey, along with several members of the Cabinet and some friendly reporters, was one of the regular players. Hoover insisted that the games go on even in the most inclement weather. At times, "the medicine ball Cabinet" assembled in driving rain or snowstorms, with its members loyally grunting and puffing along with the President until the ordeal was over. For most of the participants, the best part of the games was that they never lasted more than half an hour.

For Richey, fishing expeditions with the President offered a more congenial form of recreation. The secretary was an expert angler and he had adopted his boss as a willing pupil. Owing to Hoover's generous payments to his aide during the years at the Department of Commerce, Richey could afford to buy a rustic 1,500-acre estate in the mountains of western Maryland. Catoctin Manor featured spectacular trout streams and the President used to drive there for weekend visits. Inspired by the serenity of Richey's wooded retreat, Hoover decided to acquire a similar site for himself. He sent the secretary on a scouting expedition along the Rapidan River to find a stretch of water that could serve as a Presidential playground. When Richey found the perfect spot near Madison, Virginia, Hoover spent a great deal of his own money to build cabins, install utilities, and clear trails. At the end of his term, Hoover donated the camp to the Shenandoah National Park.

Fishing also provided a rare opportunity for the secretary to spend time with his wife. He married Mabel Hunter fourteen years before coming to the White House, but they were often separated by Richey's endless traveling on errands for his chief. The couple had no children and Mrs. Richey, a plain and unpretentious woman, shunned the press even more assiduously than did her husband. In February 1930 she accompanied Richey and the President on a leisurely fishing party to Key West. Soon after their return she developed a fever which was diagnosed as secondary meningitis. Hoover kept constantly advised of her condition and sent flowers to her hospital room every day of the illness. Mabel Richey died on February 28; the President and Mrs. Hoover attended the funeral at Washington's St. Paul's Cathedral.

Secretary Richey lived stoically with his grief: his personal tragedy only intensified the air of gloom that already prevailed at the White House. In October 1929 the bottom had fallen out of the stock market, plunging the nation into the nightmare of the Great Depression. A quarter of the work force was unemployed. Hunger riots broke out in New York, Minneapolis, and Oklahoma City. An estimated half a million men wandered the country, desperately looking for work, living in shantytowns at the edge of every major city. These pathetic assemblages of cardboard and scrap metal huts were derisively known as Hoovervilles. "Hoover Flags" were empty pockets, turned inside out. When hungry men slept in the open and wrapped old newspapers around themselves for warmth, these shreds of protection were called Hoover Blankets.

In the face of such public abuse, the President barricaded himself in the White House and suffered profoundly. William Allen White found him "constitutionally gloomy, a congenital pessimist who always saw the doleful side of any situation." Secretary of State Henry Stimson commented that a private meeting with Hoover was "like sitting in a bath of ink." Raymond Moley, after seeing the President in 1932, reported, "He seems to me to be close to death. He had the look of being done, but still of going on and on, driven by some damned duty.''

Considering his emotional state, it is not surprising that Hoover's paranoia became acute. When Congressmen clamored for relief and public works programs, the President saw only ''raids on the public treasury.'' ''As long as I sit at this desk,'' he vowed, ''they won't get by.'' Like Richard Nixon some forty years later, he began to view political skirmishes in Washington as a war to the death, and worried that others were under attack for his sake. ''It's a cruel world,'' he said, close to tears. ''My men are dropping all around me.''

Under Richey's guidance, the loyalists on the White House staff attempted to protect and isolate the beleaguered President. *The American Mercury* complained of the ''elaborate cordon'' that surrounded the chief executive, while White House veteran Ira Smith observed that his ''secretaries formed a buffer line around the President day and night.'' According to reporter Walter Liggett, the atmosphere in the White House under Hoover resembled ''the throne room of an Oriental despot.''

In this sort of environment, Lawrence Richey thrived. Sensing Hoover's psychological needs, he began to play the role of a personal bodyguard. His Secret Service experience equipped him for the job and he accompanied the President whenever possible. He also took it upon himself to reprimand the official Secret Service detail for their occasional lapses and mistakes.

By the middle of the term, it was clear to the press that Richey was ''the man closest to the President, and that takes in everybody in or out of Washington.'' Hoover called the secretary his ''trouble man'' because of Richey's ''unerring instinct for getting at the heart of irritating things.'' Almost every morning, when Richey took the sorted mail and placed it on Hoover's desk, the President had some new assignment in mind for him.

These chores often involved Hoover's deteriorating relationship with the press. ''Let a newspaper writer criticize Hoover,'' one magazine declared, ''and Larry is immediately on his trail if he thinks the incident important or dangerous enough.'' Hoover's confidential papers show that both the President and his secretary devoted an inordinate amount of time to the problem of press leaks. Richey spared no effort attempting to track down the source of the leaks and to punish the responsible parties. Richey also felt a compulsion to prepare a list of those Washington reporters who had ''turned against'' the White House. This ''black list'' became increasingly important as Hoover approached the end of his term. Richey reviewed all anonymous articles critical of the administration, researched the identity of the authors, and added those names to the master list of Hoover's enemies.

It was not the press alone that received high-handed treatment from Richey; he also knocked heads occasionally with members of Congress. At one point, Montana's Democratic Senator Burton K. Wheeler threatened to conduct a full-scale investigation of Hoover's ''detective secretary'' that would expose his questionable activities and embarrass the President. That investigation never took place, primarily because the Democrats already had an abundance of ammunition in their drive to unseat Hoover in 1932. With the Depression as the overriding issue, and Franklin D. Roosevelt as their candidate, the opposition party had no desire to distract voters with tales of Lawrence Richey's undercover operations.

After FDR's landslide victory, Hoover nursed a bitter and suspicious attitude toward his successor. Though the ex-President left Washington immediately after the inauguration, he asked Richey to remain behind on a mysterious assignment. The New York *Times* suggested only that Richey would serve as an "unofficial observer" through whom Hoover could "watch the turning government wheels." A few weeks later Attorney General Homer Cummings, no doubt using the investigative capacity of the Justice Department, discovered the true nature of Richey's presence. His dramatic announcement to the Democratic Cabinet is described in the *Secret Diary* of Interior Secretary Harold Ickes:

> The Attorney General said at the Cabinet meeting today that he was informed that a strict espionage was being maintained of Cabinet members and other officials high in the Government Service. This work is under the charge of Lawrence Richey, one of the secretaries to former President Hoover, and is supposed to be in the interest of Hoover particularly and of the Republican Party in general. Richey is maintaining elaborate offices in the Shoreham Building. He [the Attorney General] warned all of us to be on our guard against people who might thrust themselves upon our notice and he said that the same precaution should be taken by our wives and members of our families. His information is that some women are being employed to worm themselves into the confidence of our wives.

Future Washington spymasters would have taken off their hats to Lawrence Richey's ingenuity and cunning.

A political comeback never materialized for Herbert Hoover, and after 1936 Richey seemed to scale down his espionage operations. Nevertheless, he stayed on in the capital and continued to represent the interests of his chief. When Hoover headed two successive Commissions on the Organization of the Executive Branch of Government, the former secretary served him as a special assistant. During these years of semiretirement, Richey lived alone in a small house on 16th Street Northwest. He maintained his Maryland lodge as a weekend retreat, and conservative politicians, newsmen, and lobbyists occasionally assembled there. Freeman Gosden and Charles Correll, radio's famed Amos 'n' Andy, liked to visit the estate in the fall to shoot wild turkeys.

With no family of his own, Richey made it a tradition to spend Christmas every year with the Hoovers, staying at their penthouse in the tower of New York's Waldorf Hotel. After his holiday visit in 1959 he boarded American Airlines Flight 117 for the return trip to Washington, but suffered a heart attack while the plane was in the air. By the time of the landing he was already dead. Hoover, who was 85, took the news of Richey's death philosophically, issuing

a terse statement to the press in which he lamented the loss of a "loyal friend."
This description was something of an understatement: from the time Richey
was 32 until his death at age 74, Herbert Hoover had been his full-time
employer.

In the years after he left the White House, journalists often pressed Richey to
share his privileged knowledge of the Hoover administration. "If he ever cares
to write his memoirs," Walter Liggett speculated, "they should be a fascinating best-seller." Yet Richey wrote no memoirs and maintained to the end of his
life the same scrupulous silence he had observed while in power. Whatever his
shortcomings in questions of political ethics, he was always a discreet operative
who knew how to protect the reputation of his chief. It remained for a brilliant
but careless aide in the next administration to gather the storms of publicity
about his head and to win a national reputation as "the Rasputin of the White
House."

CHAPTER SEVEN

ACTIVIST ASSISTANTS

On the eve of World War II, the most lurid nightmares of nervous Republicans seemed about to come true. Under the prodding of King Franklin I, Congress passed a "Dictator Bill" calling for a sweeping revolution in the executive branch. The Reorganization Act of 1939 incorporated the recommendations made by the President's Committee on Administrative Management, chaired by Louis Brownlow. It called for a dramatic expansion of the White House staff and the consolidation of a number of federal agencies under the direct control of the chief executive. This historic legislation marked a major step on the road to what political scientists have called "the institutionalization of the Presidency." White House employees soon became so numerous (109 of them, as compared with 46 under Coolidge) that they spilled out of the executive mansion and claimed squatters' rights in the old State-War-Navy building next door.

The shape of the President's personal entourage had been changed beyond recognition. In place of the venerable position of Secretary to the President—or Herbert Hoover's tripartite secretariat—FDR employed the services of an Assistant to the President, six Administrative Assistants, a Special Counsel, an Executive Clerk, an Appointments Secretary, a Press Secretary, and a number of other aides. Despite these changes one factor remained absolutely consistent: the power of a top assistant had little to do with official title or place on an organization chart, and depended almost entirely on his personal relationship with the President. In these terms, no one could question the preeminence of the flamboyant Harry Hopkins. He held a number of prominent positions at different stages in the administration, but the only one that mattered to him was his cherished designation as Franklin Roosevelt's best friend.

Though Clark Clifford never enjoyed that kind of intimacy with Harry Truman, he managed to exercise the same sort of influence. Neither Hopkins nor Clifford supervised the mail or monitored the stream of callers as had other key figures in the history of the White House staff, but they involved themselves in every aspect of decision making and policy formulation. Both men were activists of restless temperament who refused to be confined by job assignments or formal divisions of authority. They saw White House service not as an administrative responsibility but as an undefined opportunity to shape events.

Harry L. Hopkins:
Rasputin of the White House

In January 1941, two months after losing his bid for the Presidency, Wendell Willkie paid a visit to the White House. He wanted to show his good citizenship by supporting the foreign policy of the man who had beaten him. Willkie planned a trip to England to dramatize bipartisan American backing for Britain's lonely battle against Hitler. President Roosevelt encouraged him, and in the course of their brief conversation suggested that while in London, Willkie contact FDR's friend Harry Hopkins, who was then engaged in a series of meetings with British officials.

The Republican leader smoldered at the mere mention of Hopkins' name. "Harry the Hop" represented the sort of arrogant, self-righteous liberalism Willkie hated most in the New Deal. As a long-term houseguest in the White House, Hopkins had become a symbol of dark plots in high places. His ill health added to his unsavory reputation. With two thirds of his stomach cut away to arrest the spread of cancer, the press described him as "an animated piece of shredded wheat" or "a dingy grasshopper." The notion of meeting with such a man seemed an affront to Willkie's dignity. At last he exploded at the President, "Why do you keep Hopkins so close to you? Surely you must realize that people distrust him and they resent his influence?"

Roosevelt sighed. "I can understand that you wonder why I need that half-man around me," he began. "But someday you may well be sitting here where I am now as President of the United States. And when you are, you'll be looking at that door over there and knowing that practically everybody who walks through it wants something out of you. You'll learn what a lonely job this is, and you'll discover the need for somebody like Harry Hopkins, who asks nothing except to serve you."

FDR's explanation may have stopped Wendell Willkie in his tracks, but it can hardly satisfy the thoughtful historian. If the President honestly believed that his top aide served him from purely selfless motives, then Republican propagandists were right in attributing to Hopkins the mystifying hypnotic powers of a latter-day Rasputin. Though Hopkins "asked for nothing" directly, he benefited handsomely and obviously from his association with Roosevelt. Money meant little to him, so he took other rewards—fame, power, a Cabinet post, and a chance to win the Presidency for himself. Most of all, devotion to

Roosevelt gave a sense of external purpose to a man whose personal life was chaotic and self-destructive. In contrast to many of his self-effacing predecessors, Hopkins loved to be the center of attention; he used the limelight as a refuge from his inner turmoil and tragedy.

Harry Lloyd Hopkins was born on August 17, 1890, in Sioux City, Iowa. His father was a harness maker and leather goods salesman with an uncontrollable passion for bowling. He developed remarkable skill at his sport, but unfortunately proved "unable to prevent himself from betting on what would happen when a polished wooden ball rolled down a polished wooden alley toward a number of bottle-shaped pieces of wood." His gambling difficulties contributed to the family's itinerant lifestyle, as they moved from one community to another throughout the Midwest. Finally, at the insistence of Mrs. Hopkins, they settled in Grinnell, Iowa. This straitlaced town offered two salient advantages—the presence of a respected Christian college and a local ordinance forbidding the sale of intoxicating liquors. To Anna Pickett Hopkins these features seemed to ensure the proper environment for raising her five children. An austere Methodist and former schoolteacher, she used to lead the children in family hymn sings around the pump organ and marched them off to church at least six times each week.

In later years, Hopkins took inordinate pride in these humble origins. When he became Secretary of Commerce in 1939, he told the press, "I have to pinch myself to be sure I am not dreaming. Think of it, the son of an Iowa harness maker in the Cabinet!" The New York *Times* had no patience for such comments and took Hopkins sternly to task:

> After so long a White House tradition of barefoot farm lads, rail-splitters, canal-path mule boys, fish market boys, and the like, it seems unbelievable that so comparatively minor a distinction as a Cabinet office should overwhelm the son of an Iowa harness maker. As a matter of fact, the son of an Iowa blacksmith, Herbert Hoover, was President of the United States before Franklin D. Roosevelt. If anyone has reason to be astonished it would be Mr. Roosevelt. Think of it, the son of a wealthy New York family in the White House!

The newspaper's corrective seems especially apt in light of Hopkins' easy access to higher education; he never had to struggle and sweat for an undergraduate degree as did other self-made men. His parents saved enough money to send him to Grinnell College, where he devoted himself to the pursuit of campus popularity and won election as president of his class. One of the few courses that captured his interest was a senior year offering called Applied Christianity. The professor was Edward Steiner, a Czechoslovakian Jew turned Congregational minister, who left a lasting impact on Hopkins and many of his other students. As graduation approached, Steiner told his young disciple of a job prospect in New York City. Christadora Foundation, a settlement house on the Lower East Side, needed a young man to work with boys at its summer camp. There would be no pay other than room and board, but a determined idealist would have plenty of chance to put his Christian principles to work.

In the fall of 1912 the gangly Iowan arrived in the heart of New York's teeming Jewish ghetto, ready to bring faith and enlightenment to its unwitting inhabitants. The only problem, as he later recalled, was that "I'd never seen a Jewish boy before in my life." Hopkins quickly made the necessary adjustments, tempered his missionary zeal, and became a popular and effective social worker. Like many other country boys coming to the city for the first time, he also fell in love. The object of his affections was Ethel Gross, a tough-minded, intelligent young woman who worked as secretary of Christadora House. Ethel's Jewish background and membership in the Ethical Culture Society, a group attempting to replace traditional religions with generalized moral philosophy, made her an unlikely match for the young Methodist from Grinnell. Nevertheless, the two lovers planned to be married. The consternation of Harry's parents can readily be imagined; a few years earlier his mother had broken up a collegiate romance simply because Harry's girl had not been regular enough in her church attendance.

Leaving Christadora House, Hopkins toiled at a succession of social work positions with private charities, moving steadily upward in terms of his impact and responsibilities. He and his wife moved to a comfortable home in suburban Scarsdale, where they raised their three sons far from the suffering around which Hopkins built his career. No one, however, could question the sincerity of his commitment to his work. Dr. Jacob Goldberg, who worked with him at the time, described Hopkins as "an ulcerous type. He was intense, seeming to be in a perpetual nervous ferment—a chain smoker and black coffee drinker. He was always careless in his appearance. Most of the time he would show up in the office looking as though he had spent the previous night sleeping in a hayloft. He would wear the same shirt three or four days at a time. He managed to shave almost every day—usually at the office."

Despite his disorganized personal habits, Hopkins proved a gifted administrator. In 1924 he became executive director of the New York Tuberculosis Association and immediately revolutionized the annual Christmas seals campaign. Instead of waiting for the public to order its holiday stamps, Hopkins came up with the idea of sending sheets of Christmas seals to everyone on an extensive mailing list. Even if people didn't want the stamps, he knew they would feel guilty about keeping them unless they mailed in a small contribution. His plan worked beautifully and has remained an American institution for more than fifty years.

Hopkins naturally became a hero to his office staff, including an attractive young secretary named Barbara Duncan. With her delicate complexion, finely chiseled features, and large, soulful eyes, she conveyed an unmistakable air of romance and vulnerability. The product of a well-to-do Michigan family, she had come to work at the T. B. Association after developing tubercular symptoms herself. Hopkins, who relished the poetry of Keats and remained all his life an unabashed sentimentalist, fell hopelessly in love with her. Their affair quickly became known to his wife and friends. In an effort to save his marriage he began seeing a psychoanalyst and read all the major works of Freud and Adler. He talked endlessly to anyone who would listen about his romantic troubles and used all the latest psychiatric theories to justify his behavior. At last, he fled to Europe to gain perspective on the situation, but upon his return he found himself once more unable to choose between the shy, well-bred secretary and his hard-driving wife of seventeen years. After more than twenty months of emotional upheaval, Ethel Hopkins finally settled the situation by suing for divorce. She won custody of their three sons and alimony amounting to half Harry's total income. According to the recollections of one of his sons, Hopkins seldom met his alimony payments, forcing Ethel to work as the boys grew up.

Hopkins married Barbara Duncan in 1931, at the same time that his professional career reached a crossroads. During his last years as a social worker, according to *American Magazine*, "he was like Napoleon before the French Revolution, a man of destiny fretting away at a soldier's job." The revolution that finally catapulted Hopkins into public prominence was the Great Depression. With a third of the nation impoverished, a man with Hopkins' experience in charity work became suddenly valuable to governments and politicians. In August 1931 he took charge of New York's Temporary Emergency Relief Administration (TERA), a statewide experiment initiated by Governor Franklin Roosevelt. Hopkins did not develop a personal relationship with Roosevelt at this point, but the governor seemed pleased with his performance. When FDR became President in 1933, he asked Hopkins to come along to supervise federal efforts at emergency relief.

During his first two hours as Federal Emergency Relief Administrator Hopkins startled the capital by spending $5 million of public funds. The next day the Washington *Post* heralded his controversial achievement under the headline "MONEY FLIES." Money continued to fly in the years that followed as Hopkins headed the Civil Works Administration (CWA) and then the Works Progress Administration (WPA). To those who criticized his massive programs of relief and public works, Hopkins gave a terse answer: "Hunger is not debatable." His basic goal was to put millions of unemployed Americans to work for the government as quickly as possible. If their work turned out to be trivial or unproductive it seemed a small price to pay for providing steady salaries to those who needed help. Within ten days at CWA, Hopkins accomplished the astounding feat of providing jobs for 2 million men. "Well, they're all at work," he reported to the President, "but for God's sake, don't ask me what they're doing."

Overpublicized examples of WPA employees who spent their time raking leaves or "leaning on their shovels" could not tarnish Hopkins' record of constructive achievement. Under Hopkins, federal workers built or repaired 83,000 schools, improved 400,000 miles of road, and built 11,000 bridges. Thousands of playgrounds, public pools, parks, libraries, and tennis courts were created. Hopkins enjoyed a satisfaction rare for a public man: he saw his efforts bear tangible fruits in terms of facilities that people could use and appreciate.

The press was impressed not only with the scope of Hopkins' achievements, but with his personal style as well. Reporters judged him "the frankest man in public life in Washington," and noted that he could walk into a press conference and "leave seventy newspapermen punch drunk and calling for time out." Hopkins never displayed the pretensions or self-importance generally associated with Washington bureau heads. His office, on the top floor of a run-down building a block and a half from the White House, featured exposed water pipes running along chipped and faded walls, uncarpeted floors, and a shabby, government issue desk. He maintained a small staff of youthful idealists and drove them mercilessly. They worshipped Hopkins and one of them, Corrington Gill, once advised the press that the boss "would make a swell dictator."

Visitors to his headquarters found Hopkins a beguiling combination of innocence and cynicism. He generally received guests with his feet on the desk, a cigarette dangling from one side of his mouth, and dandruff covering his shoulders. He had a bony, angular frame, slicked-down hair, and bulging, restless dark eyes. His general appearance, according to the New York *Times*, "was less that of the former farm boy he was than that of an actor made up to represent an old vaudeville conception of a farm boy." When he spoke his thin lips twisted over to the left so that he talked out of the side of his mouth in the style of a movie tough guy of the era. His smile was equally lopsided, encouraging his detractors to speak of his "perpetual leer." After reading about himself in a *New Yorker* profile, he commented that he must seem to the public "a mixture of a Baptist preacher and a racetrack tout."

This extraordinary figure was bound to make an impression on the President, but initially it was Eleanor Roosevelt who brought Hopkins into the White House inner circle. She admired his background in social work and hoped that his compassionate and uncompromising liberalism would have a positive influence on her husband. The death in 1936 of Louis Howe, the President's longtime friend and assistant who had been serving as his White House Secretary, left a vacuum in Roosevelt's life which she hoped Hopkins would help to fill.

Their relationship developed slowly after Mrs. Roosevelt began inviting Hopkins to dinner. In this social context, Roosevelt discovered that his WPA chief was more than a competent and hard-working administrator; he was also an amusing companion who knew how to laugh at himself. As White House speechwriter Robert Sherwood observed, "Despite all the differences between their characters and experience, Roosevelt and Hopkins were alike in one important way: they were thoroughly and gloriously unpompous." When a Washington newspaper ran a photo of Hopkins but identified it as Attorney General Homer Cummings, Hopkins immediately dashed off a congratulatory note to Cummings. "I am delighted to see what a fine upstanding young man you are getting to be," he declared. "Your face is beginning to show real character and I want you to know that all of your friends are delighted." A reporter once told the WPA Director that Congressional leaders complained he was no politician. Hopkins shot back, "Tell 'em thanks for the compliment." Leaders of Washington's stuffy social establishment also felt the sting of Hopkins' contempt. One evening he arrived late for a glittering affair at the home of an influential matron. Before going in to the black tie dinner he paused, pulled an electric razor out of his pocket, and proceeded to shave himself in front of an entrance hall mirror. He further shocked polite society by appearing regularly at race tracks, where he invariably lost. Late night poker games constituted an additional drain on his resources, with losses of $500 a session not uncommon.

Republican pundits insisted that Harry's lifestyle set a bad example to the millions of struggling Americans who worked for the WPA, but Hopkins only laughed at their objections. As his friend Sherwood pointed out: "He was pleased and rather proud when the hostile press denounced him as a 'playboy.' That made him feel glamorous." Hopkins' arrogant and unflinching determination to do as he pleased also sat well with Roosevelt. The President may have even felt a twinge of envy at Hopkins' ability to enjoy himself and ignore the howls of outraged conservatives. Reporter Raymond Clapper perceptively summed up Hopkins' appeal to his boss: "Many New Dealers have bored Roosevelt with their solemn earnestness. Hopkins never does. . . . Quick, alert, shrewd, bold, and carrying it off with a bright Hell's bells air, Hopkins is in all respects the inevitable Roosevelt favorite."

This favored status became apparent during the meals, cocktail hours, card games, political tours, and ocean cruises he shared with FDR. During one vacation to the Bahamas, Secretary of the Interior Harold Ickes noted that Hopkins was "very close indeed to the President. He could walk into the President's cabin without being announced or even without knocking. The President handed him apparently confidential dispatches and letters that he showed to no one else."

Even Hopkins' personal disasters served to bring him closer to Roosevelt. In July 1935 an examination by his physician turned up evidence of a duodenal ulcer. The doctor prescribed a careful diet and total abstention from alcohol —orders which Hopkins promptly and consistently ignored. Nevertheless, his illness—and the far more serious illness that followed two years later —provoked FDR's sympathy and concern. Himself paralyzed by polio from the hips down, Roosevelt had a special feeling for the infirmities of others. An astonishing number of his closest aides and associates suffered from serious health problems. It may not be too much to suggest that Roosevelt felt most secure when surrounded by those who were in some sense damaged physical specimens. His alter ego Louis Howe, Appointments Secretary Marvin McIntyre, Military Aide "Pa" Watson, Private Secretary Missy LeHand, and finally the crippled President himself all literally worked themselves to death during their years of White House service.

Though he survived other members of the inner circle, Hopkins suffered unparalleled emotional torment during the last decade of his life. Just a few weeks after the diagnosis of his ulcer his wife Barbara had her right breast surgically removed. Hopkins conspired with the doctors to convince her that the growth in her body was benign, but she knew from the beginning it was cancer. His wife had been sickly from the first days of their romance, but in the course of the marriage her health had improved sufficiently for her to give birth to a baby girl, Dianna. After the mastectomy, however, her condition deteriorated and it became clear that she was dying. Another man might have left his job and devoted himself exclusively to his wife during her last months, but Hopkins chose to go on as before, keeping impossible hours, throwing himself desperately into his work. Franklin and Eleanor Roosevelt did what they could to help. The First Lady gave the Hopkins' free use of the Roosevelt retreat at Campobello, even providing nurses and servants for Barbara's comfort. She also offered to take Dianna Hopkins, who was 5 years old at the time, into the White House during the worst of her parents' ordeal.

In the summer of 1937, Hopkins accompanied his fading wife to Saratoga Springs, New York, for what they knew would be their final vacation together. Friends who came up from New York City to help them lose money on the horses found the couple energetic and gay—but with an obviously forced quality to their gaiety. The end came in October in a Washington hospital. Hopkins sat for forty-eight consecutive hours at his wife's bedside, and he was with her when she died. The President, after completing a major speech in Chicago, announced that he would cancel his other engagements and return to Washington for the funeral.

Two months later Hopkins found himself back in the hospital—this time for a physical crisis of his own. Doctors feared that his continued digestive problems were evidence of stomach cancer. They rushed him to the Mayo Clinic, where a prominent surgeon removed most of his stomach in an effort to stop the spread of the disease. The operation proved successful—cancer never recurred. Yet the miserable state of Hopkins' remaining digestive equipment left him prey for the rest of his life to a host of painful disorders. Even in his reduced state, he worried enough about politics to lie to the press about his condition. He told reporters that the purpose of his surgery had been to relieve ulcers and formally denied all rumors of cancer.

Such deception would have been utterly pointless if Hopkins had been concerned only with his continued service as WPA Director. The bizarre fact was that even from the sobering confines of his hospital room Harry dreamed of running for President. Even more surprising is the evidence that Franklin Roosevelt encouraged his ambitions.

As he approached the election of 1940, FDR looked around for a political heir. Democratic conservatives, restless after eight years of Roosevelt's liberal reign, laid plans for recapturing the party. Most experts believed they would succeed unless Roosevelt handpicked a successor and battled actively for his nomination. "Harry the Hop" was the man closest to the President and a hero to the Democratic Left. His political liabilities were obvious—feeble health, an embarrassing divorce, and a total lack of electoral experience. But to Roosevelt these handicaps only added to the challenge of the project. In private White House conversations, he all but anointed his controversial friend, encouraging him to make the race and discussing strategy for a preconvention campaign. To ease the path to the Presidency he named Hopkins Secretary of Commerce. The swearing-in took place on Christmas Eve 1938, and the entire appointment seemed to be a Yuletide gift. Hopkins proceeded to make the most of his opportunities. He began giving speeches around the country and arranged frequent news photographs showing him side by side with Roosevelt. He gave up his sloppy clothes and careless manners and appeared in neat, conservative vested suits. He even leased a 300-acre farm near Grinnell to establish his credentials as a native son of Iowa.

The driving ambition of Hopkins' spirit, however, could not overcome the pathetic frailties of his flesh. Within three months of moving into his grandiose offices at the Commerce Department a series of digestive ailments brought him close to death. A corps of prominent physicians, personally recruited by the President, struggled valiantly to save him. "They gave me stuff they'd never given before," Hopkins recalled. "I took plasma transfusions and all sorts of drug injections through my arms, my ankles, and the back of my hands. . . . They didn't know what cured me, they tried so many things." Unfortunately, he was never cured sufficiently to return to work in the Cabinet. During his last eighteen months as Commerce Secretary he spent less than thirty days in his office. Nevertheless, he went on dreaming forlornly of the Presidency—if not in 1940, his friends reported, then in 1944.

From the bedroom of his Georgetown home he watched world events with a growing sense of helplessness and self-pity. The war raged in Europe, with Hitler's armies moving from victory to victory. On May 10, 1940, the day the Germans invaded the Low Countries, Hopkins came to dinner at the White House to discuss the situation with FDR. When he arrived he felt so weak that he could barely make it to the table. Roosevelt insisted that the ailing Commerce Secretary spend the night and ordered him upstairs to a small, unoccupied bedroom that had been used eighty years before by Abraham Lincoln. A few days later Hopkins' clothes arrived in a brown paper bag and he began to settle in. He remained FDR's guest for the next three and a half years. His status reminded many observers of Sheridan Whiteside, the obnoxious interloper in the Broadway hit *The Man Who Came to Dinner*. Whiteside, however, took advantage of confused and unwilling hosts while Hopkins stayed on at Roosevelt's insistence.

Pity for a suffering friend and his 5-year-old daughter helped explain FDR's hospitality, but his arrangement with Hopkins also had a more practical basis. Hopkins may not have been well enough to report to an office, but from his White House bedroom he conducted Presidential business on the phone. While he continued to hold the title and draw a salary as Secretary of Commerce he served, in effect, as Roosevelt's Chief of Staff. As Harold Ickes complained, "Everything must seep through Harry into the White House."

Hopkins' bedroom soon became one of the nerve centers for the entire government. He received even the most important visitors in his pajamas and did much of his work on a shaky portable card table. Those who penetrated his inner sanctum were likely to find Hopkins propped in bed, with papers and cigarette ashes scattered over the rumpled quilts. Roosevelt referred a never-ending stream of problems to his "right-hand guest," often providing only the briefest instructions. "Look into this, Harry, and let me know," he scribbled on one agency request. A letter from an angry Senator was forwarded to Hopkins with the simple notation, "Harry, do something. FDR."

Hopkins' presence in the executive mansion also gave Roosevelt the opportunity to supervise his friend's medical progress. The President offered personal instructions to both doctors and patient. On one occasion, he presented his aide with a handwritten note that included two crisp new dollar bills paper-clipped to the top of the sheet. It read:

> Dear Harry—
>   Good Boy! Teacher says you have gained 2 pounds
>   2 lbs. = 2$
>   Keep on gaining and put the reward into your little
> Savings Bank. But you must not gain more than 50 lbs.
> because Popper has not got more than 50$.
>
>   As ever
>   FDR

Despite Roosevelt's jocular tone, he knew his friend's ill health ruled out a race for elective office, and this knowledge played a part in the President's decision to seek an unprecedented third term for himself. Hopkins naturally announced early support for the third-term concept and eventually journeyed to the Chicago convention to represent his chief. He personally orchestrated FDR's renomination and the controversial choice of Henry Wallace as a running mate—an effort which won him bitter enemies within the Democratic party. Totally exhausted after the convention, Hopkins resolved to abandon public life. He knew he would be a liability to Roosevelt in the campaign ahead. Republicans had already begun complaining about his absenteeism at the Commerce Department and his residence in the White House free of charge. From a hotel room in Chicago, Hopkins wrote an emotional letter of resignation in which he described his years with Roosevelt as "the happiest time of my life." The President wrote back immediately, telling Hopkins "you may resign the office—only the office—and nothing else. Our friendship will and must go on as always." Notwithstanding these brave words, he made no objection when Hopkins prepared to move out of the White House and leased an apartment in New York. FDR even appointed him director of the newly established Franklin D. Roosevelt library in Hyde Park to facilitate his retreat from Washington.

The evidence suggests that both men wanted to terminate their working relationship but that their mutual dependence had been too deeply ingrained. Roosevelt, for instance, found it impossible to endure the last weeks of his reelection campaign without Hopkins at his side. Facing a spirited challenge from Wendell Willkie, he summoned Hopkins for help in drafting major campaign speeches. For Hopkins, the excitement of the executive mansion at the height of a campaign—especially when compared to his desolate convalescence in New York—proved irresistible. Before long, he had reestablished himself in his White House bedroom.

This time he held no official position, and power stemmed exclusively from his access to the President. No one spent more hours of the day in the President's company. They ate lunch and dinner together every day, often in total privacy. They also enjoyed the nightly ritual of a before-dinner cocktail hour in the President's study. While happily mixing liquid refreshment for his intimate friends, FDR usually downed two or three drinks himself. Hopkins reported that the President produced "a first-rate old-fashioned" and a "fair martini," though he occasionally subjected his guests to unpleasant experiments. During one bleak period lasting several weeks, he served up nightly doses of gin and grapefruit juice. Hopkins dutifully consumed the vile concoction, despite his weak stomach. He also laughed respectfully at the risqué stories FDR loved to tell over and over again.

After dinner the two men generally chatted, played cards, or watched one of the feature films that screened regularly at the White House. Hopkins even felt free to call on the President after the chief executive had retired for the night. With his own sleeping quarters just down the corridor from Roosevelt's, he often wrapped himself in a tattered dressing gown and came to the President's bedside for intimate discussion of politics and personalities. Hopkins reportedly told a friend, "I don't give a damn who sees Roosevelt during the day. I see him at night, the last half-hour before he goes to bed. . . . I see the Chief when he is alone and tired, and a half-hour then is worth two hours any other time."

Only one person in the White House rivaled Hopkins' intimacy with the President: Missy LeHand, FDR's loyal secretary. According to Roosevelt's son, Elliott, Missy had been involved in a full-blown love affair with FDR before he became President. A tall, stately blue-eyed woman with a perpetual smile and prematurely gray hair, she helped fill the sexual vacuum left by Roosevelt's troubled relationship with his wife. She never married, and her only purpose in life was to please her boss. Elliott Roosevelt claims that his mother knew the situation and accepted it. She believed it was the price she had to pay for preserving a marriage that allowed her to pursue her cherished humanitarian goals.

Hopkins' role in this domestic intrigue remains somewhat unclear. He almost certainly knew the nature of Roosevelt's relationship with Missy. On several occasions the three of them took extended vacations at FDR's private spa in Warm Springs, Georgia. During one such visit, Hopkins wrote, "There is no one here but Missy—the President and me—so life is simple—ever so informal and altogether pleasant. And why not—I like Missy—the President is the grandest of companions—I read for hours and sleep ever so well." With his own tangled experience in affairs of the heart, Hopkins made the perfect confidant for Roosevelt. Both men were romantics by nature who tried to hide their vulnerability with an air of cavalier cynicism.

Hopkins' position with Missy and the President may have helped to damage his relationship with Mrs. Roosevelt. The First Lady began to find fault with her onetime protégé, expressing distaste for the way Hopkins "agreed with the President regardless of his own opinion" or "tried to persuade him in indirect ways." Totally secure in his standing with FDR, Hopkins could afford to be rude to Mrs. Roosevelt. When she approached him with ideas for a comprehensive new health program for low-income Americans, he snapped back that he and the President were too busy to be bothered.

Near the beginning of FDR's third term, the overworked Missy LeHand suffered a stroke from which she never fully recovered. With her usefulness exhausted, she left the White House and died three years later at age 46. Her departure intensified FDR's need for Hopkins' friendship at the same time that events in Europe increased his need for practical assistance.

A year before Pearl Harbor, FDR sent his aide to England to arrange more effective American aid to the island nation. So began Hopkins' extraordinary career as the President's roving ambassador and personal representative. Over the next four years he made more than a dozen trips to world capitals and international conferences. His basic mission was to facilitate cooperation between the Allies. To do that, as he confessed in one off-the-record interview, he had to act as "a catalytic agent between two prima donnas": Roosevelt and Churchill.

The secret of Hopkins' success was his genuine intimacy with both world leaders. Churchill never achieved more than a cordial, competitive relationship with FDR, but in Roosevelt's aide he discovered a kindred spirit. During Hopkins' first visit to England they spent a weekend at the Prime Minister's country estate where the two men drank together, joked together, and laid far-reaching plans for winning the war. At first, Churchill had been wary of his guest. Hopkins, after all, represented a nation that was officially at peace and he had no experience in foreign or military affairs. Conscious of his guest's reputation as a crusading liberal, the wily Churchill tried to win his sympathy by describing plans to help England's poor after the war.

"Well, Mr. Prime Minister," Hopkins shot back before Churchill had finished, "neither the President nor I give a damn about what you've been saying. All we're interested in back in Washington is how to beat that son of a bitch in Berlin."

This sort of thinking naturally won Churchill's respect. He invited Hopkins to participate in a session of His Majesty's Cabinet—the first time a person of non-British nationality had ever attended such a meeting. The Prime Minister also asked Hopkins' aid in preparing an international radio address intended to sway American public opinion. The speech that resulted, with its memorable line "give us the tools and we will finish the job," proved a notable success. It earned Hopkins the distinction of being the only man in history to serve as speechwriter to both the President of the United States and the Prime Minister of Great Britain.

Churchill further expressed his regard with gestures of personal kindness. During one of his trips to England, Hopkins lost the battered felt hat he had been wearing for years. The Prime Minister replaced it immediately with an elegant, gray custom-made fedora that bore his initials "W.S.C." on the band. Though it was several sizes too large, Hopkins wore it proudly as he returned home. When Churchill visited the White House for conferences with the President he continued his warm relations with Roosevelt's assistant. The Englishman invariably established himself in the bedroom directly across the hall from Hopkins, and the two men made a habit of chatting and sipping brandy long after midnight. President Roosevelt declined participation in these marathon sessions. He liked to retire no later than ten o'clock and complained about Churchill's uncivilized hours and boundless energy.

Hopkins' intimacy with the British leader paid rich diplomatic dividends during the war. If Churchill wanted American approval for some new military initiative he wrote directly to Hopkins, asking if the idea should be presented to "our great and good friend." Hopkins either took the suggestion immediately to FDR or cabled Churchill that the idea would not be well-received. He thereby avoided needless strains on the top-level relationship.

The cause of allied cooperation also benefited from Hopkins' personal contacts with Joseph Stalin. Hopkins was in the midst of his second visit to England when Nazi armies crashed into Russia in July 1941. As soon as he heard the news, Hopkins called Roosevelt by transatlantic cable and asked permission to go to Moscow. He wanted to organize American aid to Russia in much the same way he had organized material support for Great Britain. Roosevelt gave his approval and Hopkins became the first Western emissary to visit the Kremlin after the German invasion. An advance letter from Roosevelt asked Stalin "to treat him with the identical confidence you would feel if you were talking directly to me." At the same time, Hopkins carried with him no written instructions from the President or the State Department. FDR trusted him to handle the negotiations entirely on his own.

The social worker from Iowa and the ruthless Soviet dictator got along surprisingly well in the course of their meetings. Hopkins was particularly impressed with his host's efficiency. "There was no waste of word, gesture nor mannerism," he reported. "Joseph Stalin knew what he wanted, knew what Russia wanted." When Hopkins returned home he became an impassioned advocate of all-out aid to the Soviet Union and persuaded Roosevelt to provide emergency supplies. At the Teheran Conference in 1943, Stalin showed his gratitude by crossing the crowded room to shake hands with Hopkins, an honor that the dictator conferred on no one else there.

Hopkins' familiarity with all of "the Big Three" allowed him to play a unique role at major wartime strategy sessions. As Winston Churchill observed, "I have been present at several great conferences where twenty or more of the most important executive personages were gathered together. When the discussion flagged and seemed baffled, it was on these occasions he would rap out the deadly question: 'Surely, Mr. President, here is the point we have got to settle. Are we going to face it or not?'" To honor his persistent focus on wartime essentials, Churchill promised to grant Hopkins an English title after the war: Lord Root-of-the-Matter. FDR offered a similar tribute to his friend's no-nonsense diplomacy. "He doesn't even know the meaning of the word 'protocol,'" the President announced. "When he sees a piece of red tape, he just pulls out those old garden shears of his and snips it. And when he's talking to some foreign dignitary, he knows how to slump back in his chair and put his feet up on the conference table and say, 'Oh, *yeah*?'"

Hopkins' top-level globe-trotting without benefit of formal governmental commission reminded many observers of Colonel House. Yet unlike House, Hopkins did not possess independent means; he needed to earn a living while serving his country. In March 1941, FDR placed him on the federal payroll as Special Assistant for the Lend-Lease Program. The new title did nothing to increase his power or prestige, but it did provide a much-needed $10,000 a year. In the informal, loosely structured atmosphere of the Roosevelt White House, official titles had become increasingly irrelevant. The power of the Presidency had expanded so quickly that organization charts could hardly keep pace with shifting realities.

FDR's last attempt to work within the established traditions had been the appointment of his son James as Secretary to the President. Succeeding to the office on the death of Louis Howe, the dapper, amiable Jimmy hoped to use the position to further his political ambitions. From the beginning, his favored status was resented by other White House aides and the public at large. "The Crown Prince" lacked both the experience and the temperament to carve order out of the administrative chaos. Certainly, the presence of a powerful figure such as Hopkins made his job all the more difficult. While trying desperately to please his father, Jimmy developed a severe case of gastric ulcers and wound up in the Mayo Clinic.

So it was that the old, honorable position of Secretary to the President died not with a bang, but with a whimper. FDR released his suffering son from White House responsibilities and soon created a totally new structure for the Presidential staff. The Reorganization Act of 1939 provided for six "Administrative Assistants" with wide-ranging and occasionally overlapping authority. This arrangement reflected Roosevelt's theories of personnel management. "A little rivalry is stimulating, you know," he once explained to Secretary of

Labor Frances Perkins. "It keeps everybody going to prove he is a better fellow than the next man. It keeps them honest too."

Despite the intensely competitive environment in the executive mansion, Hopkins maintained his position as the President's one indispensable aide. He was sitting at lunch with FDR on Sunday, December 7, when news arrived that the Japanese had attacked Pearl Harbor. From that point to the end of his government service, military victory became Hopkins' single obsessive concern. His friend Marquis Childs observed that Hopkins seemed "relieved, happy almost, at having found something in which he could abandon his own personal destiny; submerging himself in a task of immeasurable magnitude and immeasurable risk." Interior Secretary Harold Ickes wryly reported that "we don't have to worry any more about the war; Harry Hopkins will take it on as his responsibility and run it." At times, Hopkins' disregard for all "lesser matters" could be positively brutal. Mrs. Roosevelt once told him she worried that Dianna's lonely life in the White House might prove unhealthy for a little girl. "That's totally unimportant," Hopkins snapped. "The only important thing is the war."

With all the strength left in his emaciated body, he threw himself into diplomatic missions and his new responsibilities as head of the Munitions Assignment Board. This Anglo-American agency, recently created by Roosevelt and Churchill, determined the allocation of war materiel to Allied forces throughout the world. Hopkins spent hours on the telephone badgering industrialists into meeting the impossible production schedules required for victory. When the Navy delayed in sending vitally needed planes to Russia, FDR dashed off a note that summed up Hopkins' role. "Say to them for me," the President commanded, "Hurry, Hurry, Hurry!" For scores of generals and bureaucrats who wanted to push their pet projects the key question in Washington was, "Can you get the 'HH' on it?" By the end of the war this civilian coordinator had won the respect of even the most skeptical military men. Dwight Eisenhower declared that "he had a grasp of the broad factors in military problems that was almost phenomenal."

Hopkins' heroic achievements were made possible to a great extent by his mastery of palace intrigue in the White House. As Winston Churchill noted in a classic understatement, Hopkins "did not encourage" rivals. He also knew the value of placing mediocre and easily manipulated men in key government positions. One such individual was Edward R. Stettinius, the handsome, well-bred former board chairman of U.S. Steel. At Hopkins' urging, Stettinius was appointed administrator of the Lend-Lease in September 1941. Hopkins went on running the program just as he always had, but the soft-spoken Stettinius served as his shield in dealings with Congress. In 1944, when the aging Cordell Hull at long last retired as Secretary of State, numerous powerful politicos aspired to succeed him. Hopkins had his own candidate for the position: that reliable foil, Edward Stettinius. As usual, FDR followed his aide's advice.

Only once during the war years did Hopkins conspire to win high office for himself. Increasingly concerned about his ultimate place in history, he hoped to become Secretary of War during the climactic phase of the conflict. This meant displacing Henry L. Stimson, a distinguished Republican who enjoyed bipartisan popularity. FDR seems to have been aware of Hopkins' ambition. He must have suspected his aide as the anonymous source for frequent magazine stories about the 76-year-old Stimson "losing his grip" and growing too senile to handle his responsibilities. Stimson, however, had no intention of retiring and Roosevelt would not risk a Congressional furor by forcing his resignation.

Though denied the prestige of the War Department post, Hopkins received considerable press attention as "one of America's most eligible bachelors." During his weekends away from Washington he enjoyed total escape: making a splash with his tangos and sambas at the El Morocco or the 21 Club. *Time* magazine described him as "a hot-eyed social reformer with an eye for a pretty face." For a while he dated movie star Paulette Goddard, the glamorous ex-wife of Charlie Chaplin. Of even greater interest to the gossip columnists were his public appearances with Anna Roosevelt, the President's handsome and recently divorced daughter. Some of Hopkins' close friends believed that he might have actually married into the Roosevelt family except for the fear that a union with Anna would have complicated his all-important relationship with FDR. The most substantial rumors concerning his love life linked him to Mrs. Dorothy Donovan Thomas Hale, a wealthy widow who owned mansions in the United States and Europe. Hopkins told the press that it was "nobody's God-damned business" whether or not he was engaged to her. Whisperers nonetheless blamed "lover boy" Hopkins when Mrs. Hale leaped to her death from the window of her sixteenth-floor Manhattan penthouse.

In the summer of 1942 announcement of Hopkins' engagement to Louise Macy temporarily stifled the bad publicity. The third Mrs. Hopkins, like most of Harry's love interests of the period, was a divorcée and a member of New York's smart set. She was also a successful career woman and former Paris editor of *Harper's Bazaar*. Slim, athletic, stylish, and poised, she offered a striking contrast to the sick and slovenly Hopkins. The wedding took place in the Oval Study of the White House, with President Roosevelt giving away the bride. Originally, Hopkins had wanted his boss to perform the ceremony, but Roosevelt's authority as Commander in Chief extended only to weddings at sea. For their honeymoon the newlyweds vacationed on a small farm in Connecticut, though the Republican press, missing no chance to hit its favorite target, reported that Hopkins had commandeered a Navy ship for a romantic pleasure cruise.

No one was more delighted at Hopkins' wedding than Eleanor Roosevelt. The First Lady reasonably expected that the happy event would rid her of a houseguest whose presence had become increasingly onerous. With his special dietary requirements at each meal, his habit of dropping cigarette ashes everywhere, and the unrelenting rudeness, Hopkins had long ago worn out his welcome. Mrs. Roosevelt was therefore dumbfounded when Harry blandly in-

White House secretary John Nicolay (seated left), assistant secretary John Hay, and friend: "Lincoln was fond of reading Shakespeare aloud, and would often keep the young men awake long past midnight, declaiming favorite passages from *Macbeth* or the history plays."

Robert Johnson, ill-fated private secretary to his father, President Andrew Johnson: "One Illinois politician reported that 'there is too much whiskey in the White House, and harlots go into the private secretary's office unannounced in broad daylight.'"

U.S. Grant's unscrupulous and illustrious courtier, Colonel Orville Babcock: "'He fished for gold in every stinking cesspool and served more than any other man to blacken the record of Grant's administration.'"

William K. Rogers, long-time friend and White House aide to Rutherford B. Hayes: "When he arrived at the capital, Rogers received the traditional greeting Washington reserves for rank outsiders suddenly elevated to positions of power: he was socially snubbed and bitterly criticized."

Joseph Stanley-Brown, private secretary to James A. Garfield: "By the time the bleeding President arrived at the White House on a pile of mattresses loaded on the back of a wagon, his 22-year-old secretary had already taken firm command."

Daniel G. Rollins, who exercised a decisive, long-distance influence on the administration of Chester A. Arthur: "It is doubtful that the public reaction would have been as favorable as it was if the nation had known the truth about the President's message — that every word of it had been written by another man."

Daniel Lamont, much admired "Assistant President" to Grover Cleveland: "It wasn't until 1917, long after the death of all the principals, that the public learned the truth about the President's cancer operation.... Lamont had successfully engineered one of the most remarkable cover-ups in White House history."

Elijah Halford, Benjamin Harrison's dour private secretary: "During his first year of White House service, Halford proved the first, but by no means the last Presidential aide to break under the strain of his official responsibilities."

William McKinley's popular and resourceful assistant, George B. Courtelyou: "Ike Hoover, who worked as an usher in the White House for forty-two years, believed that Cortelyou was the most effective aide ever to serve an American President, and today that still seems a reasonable judgment."

William Loeb, Jr., Teddy Roosevelt's devoted friend and secretary: "An obscure plugger from the wrong side of the tracks...Loeb did his best to remake himself in Roosevelt's image." (Courtesy of the New York *Times*)

Charles Dyer Norton, the charismatic assistant who helped ruin the administration of William Howard Taft: "Cabinet members continued to complain that 'the President won't let us say a word against Norton' and an eerie atmosphere of plot and counterplot prevailed at the White House." (Courtesy of the New York *Times*)

Woodrow Wilson with his intimate friend Colonel Edward M. House: " 'He is not the biggest man I have ever met,' House wrote to his brother-in-law, 'but he is one of the pleasantest and I would rather play with him than any prospective candidate I have seen.' " (Courtesy of the New York *Times*)

White House aide George B. Christian stands admiringly behind his boss, Warren G. Harding: "...if Christian had grown up any place on earth other than Mount Vernon Avenue in Marion, Ohio, his chances of serving in the White House would have remained as remote as his chances of reaching the moon."

President Coolidge, left, with his controversial assistant C. Bascom Slemp: "For two days in a row, the New York *World* ran editorials under the headline, 'Why Mr. Slemp is a Blunder.' To summarize the arguments, the newspaper's editor offered a bit of doggerel:

In picking Slemp, I think, Cal's bump
Of acumen has taken a Slump.

Herbert Hoover poses with Lawrence Richey, his "confidential snooper" and principal assistant: "As early as 1929, a White House aide spied on the opposition party, blackmailed a troublesome Senator, dispatched private detectives to plug press leaks, and compiled 'black lists' of administration enemies."

Harry Hopkins, relief administrator, Commerce Secretary, Assistant to the President, and FDR's "right-hand guest": "At last Wilkie exploded at the President, 'Why do you keep Hopkins so close to you? Surely you must realize that people distrust him and they resent his influence?'" (Courtesy of the New York *Times*)

Clark M. Clifford, the youthful, ambitious leader of the Truman White House staff: "When asked who proved the most effective poker player in this august assemblage of wheeler-dealers, Clifford only chuckled in reply. 'Now, modesty forbids me from answering that,' he said." (Courtesy of the New York *Times*)

Sherman Adams, all-powerful Chief of Staff to President Dwight Eisenhower: " 'Just imagine,' said the first one, 'what a disaster it would be if Eisenhower died and Nixon became President!'

'Or even worse,' answered his companion, 'what if Sherman Adams died and Eisenhower became President?' " (Courtesy of George Tames/the New York *Times*)

Presidential alter-ego Ted Sorenson confers with JFK in the Oval Office: " 'I had given eleven years of my life to John Kennedy,' he commented after his patron's death, 'and for those eleven years he was the only human being who mattered to me.' " (Courtesy of George Tames/the New York *Times*)

(*Right*) Bill Moyers, staff coordinator and, later, White House Press Secretary, keeps in step with his demanding boss: " 'I loved Lyndon Johnson,' he said. 'As much as a man can love another man, I loved Lyndon Johnson.... But I wish I had known him later and worked for him at a more mature period of my life.' " (Official White House photograph)

"Zero-defects man" Bob Haldeman taking orders from his chief aboard Nixon's campaign plane in 1968: "All Washington recognized the President's practical reliance on Haldeman for the day-to-day running of the White House, but few observers would have guessed the intensity of his emotional dependence on the Chief of Staff." (Official White House photograph)

(*Right*) Dick Cheney, the capable but publicity-shy Chief of Staff to President Gerald Ford: "As one senior Democratic Congressman observed: 'Nobody talked about him at the time, but if you look back on it, that kid Cheney did a hell of a job.'" (Courtesy of Richard Cheney)

Hamilton Jordan: ranking Georgian in the Carter White House: " 'Jimmy Carter's got God, and Hamilton Jordan's got Jimmy Carter.' " (Courtesy of Mike Keza/the New York *Times*)

formed her that his new wife would be joining him in residence at the White House. According to Hopkins, he and the President had decided that his continued presence was essential for the successful conduct of the war. With Louise Hopkins taking over a bedroom adjoining her husband's, Mrs. Roosevelt felt she had ceased to be mistress under her own roof. The press began running stories of nasty scenes between Mrs. Hopkins and the First Lady. Eleanor Roosevelt strongly disapproved of the lifestyle Hopkins pursued with his gay young wife. She noted that every afternoon they sipped drinks in their rooms before joining FDR for the regular cocktail hour. The First Lady complained that "they really are quite *high* sometimes before they sit down to dinner."

The couple's occupation of the White House lasted a full year before Hopkins decided to find a home of his own. For the sake of his wife and daughter he rented a house on N Street in Georgetown. Hopkins' critics naturally rejoiced when he moved out of the White House, hoping that his departure would end his "mystifying hold" on the President.

Hopkins' influence did in fact go into a temporary eclipse, but the main reason was physical collapse. On New Year's day 1944 he was entertaining friends at home when he suddenly felt ill and went upstairs to rest. He remained in bed for most of the next seven months, fretting away his time at the Mayo Clinic, Miami Beach, and Washington. FDR, whose own health had deteriorated as the long war neared its conclusion, seemed impatient with the physical limitations of his aide. Hopkins played no substantial role in Roosevelt's fourth-term campaign and his responsibilities as a coordinator of military strategy passed largely to others. It was only when FDR needed his special skills to set up another Big Three conference that Hopkins returned to his cherished role at the center of the world stage.

The historic meeting that resulted largely from his efforts was plagued by controversy from the moment of its conception. Stalin refused to leave Soviet territory and insisted that the ailing American President travel halfway round the world to meet him on his home soil. Many of FDR's advisors considered this demand humiliating and unreasonable, but Hopkins took another point of view. "The all-important thing was to get the meeting," he declared.

Eventually, Roosevelt and Churchill agreed to come to the Black Sea resort of Yalta. When FDR arrived he showed the strain of his exhausting 13,000 mile flight. "The President seemed flaccid and frail," Churchill reported. "I felt that he had a slender contact with life." Hopkins' condition was even worse. Secretary of State Stettinius recalled that "he was so sick that we put him to bed" and noted that Hopkins survived on "coffee, cigarettes, and amazingly small amounts of food and paregoric."

The poor health of both American leaders undoubtedly contributed to their diplomatic failures at Yalta. Hopkins knew he was a dying man and concerned himself with the present rather than the future. Churchill and others warned that sweeping concessions to the Russians would only sow the seeds for postwar confrontations, but Hopkins and Roosevelt disagreed. Hopkins favored granting Stalin's demands in order to ensure cooperation during the final stage of the war.

On the way home from the Yalta Conference the Presidential party sailed at a leisurely pace across the Mediterranean. FDR wanted Hopkins' help in drafting a report to Congress on the recent negotiations, but Hopkins was in no condition to work. One day after lunch he sat down with his chief on the main deck. "I'm sick," he insisted. "I mean really sick. I want to stop off and go to Marrakech and rest."

Roosevelt showed his irritation and said that anyone could rest more peacefully on an ocean cruise. "No, no," Hopkins sighed. "I can't rest on a ship. That's the problem." FDR, wrapped in his blue Navy cape, slouched back in disgust and turned away. Later he asked his daughter Anna to persuade Hopkins to change his mind. She went down to his cabin and tried to influence her old friend, but he remained adamant.

A few days later, with his bags packed and a Navy launch waiting to take him ashore, Harry went to the President to say goodbye. FDR sat on his favorite deck chair going over a stack of papers. His pince-nez spectacles glinted in the sun. As Hopkins walked over to him, the President looked up and mechanically offered his hand. "Goodbye," he said without emotion and then returned immediately to his reading. He expressed no good wishes, no words of thanks, no hopes for future meetings.

After four days of rest at Marrakech, Hopkins flew back to the States and checked himself into the Mayo Clinic. He was still hospitalized six weeks later when he received an urgent call from the capital. Franklin Roosevelt, while vacationing at Warm Springs, had just died of a cerebral hemorrhage. For several moments Hopkins held the phone in his hand but could not speak. At last he said, "I guess I'd better be going to Washington."

He arrived in time for the funeral where, according to his friend Robert Sherwood, he "looked like death, the skin of his face a dreadful cold white with apparently no flesh left under it." When the Bishop of Washington announced the opening hymn and the mourners began to sing, Hopkins burst into noisy sobs.

After the ceremony he asked Sherwood to come with him back to his Georgetown home. Hopkins immediately went upstairs to rest and asked his friend to keep him company. Sherwood sat by the bed and noted the fiery intensity of Hopkins' dark eyes as he rattled on for hours about the past and the future. "God damn it," he said, "now we've got to get to work on our own. This is where we've really got to begin. We've had it too easy all this time, because we knew he was there, and we had the privilege of being able to get to him. Whatever we thought was the matter with the world, whatever we felt ought to be done about it, we could take our ideas to him. . . . Well—he isn't there now, and we've got to find a way to do things by ourselves."

With this determination in mind, Hopkins spent the next few days in meetings with President Truman. He briefed the new chief executive on the Yalta negotiations, the personalities of Churchill and Stalin, and Roosevelt's secret ideas on winning the war and organizing the United Nations. No other human being could have given Truman the sort of in-depth information that Hopkins provided. Deeply impressed with the frail but fast-talking aide, Truman wanted him to "continue with me in the same role he had played with my predecessor." Hopkins declined for the sake of his health and because he knew that a relationship such as the one he enjoyed with Roosevelt could never be recreated. "Truman has got to have his own people around him, not Roosevelt's," he said. "If we were around, we'd always be looking at him and he'd know we were thinking, 'The *President* wouldn't do it that way!'"

Despite his reservations, Hopkins agreed to perform a crucial diplomatic mission for Truman before he left government service. Within a month of Roosevelt's death, a series of disagreements with the Soviet Union —particularly regarding the future status of Poland—had begun to threaten world peace. Unless the disputes could be settled amicably, the newly constituted United Nations might never get off the ground. Averell Harriman, American Ambassador to Russia, believed that Stalin's long-standing trust and affection for Hopkins made him the indispensable man for handling the negotiations. Though his friends thought him "too ill even to get out of bed and walk across N street," Hopkins flew to Moscow at Truman's request. In ten days of conferences with the Soviet dictator, he smoothed over the differences between the two nations without settling any of the substantive problems. In retrospect it is hard to justify Hopkins' naive faith that American goodwill and conciliation would automatically be reciprocated by the Russians. Nevertheless, his contemporaries universally applauded his achievements in Moscow and welcomed him home as a hero. Never before had he received such favorable treatment in the press.

The glowing accounts did wonders for Hopkins' ego, but they did not pay his bills. Having given up his salary as a White House aide, he needed a job that would support him while he worked on the book—or books—he planned to write about his years with Roosevelt. Some of his friends in the labor movement came to the rescue, finding him a place as "Impartial Chairman of the Clothing Industry." This meant that labor and management got together to pay him $25,000 a year for arbitrating their occasional disputes. His new responsibilities seldom required more than one day a week of his time.

As he moved to New York, Hopkins looked forward to relaxed and contemplative years with his wife and daughter. At last he could enjoy some of the material comforts he had long been denied. Yet taking him away from the hysterical pace of life in Washington was like letting the air out of a balloon. For years the grueling demands of his position had kept him alive. When he tried to adjust to "normal" life, without desperate, world-saving missions to take him from his sickbed, the miraculous recoveries of the past no longer seemed possible. A mere five months after leaving the capital Hopkins entered

Memorial Hospital for his final struggle for survival. He lingered for weeks, writing jaunty letters and laying future plans, before he entered a period of extended unconsciousness at the end. On the morning of January 29, 1946, his tortured body finally gave up its fight.

After his death tributes poured in from around the world. "He rendered a service to his country which will never even vaguely be appreciated," declared Army Chief of Staff George Marshall. "His was a soul that flamed out of a frail and fading body," said his friend Winston Churchill. "He was a crumbling lighthouse from which there shone the beams that led great fleets to harbor."

Hopkins' extraordinary power was based not on brilliance, wealth, or popular support, but exclusively on his talent for friendship. His personal bond with FDR was all the more remarkable because it had not existed before Roosevelt entered the White House. As with other Presidents and their aides, the overwhelming pressures of the office helped to forge a special sort of camaraderie—a relationship somewhat akin to that of two front-line soldiers who face combat together. Since Roosevelt held office for an unprecedented twelve years, Hopkins had the chance to develop that intimate dependence to an unprecedented extent.

The day after Hopkins' death the Los Angeles *Times* ran a bitter editorial which repeated the familiar charge that he was "never elected by the people to a public office" and that his work as a Presidential assistant was "out of bounds by any constitutional concept." The *Times* solemnly concluded: "Americans need not concern themselves now whether Harry Hopkins was great or little or good or bad; their care should be that the phenomenon of a Harry Hopkins in the White House does not recur."

If the anonymous editorialist expected that the role of aggressive and freewheeling Presidential confidant had died with Hopkins then he would be sorely disappointed—particularly by the smooth maneuvers of the President's lawyer in the next administration.

Clark M. Clifford:
The Very Special Counsel

The young officer had been in the White House three days before he was formally introduced to the President. "This is Lieutenant Clifford from St. Louis," said Jake Vardaman, White House Naval Aide. "He's going to look after my office while I go with you to Potsdam."

Harry Truman cast an appraising eye on the handsome newcomer. Wavy golden hair framed a high forehead while blue eyes gleamed out of a boyish face. The Navy uniform accentuated broad shoulders and a 6'2'', 185-pound frame. After a moment's hesitation, Truman delivered his opinion: "Big fella, isn't he?"

Clark Clifford, meanwhile, formed his own impressions of the President. He had seen Truman at a few political gatherings back in Missouri, but "he now seemed a substantially more impressive figure than I remembered him. This may be part of the mystique of the Oval Office. His manner was affable and brisk. He seemed to radiate confidence which, as I later learned, was perhaps a facade." A deep chuckle came into his voice as Clifford continued his recollections with the author of this book. "In those early days at the White House we were really just living from day to day, you see, because of the tasks we assumed. We were in the process of learning it together. I was learning awfully fast in 1945 and that first half of '46." He had to learn quickly—the future of his President and his country depended on it.

Clark Clifford was born on Christmas Day 1906—an appropriate date, his admirers insist, for a man of such messianic gifts. He was named for his uncle Clark McAdams, a celebrated reformer and editor of the St. Louis *Post-Dispatch*. His father earned a comfortable living as an auditor for the Missouri Pacific Railroad and played a role in local high society. His mother worked occasionally as a professional lecturer and used to draw large crowds for her recitation of original fairy tales.

As a child, Clark sold magazines and sang in an Episcopal Church choir. At Washington University in St. Louis he became a big man on campus while his academic performance remained merely respectable. A stalwart of the tennis team and the dramatic society, he starred in several theatrical productions. Student actresses reportedly cut one another's throats to get the female lead opposite him.

Clifford went on to Washington University Law School, receiving his LL.B. in 1928. When he took the bar examinations later that year he scored second among 350 applicants in the state of Missouri. Before settling down to the practice of law he gave in to wanderlust and toured Europe with a friend, Lewis McKuen. "We called our trip the Lewis and Clark Expedition. We had a perfectly wonderful time, and I met Margery Kimball on a river steamer as we were going up the Rhine one day. She was with a Wellesley tour. And we saw them a great deal in different places in Europe." Clifford found himself instantly drawn to the elegant "Marny" Kimball. She was a gifted student pianist at the New England Conservatory of Music who had once played the Grieg Concerto with the Boston Symphony. Along with the dashing young attorney from St. Louis her most persistent suitor was the well-known professional bridge player Oswald Jacoby. When, after a courtship of two years, Clifford finally prevailed Jacoby attended the wedding and proved himself a first-rate sportsman. "As a semifinalist to a finalist," he said to the beaming bridegroom, "I'd like to congratulate you."

At the time of his marriage, Clifford earned $175 a month with a corporate law firm in his hometown. He specialized in trial work, handling up to forty cases a year. As one of his colleagues observed: "Juries find Clark well-nigh irresistible." Within a decade the budding advocate was earning an annual salary of $30,000. "It's the hardest kind of work," he recalls, "but it is the most extraordinary kind of training a young man can go through. You are forced to discipline yourself, organize material, and then present a proposition persuasively. When I came to the White House I found very early this was an enormous asset."

The contact that brought him to Washington developed, oddly enough, through his wife's interest in music. For several years Clifford served as a director of the St. Louis Symphony Society while Marny headed the Grand Opera Guild. Jake Vardaman, a shoe company executive and personal friend of Senator Harry Truman, shared their commitment to the classics. During the winter months Vardaman invited the Cliffords to his farm every Saturday afternoon to listen to radio broadcasts of the Metropolitan Opera. When he joined the Navy after Pearl Harbor, Vardaman left his legal affairs in Clifford's hands. He did not expect that Clark, who was past draft age and had three small daughters to support, would himself enter Naval service a year later.

Their friendship, interrupted by the war, was resumed under dramatic circumstances in April 1945. When FDR died and Harry Truman suddenly became President, he ordered Jake Vardaman to Washington to be his Naval Aide. Vardaman, in turn, summoned Clifford from an administrative post in San Francisco for temporary duty at the White House.

According to the original schedule his stay in Washington would last only five weeks while Vardaman accompanied the President to a series of European conferences. Lieutenant Clifford, however, made the most of his opportunities. During the absence of his superiors he found his duties as Naval Aide so trivial that he looked around for better ways to occupy his time. He noted that Judge Sam Rosenman, a holdover from the Roosevelt years, seemed grossly over-worked as Special Counsel to the President. "The Judge was a very able man, but he had no one helping him. I indicated to him that there was very little to do in my office and I would certainly be available if he had any assignments for me. He did immediately." Clifford prepared memos and speeches on various issues and proceeded to make himself indispensable. "When Truman and Var-daman returned, Rosenman said, 'Why not keep this young fellow here? He might be helpful.' Well, that started me."

Before long Clifford was working directly with Truman. "The whole rela-tionship between the President and me was a highly personal one. It developed because there was a vacuum in the White House. I think the fact that I came from Missouri helped a little, and the fact that I began to understand the man-ner in which he wanted to express himself. He was not comfortable with Eastern—to use a word much abused—elitism. And he was comfortable with me." Clifford certainly gave the President every reason to feel comfortable. Washington columnists Robert Allen and William Shannon described him as "an outwardly calm, even-tempered, hard-working, dependable young man who can get others out of trouble and who never gets into it himself."

Clifford dramatically demonstrated his value to the President during the crisis over a nationwide rail strike in May 1946. Enraged at the refusal of two unions to accept the recommendations of a federal fact-finding board, Truman wrote out a longhand draft of a bitter, hysterical speech attacking the strikers. His statement lambasted "effete union leaders" for receiving "five to ten times the net salary of your president. . . . Let's give the country back to the people," Truman declared. "Let's put transportation and production back to work, hang a few traitors, make our own country safe for democracy, tell Russia where to get off, and make the United Nations work. Come on, boys, let's do the job!"

Fortunately, Truman showed the speech to his aides before delivering it. Press Secretary Charlie Ross realized immediately that the proposed address would expose the President to censure and ridicule. Someone would have to rewrite Truman's words without wounding the President's pride—a task requir-ing consummate tact and total self-assurance. Clark Clifford proved more than equal to the challenge. He wrote a tough but dignified speech which Truman presented on the radio with telling effect.

He also played a key role in the President's dramatic appearance before Con-gress to demand special legislation to deal with the strike. At the moment that Truman walked to the rostrum, Clifford disappeared into a small anteroom off the House floor to check on the progress of last-minute negotiations. Truman railed against the "obstinate arrogance" of union leaders at the same time

Clifford learned, through a series of phone calls, that those leaders had just capitulated to White House demands. The President's alert aide scribbled the news on a scrap of paper and handed the note to the secretary of the Senate. The messenger scurried back onto the House floor just as Truman reached the climactic portion of his speech: "As a part of the temporary emergency legislation, I request the Congress immediately to authorize the President to draft into the Armed Forces of the United States all workers who are on strike against their government." Congress applauded, and once the words had been spoken the President looked down and read Clifford's note. He paused for a few seconds, savoring his moment of triumph and drama before announcing, "Word has just been received that the railroad strike has been settled—on terms proposed by the President!" The members of Congress stood and cheered.

Not surprisingly, Clark Clifford received a promotion as reward for his role in the triumph. On June 1, one week after the remarkable speech to Congress, Truman ordered Clifford to leave the Navy and accept the post of Special Counsel to the President. Sam Rosenman had left the job vacant some months before when he returned to the private practice of law. Clifford had already begun taking over Rosenman's responsibilities and the new title gave formal recognition to his emerging primacy within the staff.

One of the reasons that Clifford rose to the top so quickly was the lack of competition from the President's other advisors. "The Missouri Gang" that populated the White House under Truman was, in the words of Atomic Energy Commission Director David Lilienthal, "as sorry a bunch of third-raters as I have seen in many a moon." Journalist I. F. Stone rendered an even harsher judgment. "The composite impression," he wrote, "was of big-bellied, good-natured guys who knew a lot of dirty jokes, spent as little time in their offices as possible, saw Washington as a chance to make useful 'contacts,' and were anxious to get what they could for themselves out of the experience." The petty indiscretions by Truman's aides and cronies, dubbed by Republicans "the mess in Washington," never involved Clark Clifford. Yet long before the disclosures about dubious favors for friendly businessmen, the Special Counsel stood out from his colleagues. "Alone of all the Truman entourage," wrote Allen and Shannon, "Clifford has the brains, the personal élan, and the savoir faire required for a big leaguer. He is really of the White House class. None of the others are, or ever can be."

This did not mean that Clifford's influence went uncontested within the administration. John Steelman, a hefty, gregarious Southerner who specialized in labor relations, held the title Assistant to the President and had his own very definite ideas on the way things should run in the White House. Steelman led a group of conservatives among Truman's friends and members of the Cabinet who wanted the President to moderate the crusading spirit of the New Deal. Clifford, meanwhile, served as pivotman for administration liberals. These Roosevelt Democrats gathered for dinner every Monday night and Clifford later presented their concerns to Truman. Because of the Special Counsel's "attaché case full of tricks,'' the liberals most often won the upper hand in formulating policy.

On one issue, at least, Clifford and Steelman seemed to switch ideological roles. In October 1946, when mine union leader John L. Lewis repudiated a prior agreement and threatened the nation with a devastating coal strike, the conservative Steelman urged conciliation. Clifford, on the other hand, wanted a showdown with Lewis that would refurbish Truman's public image. Despite the pro-labor orientation of most liberal Democrats, Clifford understood the political benefits of total war against an unpopular union chief. The internal debate raged for days at the White House before the Special Counsel succeeded in appealing to Truman's fighting instincts. The President refused to negotiate with Lewis and launched a legal battle that culminated in a $3.5 million contempt of court judgment against the United Mine Workers. The praise for Truman that poured into the White House proved even more extravagant than Clifford had predicted. *Newsweek* magazine exulted that "the mild-looking, often indecisive man from Missouri was stubborn in his determination that no man, not even John L. Lewis, could push the United States of America around.''

In the afterglow of this success the press discovered a pleasing new subject for its White House reporters: the new golden boy of the President's staff, Clark Clifford. Having tired of endless discussions of Truman's ill-fated haberdashery in Kansas City, newsmen turned to the question of Clifford's remarkable good looks. *Life* magazine repeated rumors that the Special Counsel's hair had been professionally curled with the aid of a micrometer. The nationally syndicated column Washington "Merry-Go-Round" declared that "somewhere there must be a flaw, a glaring weakness, an idiosyncrasy. But so far Washington hasn't discovered it.'' White House Press Secretary Charlie Ross felt mildly exasperated at the sudden gush of favorable publicity concerning the Special Counsel. "All I do around here is answer questions about the great Clark Clifford,'' he complained.

Clifford knew that too much attention could jeopardize his standing with the President and so began to avoid public appearances and radio interviews. "Truman did not like showoff people,'' he recalls. "He wasn't one himself. He didn't like people who projected themselves out. Mr. Roosevelt had some problems in that regard, you know.'' The President once told Clifford that in his opinion most of FDR's advisors had been "crackpots and lunatic fringe.''

No one could accuse Clifford of lunacy, but he did have a difficult time stopping exaggerated accounts of his importance. The annual banquet of the Gridiron Club proved particularly embarrassing on this score. Each year, members of this venerable Washington institution watch reporters perform irreverent and occasionally drunken skits satirizing the nation's leaders. With both Clifford and Truman in the audience the newsmen offered one particularly biting scene depicting the President as a ventriloquist's dummy controlled by a smug, all powerful Clark Clifford. At the end of the performance Clifford, upset beyond words, rushed up to Truman and poured out emotional apologies. "It wasn't your fault, Clark,'' the President replied. "What could you do about it? They're just jumping over your back to get at me." At that point Clifford "could have thrown my arms around him and kissed him."

This small incident reflected the developing personal attachment between the two men. Clifford could never be as close to Truman as old friends like Treasury Secretary John Snyder or Military Aide Harry Vaughan, but he did enter the charmed circle of the President's poker partners. "Every third weekend or so we'd get together the group he was most comfortable with and sail down the Potomac in the *Williamsburg,* the President's yacht. We'd meet, say, late Friday afternoon and have Friday evening, Saturday, and sometimes Sunday." Cruising at a leisurely pace through the green tidewater country of Virginia, the President and his guests sipped bourbon and played cards. "I was the only staff man who participated in these particular poker games. Then it became my function to get up the games and make the arrangements. Those were very close relationships and he loved to have Chief Justice Vinson, Senator Robert Kerr, and Senator Stuart Symington. Occasionally, Averell Harriman went and sometimes a new Senator he liked—Lyndon Johnson."

When asked who proved the most effective poker player in this august assemblage of wheeler-dealers, Clifford only chuckled in reply. "Now, modesty forbids me from answering that," he said, "though I think at the end of each year that I was maybe more ahead than the rest of them. To a great extent, the poker games were just a medium at which Truman could get his friends together and sit them around a table. Coupled with the game was a great deal of conversation. Somebody would remember an incident and then the poker would stop for quite a while.

"Mealtime during these weekends was perfectly fascinating. Breakfast, lunch, and dinner the President would recount his experiences. Oh, I guess I've heard twenty times his recounting of what took place at Chicago in 1944 when he turned out to be the Vice-Presidential nominee. And others would remember. My presence in that group was valuable to me. I got to know him better. I got to know the men that he liked to be with. It greatly furthered our relationship."

The poker parties were purely stag affairs since, according to Clifford, "the President was not particularly comfortable in the presence of women." Truman, nevertheless, developed warm relationships with some of the females in the Clifford family. With Mrs. Clifford he shared a strong interest in the piano. "Sometimes we'd be there at the White House and it would be just a family evening with close friends, and he might play and then she might play some. He played, as you know, very badly. But he loved the piano and knew a good deal about famous pianists. He certainly could appreciate the way my wife played." On several occasions the President and First Lady paid Mrs. Clifford the ultimate compliment a Washington hostess can receive by visiting her Chevy Chase home as dinner guests. They also invited the Cliffords—including

Clark's aged but talkative mother—for Thanksgiving meals and other occasions at the White House. In the course of these family gatherings, Truman became particularly fond of Clifford's youngest daughter. "She was a little girl at the time, maybe nine years old, awfully pretty. And I think he told her once that he'd like to have a photograph of her. So she gave him a photograph and he kept it on the table in back of his desk. It was kind of a preferred place. He was just drawn to her. Interestingly enough, I noticed that when they constructed a model of his office at the Truman Library out in Independence, there, sure enough, on the table behind the desk was still the photograph of Randall, our youngest daughter."

This sort of intimacy facilitated Clifford's role as the unofficial kingpin of the White House staff. He never lorded it over his colleagues as did future aides Sherman Adams and H. R. Haldeman nor attempted to obstruct communication with the President. Nevertheless, members of the official family began to realize that using Clifford as a go-between helped ensure a favorable hearing from Truman. Defense Secretary James Forrestal, for example, made a point of eating breakfast with the Special Counsel at least once a week. Clifford defined his own position as "a focal point in the White House to which the defense and foreign policy establishments could bring their special problems."

Clifford proved his effectiveness as a conduit for vital information in a confidential 1946 memo concerning U.S. policy toward the Soviet Union. At Truman's request, he met with a series of top officials and "picked their brains" concerning deteriorating relations with the Russians. The resulting seventy-page document, prepared with the assistance of Clifford's personal aide George Elsey, helped shape American decisions for decades to come. "The key to an understanding of current Soviet foreign policy," he wrote, "is the realization that Soviet leaders adhere to the Marxian theory of the ultimate destruction of capitalist states by Communist states. . . . The language of military power is the only language which disciples of power politics understand. The United States must use that language in order that Soviet leaders will realize our government is determined to uphold the interests of its citizens and the rights of small nations. Compromises and concessions are considered by the Soviets to be evidence of weakness." Clifford's historic memorandum pushed the administration toward such major commitments as the Truman Doctrine, Marshall Plan, formation of NATO, and defense of Korea. It stated, in succinct and persuasive terms, the intellectual framework of the Cold War. With the benefit of thirty years of hindsight, some observers question these assumptions but Clifford is not among them. "I have recently looked at that memorandum and I will stand today by every word of it. It has stood up wonderfully well. In my opinion, that was one of the proudest periods in American history. I know it saved freedom in the world. I *know* because I was there."

Clifford was also there at the birth of the state of Israel, playing the part of a helpful midwife. Alone among the President's principal foreign policy advisors, Clifford urged immediate recognition and support for the new nation. In so doing, he braved a head-to-head confrontation with one of the most respected Americans of his generation, General George C. Marshall.

Unfortunately, Clifford's role in the affair has been overshadowed by a popular story concerning Truman's relationship with his World War I comrade and onetime business partner Eddie Jacobson. Jacobson, a Kansas City Jew, made several trips to Washington to plead his people's cause with the President. These emotional appeals brought about a meeting between Truman and Zionist leader Chaim Weizmann at one crucial juncture, but Jacobson had little impact on the all-important question of recognition. He was not on hand when that decision was made; nor would even so compassionate a human being as Harry Truman have disregarded the unanimous opinion of the State Department solely for the sake of an old friend from Missouri.

The fact was that by 1948, Truman had little patience for attempts by American Jews to influence his decisions. "Jesus Christ couldn't please them when he was here on earth," he told Commerce Secretary Henry Wallace, "so how could anyone expect that I would have any luck?" During U.N. debate over the partition of Palestine, Truman wrote to Senator Claude Pepper: "I received about thirty-five thousand pieces of mail and propaganda from the Jews in this country while this matter was pending. I put it all in a pile and struck a match to it—I never looked at a single one of the letters. . . ." Though Truman maintained an affectionate regard for David Niles, a Jewish member of his staff, he began to discount Niles' advice on the Middle East situation. The President complained to the Democratic national chairman that Niles could not even discuss the Palestine issue without bursting into tears.

In this atmosphere, the cool reasoning of a suave St. Louis Episcopalian carried more weight than anyone's passionate petitions. Clifford maintained that the Jewish state was already a de facto reality and that the United States should get the jump on the Soviet Union by granting immediate recognition. To delay would not appease the Arabs—in fact, it would only encourage them to increase the scale of their violence against the Jewish settlements. Above all, Clifford insisted that U.S. policy should be shaped "by sheer human concern for a people who had endured the torments of the damned and whose instincts for survival and nationhood still refused to be extinguished." To provide a homeland for holocaust survivors, Clifford believed, "would be an act of simple humanity and entirely symbolic of what this country should represent in world affairs."

The chief officers of the Cabinet strongly disagreed. James Forrestal, Secretary of Defense, worried that the Jewish armies would be quickly wiped out by the Arabs and that American forces might be dragged into the fighting. "It's just a question of mathematics," he told Clifford. "There are 30 million Arabs. There are only 600,000 Jews. The 30 million Arabs are going to push the 600,000 Jews into the Mediterranean." George C. Marshall, the former Army Chief of Staff who served Truman as Secretary of State, opposed Clifford's position even more vehemently. Deeply influenced by pro-Arab careerists in the State Department, he emphasized the strategic importance of Middle Eastern oil. He also warned that the socialist leanings of most Zionist leaders would allow Israel to become a base for Communist subversion.

The bitter argument reached its climax at an extraordinary White House meeting on May 12, 1948, with Clifford, Marshall, and State Department Near East specialists in attendance. The President opened the session by announcing what they all knew—that the state of Israel would officially declare its independence in two days. The question before the group was how the United States should respond. Clifford, who had been practicing his speech for several days, presented the arguments for instant recognition. "I was deeply immersed in the subject. I prepared as though I were going to argue a case before the Supreme Court of the United States. And I like to think that I presented my views very effectively, too. But something about the presentation of my views infuriated General Marshall." Turning red in the face, the Secretary of State snapped at the President, "This is not a political matter. Unless politics were involved, Clifford wouldn't even be at this conference. This is a very serious matter of foreign policy determination."

The Special Counsel, who had not mentioned political considerations in his remarks, waited for Truman to respond. "Mr. Clifford is here," the President said softly, "because I asked him to be here." That simple statement settled the question of Clifford's presence, but debate continued on the substantive issues. The representatives of the State Department ran through a long series of arguments and statistics in an attempt to counter Clifford's advice. Sensing the President's continued ambivalence in the face of this evidence, General Marshall brought the meeting to a stormy conclusion. "I remarked to the President," he recalled, "that, speaking objectively, I could not help but think that the suggestions made by Mr. Clifford were wrong. . . . The counsel offered by Mr. Clifford was based on domestic political considerations, while the problem that confronted us was international. I said bluntly that if the President were to follow Mr. Clifford's advice and if in the elections I were to vote, I would vote against the President."

For all those who knew Truman's profound respect for General Marshall this seemed to settle the issue. After the others left the room, Clifford gloomily gathered up his papers, convinced that the new Jewish state would have to face the world without the backing of the United States. The President came over to comfort him. "Clark, don't feel too bad about this," he said.

"Mr. President," Clifford replied, "I was a trial lawyer for many years and I've lost cases before and I'll lose them again. It's all right."

"But you haven't lost this case yet," Truman insisted.

Encouraged by these words, Clifford worked feverishly in the next two days to reverse the trend in the administration. He had a drink with the Undersecretary of State and won him over to the pro-Israel position. He contacted the official representatives of the Zionist movement in New York and asked them to prepare a formal request for recognition. Most importantly, he urged Harry Truman to follow his own humanitarian inclinations and ignore the counsel of the "striped-pants boys" at the Department of State. Despite his irritation at pressure from Zionist leaders, Truman's reading of the Bible and his instinctive sympathy for the underdog disposed him kindly to the idea of a Jewish state. After all, this was the same man who had written a Southern Senator just eight months before: "I sincerely wish that every member of the Congress could visit the displaced persons camps in Germany and Austria and see just what is happening to five hundred thousand human beings through no fault of their own."

On May 14—an epic day in the long and sorrowful history of the Jewish people—Clifford's efforts bore fruit. The nation of Israel came into being at 6 P.M. Washington time, and exactly sixteen minutes later the United States granted full recognition. So began an international friendship that has lasted more than thirty years and changed the course of world affairs.

Revisionist historians today question Clifford's part in this decision, echoing George Marshall's charge of political opportunism. Clifford deeply resents such criticism. "To say that the President came out for this policy for political reasons has no basis at all. The situation was entirely different in 1948 than it is in the 1970's. Today there is an almost unanimous opinion on the part of the American Jewish community about Israel. There wasn't in 1948. That community was divided into Zionists who were in favor of an independent homeland, and many other Jews who did not favor it. I think they felt it could lead to all kinds of difficulties, anti-Semitism and so forth. So the political impact of our policy was not at all clear." Clifford further points out that New York, the only state in which Jewish voters were numerous enough to play a decisive role, had been written off by the administration several months before the Israel decision. Governor Thomas Dewey, Truman's likely opponent, enjoyed strong home state support, while the third-party candidacy of Henry Wallace deeply divided New York Democrats. Truman could never outbid Wallace, an ardent Zionist, in appealing to hard-core pro-Israel votes. On election day Dewey swept New York as predicted, along with most of the other populous northeastern states. Truman won the nation with a surprising combination of rural and far western states—areas in which Jewish votes had negligible impact.

In discussing Truman's political strategy, Clark Clifford speaks with authority—he devised that strategy himself a year before the election. In an astonishing memorandum he explained to the President how he could restore his popularity and score the greatest political upset in U.S. history. This document reveals the hard-nosed and occasionally cynical calculations behind some of Truman's most flamboyant public actions. "A President who is also a candidate must resort to subterfuge," Clifford wrote. "He cannot sit silent; he must be in the limelight. . . ." The Special Counsel recommended an all-out attack on the Republican-controlled 80th Congress. "The High Cost of Living will be the most controversial issue of the 1948 campaign—indeed the only domestic issue. Whichever party is adjudged guilty of causing it will lose the election. . . . The administration's recommendations—in the State of the Union message and elsewhere—must be tailored to the voter, not the Congressman; they must display a label which reads 'No Compromises.'" Clifford correctly anticipated Truman's unique winning combination, urging administrative "concentration on the West and its problems, including reclamation, floods, and agriculture." The issue of civil rights could also serve Truman's purposes: "It would appear to be sound strategy to have the President go as far as he possibly could go in recommending measures to protect the rights of minority groups." Clifford even found political value in the dangers of the Cold War, seeing "the Battle with the Kremlin" as a substantial plus. "The worse matters get the better, up to a point—in crisis times Americans tend to back up the President." Given the nation's suspicious mood, Clifford knew that the threat of Henry Wallace's Progressive Party campaign could easily be defused. "Every effort must be made *now*," he wrote, ". . . to identify him and isolate him in the public mind with the Communists." This advice Truman followed with a vengeance. To Clifford, such brutal tactics seemed appropriate because of the transcendent importance of the President's political survival. "The future of the country and the future of the world are linked inextricably with his reelection," he declared at the end of his memo.

Once again, Clifford's advice struck a responsive chord with his boss. Combative by nature and stung by the widespread assumption that his campaign could not be taken seriously, Truman lashed out at his opponents. As Clifford remembered the election years later: "We were on our own twenty-yard line. We had to be bold. If we kept plugging away in moderate terms, the best we could have done would have been to reach midfield when the gun went off. So we had to throw long passes. . . ." Clifford himself helped execute many of those pass plays, preparing speeches and state papers that created the image of "Give 'Em Hell Harry." During the President's whistle-stop tours he rode along on the train, scribbling out new material for Truman to fire at his audiences. As they pulled into backwater stations, Clifford and his colleagues used to jump out of the train, dissolve into the crowds, and applaud energetically at speeches they themselves had written.

With this sort of enthusiasm the Democratic campaign overcame all obstacles. An article in *Life* magazine early in 1947 had suggested that Clifford might "help Mr. Truman erase his early mistakes and become one of the best lame-duck presidents in history." Clifford did more than that. He helped his boss confound the pundits and win a full term of his own.

To make sure that this term began auspiciously, the President asked Clifford to draft the inaugural address. "We'd just won the biggest election upset in history and the President said, 'We've really got to have an outstanding inaugural address.' I began to think about what we could do to seize the attention of the world. Then—Bong!—I thought of that memo." The memorandum in question had been sitting in Clifford's desk for several months. Originally drafted by a State Department official who had been unable to get the attention of his superiors, it recommended that a minor technical assistance program in Latin America be expanded to global proportions. Clifford raised the idea with Truman, who liked it well enough to make it one of the major thrusts of his inaugural. This "bold new program for making the benefits of our scientific advances and industrial progress available for the improvement and growth of underdeveloped areas" won praise throughout the world. Since Clifford listed it fourth among the basic foreign policy points outlined in the speech, it became known as Point Four. By 1953 the program drew on a budget of $155 million for technical aid programs in thirty-three countries. This breakthrough concept, rescued by Clifford from the obscurity of his desk drawer, remained a cornerstone of U.S. policy for decades to come.

Such achievements brought Clifford personal satisfaction, but they did not relieve the mounting pressures of life in the White House. "In almost every other kind of place, even in government, there are periods when the pressures abate. But they never abate in the White House. One day it's a problem with the Soviet Union, the next day it's some very bad strike that affects the economy. We used to talk about what time of day our 'daily crisis' would come. And sure enough, without fail it would come. Five years of that kind of pressure does something to you. I've even looked at some photos that were taken before I went in and at the time I left. The change . . . well, the change is a marked one."

Clifford's job not only put worry lines in his handsome face but eventually gave him an ulcer. "I had gone through all those years of trials in St. Louis without one. I had two years in the Navy but there's no pressure involved in that. But those five years at the White House—about the third year, I got one."

He acted immediately to protect his health, giving up alcohol and coffee and observing a strictly regulated diet. There was no easy remedy, however, for the emotional strain of his work. "It was unrelenting. The world goes on, the country goes on. You can't say, well, I'm going to take some time off. I never took any time off in those five years unless I went away with the President on a brief holiday. . . . Mrs. Clifford was exceedingly understanding about the demands that my professional life made upon me. During the time I was in the White House my wife and family were pretty much on their own. We put in a special warming oven at our house because I was so rarely home for dinner. When I'd come in—it might be ten, eleven, or twelve o'clock in emergency times—Mrs. Clifford might have gone to bed. She developed kind of a separate life."

No wonder that by December 1948, after the excitement of the successful election campaign, Clifford began to weary of his job. His friend David Lilienthal reported in his diary: "Clark seemed tired and very thoughtful. He spoke in a worried tone—quite unusual for him—about the conflict within the President's own family about future policy, between the conservatives and the 'forward-lookers.' He said he was 'tired, awfully tired; not physically, but emotionally, psychologically.' Felt that the lift that came from doing new things, of learning, is no longer there. He spoke of the awful exhibition one sees around the White House of self-seeking, etc., and seemed rather depressed by it, not as if it were something new but that he was getting his fill of it.''

An awkward financial position compounded Clifford's depression. His Special Counsel's salary of $12,000 provided less than half the money he had earned as a trial lawyer. He and his wife, who had grown accustomed to gracious living, found it impossible to pay their bills. Clifford developed a dependence on "a friend in St. Louis, an older man. We had kind of a father-son relationship. He'd never had a son, and we met when I was a young lawyer and he was a representative of a large insurance company. When I went to Washington he entered into an arrangement with me. If I ran short, I would fill out a promissory note for a thousand or two thousand, sign my name to it, mail it to him, and I'd get a check by return mail. That carried us through the years in the White House. Of course I had no security. So by the time I left the debt amounted to somewhere near $35,000, which in those days was a rather substantial obligation.''

Clifford could never earn enough to pay off that sum while working at the White House, and so in mid-1949 he informed Truman of his plans to leave government. The President accepted his aide's decision with regret, but with none of the bitterness that characterized Lyndon Johnson's reaction to Bill Moyers' departure some eighteen years later. Truman, in fact, talked of providing his counselor with a generous reward for devoted service. According to Clifford, "One time when we were down at Key West, he asked me if by any chance I'd ever had an interest in serving on the Supreme Court of the United States. Interestingly enough, even at that young age I knew I was an advocate and not a judge. And I answered him very frankly at the time and said, 'No, I'm not a judge. I want to be down in the pit where the action is.' ''

For Clifford, this desire for action led to the practice of law rather than a candidacy for electoral office. In 1948 a group of prominent Missouri Democrats had asked him to run for U.S. Senator but he turned them down. It was a fateful decision because in the Senate Clifford, with his dazzling good looks, persuasive abilities, and national stature, would have been an automatic Presidential contender. "I've never run for political office because I was not that interested in politics. I still am not interested in politics," he insists, "but I'm enormously interested in government.''

His critics point out that he has been even more interested in making money. After his resignation as Special Counsel in January 1950, he entered a new phase of his career as a private attorney with a government-related practice. The law firm he set up in Washington proved a spectacular success from the very beginning. Corporations with governmental problems to solve learned that an advocate with Clifford's experience and connections could be a powerful ally. His clients over the years have included Standard Oil of California, Hughes Tool and Die, General Electric, Phillips Petroleum, Time Incorporated, Dupont, and Trans World Airlines. Since leaving the White House, "Superclark" has earned more than $500,000 annually; in several "good years" his personal income exceeded $1 million.

One of the reasons for his remarkable success has been his continued status as a Presidential advisor. Truman remained in office for three years after Clifford's resignation and continued to call on his former aide for advice and companionship. "We still had those poker games every few weeks and I was still the fellow who got the games up. So we had weekends together. Then the custom came up that every year I had the birthday party for Chief Justice Vinson. That was always dinner at my house and a poker game." These festivities continued even after Truman left the White House. "Through the first part of the fifties he used to come back to Washington at reasonably frequent intervals. Usually he'd call me ahead of time to get up the old poker games. That was my permanent responsibility—to bring his old pals together again."

Dwight Eisenhower's two terms as President brought lean years to most Washington Democrats but not to Clark Clifford. His law firm continued to prosper as he cultivated the friendship of leading members of Congress. He placed special emphasis on his relationships with Senators John Kennedy of Massachusetts and Lyndon Johnson of Texas. In 1957, Clifford helped Kennedy force a retraction from ABC television of the charge that the Senator's aide Ted Sorensen had ghostwritten the book *Profiles in Courage*. Clifford's deft handling of the case won the special gratitude of Joseph P. Kennedy. In 1960, however, he disappointed the Kennedys as well as Lyndon Johnson by endorsing his friend and fellow Missourian Stuart Symington for the Presidency. In so doing, Clifford followed the lead of his old mentor Harry Truman, but wound up making one of the few major political mistakes of his career. Senator Symington fell far short of the nomination, leaving the adaptable former aide to scramble aboard the Kennedy bandwagon at the last moment. He tried to make himself useful in the campaign, playing his familiar role of "senior advisor." JFK appreciated these efforts and once the election was over he asked Clifford, with his insider's knowledge of the White House, to supervise the transition from the Eisenhower to the Kennedy regime. JFK later teased Clifford about the fact that he did not request appointive office in return for his services. "Clark is a wonderful fellow," the President said. "In a day when many are seeking a reward for what they contributed to the return of the Democrats to the White House, you don't hear Clark clamoring. All he asks in return is that we advertise his law firm on the backs of one-dollar bills."

President Kennedy did not change the currency, but he did invite Clifford into the highest councils of government. He appointed the veteran attorney Chairman of the Foreign Intelligence Advisory Board, a position Clifford held for five years. JFK also asked Clifford to represent the administration in the delicate negotiations over a possible steel industry price hike in 1962. In two days of meetings, Clifford used his patented blend of threats and cajolery to convince the president of U.S. Steel to hold down prices—an accomplishment that gave Kennedy one of his major public relations triumphs.

Shortly after JFK's assassination, Lyndon Johnson asked for Clifford's help in reorganizing the administration. With his experience as a White House speechwriter, Clifford also helped draft LBJ's first State of the Union address. Before long, *Newsweek* magazine singled out Harry Truman's onetime Special Counsel "as probably the most influential member of Lyndon Johnson's kitchen cabinet." As one senior member of the staff observed, "The President likes to get advice from men like Clark who are cold and shrewd and aren't swayed by moralistic arguments." Five to ten calls a day would often pass between Clifford and the White House. When particularly thorny problems arose, LBJ asked his aides "to see if Clark can come over." On these occasions, Clifford would cancel his afternoon appointments and walk the single block that separated his law offices from the executive mansion.

During the period 1965–67, Johnson was particularly pleased by Clifford's hawkish approach to the war in Vietnam. In line with his energetic anti-Communism, Clifford fully supported the administration's escalation of the war and opposed early proposals for a bombing halt. Since his position showed no traces of "weakness," Johnson enthusiastically turned to him in January 1968 as a replacement for the wavering and tormented Defense Secretary, Robert McNamara.

Shortly after Clifford took over the Department of Defense, Johnson asked him to provide 200,000 troops to reenforce the 525,000 already assigned to Vietnam. He was not supposed to question the wisdom of this Presidential decision, but Clifford was not the sort of man who blindly followed orders from his chief. "He had a great sense of his own value and did not believe that anyone hired Clark Clifford except to gain the full benefit of Clark Clifford's services," wrote David Halberstam in *The Best and the Brightest*. "A great lawyer is paid for telling a rich and powerful client the truth, no matter how unpalatable." To find the truth, Clifford commenced an in-depth investigation of the war, soon realizing that neither 200,000 nor 300,000 nor even 400,000 new men could permanently secure American objectives. Reversing his previous position, he became convinced that sanity demanded an end to the policy of escalation, and the beginning of serious negotiations.

When Clifford began pressing this point of view he was alone among the President's chief advisors—every bit as alone as he had been in battling the foreign policy establishment over recognition of Israel in 1948. Clifford never shied away from these confrontations; he knew that he had few equals when it came to palace politics. In 1968 a startling series of events helped push the President in Clifford's direction: the Tet offensive, the intensification of domestic unrest, and Eugene McCarthy's strong showing in the New Hampshire primary supported the arguments of the Secretary of Defense. In his dramatic announcement of March 31, LBJ withdrew as a candidate for reelection while declaring a partial bombing halt and a reversal of administration policy. As David Halberstam reported, "Clifford forced Johnson to turn and look honestly at the war; it was an act of friendship for which Johnson could never forgive him."

For Clifford, the end of his warm relationship with Lyndon Johnson was an affordable price to pay for changing the nation's course in Southeast Asia—an achievement which may rank as his greatest contribution to his country. Moreover, with a Presidential election pending and Hubert Humphrey the Democratic candidate, the Defense Secretary had reason to believe that he could continue to play a leading role in government. Clifford notes that "sometime after his defeat in '68, Humphrey was asked by a reporter, 'If elected, who would you have put in your cabinet?'

"And he said, 'The first thing I would have done would have been to transfer Clark Clifford from Defense to State.' Now *that* would have been a very logical development. I could have taken a team over to the State Department and, my God! We could have done a great job over there!' "

But it was not to be. Richard Nixon won the Presidency, and Clifford returned to private life where he had to content himself with being one of the country's richest lawyers and most influential citizens. When he saw the Republicans dragging their feet on Vietnam he gave quiet but crucial support to the peace movement, advising dovish Congressmen and signing his name to a national lawyers' petition against the war. In 1972 he participated in Edmund Muskie's ill-fated Presidential campaign, acting the part of Secretary of State in the Maine Senator's "shadow cabinet." Four years later the Democrats finally succeeded in recapturing the White House, but they did so under the banner of a candidate who proclaimed his contempt for Washington "insiders." Clifford could hardly have welcomed these declarations—who, after all, could be more of an insider than he was? Once established in the White House, however, Jimmy Carter proved just as vulnerable as the other Democratic Presidents of his generation to the temptation to make use of Clifford's services. In the early days of the administration, he dispatched Clifford on a special diplomatic mission to Cyprus. Later, when the President's Budget Director Bert Lance ran into trouble, the phone rang again in Clifford's office. On the day that the good ol' boy from Calhoun, Georgia, faced a Congressional investigating committee, the best established of all establishment lawyers sat at his side. This was, in *Newsweek*'s phrase, truly "a man for all Caesars."

A visit to Clifford's office today brings with it the sense of a pilgrimage to a national shrine. The physical surroundings are modest enough—courtly, old-fashioned furnishings suggesting the comfortable air of an English country inn. Nor are the walls covered with autographed pictures and other mementos that decorate the offices of most other men who have served their time at the White House. It is Clifford himself who is the monument, as he tilts back behind his antique desk, spinning out lucid sentences in his patient Missouri drawl, describing decisions that changed the face of the world. The once blond hair has turned to gray, but the lanky frame is still trim and well-muscled in its immaculate vested suit, and the cool blue eyes are as riveting as ever. It is not his past association with Presidents and princes that gives Clifford his awesome air of power and authority; it is the sheer physical magnetism of the man, undimmed as he pushes into his seventies. No wonder that clients pay so royally to enjoy the comfort of his presence.

As precious minutes tick away, the mind reverts to some of the enduring legends concerning Clifford's practice of law. According to one well-known Washington story, a corporation counsel once wrote to Clifford for advice on what his company should do concerning pending tax legislation. After three weeks Clifford telegrammed a two-word response, "Do nothing," and the next day sent a bill for $10,000. Feeling that his corporation's money entitled him to a more complete explanation, the executive demanded to know why he should follow Clifford's recommendation. "Because I told you so," the Great Man answered and forwarded a bill for an additional $5,000.

Clifford has little desire to discuss these aspects of his career; he prefers to talk of his work with Harry Truman. He seems to be worried that a younger generation of Americans will think of him only as a millionaire lawyer and elder statesman, forgetting about his days as a youthful idealist in the White House. He is particularly proud of a letter Truman wrote him three days before he left government service—a letter not mentioned in previous articles about him. "I have that letter framed at home because I prize it so," he says. "You ought to have it. I'll send you a copy as soon as possible."

The letter from Truman stresses the selfless aspects of Clifford's contribution. "Through six years of public service," the President wrote, "and those potentially among the most fruitful of your professional life—you have devoted your talents and superb abilities exclusively to your country's welfare. That is a long time for you to be away from the practice of law."

Truman also praised Clifford for his poise and clear thinking. "Your reports on the various problems on which I asked for your advice were models of lucidity and logic. . . . Your final opinions were always models of brevity and accuracy, as well as clarity and strength." These words highlight the most passionate commitment of this cool and calculating man: a commitment to reason, to competence, and to sanity. Time spent with Clifford is a powerful and soothing tonic. It offers reassurance that the quiet maneuvers of gentlemen of goodwill may yet solve the problems of a sorely distracted world.

At the same time there is a lingering aftertaste, a dim suspicion that you may have been conned along with the rest of the world. As Richard Cohen of the Washington *Post* reported after one typical session with Clifford, "He was smiling. He continued to talk. He was on his feet. So was I. He led me to the door. We shook hands. . . . The elevator arrived. The questions were still in my pocket. I should check to see if I still had my watch."

CHAPTER EIGHT

THE SUMMIT OF POWER

The U.S. Army may not be the world's most smoothly run institution, but when compared to the federal government it is efficiency itself. Dwight Eisenhower made that discovery during World War II when forced to work closely with top civilian authorities. As President, he resolved to improve the often haphazard operations of the White House by introducing military concepts of order and organization.

The result was the introduction of the "Chief of Staff" system—one man would be responsible for supervising all the other aides and for reporting directly to the President. The press treated the change as a startling innovation, though in a sense it marked a return to an arrangement that had existed for some seventy years before the administration of Herbert Hoover. Ike's top aide, Sherman Adams, had the same responsibility for overall coordination as a nineteenth-century Secretary to the President. The vast increase in the number of aides and the dramatic expansion of Presidential power, however, made him a far more formidable figure than, say, a Daniel Lamont.

The era that began with Adams and ended with Bob Haldeman's untimely departure marked the summit of power and prestige for top White House aides. Kennedy and Johnson attempted to do away with the Chief of Staff concept, but neither President could prevent a remarkable individual from dominating the internal workings of the White House. As always, personal factors undermined organizational guidelines and propelled a single aide into a central role.

During the period under discussion those who had wrung their hands at the "imperial" dimensions of FDR's staff must have finally abandoned all hope. By the time Richard Nixon left the White House he employed four times the number of aides that had served Roosevelt, and required sixty times the annual appropriation to support them. Whether Nixon received fair value for his money is a matter that is seriously open to question.

Sherman Adams:
The Indispensable Man

According to a popular gag of the 1950's, two Democrats met at a Washington cocktail party and exchanged dire speculations. "Just imagine," said the first one, "what a disaster it would be if Eisenhower died and Nixon became President!"

"Or even worse," answered his companion, "what if Sherman Adams died and Eisenhower became President?"

This punch line reflected a well-publicized reality—that Dwight Eisenhower delegated more of his authority to a single assistant than had any of his predecessors. Two potential rivals for the title of history's most powerful White House aide are ready to concede the honor to Adams. "He was really an alternate President," says H. R. Haldeman. "I had little to do with the substance of policymaking, whereas I understand that Adams had a great deal to do with substance. If you put Ehrlichman, Kissinger, and me all together, then you might have a Sherman Adams."

"His position was unique because of Eisenhower's background," Clark Clifford maintains. "I got to know the General quite well when I was Special Counsel at the White House and he was Chief of Staff of the Army. Occasionally he and Mrs. Eisenhower would have dinner at our home. We also had dinner at their Army quarters. We developed a very pleasant relationship. But I always had the feeling that by reason of his background and training, he did not have an understanding of the institution of the Presidency.

"Now, why should he? At age 18 a boy gets out of high school. He goes to West Point. He spends four years at the Academy. From that time on he leads the most protected life of anybody you've ever seen. He's on Army bases. His children go to Army schools. He doesn't concern himself with finding a job or joining a labor union. President Eisenhower admitted he'd never joined a political party. I think he said he never even voted. So you don't take part, you don't have the normal problems that an ordinary individual has. You never get interested in governmental matters. Then suddenly this man is projected into the White House. That means that he has to depend very much on somebody else. And that somebody happened to be Sherman Adams."

But why Adams out of all the hundreds and thousands of talented individuals who would gladly have served the hero-general in his quest for the Presidency?

In part, the answer to that question lies in the fact that Adams managed to be in the right place at the right time. Beyond that stands the strength of his personality—a personality so powerful and so unusual that it appeared to overwhelm his contemporaries. At his peak, Adams seemed as inevitable as a force of nature. Yet today, he is remembered by most people only in the sordid context of an illicit vicuna coat, a borrowed oriental rug, and improperly paid hotel bills. We have lost sight of the complex human being beneath the scandal, whose virtues were at least as remarkable as his faults.

Henry Adams, the first individual with that last name to settle in North America, established himself near Braintree, Massachusetts, in the 1630's. He bore several sons, one of whom sired the famous line of statesmen and intellectuals which included two Presidents of the United States. Another son produced less distinguished progeny—farmers and merchants who lived quietly in various corners of rural New England. This obscure branch of the Adams family offered no one of historical significance until Sherman Adams appeared on the national scene in the 1950's. As Assistant to the President he never stressed his connection with America's most celebrated dynasty, but he did hang small portraits of his distant relatives John and John Quincy Adams on the walls of his White House office.

Adams' mother's family—the Shermans of East Dover, Vermont—played the leading role in his upbringing. He was born on January 8, 1899, at the village parsonage of his grandfather, the Reverend Cyrus Sherman. This stern, bearded Baptist managed to raise five children on an income of $500 a year while serving as patriarch to assorted nephews and grandchildren. When Sherman was three his father, a frustrated grocer named Clyde Adams, decided to leave this extended family and try his luck in Providence, Rhode Island. He took his wife and two infant children with him, but the marriage did not survive. Clyde went his own way, leaving his dependents to fend for themselves. Biographical articles on Sherman Adams seldom mention these painful facts, thereby ignoring one of the keys to his character. The episodes of early childhood left emotional scars that were still evident when Adams was interviewed for this book at age 77. He began shouting and pounding his desk the moment he was asked to describe his father. "Young man, that's a personal question, and it has nothing to do with the Presidency. If you're going to ask me questions like that, this interview is going to be over right away. It's my business, not yours!"

Though many details of his early years remain obscure, we do know that Sherman's mother faced a desperate financial situation before her brother stepped in to support the struggling family. This Providence businessman became "a second father" to the children and encouraged them to stay in the city. His generosity kept the Adams from poverty, but they remained far from comfortable. "The first job I ever had," Sherman recalls, "was working for 12½ cents an hour at the Providence Public Market. I was working so I could get enough money for carfare and tickets to the Boston Opera Company. At that time they had some of the best bel canto artists in the world—probably the best bel canto troupe ever assembled in one place. I still remember some of those performances.'' In addition to his devotion to music young Adams developed a passion for the outdoors. He devoured the novels of James Fenimore Cooper and spent his summers tending to farm chores at his grandfather's Vermont home.

A fondness for the hill country of northern New England led him to choose Dartmouth for his college education—a choice financed by his uncle and his own accumulated savings. As a hiker, skier, and mountain climber with the Dartmouth Outing Club, Adams had few equals, winning for himself the nickname "Old Man of the Mountains." A campus fad at the time involved an ongoing competition to see which young man could hike the longest distance over rugged mountain trails in a 24-hour period. Adams set the all-time record, marching 83 miles from Skyline Farm to Hanover. He refused to stop even when wracked by stomach cramps during the last 10 miles of his journey and hobbled in to his destination at the point of physical collapse.

This need to prove his manhood through harsh displays of stamina and will-power became a consistent element in his personality. Having grown up in a fatherless household with his mother and younger sister as his constant companions, his insecurities are easy to understand. They were intensified by his small size—as an adult he was only 5'7'' and weighed 140 pounds. To compensate, he developed a tough, wiry well-muscled body and posture that was ramrod straight. Sharply chiseled features, a characteristically grim expression, and icy blue eyes further complemented a personal style that can be described only as Yankee macho.

In line with that style, Adams enlisted in the Marine Corps shortly after the United States entered World War I. He survived the legendary rigors of Marine training, but the Armistice arrived before his division could be shipped to Europe. Returning to Dartmouth, he completed his studies with an academic standing well above average. Though he might have followed the lead of most of his classmates and snapped up one of the attractive business opportunities available in New York or Boston, Adams wanted to remain in his beloved White Mountains. He signed on as a scaler at a logging camp and fought to win acceptance from the rough and tumble lumberjacks. "He was a cocky little devil," one of his colleagues recalled. "He'd pitch in and do anything, whether he knew anything about it or not. On river drives he'd be right out there with a pickaroon, keeping the logs moving. Being a little guy, he'd be right up to his belly in that cold water.''

Adams still bears the marks of some of his logging experiences. He lost his two front teeth when a log-skid shot out of the river and smacked him in the face. A few weeks later a flying chunk of maple caught him behind the ear and left him partially deaf on the left side. Then one day an old nag named Snowball kept getting in his way. Adams swatted the animal on the rump to move it aside and the ancient horse responded by kicking him between the eyes, fracturing his frontal sinus.

His endurance naturally impressed his superiors. Adams rose quickly within the company as woods superintendent, general woods manager, and finally treasurer. In the course of his progress he worked for a time near Healdville, Vermont, where he met Rachel White. This pert 17-year-old, home from school on a vacation, enjoyed a local reputation as the best square dancer in town. Adams, who had a high opinion of his own dancing skills, one night challenged her to display her prowess. She did, and a year later they were married.

Despite her tender years and tiny size (she was less than five feet tall) Rachel Adams could be nearly as stubborn as her husband. Their marriage became at times a contest of wills. When Adams angered his wife by ignoring her at the dinner table, she retaliated by packing his lunch the next day with sandwiches made of string and laundry soap. Enduring such occasional hardships, Adams took pride in the defiant spirit of his diminutive spouse and in her willingness to accompany him on hiking, fishing, and snow-shoeing expeditions. He called her "Plum," a term of endearment which she stoically accepted. As his career advanced they settled in Lincoln, New Hampshire, headquarters of the Parker-Young Company. They raised four children—one son and three daughters—in a barn-red house that looked out on the steep, wooded slope of Loon Mountain.

Adams enjoyed his life as a lumber company executive and might have continued indefinitely in that capacity had not the Great Hurricane of 1938 literally swept him into politics. This natural disaster blew down tens of thousands of trees and created an enormous fire hazard in the New Hampshire timberlands. With the approval of his superiors in the company, Adams became a leader in the statewide effort to clear and salvage the fallen lumber. He addressed a series of public meetings, preaching the need for commitment and cooperation. Martin Brown, president of Parker-Young, remembered Adams' performance a year later when "some of the men at the mill said we ought to send a better type down to the capital." Brown called a meeting of twenty-five top company officials, who promptly agreed that Adams would make a fine legislator. The following day the company president walked into Adams' office and brusquely announced: "Sherm, I guess we've got to send you down to Concord this fall." The sparse voting population in the district dutifully ratified this corporate choice and Adams entered the New Hampshire House of Representatives in 1940.

From this modest beginning his political career progressed rapidly. Reelected two years later, he served part of his second term as speaker. He ran the assembly with a heavy hand and many of his colleagues felt relieved when he went on to the federal Congress in Washington. On Capitol Hill he preserved the obscurity traditionally associated with freshman Representatives but nonetheless made a pleasing impression on his constituents. He returned home after a single term to contest the Republican nomination for governor, losing to the incumbent by a mere 157 votes. At the next election, in 1948, Adams faced a new opponent and won handily.

He brought to the office of governor no sweeping program or fixed ideology; he felt only a general sense that he could do the job more efficiently than his predecessors. After setting up a commission on bureaucratic reorganization, Adams briskly pushed through its recommendations. He succeeded in consolidating 83 existing state agencies into 43 but failed to save money for the taxpayers. His abrasive personality also created unnecessary political problems. Near the end of his two-year term, a delegation of citizens lobbying for special legislation invaded his office. "We represent more than 30,000 votes for governor," declared the group's leader. "Who the hell wants to be governor?" Adams replied. It was this sort of exchange that led reporters to dub him "One Term Sherm." Nevertheless, he confounded the cynics by winning reelection in 1950 with a thumping majority. His feisty and frugal personal style appealed to the people of New Hampshire.

Adams' most important decision as governor involved not the state of New Hampshire but the Republican nomination for President in 1952. Because of the quaint tradition under which the Granite State invariably leads off the Presidential primary season, Governor Adams found himself in a strong position to influence events. Republican conservatives supporting Senator Robert Taft competed with pro-Eisenhower moderates in attempts to win the governor's support. Adams ended the suspense at the national governors' conference in 1951 by announcing that he would enter Dwight Eisenhower's name in the New Hampshire primary. No one knew at the time whether Ike actually planned to run or whether he even considered himself a Republican. None of this deterred Adams, who had reached the conclusion that Eisenhower "looked like the fastest horse in the stable."

In the primary campaign that followed, Senator Taft stumped New Hampshire while Eisenhower remained above the fray as commander of NATO forces in Europe. Adams served as a stand-in for Ike, campaigning tirelessly and earning much of the credit when the absent general won his first electoral test. Three months later, with Ike back in the United States and fighting actively for the nomination, Adams had a chance to meet his candidate. Over a quiet lunch at Eisenhower's residence in New York, Adams realized "right away that I had not been wasting my time in working for his nomination. . . . He seemed on first impression a remarkably straightforward and uncomplicated man, with nothing devious or complex about him. I noticed that he had no time for trivialities. He focused his mind completely on the big and important aspects of the questions we discussed, shutting out with a strongly self-disciplined firmness the smaller and petty side issues when they crept into the conversation."

Eisenhower was similarly impressed. "From our first meeting in 1952, Sherman Adams seemed to me best described as laconic, abrupt, businesslike, and puritanically honest," he declared in his memoirs. Within weeks of that meeting, Ike approved the choice of Adams as his floor manager at the Republican convention. The governor received notification of this assignment in a bathroom at Chicago's Conrad Hilton Hotel—the only place in the crowded Republican headquarters where Eisenhower's lieutenants could talk with him privately. Adams' lack of ideological identification helped qualify him for the job. In past party battles he had been known as neither a "Taft man" nor a "Dewey man" and so could approach all factions on the convention floor. During the crucial fight over delegate credentials, Adams steered the Eisenhower forces with consummate skill. The candidate, who was a connoisseur of battlefield reports, particularly appreciated the governor's dispatches from the front: concise, shrewd, and consistently reliable. He also appreciated Adams' advice in a series of postnomination meetings to plan future strategy.

After the convention Adams retreated to the mountains of Wyoming for a brief vacation. He expected to return to his duties as governor of New Hampshire and to play only a minor role in the campaign. Before he could head east, however, Eisenhower intercepted him with a phone call. The general wanted Adams to drop everything and work at his side for the duration of the electoral battle. Such a request, coming from a Presidential nominee, can be the most intoxicating form of flattery. Adams had less than six months left in his gubernatorial term and no dramatic issues confronted his state. After a few days' hesitation, he took a leave of absence without pay from his post in New Hampshire and reported for duty at Eisenhower headquarters.

"During the campaign, as later in the White House," Adams wrote, "Eisenhower never defined or outlined the precise duties and responsibilities he wanted me to assume. Evidently I was supposed to know what I was supposed to do. Sometimes, in taking a line of action on my own, I may have overstepped or fallen short of what Eisenhower had in mind, but I did not hesitate nor did I ever feel confused." In other words, as his associate Robert Gray reported, "Adams soaked up responsibilities like a sponge." Arthur Summerfield, Republican national chairman, held the official title of campaign manager, but reporters knew Adams to be the man closest to the candidate. As Eisenhower confessed in a conversation with a friend, "I think of Adams as my Chief of Staff, but I don't call him that because the politicians think it sounds too military."

Over the course of 40,000 back-breaking miles, Adams shaped some of the major decisions of the campaign. One of the most ticklish issues he faced concerned the candidate's posture toward Wisconsin Senator Joseph McCarthy. Eisenhower felt genuine distaste for the anti-Communist demagogue, but McCarthy, running for reelection in his home state, was officially part of the Republican ticket. When Eisenhower toured Wisconsin he could hardly avoid appearing on the same platform with him. The general therefore felt relieved when his speechwriters devised a subtle but effective means to emphasize his differences with McCarthy. The Senator had recently questioned the loyalty of General George C. Marshall, Eisenhower's friend and wartime superior. Ike admired Marshall, and if he expressed that admiration in his major Wisconsin address it would serve as a public rebuke to the witch-hunting hysteria.

The scheme went forward until Adams reviewed the text of the speech, a bland document dealing in general terms with the issue of domestic Communism. When the governor came to the single paragraph praising George Marshall he suggested that it be dropped. He had no more sympathy for McCarthy than did Eisenhower, but he believed that the slap at the Wisconsin Senator on his home turf would stir up trouble among Republican right-wingers. Eisenhower, a political novice, immediately deferred to Adams' judgment and delivered his Milwaukee speech without the controversial passage. Somehow the entire story of the last-minute deletion found its way into the press and Eisenhower came in for heavy criticism. Liberal columnists charged that the battlefield hero had displayed a singular lack of courage in the political wars. Arthur Hays Sulzberger, publisher of the New York *Times* and an early supporter of Eisenhower, cabled Adams: "Do I need to tell you I am sick at heart?" Despite such reactions and the horror of subsequent historians at the excesses of McCarthyism, Adams makes no apologies for the incident. "I didn't see any point in getting tangled up in that whole mess. I still don't. McCarthy, like Eisenhower, was a Republican candidate who wanted support from the people of Wisconsin. It wasn't a moral issue, it was a political issue. I would stand by that decision today."

Though Republican ultraconservatives later denounced him as a "liberal" influence, on yet another occasion in the campaign of 1952 Adams served their interests. When young Richard Nixon, the favorite of the anti-Communist Right, ran into trouble over the "Nixon Fund," Adams stepped in to rescue him. Leading newspapers and politicians demanded that Nixon be dumped immediately as Eisenhower's running mate and Ike was inclined to agree. Adams and Herbert Brownell, a New York lawyer who subsequently served Eisenhower as Attorney General, recommended another course. In a secret meeting in the candidate's private train car, with doors locked and shades drawn, they persuaded the general to adopt a "wait and see" attitude until Nixon had a chance to defend himself. Meanwhile, Adams made arrangements for the nationwide television broadcast that resulted in Nixon's celebrated "Checkers" speech. This emotional appeal proved so successful that it vindicated Adams' advice and saved Nixon from a premature political demise.

Within a few weeks of Ike's election, he called Adams into his office and said to him, "I could visualize you as a member of the Cabinet, but I need somebody to be my assistant in running my office. I'd like you to continue on at my right hand, just as you've been in the campaign. You would be associated with me more closely than anybody else in government."

Eisenhower had in mind something more than a Presidential troubleshooter in the tradition of Harry Hopkins and Clark Clifford. Though entering the Presidency with few burning commitments on political programs he did have strong feelings about the organization of the White House staff. "With my training in problems involving organization," he wrote, "it was inconceivable to me that the work of the White House could not be better systemized than had been the case during the years I observed it."

To achieve the system that he wanted, Eisenhower drew on his own experience in the Army as well as recommendations from a special advisory commission headed by young Nelson Rockefeller. In the resulting transformation, the competitive chaos of the Roosevelt White House and the pervasive informality of the Truman years gave way to a series of clearly defined organization charts. These charts all had one element in common: Adams' position at the top of the pyramid, just below the President. With his official title "Assistant to the President," he reviewed virtually every decision before it went to Eisenhower. If an official paper lacked Adams' familiar notation "O.K., S.A.," Ike automatically withheld his approval until he had checked with the governor.

The President placed an enormous premium on what he called "completed staff work." This meant that all questions reaching his desk must be accompanied by a definitive recommendation from his aides. Adams proved absolutely ruthless in protecting the President from indecisive subordinates. Two Cabinet members who argued over a major agency appointment wanted to take their disagreement to Eisenhower for final resolution. The governor blocked their path. "Either you make up your minds," he snapped, "or else tell me and I will do it. We must not bother the President with this. He is trying to keep the world from war."

Actions of this sort naturally led to charges that Adams unduly isolated the President from outside influences. Senator Joe McCarthy railed against "the palace guard" at the White House—using the same phrase applied years later to Richard Nixon's Presidential staff. In Adams' case, his role never reflected a manipulative or conspiratorial intent; it stemmed from the temperament, health requirements, and administrative preferences of the man he served.

No President had as great an appetite for leisure and relaxation as Dwight Eisenhower. In addition to his almost daily sessions on the golf course, Ike spent fully 25 per cent of his time in office on various excursions away from the capital. Those who normally would have taken their business to the President were scared away more by Eisenhower than by Adams. "Whenever I had to make a decision that properly belonged to a subordinate," the general wrote in his memoirs, "I admonished him at once, but if he failed again it was time to begin looking for a replacement." This approach encouraged members of the staff to avoid the President at all costs and use Adams as the court of last resort. The governor once summed up the situation when he stared in disgust at the papers, letters, memos, and requests of every description that littered his White House desk. "This damn thing isn't a desk, it's a swill barrel," he growled. "If they can't find any place to dump their junk, they dump it here."

The enormous desk itself dominated his office and dwarfed the fidgety little man who swiveled and tilted behind it. On its front panel it bore a large carved replica of the Presidential seal—a pointed reminder to visitors of the source of

Adams' authority. At the edge of his desk, crowded to one side by papers and clutter, were miniatures of New England birds, three framed photographs of Mrs. Adams, and two elaborate telephone consoles.

These telephones consumed much of Adams' energy. A reporter who monitored his schedule kept a careful count of incoming and outgoing calls and noted that they averaged 250 a day. On occasion, Adams handled two conversations simultaneously, with a phone at either ear. To save time he invariably dispensed with telephone amenities. He hung up without saying goodbye when finished with a conversation, leaving the listener at the other end to contemplate the sound of a line suddenly gone dead.

Adams' telephone responsibilities stemmed in part from Eisenhower's distaste for that instrument. The President avoided phone calls whenever possible, insisting that aides and Cabinet officers speak with him face to face. Adams made the pilgrimage to the President's office at least six times a day. The only person in government to enjoy the privilege of frequent phone contact with Eisenhower was Secretary of State John Foster Dulles, whose far-flung diplomatic errands made such communication a necessity. A call from Eisenhower on a nonessential matter was so extraordinary an event that Adams made special note of one such occurrence. The call came on a summer's day while the President vacationed in Newport and his assistant "minded the store" at the White House. "I picked up my telephone in Washington, and after he had disposed of a small item of business, I was astonished to hear him ask, 'Are your eyes blue?' He was painting a portrait of me from a color photograph in which the color of my eyes was indistinct."

Ike's call spoiled the surprise element, but Adams welcomed the gift nonetheless at Christmas 1957. When pressed, he admits that the oil portrait, which hangs today in his New Hampshire home, is something less than an immortal work of art. "I remember when Eisenhower gave it to me he said, sort of apologetically, 'I'm afraid I made it too gray.' Well, it was. It was sort of gray all over. Much too gray. Maybe a painter like Mr. Copley—whose work you can see in the Boston Museum—wouldn't even think it was much of a portrait. But I had to remember who the artist was. The artist was President of the United States." Adams did his best under the circumstances to pay gracious tribute to Eisenhower's artistic skill. "Already the painting you did of me is a family heirloom," he wrote in a note to his boss, "and Rachel says I grow to look more like it every day."

Despite such friendly interchanges, Ike and his top assistant never developed a genuine intimacy. Adams' ineptitude as a golfer and bridge player excluded him from the President's preferred pastimes and the two men seldom relaxed together. A casual comment one afternoon while the President practiced golf shots on the back lawn of the White House revealed his attitude toward his hardworking aide. As Ike chipped away at the ball and chatted with Secretary of State Dulles, he spotted Adams walking toward him with a file of papers in hand and the customary grim expression on his face. "Look, Foster," the President sighed, "here comes my conscience!"

Eisenhower felt such complete confidence in his Chief of Staff's dedication that he ignored occasional complaints about Adams' power. "The trouble with these people," the President declared to an associate, "is they don't understand integrity." In a public statement, Ike went even further in praise of his assistant. "The one person who really knows what I am trying to do is Sherman Adams," he announced.

At Eisenhower's request, Adams sat in on all meetings of the Cabinet and the National Security Council. Adams' comments occasionally helped to guide these sessions but not even his careful vigilance could ensure smooth operations at all times. One minor foul-up involved the practice of beginning each Cabinet meeting with a moment of silent prayer. Agriculture Secretary Ezra Taft Benson, a leading member of the Mormon Church, had suggested these devotions to Eisenhower "because of my love for you, members of the Cabinet, and the people of this great Christian nation." Despite his good intentions, Ike unwittingly omitted the prayer at the beginning of one meeting early in his administration. When an executive clerk quietly passed him a note calling his attention to that fact, the President exclaimed aloud, "Oh, goddamnit, we forgot the silent prayer!"

For Adams, the twice-weekly meetings of the White House staff were even more important than the meetings of the Cabinet. These gatherings replaced the loosely structured staff sessions that Truman had conducted every morning with the six aides closest to him. Under Eisenhower, an unprecedented total of 412 government employees toiled at the White House and the President left their supervision entirely to Adams. At their regular meetings, the Assistant to the President stood behind a huge oak table and lectured his upper echelon associates on hundreds of administrative details. While his subordinates sat taking notes like obedient students, the governor laid down the law on the proper use of staff cars, the danger of press leaks, the scheduling of personal vacations, the importance of eight hours' sleep each night, or the necessity for charging all calls of a political nature to the Republican National Committee.

No one challenged his orders because his position with the President was so clearly beyond question. Alone among major aides of this century, Adams had no serious rivals on the White House staff. Richard Strout reported in the *New York Times Magazine:* "Under Adams' firm rule there is less of jealousy and palace intrigue in the White House today than there have been for many a year; instead, there is a high sense of team play and collective élan." This situation also had its negative aspects. Richard Rovere described the Eisenhower White House as "a place in which the novel, the unexpected, and the unforeseen were seldom to be found. There was no tension there, no rub, no friction, no excitement."

Those who served directly under Adams found no lack of excitement in their work. Robert Gray noted that Adams' imperious style "made a potentially memorable act of every memorandum sent to him, of every statement made in his presence, and of every answer to his questions." Gray recalled innumerable on the carpet sessions in which he stood before the governor's desk "afraid to inhale for fear of breathing fire."

Adams' habitual abuse of his subordinates became a legend in official Washington. Much of his bad temper centered on the inability of other staff members to emulate his example of appearing at the office by 7:30 every morning. When one senior aide had not arrived by 7:50, Adams called him at home. "Look, I can't do my job with half a staff," he shouted. "If you're going to keep banker's hours you'll have to submit a schedule so I'll know when I can do business with you." Most often, Adams' five secretaries bore the brunt of his idiosyncrasies. One or another of them frequently burst into tears and a newsman once walked into the outer office to find all five sobbing simultaneously. The governor's number one secretary, a brilliant woman who later became administrative assistant to Nelson Rockefeller, used to storm out of sessions with her boss shouting "that impossible beast!" or "He's a madman—he's insane!" Simple and unmitigated rudeness contributed to her difficulties. Adams, for instance, never said "good morning" to his personal staff. When asked why he omitted such courtesies he replied, "Why should I say hello? They know I'm here." His secretaries unanimously relished those infrequent occasions when Adams left Washington on errands for the President. During one such absence, three of them celebrated by kicking off their shoes, reclining on the boss's private couch and enjoying a leisurely cigarette. Suddenly, the President of the United States walked into the office. Surveying the situation and noting their horrified expressions, Eisenhower smiled. "Don't worry, girls," he said. "I won't tell the governor."

For all his impossible ways, Adams inspired great loyalty in his staff. His male associates developed an attitude toward him resembling the devotion Marine recruits might feel toward a sadistic drill sergeant. The fact that they survived the ordeals imposed on them proved to the world that they were tough; they took pride in their designation as "Sherm's boys." As one former subordinate commented, "You either quit Adams on the second day, or you go through hell for him."

His colleagues eventually discovered significant virtues in the governor's gruff and uncompromising manner. "He is a man you can get an answer from," said a fellow staff member, "a quality that is rather rare in government." Adams seemed immune to the more obvious forms of flattery. An underling once attempted to win points by clipping out and handing to Adams a highly favorable newspaper article. The governor read it carefully and frowned at key passages. "'Able' is a damning word," he mumbled. "Your worst enemy you call 'able.' 'Dedicated'—that's a pukey word."

Adams had difficulty accepting praise because he applied the same impossible standards to himself that he did to his subordinates. "In the two years I worked under him," his special assistant Robert Gray recalled, "I never once sent a memorandum to which he failed to reply the same day." That record was little short of miraculous, considering the volume of work encountered by the chief White House aide. Administrative experts agreed that the capital had never seen a man who could reach decisions or "move papers" as quickly as Adams. White House speechwriter Emmet John Hughes, who became disenchanted with the President and many others in the administration, always maintained his respect for Adams. "The man hurled himself at his work with a kind of headlong force," he wrote, "a stoic disregard to self and a cold clarity of judgment that seemed almost to beat matters into decent submission."

Deeply imbued with the work ethic of his Puritan ancestors, Adams derived spiritual satisfaction from the performance of his duties. The system of pragmatism developed by William James helped mold his personal philosophy. "Have you read *The Varieties of Religious Experience*?" he asked the author of this book. "If you have, then you know that public service is one of the possible varieties. It can be almost a religious experience, even if not specifically godly. It ought to be if you're going to do the job."

The most important test of Adams' inner strength took place in September 1955. The month began innocently enough, with the governor flying to Europe for a much needed break. "One day Eisenhower called me into his office and said, 'What do you know about NATO?' I said, 'Very little.' He said, 'Well it's time you learned.' So I went over to Western Europe and I met with the generals and I visited the various countries." The trip proceeded smoothly until Adams and his wife arrived in Scotland and learned that Eisenhower, who was vacationing in Denver, had just suffered a heart attack. Though he received no medical details of the President's condition, Adams never doubted that his chief would recover. He boarded the first plane back to the States and on the bumpy, rain-drenched flight "began to think of how the President would expect his staff and Cabinet to act while he was disabled. He had never given me directives for such an emergency, but then he had never given me many directives of any kind and we had gotten along all right."

Other members of the official family, paralyzed by confusion and doubt, welcomed this unquestioning assumption of authority. Press Secretary James Hagerty, who handled the swarms of reporters while the President lay immobilized under an oxygen tent, said he would never forget what it meant when Adams arrived in Denver. "When I saw that little guy step off the plane, I could have kissed him. I would have—but for the photographers." Adams set up his command post in an Air Force administration building a few blocks from the President's hospital room. He spent every day on the phone to Washington, channeling information to and from his stricken chief and making the decisions necessary to keep the government running. Once a week he flew back to the capital to attend meetings of the Cabinet and the National Security Council. With the Twenty-fifth Amendment more than a decade away and no constitutional provision for the Vice-President to take over for a disabled chief executive, Adams became, in a sense, the acting President. During Eisenhower's illness, even those who had previously complained of Adams' influence acknowledged the value of a single, dominant White House aide who was used to acting in the President's name.

The governor's smooth performance combined with Eisenhower's speedy recovery to minimize political ramifications of the heart attack. Following two months of rest and hospital care the President returned to the White House; three months after that he announced his intention to run for reelection. Doubts about his health did nothing to diminish his phenomenal popularity, even after he returned to the hospital in June 1956. This time it was an acute ileitis condition that threatened Ike's well-being, and doctors performed emergency surgery to remove part of his small intestine. Adams and Press Secretary Hagerty stood at the door of the operating room to "watch the surgeons as they worked on the body of the President of the United States. It was an eerie and striking experience. . . . Nothing mattered to us except how The Old Man, as we called him, was going to get out of this one. With two major physical misfortunes within a year, how could he be expected to go through the coming 1956 Presidential election campaign and four more years of the hardest strain to which a human being can be subjected?"

Without Adams to lean on, Eisenhower might not have attempted—or survived—the ordeal. During the campaign for reelection the governor fielded all major problems as they arose, including a bitter dispute concerning the renomination of Vice-President Richard Nixon. Harold Stassen, the former governor of Minnesota who served the administration as Director for Mutual Security, led a public drive to "Dump Nixon" from the ticket and replace him with Massachusetts Governor Christian Herter. Adams decided to save the administration embarrassment by pressuring Herter to renounce the movement forming behind him. Knowing the Bay Stater's long-standing interest in foreign policy, he told him on the phone that "in making his future plans, he could take into account the fact that he would be given favorable consideration for a position of responsibility in the State Department." At the same time, Adams hinted broadly that Eisenhower "had no objection" to Herter's going before the convention to make the nominating speech for Nixon. The Massachusetts governor had been in politics long enough to recognize the outlines of a deal when he saw one. He called Adams back and told him he had decided to make the speech for Nixon; a few months later he became Under Secretary of State.

Despite his defense of Nixon's interests in both the 1952 and 1956 campaigns, rumors persisted of a strained relationship between Adams and the Vice-President. Nixon may well have envied the governor's access to Eisenhower and his authority in the White House. Adams, however, denies the existence of a rift. "We weren't really thrown together all that much. When we did come together there was no particular problem. We had very different jobs. Nixon was world errand boy. I worked in the kitchen."

One of his kitchen responsibilities involved the dispensation of federal patronage. During the six years that he served the administration, Adams reviewed some 15,378 executive appointments. In nearly all of these cases, his recommendation amounted to final approval. His negative verdict carried similar authority. GOP politicos occasionally protested when he blocked the appointment of otherwise deserving Republicans for no other reason than their inability to do the job. "Nuts!" Adams said to one such complaint. "We're doing quite enough for the goddam Republican Party."

He displayed his partisan commitment, for example, by delivering slashing attacks on the Democrats in a number of political speaking tours. "Eisenhower sent me to give speeches because he knew I enjoyed it. I liked getting away. Speaking for the party—that was relaxation for me." The tone of his rhetoric was by no means relaxed; along with Richard Nixon he emerged as one of Ike's most effective hatchet men. In 1954 he lambasted the opposition party as "an addle-brained donkey" that was "fused by lust for privileges of public office." He warned that unless a Republican Congress were elected the country would be "turned back once more to the spending sprees and political orgies to which the American people called a halt in 1952." A friend on the White House staff once advised him to tone down the fervor of his oratory, but Adams stoutly refused. "I will not give a namby-pamby speech," he snarled.

In addition to his strenuous speechifying, Adams drew other pleasant assignments from his chief. "Twice he appointed me to represent him at the Academy of Music in Philadelphia for the annual concert-celebrations of the Philadelphia Orchestra. In Washington I also went to concerts quite often, and sometimes I would be officially representing the President." In general, Adams shunned the glittering social world of Washington, but he did take advantage of his position to hobnob with great musicians. Among his guests for lunch at the staff cafeteria in the White House were pianist Artur Rubinstein, violinist Isaac Stern, and conductors Charles Munch and Leonard Bernstein.

Another distinguished visitor to the lunchroom was the poet Robert Frost, a favorite of the governor's because of his ties to the New Hampshire soil. For nearly an hour the hardy, 84-year-old Frost stood at one end of the small cafeteria and recited his poetry to the assembled aides. For once, Adams did not worry about the staff's wasting time during a break. The impromptu and unpublicized reading would have surely surprised the nation's intellectuals, who did not spontaneously associate the Eisenhower administration with a commitment to high culture.

Even more surprising was the manner in which Adams returned Frost's favor. The New England bard had interested himself in the case of Ezra Pound, an eccentric genius who had been incarcerated in a Washington mental institution since the end of World War II. Pound, one of the major poets of the twentieth century, had broadcast pro-fascist propaganda from Italy during the war. Captured by American troops, he spent a decade locked in St. Elizabeth's Hospital without trial and without hope. Frost had no enthusiasm for Pound's political views, but he pleaded with Adams to end the senseless ordeal. The

governor agreed to help, and set up meetings between Frost and Justice Department officials that eventually resulted in Pound's release.

Despite interludes in the world of poetry, Adams' daily schedule remained
decidedly prosaic. At 6 A.M. each morning his hi-fi automatically
awakened him with a classical record that he had selected the night before. At 7
he packed his bulging briefcase into a green Oldsmobile convertible and drove
himself to work. He declined the use of an official limousine as a waste of the
taxpayers' money. He worked six full days a week and also came into the
office on Sundays after church. Each evening he returned home by 6:30 for a
quiet dinner with his wife. Unlike Clark Clifford and other aides of the past, he
refused to keep late hours. With his four children either married or away at
school, the governor relished his time alone with Mrs. Adams. After dinner
they played scrabble, or he looked over papers from the office, before turning
in by nine o'clock.

According to their Washington acquaintances, the governor and Plum con-
formed almost perfectly to the stereotype of tightfisted New Englanders. One of
his assistants noted that some of Adams' suits "must have dated back to his
freshman days at Dartmouth, over three decades ago." His attitude toward free
cigars further reflected his obsessive opposition to waste. Though he did not
smoke, and barely tolerated the habit in others, he never refused a cigar when it
was offered. He accumulated them in all varieties and sizes and then handed
them out as tips to White House ushers who opened doors for him and performed other favors.

The governor's thrifty ways seemed well-suited to an administration which
had always made a point of its scrupulous integrity. During the 1952 campaign,
Ike attacked the sloppy morality of some of Truman's aides who had accepted
mink coats and deep freezes from businessmen hoping to improve their government "connections." Under the new regime, the general promised, "the
mess in Washington" would disappear and the people would see a government
"as clean as a hound's tooth." He reiterated this promise several times after he
became President. In 1956 he declared, "I cannot believe that anybody on my
staff would ever be guilty of anything indiscreet, but if ever anything came to
my attention of that kind, in any part of this government, that individual would
be gone."

Adams vigorously endorsed these standards in principle and helped to enforce them in practice. When Air Force Secretary Harold Talbott became involved in an apparent conflict of interest, the governor secured his immediate
resignation. He meted out the same stern and ruthless justice to several lesser
officials at even the slightest whisper of impropriety. It therefore seemed absolutely incredible when national headlines in June 1958 implicated the governor
himself in an influence-buying scandal. The House Subcommittee on Legislative Oversight charged that Adams had intervened in behalf of a shady Boston
businessman in exchange for a few expensive gifts. At first, Washington insiders wrote these charges off as so much partisan grandstanding and expected the

Chief of Staff to disprove them without difficulty. After all, Adams' personal integrity seemed "as apparent as his New England accent."

The case against Adams stemmed from an investigation into the murky affairs of textile manufacturer Bernard Goldfine. Goldfine, who operated mills throughout New England, had run into trouble with federal regulatory agencies for improper labeling and other questionable business practices. On three different occasions Goldfine had asked his friend in the White House, Sherman Adams, to report on the specific charges against him. On all three occasions Adams complied. He placed a few quick phone calls to learn the current status of the case, but never suggested to any federal official that the charges against Goldfine be either dropped or altered.

The governor's inquiries would have done little more than raise eyebrows had it not been for the fact, as revealed by the Congressional committee, that he had accepted gifts worth thousands of dollars from the man under investigation. Since 1955, Goldfine had paid nearly $3,000 in hotel bills for Adams and his family. He also presented them with a vicuna coat worth $700 and an oriental rug valued at $2,400.

Adams never disputed these facts, but he attempted to explain them away. In a dramatic appearance as a volunteer witness before the Legislative Oversight Subcommittee, he revealed that he and Goldfine had been friends for years and that the exchange of gifts had been a natural part of their relationship. Nor had the generosity been limited to one party to the friendship: during his trip to Europe in 1955, Adams bought Goldfine a beautiful gold watch, and later Mrs. Adams gave the Goldfines one of the best of her amateur oil paintings. Moreover, the value of Goldfine's favors had been grossly exaggerated. The vicuna coat, which came from one of his mills, had actually cost the industrialist less than $100, despite its high retail price. The oriental rug that graced the floor of the Adams' living room had been intended as a loan, and the governor planned to return it when he left Washington. As to the hotel bills, Adams had assumed that Goldfine maintained the choice rooms in Boston on a permanent basis to play host to associates and friends. He therefore concluded—mistakenly, as it turned out—that by occupying those rooms every now and again he had not cost his friend an extra penny. Most importantly, Adams insisted again and again that he had done nothing wrong, that the gifts from Goldfine had been received "without strings attached." As he summarized his presentation to the committee, "I have no excuses to offer. I did not come here to make an apology." He admitted, however, that if he had the opportunity to do it over, "I would have acted a little more prudently."

Though the press continued to howl, the governor's rationalizations seemed to satisfy Eisenhower. Press Secretary Hagerty told reporters that the President maintained "full confidence" in his aide and the White House now considered the incident "a closed book." Ike himself made a statement to the press the day after Adams' Congressional testimony. A gift, the President declared, "is not necessarily a bribe. One is evil, the other is a tangible expression of friendship.'' He conceded that Adams may have been imprudent, but found no grounds for firing him. ''I believe that the presentation made by Governor Adams to the Congressional committee yesterday truthfully represents the pertinent facts. I personally like Governor Adams. I admire his abilities. I respect him because of his personal and official integrity. I need him.''

This last statement, intended as a frank and manly confession of the governor's importance to the administration, struck many observers as a sign of Presidential weakness. Most Americans remained ignorant of the long history of executive reliance on powerful White House aides; they found something unseemly in the idea that the President should ''need'' any one individual. After Eisenhower's declaration of dependence, the outcry against Adams expanded to include a general critique of his relationship with the President. Approaching the 1958 Congressional elections, Democrats had a field day with a President whose personal reliance on a controversial aide led him to abandon his previously proclaimed standards of political morality.

The governor might have weathered these partisan attacks had not leaders of his own party added their voices to the chorus of denunciation. Republican conservatives in particular had been waiting for years to ''get'' the governor. They resented his authoritarian rule at the White House, his moderate position on social issues, and his outspoken advocacy of civil rights. Any man who enjoyed a warm working relationship with Representative Adam Clayton Powell, conservatives reasoned, deserved their hostility with or without the Goldfine affair. More moderate party chieftains worried about Adams from a purely practical point of view. Unless he resigned his White House post the scandal associated with his name might drag scores of GOP Congressional candidates down to defeat.

These concerns intensified as major Republican contributors cut off their donations pending resolution of ''the Adams mess.'' One well-known big giver, Sidney Weinberg of New York, summed up the feelings of the disgruntled money men: ''When Adams used the world 'imprudent' regarding his conduct, he was using a word meaning 'stupid.''

While the governor clung stubbornly to his position through the summer of 1958 the ground slowly eroded beneath his feet. ''Sherm's Boys'' in the White House, who had once stood in awe of their powerful leader, began to avoid him whenever possible and to reach major decisions on their own. The President, instead of using the phrase ''Check it with the governor'' as he had in the past, relied increasingly on his Cabinet for substantive advice. To nearly all his close associates, Adams became an object of pity; he ceased to inspire reverence or fear.

The governor responded to these changes by retreating from the feverish activity around him. During his last month at the White House he spent hours quietly sorting through the mountain of papers he had accumulated. As his assistant Robert Gray reported: ''He was tired in spirit now as well as in body, his mood was mellow and his speech was slow. The old bark and bite were gone. The demanding commander issued few orders and those pathetically petty and awkwardly tempered with apology.''

The end finally came in September, when Adams took a few days off for a fishing expedition in Canada. During his absence Meade Alcorn, chairman of the Republican National Committee, went to the President to warn of an impending electoral disaster if Adams remained at his post. Eisenhower no longer had the stomach to protect his embattled aide, nor could he bring himself to fire him directly. Disgusted with the whole sordid affair, the President shrugged off his responsibilities and asked Alcorn and Vice-President Nixon to "have a talk" with Adams.

Following this quiet capitulation, events moved swiftly to their conclusion. Alcorn contacted Adams in the backwoods of New Brunswick and asked him to return to Washington immediately. Back in the capital the governor sat down with Nixon and Alcorn to learn some of the grim facts of political life. Nixon, in his 1977 interviews with David Frost, recalled this conversation as one of the most unpleasant duties he ever performed. The two bearers of bad tidings left the governor with little doubt that Eisenhower would welcome his resignation.

Looking back on those hectic days, Eisenhower took great pains to exonerate himself from the charge of having betrayed his faithful aide. At a press conference the President insisted: "I did not instruct anyone to ask for a resignation. He did resign voluntarily. Now, there is no question that other people advised him very strongly at this time, during these last weeks and months, I guess it is now, but he was never advised by me to resign.'' This response begged the question, to say the least. By the time Adams drafted a resignation statement and flew up to Newport to show it to the vacationing President, Ike had already prepared a carefully worded letter accepting the governor's decision and thanking him for his years of faithful service. Seated behind his desk, Eisenhower read the letter aloud and then looked up with a smile. "Will this be all right?'' he asked.

Adams thanked him. "There was nothing else I could do,'' the governor later recalled.

Several reporters maintained that the handling of the Adams case showed the Eisenhower administration at its worst. Former speechwriter Emmet J. Hughes wrote: "When the crisis, at its onset, might have been sternly construed by a righteous President to be a matter of principle, Eisenhower had defended Adams. When the issue became a crude matter of vengeful insurrection by the most wealthy and vocal of the extreme Republican Right, he had left Adams alone—to write his own resignation.'' The timing of the governor's departure—three full months after the facts of the case had been revealed —made it clear to everyone that Eisenhower had acted out of political expediency rather than a genuine concern for official integrity.

Hughes happened to speak with Adams the day before he left the White House. "I called upon him to chat for a few moments as he quietly, methodically cleaned off his desk in the large office of the West Wing. And I could not refrain from bitterly remarking, 'Well, the vultures of the Grand Old Party finally descended.' He only smiled tightly and shrugged: 'That's the great game of politics.'''

The next day Adams left town. Eisenhower had wanted to send him off with a farewell dinner and square dancing at the White House but the governor, understandably, had no appetite for dancing. He returned to New Hampshire with little fanfare, carrying in his bags a shiny new possession—an enormous sterling silver punch bowl. Under the circumstances, the inscription on the bowl's face contained more than a touch of irony. It cited Adams' "unsurpassed dedication" and "tireless service" and bore the engraved signature of "his devoted friend, Dwight D. Eisenhower."

In retirement, Adams looked back and began to admit his mistakes. "I never intended to seek special favors for Goldfine nor did I ask anybody to do anything for him," he wrote. "But I did not stop to consider that in making a personal call or an inquiry concerning a matter in which he was involved I might be giving the officials in the federal agency the erroneous impression that I had a personal interest in their ruling or decision in the case. . . . This was a blind spot of which I was not sufficiently aware, but those were busy days for me and I was continually working under intense pressure."

Other White House aides experienced similar pressure, but they avoided the costly mistakes that Adams made. What flaw in the governor's character led to his fatal vulnerability? How could a man of his experience and intelligence have behaved so foolishly? His White House colleague Robert Gray suggests that his preoccupation with thrift proved the governor's undoing—he saw the gifts from Goldfine as "money saved" and couldn't resist them. Another factor, rooted even more deeply in his character, further helps to explain his blunders. The Adams who intervened for Bernard Goldfine was the same Adams who felt the need to prove himself as a long-distance hiker, a lumberjack, and a Marine—the same Adams whose manhood seemed constantly to be on the line. The sort of male bond he established with Goldfine became a solemn trust; he would not abandon his friend in the way his father had long ago abandoned him. He accumulated power as means to potency and security, but what good was that power if he could not use it to aid a comrade in trouble? Under the stern code he lived by, snap judgments were a sign of strength and all decisions must be reached in a hurry. An understated bravado was as much a part of his personal style as his contempt for his enemies, and both qualities contributed to his carelessness.

When interviewed for this book, Adams revealed a heretofore unpublicized aspect of his White House service that raises new questions concerning his curious fall from grace. In 1957, the governor recalled, Eisenhower became concerned about the extensive operations of the Central Intelligence Agency. "In the mornings, at seven o'clock, Eisenhower would get special intelligence briefings from General Andrew Goodpaster, and some of these briefings indicated to him that we should look into how the CIA was spending the tremendous amount of money it was getting. Just how was this money being used? How effective was the operation? He knew that people would start asking these questions some day and he wanted to be ready to answer them when they did. Because we need a covert operation, he wanted to have all the answers ready, so that when the questions were asked, it wouldn't wreck the operation.

"Eisenhower asked me to head the investigation—and he wanted it done quietly. I was surprised he put me in charge, because there were some extremely knowledgeable people involved who knew a lot more about intelligence than I did. He said to be sure to get some of our worst enemies on that investigation, or else we wouldn't find out the truth. That's why I got Joe Kennedy and asked him to be on it. There were also a number of retired generals and admirals—I don't remember all the names—but it was quite a crowd. It was entirely covert. I was very careful about that. We were asking a lot of the same questions they are asking today, but without the very destructive effects on the agency that Senator Frank Church's committee has brought about.

"I can't really say what our conclusions were, because the final report came out after I left the administration. At least I assume it came out, I assume they followed through with it and sent a report to the President. But I can't say for certain that they finished the job, because the whole thing was completely covert, and as far as I know, none of it's been declassified yet."

Could it be that Adams' memory is playing tricks on him? The official records show two investigations on intelligence activities in the latter part of the Eisenhower administration. On January 13, 1956, the President set up the Board of Consultants on Foreign Intelligence Activities with James R. Killian, president of MIT, as chairman. Joseph P. Kennedy served for a time as a member of the board, but Sherman Adams apparently did not. Then, in December 1960, came the Sprague Report of the President's Committee on Information Activities Abroad. Once again, no mention could be found of Adams ever having chaired the committee. This means that the governor either imagined the entire episode or else it has remained totally classified as he suggests. If so, it is possible that the secret committee he chaired failed to complete a report after his departure. Perhaps its task was reassigned to one of the other two committees, both of which submitted recommendations strongly supportive of the CIA and its appropriation requests.

We do not know what areas Adams explored in his allegedly thorough and covert investigation, and it may be pure coincidence that he was driven from office before he could complete his work. Yet considering the nature of recent revelations about the CIA it is at least conceivable that "the Company" had a role in hastening his departure. Could Adams have been "set up" to embarrass himself with Bernard Goldfine? Or might the agency, at precisely the moment that it suited its interests to do so, have passed on to Congressional investigators damaging information concerning the governor's indiscretions? These ideas seem bizarre and farfetched, but the intelligence community has recently admitted its involvement in projects considerably more farfetched than this one. The facts concerning Adams' fall and the intriguing investigation he purports to have headed may never be fully revealed.

After leaving the White House, the governor received a number of flattering offers from major corporations. He turned them all down because a job as a business executive would have meant giving up rural New England. After his Washington ordeal, "our red house in the White Mountains looked pretty good to my wife and to me." Living in semiretirement, he worked on a book about his experiences with Eisenhower. *Firsthand Report,* published in 1961, proved a modest success and helped fill his financial needs. Adams also taught a seminar at Dartmouth on the Eisenhower years and made regular appearances at other campuses.

Politically, he lay low for ten years, then emerged in 1968 to offer public support for Nelson Rockefeller's Presidential bid. During the New Hampshire primary of 1976, President Gerald Ford called Adams from Air Force One. "He said he was very worried about the primary and thought that Reagan might actually win. He wanted me to help him out, to talk to some of my friends up here. But I told him I had no intention of recruiting myself for this sort of thing any more. I'd had my day in politics. Like every dog has."

Since the mid-sixties the governor has spent most of his time on a project to develop Loon Mountain near his home as an up-to-date ski resort. As president of the Loon Mountain Recreation Corporation, he supervised the building of chair lifts, rope tows, a restaurant and hotel. These efforts have transformed the local economy and his neighbors speak with gratitude of his business skills.

Still spry and sharp as he approaches 80, Adams comes into his Loon Mountain office every day. The windows behind his desk look out onto a busy ski slope, with sportsmen whooshing past every few seconds and occasionally waving hello to "the Old Man of the Mountains." Though far from the center of action and power he still bullies his secretaries and can still give an interviewer a taste of the rough treatment that had been his White House stock-in-trade. Nor has his conversation lost its partisan bite. "I'm very distressed at this tendency of academics to look down their noses at the Eisenhower administration," he says. "It's a common sort of thing with the intelligentsia. It's just typical. Look at Mr. Roosevelt. He's a great favorite with the academics, and he's probably a great man. But he lost a lot of battles, didn't he? The NRA was struck down. He lost the battle over the Supreme Court. Then he got us into World War II. Well, we may not have done as much, may not have been as spectacular in terms of our willingness to break with the past, but we didn't lose a lot of battles either. A lot of our most important accomplishments were negative—things we avoided. We maintained a peaceful front and adjudicated a lot of issues that seemed ominous and threatening at the time. Eisenhower didn't claim to be a purveyor of miracles. He never represented himself to do things he couldn't do."

The governor's skills blended perfectly with this government of limited intentions. His forte, as one of his White House associates observed, "was organizing and expediting. He could keep track of all the timber in the forest and fight fires with perfection, but it was up to others to plant the trees."

For all his White House power, he left no distinctive mark on the course of twentieth-century history. "I wasn't there to accomplish things," he admits. "I was there to help the President. Good staff people have to be measured by their dedication, by their hard work, by their sense of proportion. But not by their accomplishments. All the accomplishments belong to the President. Good staff people don't go down to Washington with the idea of accomplishing something."

The young idealist who became a guiding spirit of the next administration would strenuously disagree with this assessment.

Ted Sorensen:
Kennedy's Co-Author

Clark Clifford came to Washington with a sense of adventure and the hope for advancement; Sherman Adams came with a dour, puritanical commitment to serving his boss; Ted Sorensen came to change the world.

He was only 22 when he arrived, fresh out of the University of Nebraska Law School. Already a veteran of liberal causes and campus organizations, he wanted a job in which he could challenge the racial and economic injustice he saw in American society. The best he could manage, however, was a post as a lowly lawyer for the Federal Security Agency, quickly followed by a staff assignment with a Congressional committee investigating railroad retirement legislation. It was not, as Sorensen admits today, "the most fascinating subject in the world." What's more, the committee finished its work within eight months, leaving Sorensen once again without a job.

This time he turned to the newly elected crop of Democratic Senators—"the Class of '52"—hoping that one of them could use his services on Capitol Hill. Among the names on his list was that of John Kennedy, who had overcome the Eisenhower landslide in Massachusetts and unseated the deeply entrenched Senator Henry Cabot Lodge. Most Washington insiders sniffed at Kennedy's success, attributing it exclusively to the wealth and connections of his father. During three terms in the House of Representatives, the young bachelor had achieved a reputation as a dilettante and lightweight with little interest in the legislative process. These reports could hardly have encouraged Sorensen as he walked into the new Senator's office for an interview in January 1953. Nevertheless, he found himself favorably impressed with young Kennedy. "As a human being he had an extraordinary ability to communicate and get directly to the point, not to put on airs of any kind, not to try to overwhelm me or overimpress me with his importance." At the first meeting, the Senator-elect restlessly tapped his fingers against his teeth and his knee while they discussed Sorensen's background and Kennedy's needs in the office. "I felt I could have had the job right then and there if I wanted it," Sorensen recalls. "But I also felt that if I was going to throw in with him, then there were things I wanted to know. I didn't want us to be too far apart on basic policy, and so we had another interview and this time I asked the questions—about his father, Joe McCarthy, the Catholic Church. He must have thought I was an odd duck and I don't remember exactly what I asked or exactly what he said, but I know we satisfied each other.'' Kennedy offered Sorensen a job as his number two legislative assistant on a one-year trial basis. The Nebraskan quickly accepted.

Their working relationship lasted for the rest of Kennedy's life and for Sorensen it became an obsession rather than a job. As he commented after his patron's death, ''I had given eleven years of my life to John Kennedy, and for those eleven years he was the only human being who mattered to me.''

Armchair historians are fond of asking questions that begin with, ''What if? . . .'' What if Napoleon had started the Battle of Waterloo a few hours earlier? What if John Wilkes Booth's revolver had misfired? What if young Adolf Hitler had not been prematurely released from Landsberg prison? To this fateful list, we can rightfully add the question: what if Ted Sorensen had not walked through Kennedy's office door in 1953? What if the youthful aide had accepted a job with another U.S. Senator? The answer might well be that John Kennedy would never have become President of the United States. Certainly, Kennedy had substantial assets with or without Sorensen, including brains, good looks, ambition, and enormous wealth. But what Ted Sorensen provided him was the one indispensable ingredient, the bit of yeast that allowed the cake to rise. Sorensen gave Kennedy the power of words. Though he performed many functions for his chief, Sorensen remained above all the candidate's speechwriter and coauthor. He made possible the books, articles, and speeches that transformed JFK in the public mind from ''a playboy Senator'' to ''a profile in courage.''

There is little question that the lofty style of speaking and writing that became so firmly identified with JFK was more Sorensen's doing than Kennedy's. In his high school valedictory address, long before he had even heard of John Kennedy, Sorensen included the phrase, ''To prove ourselves, we must improve the world.'' This poised, euphonious declaration would have fit comfortably in the 1961 inaugural. Kennedy's own pre-Senate and pre-Sorensen speeches, on the other hand, were a drab, workmanlike lot. Reading through the *Congressional Record,* one can understand why the young Congressman from Boston made so little impression on his colleagues. A comparison of *Profiles in Courage* with Kennedy's earlier book *Why England Slept* shows the profound impact of Sorensen's assistance. Written as a student exercise at Harvard and published through the intercession of his father, *Why England Slept* features clear and for the most part readable prose, but with scarcely a hint of the drumtaps and bugles of his later style. *Profiles in Courage,* on the other hand, won the Pulitzer Prize and helped shape the image that made Jack Kennedy so irresistible a political commodity.

This same elevated, inspiring style appeared in all of Kennedy's public pronouncements—even routine statements about federal construction grants for his Massachusetts constituents. His 1960 speech accepting the Democratic nomination offers a glittering example. ''I think the American people expect more from us than cries of indignation and attack,'' the candidate thundered.

"The times are too grave, the challenge too urgent, the stakes too high to permit the customary passions of political debate. . . . We stand today on the edge of a New Frontier—the frontier of the 1960's—a frontier of unknown opportunities and perils—a frontier of unfulfilled hopes and threats. . . . The New Frontier of which I speak is not a set of promises—it is a set of challenges. It sums up not what I intend to offer the American people, but what I intend to ask of them. It appeals to their pride, not their pocket book—it holds out the promise of more sacrifice instead of more security."

It is easy to ridicule that style—the hypnotic staccato of short phrases, the balanced, alliterative sentences—but it is impossible to deny its effectiveness. Reporter Patrick Anderson, among others, decries the "hollow pomposity" he finds in Kennedy's speeches and blames Sorensen for the mock-heroic pose. "The banality of Kennedy's formal style," Anderson writes, "was underscored by his wit and spontaneity in press conferences." Yet even Anderson admits that Sorensen, despite his "mania for contrapuntal sentences . . . fashioned an oratory that not only won the election, it inspired a generation of Americans." The Kennedy-Sorensen addresses, even when they descended into constructions of dubious sense and taste ("While we do not intend to see the free world give up, we shall make every effort to prevent the world from being blown up") had the enormous advantage of sticking in the mind. How many political leaders of the last generation have delivered speeches, regardless of their literary merits, that could be remembered by the multitudes? Those who attended even the most minor Kennedy rallies recall them today as great events. Hysterical crowds believed, even at the time, that they were watching history in the making. The candidate provided the physical magnetism; Sorensen's prose provided the sense of grandeur; both were essential ingredients in the fabled Kennedy charisma. The young aide, according to one of his friends, saw Kennedy as "his work of art."

What made Sorensen so effective as an image-maker was the bedrock of idealism in his commitment to Kennedy. He came by that idealism honestly —for all the Sorensen boys, it was as much a matter of inheritance as inclination. Ted's father, a Nebraskan of Danish ancestry, had been expelled from fundamentalist Grand Island College in 1912 for making a "radical" speech in an oratorical contest. Following that incident he joined the Unitarian Church, studied law at the University of Nebraska, and spent the rest of his life shaking the complacency of his conservative midwestern neighbors. During World War I, with patriotic hysteria at its height, C. A. Sorensen successfully defended a number of pacifists who had criticized government policy. He also fell in love with a member of the group—Annis Chaikin, daughter of Russian Jewish immigrants, a former social worker and a leader of the women's suffrage movement in the state. Their common political vision proved a strong enough bond to overcome differences in background, and the two were married in 1921.

Their gray stucco home in Lincoln soon became a lonely outpost of liberal ideas in the often inhospitable environment of the great prairie. At the dinner table each night, the Sorensens and their five children argued about reshaping the world while discussing the latest articles in *The New Republic* and other journals imported from New York. An activist by nature, C.A. played a prominent role in state politics, where he found himself irresistibly drawn into the orbit of Senator George Norris, Nebraska's maverick progressive Republican. On several occasions, C.A. managed the Senator's campaigns, helping him win an upset reelection victory as an independent when he was denied the Republican nomination in 1936. Sorensen also waged several campaigns on his own, winning two terms as the state's attorney general. In office, he earned a reputation as a fire-eating "crime-buster" and foe of corporate wealth.

His four sons inevitably shared their father's interest in politics. As one friend commented, "The Sorensens came campaigning from the womb." In a sense, this athletic, competitive brood resembled the Kennedy brothers growing up at the same time in Massachusetts. Like the Kennedys they all achieved distinguished careers. Robert, the oldest, is a management consultant who once headed Radio Free Europe. Thomas, the second son, became an official of the U.S. Information Agency and vice-president of the University of California. Phil, the youngest, won election as lieutenant governor of Nebraska.

Theodore was the third son and considered by most of his teachers to be the brightest of the lot. He starred on his high school debate team and earned a Phi Beta Kappa key at the University of Nebraska. At the university's law school, he graduated first in his class and edited the law review. In addition to his academic achievements, he found time for political and social activism. With a few friends he organized a Lincoln chapter of the Congress of Racial Equality (CORE) and successfully integrated the municipal swimming pool and roller skating rink. He also put together a Nebraska branch of Americans for Democratic Action and corresponded "rather pathetically" with national headquarters about the desperate condition of liberalism within the state.

In 1949, while still in law school, Ted married Camilla Palmer, a college classmate and daughter of a professor at the university. Ted and his wife produced three sons in the space of three years, but the distractions of family life in no way diminished his crusading spirit.

For a man of Sorensen's talent and ambition, Washington was an inevitable destination, and after he secured his position with Kennedy he believed he had found his niche. He was 24 and JFK was 35 when their partnership began, and Sorensen carefully concealed his age from his employer. When the Senator learned the truth two years later, "he seemed more amused than astonished." Kennedy by that time had learned the value of the intense young man who toiled in his office. Sorensen's first assignment was the preparation of a program of economic development for the depressed areas of New England—a task he performed so effectively that he received an immediate raise in pay. The following spring, when the young Nebraska Unitarian turned out a St. Patrick's Day address whose idiom and emphasis were perfectly suited for Boston's Irish, Kennedy became convinced that his new aide could do anything.

What Sorensen wanted to do, above all, was help the Senator establish himself as a leader of national standing. Kennedy took his first halting steps in that direction in 1954 when the proposed St. Lawrence Seaway came before the Senate. On six previous votes over the course of twenty years, all elected representatives from Massachusetts, regardless of party or district, had voted against the project. New England dockworkers and shipping interests believed it would hurt them and exerted pressure on all the state's politicians. In his Senate campaign in 1952, Kennedy specifically opposed the seaway.

Nevertheless, he asked Sorensen to make a careful study of the merits of the plan. His aide reported that the seaway was unquestionably in the national interest and drafted a dramatic Senate speech explaining that position. Kennedy hesitated several days about delivering the address—he was not required to speak, or even to vote, on either side of the issue. At the last moment, he decided to follow his conscience and walked with Sorensen to the Senate floor to address his colleagues. His remarks, emphasizing that the welfare of the nation must come before the wishes of his constituents, forecast the theme of *Profiles in Courage*. Sorensen stood proudly at the back of the chamber as Kennedy spoke, and later handed out copies of the address to the crowd of reporters that surrounded him. The Senator's independent stand won respect from his fellow legislators and from the national press, while home state voters quickly forgave his heresy.

Though Sorensen pushed Kennedy to take a risky position on the issue of the St. Lawrence Seaway, on the far more important issue of the censure of Joseph McCarthy he contributed to his employer's well-known equivocation. During his years in the House of Representatives, Kennedy had voted for repressive internal security measures and generally supported the red-baiting Senator from Wisconsin. His father frankly admired McCarthy and his brother Robert once worked for the Senator. Under Sorensen's subtle prodding and in the hopes of winning a national constituency, Kennedy as Senator moved in a perceptibly more liberal direction. As a member of McCarthy's Government Operations Committee, JFK occasionally defied the chairman and spoke out for civil liberties. When the Senate discussed measures to censure McCarthy in July 1954, Kennedy planned to line up with the majority of his colleagues. He asked Sorensen to write a speech supporting the formal resolution of censure, but before he had a chance to deliver it the Senate referred the entire matter to a special committee. By the time the question came back to the floor, Kennedy lay in a New York hospital bed, recovering from spinal surgery. Critics later claimed that his illness was only a ruse to allow him to duck a controversial issue, but medical records make it clear that the Senator was genuinely close to death. He could not take phone calls, read memoranda, or even sit up—let alone make an appearance on the Senate floor.

Still, his vote could have been recorded against McCarthy—it was up to Sorensen, as the absent Senator's legislative aide, to do so. When the young assistant refrained from taking such action, he made a decision that haunted Kennedy for the rest of his career. In all his subsequent campaigns, liberals attacked him for his cowardice on the McCarthy issue, claiming that he had sacrificed principle for temporary political advantage. The problem with these charges was that no advantage had been gained. By failing to record Kennedy's vote, Sorensen won his chief no friends and many enemies. Kennedy and his aide may have had many failings but they were not political bumblers. Sorensen knew that all the Democratic Senators were voting against McCarthy and that Kennedy's name would be conspicuous by its absence. But he also knew that the Senator had not seen the revised text of the censure resolution and that there was no way to show it to him during his hospitalization. Better to brave the howls of outraged liberals, Sorensen reasoned, than to make a decision that his chief had never specifically authorized.

Sorensen's behavior in this matter speaks volumes about his relationship with Kennedy. Aggressive aides in the past like William Loeb and Harry Hopkins had frequently taken bold initiatives to save their employers from embarrassment. Hopkins once stopped a letter to Churchill that the President had personally composed because he knew its contents would compromise FDR's relationship with Stalin. Roosevelt later thanked his aide for this unprecedented intervention. The Kennedy-Sorensen partnership, however, was cut of different cloth. In the eyes of the young Nebraskan, the Senator could make no mistakes. If Kennedy had not already delegated a responsibility to Sorensen, the Senator's collaborator would never seize it on his own. When asked recently how a young man could climb to a place of importance in the White House, Sorensen derided all showy or assertive stratagems. The only way to become a Presidential aide, he declared, "is to make yourself indispensable to a man who is going to be President."

Sorensen continued on that path during the writing of *Profiles in Courage*. The basic idea for the book was Kennedy's. While reading *The Price of Union* by Herbert Agar, he became fascinated with the account of John Quincy Adams' defiance of Massachusetts maritime interests while serving as Senator from that state. Kennedy recognized the similarity between Adams' stubborn independence and his own experience on the St. Lawrence Seaway issue and suggested to Sorensen that they collaborate on an article about Senators over the years who had courageously resisted constituent pressures. Almost immediately Sorensen began collecting a file for the project, but nothing serious came of it until Senator Kennedy's hospitalization in the fall of 1954. A football accident from his youth, aggravated by a wartime injury aboard PT-109, left him with back pains that became literally unendurable. After deciding on major surgery, he spent seven months away from his Senate duties and needed a diversion to keep his mind from his troubles. During this period of recuperation, Kennedy turned with enthusiasm to the historical research Sorensen had already begun to prepare. The aide remained in Washington, running the Senator's office and combing the Library of Congress for relevant sources, while the Senator received suggestions, memos, and detailed research reports at his Florida bedside. Later, Sorensen traveled to Palm Beach and worked directly with his boss in hammering out final organization and wording. The project, meanwhile, had grown from the originally intended article into a full-scale book. In later years, some of Kennedy's critics, including columnist Drew Pearson, claimed that Sorensen had secretly "written" that book for him. These were foolish charges, and the Kennedy family, with the help of attorney Clark Clifford, succeeded in winning retractions and apologies. John Kennedy was much too articulate and intelligent a man to require a ghostwriter, but like many another literary craftsman he benefited by working with a coauthor. That was a role Sorensen filled with admirable skill. If their positions had not been those of Senator and aide, employer and employee, there is little doubt that they would have been billed as collaborators on the book's cover. The final product bore the clear imprint of Kennedy's personality, but it also showed unmistakable traces of Sorensen. One of the most compelling chapters in the book concerned George Norris, Ted's boyhood hero, and drew heavily on private papers in the possession of Sorensen's father.

The publication of *Profiles in Courage* in 1955 proved the turning point in Kennedy's career. Praised by critics and awarded several literary prizes, it also zoomed to the top of the best-seller lists. The photograph of its handsome young author graced bookstores and magazines across the country. Among a sizable segment of the populace, Kennedy's name became a byword for intellectual ability and thoughtful dedication to public service. The theme of the book, and the circumstances of its composition, also called attention to his wartime heroics.

None of this changed his effectiveness as a member of the U.S. Senate. Even Sorensen, whose judgments of his boss are always on the far side of generous, freely admits that "John Kennedy was not one of the Senate's great leaders." JFK's colleagues tended to resent the wealthy celebrity in their midst and never granted him full admission into "the most exclusive club in the world." Sorensen similarly remained something of an outsider on Capitol Hill. Other Senate aides instinctively disliked the stiff, arrogant young man who often passed them in the halls without so much as a nod of recognition. His social problems stemmed in part from the fact that he was a teetotaller in one of America's hardest-drinking fraternities. His father had promised him a silver dollar if he neither drank nor smoked before his twenty-first birthday.* Sorensen not only won the wager; he maintained the habits. In Washington his abstemious ways only complemented the dour, priggish impression made by his physical appearance. Though his athletic, 6'1'' frame makes him a far more attractive man in

---

*Joseph Kennedy made a similar offer to his son Jack. In line with the family's financial status, the stake in this instance was $1,000 in cash. JFK forfeited this substantial reward because of a youthful weakness for beer.

person than his photographs would indicate, there is in Sorensen's habitual expression a note of vaguely worried smugness suggesting a high school vice principal in charge of discipline. Columnist Murray Kempton wrote of him: "That wintry face and those thin lips will always remind us that the pioneer women of Nebraska pulled the plow and chopped the wood while their husbands complained all the while about the service." As one of his colleagues on Capitol Hill reported, "He's a dreadfully cold fish."

Sorensen's one reigning passion was his work. He organized his days and weeks with detailed lists drawn up on sheets of yellow legal paper. He also compiled special notes on long-term goals, and in 1956 one of those projects involved the possibility of winning the Vice-Presidential nomination for his boss. The Senator's father opposed the idea from the beginning. Joe Kennedy believed that Eisenhower would beat any Democrat in 1956 and that if JFK were part of the ticket his Catholic faith would be blamed for the defeat. Sorensen nonetheless pressed forward with his plans, mightily encouraged when Presidential front-runner Adlai Stevenson mentioned Kennedy's name as one of four potential running mates. To answer objections concerning the Senator's religion, Sorensen prepared a persuasive statistical analysis showing that a Catholic Vice-Presidential candidate would help rather than hinder the Democratic ticket. This memorandum provoked widespread discussion among party leaders, political columnists, and members of the Stevenson staff.

At the Democratic convention, the inexperienced but enthusiastic Sorensen remained undisputed manager of Kennedy's quiet campaign. "You're responsible for this whole thing," the Senator told him. "No," the aide replied. "I'm only responsible if you lose. If you win, you will be known as the greatest political strategist in convention history." When Stevenson left the choice of a running mate to open balloting by the delegates, Kennedy lost a tight seesaw battle to Senator Estes Kefauver. Nevertheless, the grace with which he rushed to the convention floor to concede defeat greatly advanced his political fortunes.

Sorensen registered that advance and began planning almost immediately for a Presidential race in 1960. His Christmas gift to Kennedy in 1956 was a map of the United States showing the sources of his delegate support in the Vice-Presidential balloting. The large blank areas west of the Mississippi indicated the need for Kennedy to travel extensively in order to broaden his national base. One night, as they worked out the scheduling of a Western speaking tour, the Senator said suddenly, "Why don't you come along?" Sorensen jumped at the chance. Over the next three years the two men visited all fifty states, campaigning for Democratic candidates, attracting national press attention, addressing college campuses, meeting local political leaders, building support for the campaign to come. Sorensen not only wrote and scheduled all the speeches, but also acted as the candidate's traveling press secretary and political advance man. He scheduled interviews and fielded questions from reporters, briefed the Senator on local issues and personalities, and handled follow-up phone calls while assembling a card file with the names of 30,000 Democratic activists.

The time they spent on the road together cemented their personal relationship. "We traveled together constantly," Sorensen wrote, "and long hours of conversation and observation in airplanes, airports, and hotels forged a bond of intimacy in which there were few secrets and no illusions." Looking back on those times, Sorensen told me: "I called him Jack and he called me Ted. We joked a lot and we kidded each other a great deal. We talked about sports, women, literature, family life, almost any other subject people ordinarily talk about. There would be a certain amount of kidding about one's personal life, that sort of thing. But I don't think I'll repeat that for publication."

Did this banter between them mean that their relationship developed into an ordinary sort of friendship? "He certainly looked to me for companionship. He also looked to me for a great deal of advice and recommendations. But I don't think that I ever regarded myself as his equal." In addition to his other responsibilities, Sorensen functioned at times as a glorified valet, and Kennedy, with his background of privilege, felt perfectly comfortable with that arrangement. Sorensen handled the baggage at airports, hailed cabs, made hotel reservations. He sent out Christmas cards and other personal greetings in the Senator's name. On the road he even ordered breakfast for Kennedy. Only once did the two men share the same bedroom. On that occasion, Sorensen's constant fidgeting proved so destructive to Kennedy's sleep that they never repeated the experiment.

Seen from the distance of twenty years, even such mundane details take on the glow of nostalgia. Their informal campaign tours, especially in contrast to the pomp and seriousness of the Presidency, seemed a carefree and boyish adventure. "We flew in all kinds of little planes," Sorensen recalls, "in all kinds of weather, with all kinds of pilots. . . ." On a flight from Phoenix to Denver the plane door flew open and Sorensen had to hold it closed until they landed. In order to show up on time at a corn-picking contest, they once managed a hazardous touchdown in an Iowa cornfield. On a flight to Rockport, Maine, the pilot lost his way and could not find the landing strip. With fuel running low, they circled the area while the pilot peered out one side of the cockpit and Kennedy, in the copilot's seat, looked out the other.

They also experienced some close calls on the ground. Desperately overworked, Sorensen occasionally finished his drafts of Kennedy's speeches just moments before the Senator was supposed to deliver them. Once, JFK's reading copy of a major California address was handed to him as he sat calmly on the dais listening to the master of ceremonies introduce him. Small wonder that the two men often found themselves so keyed up after a speech that they sought out all-night cafés in order to relax.

Whatever other services he performed for the Senator, Sorensen's chief value to Kennedy continued to involve the preparation of speeches. As he reported rather smugly in his book about JFK, "We tried repeatedly but unsuccessfully to find other wordsmiths who could write for him in the style to which he was accustomed. The style of those we tried may have been very good. It may have been superior. But it was not him.'' One weary night in 1959 in an Indianapolis hotel room, Kennedy told him, ''I know you wish you could get out of writing so many speeches. I wish I could get out of giving so many, but that's the situation we're both in for the present.''

Sorensen not only accepted that situation—he relished it. Those years in which the Senator relied upon him almost exclusively, in which they traveled alone and not even their wives could stand between them, were precious rather than onerous. Sorensen remained acutely aware of his privileged position. Wherever they went, crowds gathered to see The Great Man and political leaders begged for a few moments of his time. Sorensen, however, enjoyed his company constantly and listened to his private judgments on the rest of humanity. Reporters incessantly clamored for details about the Senator's personal life, about the little human interest items that would make their stories come alive. Sorensen, on the other hand, knew and shared everything—even those intimate aspects that would never find their way into the press. Reflected glory, proximity to a center of attention and power, can be a powerful intoxicant; Theodore Sorensen definitely imbibed.

Unconsciously, he began to imitate Kennedy in his speech and mannerisms. Suggestions of a Boston accent crept into his conversation, as he used ''hahf'' for half and ''mo-weh'' for more—pronunciations he never learned on the plains of Nebraska. He also came to gesture as Kennedy did, jabbing the air with one forefinger while he held the other hand in the side pocket of his jacket. He even compromised his opposition to alcohol, developing a taste for Heineken's beer and an occasional daiquiri—the Senator's two favorite drinks. These changes in his personality did not escape notice. A friend of Kennedy's once told Sorensen, ''Say, you're getting more like Jack than Jack himself.'' On occasion, JFK saved time by mischievously asking his aide to assume the Senatorial identity on the telephone. None of the callers Sorensen handled ever caught on to the masquerade. These lighthearted impersonations reflected an ongoing merger of two personalities. ''They're in each other's skin more than any superior and subordinate I've ever seen,'' a leading Democrat observed. An unidentified Senate source summed up the situation for the New York *Times:* ''When Jack is wounded, Ted bleeds.''

Considering the nature of the bond between them it is not surprising that Sorensen felt uneasy when their operation expanded into a full-scale Presidential campaign in the fall of 1959. For the first time, Sorensen had to ''share'' Kennedy. Robert Kennedy took over as campaign manager and brought with him Ken O'Donnell, Larry O'Brien, and other members of the so-called Irish Mafia. Sorensen continued to hold special status as ''an extra lobe of Kennedy's mind,'' but he could not avoid a certain amount of tension in his dealings with the Senator's brother. It always infuriated Bobby when members of the staff went to Sorensen for directions or asked the speechwriter, rather than the campaign manager, to clarify the Senator's wishes. Both men had to struggle to accept the intimate standing the other enjoyed with JFK. The competition between them, though never bitter or destructive, continued to some extent after the election. "Bobby and Ted got along in the White House," reported one friend of both, "but they were rivals for the President's ear. Sorensen was the staff liberal while Bobby was the pull to the right."

For the most part, Kennedy seemed amused rather than concerned by tensions within his staff. In the last month of the campaign he discussed the problem with Arthur Schlesinger, complaining that "the Senatorial group . . . tended to suspect every new face" but adding, with great emphasis, "Ted is indispensable to me." He expressed similar sentiments to a reporter from *Time* magazine. "I want to keep Ted with me wherever I go in this campaign," he said. "You need somebody whom you can trust implicitly."

Many times in the course of the grueling campaign Sorensen proved his value to his boss. When Kennedy lost his voice for a few days in the midst of the primary battles, Sorensen managed to pinch-hit for him. He delivered the candidate's speeches with the distinctive Kennedy inflections, as well as offering the "impromptu" jokes and literary quotations that had become JFK trademarks. Meanwhile, he continued to grind out new addresses day after day, sometimes working on as many as three speeches simultaneously. He also helped prepare the candidate for his all important televised debates with Richard Nixon. Sorensen and his two research assistants, Meyer Feldman and Richard Goodwin, sorted through the mass of statements and information accumulated during the campaign and prepared a tight, factual fifteen-page summary anticipating all questions likely to be raised by Nixon or by the panel of newsmen quizzing the candidates. Kennedy's performance in the fateful first debate, in which he had a wealth of detailed information at his fingertips, erased in one stroke the image of inexperience and immaturity that had been his major campaign liability.

Kennedy's success on television convinced Sorensen that the Democrats would win by a landslide. Certainly, he never expected that his hero would be involved in an election night cliff-hanger with Richard Nixon. At Hyannis Port with the rest of the Kennedy entourage, Sorensen faithfully watched the returns until eight the next morning, when he was the first one to wake the Senator with the news that he had carried the state of Minnesota and with it the election. When Press Secretary Pierre Salinger reached Kennedy a few minutes before nine, he found the President-elect happily sudsing himself in an upstairs bathroom while Sorensen perched at the edge of the tub, reading him the latest returns.

Shortly after the election, Kennedy announced the first of his major appointments, naming Ted Sorensen as his White House Special Counsel. The decision provided Sorensen with a new title but with little change in his responsibilities. His initial assignments from the President-elect emphasized the essential continuity in his role. First, Kennedy asked him to begin writing out ideas for the inaugural and State of the Union addresses. Second, he ordered his aide to supervise a special task force in preparing a master checklist of all major questions awaiting Presidential action. In December, Sorensen handed Kennedy a detailed list of over 250 items, ranging from proposed new national parks to crucial decisions in military technology. In a wearying all-day session in Palm Beach, Sorensen reviewed the issues with his boss. "Now I know," Kennedy said after the ordeal, "why Ike had Sherman Adams."

Joking aside, the new President had no intention of allowing anyone on his staff to duplicate Adams' all-powerful role. As Sorensen observed, "Kennedy was his own chief of staff." In the Eisenhower administration, Sherman Adams had conducted the staff meetings; under Truman, the President himself presided over daily sessions with his aides. Kennedy decided to eliminate group meetings entirely. He wanted to arrange his relationship to his assistants in the image of "a wheel and a series of spokes" with the President at all times at the hub of the wheel. Other administrations, notably Ford's and Carter's, have tried JFK's "spokes of the wheel" model and even used the same terminology, but none of his successors have been able to make it work. JFK's unique success stemmed in part from his first-class managerial skills and warm personal relationships with a number of assistants. But some of the credit also belongs to Sorensen. He was the Presidential aide with the longest record of service and the broadest grant of authority, but he never allowed ego problems to interfere with his selfless devotion to his chief.

The initial division of White House responsibilities seemed clear-cut and sensible. Kenny O'Donnell handled scheduling and appointments and Pierre Salinger handled press, as they had in the campaign. Political operative Larry O'Brien took charge of the President's relations with Congress. National Security Advisor McGeorge Bundy presided over foreign affairs and defense concerns while Sorensen handled the shaping of domestic policy and the drafting of a legislative program. As it turned out, the Nebraskan's exclusive concern with domestic issues lasted only a few weeks. After the Bay of Pigs fiasco, Kennedy wanted Sorensen to become actively involved in foreign policy decisions; he naturally had more faith in his longtime alter ego than in the CIA and State Department professionals who had advised him so disastrously about the refugee invasion of Cuba. By the end of the administration's first year, Sorensen's influence stretched across the board. The President's frequently repeated question, "What do you think, Ted?" became something of a White House byword. Sorensen's continued role as the President's main speechwriter reinforced his formidable position. For no other President was the making of speeches so closely related to the making of policy as it was for Kennedy.

Unfortunately, Sorensen paid for his White House influence by compromising his normally robust health. Like Hopkins and Clifford before him, he developed an ulcer while serving the President. His first ulcer came in 1962 and was soon followed by two others. "I don't know whether ulcers go with a certain type of personality which is likely to be found in a top position," he speculates, "or whether ulcers are the result of the position. If it comes with the personality then it's hard to blame the job in the White House. But there is no doubt that the hours and the tension, the stress, the sense of constant responsibility, can be very powerful.''

These same unremitting pressures contributed to the breakup of Sorensen's fourteen-year marriage. He and his wife had been separated since the early stages of Kennedy's Presidential campaign and in July 1963 they were formally divorced. During his years in the White House, Sorensen lived alone in a bachelor apartment in Alexandria, Virginia. *Life* magazine politely described this habitation as ''austere'' while some of his personal friends saw it as ''positively grim.'' Despite his straitlaced style and reputation, Sorensen admits that he ''maintained a certain amount of social life with a variety of young ladies.'' Given his youth and the glamour of his position he enjoyed any number of options, but he had neither the time nor the energy for serious relationships. For Sorensen, the only human contact that mattered in the long run was his ongoing relationship with the President of the United States.

As he recalled in *Kennedy,* his massive memoir of their partnership: ''He and I continued to be close in a peculiarly impersonal way.'' When interviewed for this book, Sorensen explained: ''There was a somewhat artificial dichotomy in my relationship with the President. I was totally involved in the political, governmental, substantive side of his life and almost totally noninvolved in the social and personal side of his life. Except for a few formal banquets, we never even ate dinner together while I worked at the White House. The social life, the personal life of the President was a completely separate area in which I did not intrude.''

There is little doubt that for Sorensen this situation was largely a matter of choice. He simply did not share the Kennedys' taste for elegant society. Once he did attend a New Year's Eve party given for JFK by the Charles Wrightsmans—and went home by 10:30. ''In Sorensen,'' Murray Kempton declares, ''we are never away from a presence for whom to be casual for one hour at a time was to risk feeling oneself not a serious person for all time.''

The intensity with which he approached his job won him few friends among the Washington elite. Said one prominent Democrat: ''He is one of the toughest and most ruthless people I have ever dealt with, insulting, belittling, condescending. More than once I have wanted to hang up the phone on him. He thinks the way to make people realize his importance is to talk like Sherman Adams. . . .'' As in previous administrations, some members of the Cabinet questioned the legitimacy of the top aide's wide-ranging power. Commerce Secretary Luther Hodges, upset by his inability to see the President as often as he wanted, planned to air his complaints at a Cabinet meeting. The formal agenda for the session of June 15, 1961, contained an item headed, ''A candid discussion with the President on relationships with the White House staff.'' Spotting this notation on the schedule at the meeting, Sorensen passed Kennedy a slip of paper with the question, ''Shall I leave?'' The President ignored his note and never allowed the matter to come up. He similarly ignored complaints from leading legislators. ''Congressmen are always advising Presidents to get rid of Presidential advisors," Kennedy told a press conference. "That is one of the most constant threads that runs through American history." Among the attacks the President found it easiest to dismiss was the crude, partisan attempt by Senator Barry Goldwater to make an issue of Sorensen's draft record. "I can't help but wonder at the thought of the fathers and mothers of American boys who right now are being called up for active military service," the Arizona Republican melodramatically intoned, "when they learn that one of the President's closest advisors is an objector because of conscience." Though too young for service in World War II, Sorensen inherited enough of his mother's pacifist convictions to register with the Selective Service as a conscientious objector. He was prepared to serve in a nonmilitary capacity, but at his draft physical during the Korean War he received a IV-F classification because of a recently removed tumor behind his ear.

None of this concerned Kennedy, but it did point up the advantages of a White House aide's maintaining a low profile. A careful student of history, the President wanted his Special Counsel to learn from the experience of his predecessors. Shortly before entering the White House, he told Sorensen, "Every man that's ever held a job like yours—Sherman Adams, Harry Hopkins, House, all the rest—has ended up in the shithouse. Congress was down on them or the President was hurt by them or somebody was mad at them. The best way to stay out of trouble is to stay out of sight." The President took his own advice so seriously that he ordered Sorensen to turn down all speaking invitations he received. He even vetoed the idea of his aide's appearing one year as the featured guest at the banquet of the Gridiron Club. "It will take too much time to work up a funny speech," Kennedy told him. "Besides, we don't have enough jokes for our own speeches."

Sorensen's natural flair for the undramatic helped him to follow the President's wishes. Not since Hoover's assistant Lawrence Richey had a major aide worked so comfortably in the shadows. Sorensen was never a "mystery man"—the glare of publicity on every aspect of "Camelot" made that impossible. Yet he remained an indistinct, elusive figure in the public mind who received fewer headlines than Hopkins, Clifford, Adams, Haldeman, Jordan, or other contemporary aides. The press found little of interest in his matter-of-fact personal style and preferred to concentrate its attention on the antics of Pierre Salinger. "Plucky Pierre," with his comical, rotund form, omnipresent cigars, and daily meetings with reporters, made wonderful copy even though he exerted little influence on major decisions.

Sorensen, on the other hand, played a steadily increasing role in the formulation of policy, particularly in the area of foreign affairs. For the most part, his dovish recommendations helped to moderate the aggressive, hard-line approach of some of Kennedy's other advisors.

Sorensen also helped Kennedy correct a potentially costly blunder during his visit to Berlin in 1963. The crowds that greeted the American President on that occasion were as large and enthusiastic as those at any political rally. Chanting his name, surging forward by the hundreds of thousands into the square in front of the city hall, they hailed the young leader as if he were a Messiah. Swept up by the frenzy of the moment, Kennedy departed from his prepared text to deliver a ringing series of challenges to apologists for the Communist system. Each one ended with the words, "Let them come to Berlin!"—a rhetorical device that captured the imagination of the world. The problem was that one of JFK's declarations seemed to go too far, stating: "And there are some who say in Europe and elsewhere we can work with the Communists. Let them come to Berlin!" This bellicose pronouncement threatened to undermine recent administration initiatives for a thaw in the Cold War and a nuclear test ban treaty. Sorensen saw the dangerous implications at once, and during the short break between Kennedy's speech and his next appearance at the Free University of Berlin he discussed them with the President. JFK quickly agreed with his aide on the necessity of inserting a hastily composed passage into his university speech that tempered and reinterpreted his previous words: "As I said this morning, I am not impressed by the opportunities open to popular fronts throughout the world. I do not believe any democrat can successfully ride that tiger. But I do believe in the necessity of the great powers working together to preserve the human race."

Despite Sorensen's low visibility at home, the Soviets readily understood that he was Kennedy's right-hand man. When Premier Nikita Khrushchev wanted to transmit personal letters to the President, Sorensen occasionally acted as go-between. Elaborate cloak-and-dagger precautions helped to protect the secrecy of the correspondence. Once, Sorensen was asked to meet an obscure Soviet official named Grigori Balshakov in downtown Washington. As they walked together, the Russian handed him a folded newspaper which contained a letter from Khrushchev, already translated. Balshakov insisted that the message, concerning a minor concession on Berlin, came from Khrushchev himself and not from Foreign Ministry bureaucrats "who specialized in why something had not worked forty years ago." The Soviet representative said he assumed that Kennedy preferred to operate on the same informal basis.

With that assumption in mind, Ambassador Anatoly Dobrynin summoned Sorensen—and not the Secretary of State or some other relevant official—on September 6, 1962. The ambassador explained that he had an urgent personal message from Chairman Khrushchev and suggested that Sorensen take notes in order to transmit its contents precisely to the President. Responding to administration concerns, the Soviet chief promised Kennedy that "nothing would be undertaken before the American Congressional elections that would complicate the international situation. . . . The Chairman does not wish to become involved in your internal political affairs."

At the same time that the Soviet ambassador passed on this reassurance, forty-two medium- and intermediate-range ballistic missiles were making their way to Cuba. When American reconnaissance planes discovered their presence five weeks later, it provoked the major crisis of Kennedy's Presidency. JFK and his advisors had less than two weeks to decide on a course of action that could determine the survival of Western civilization. At the end of that time the Soviet missiles in Cuba would become operational, decisively upsetting the strategic balance. Passive American acceptance of their installation would give the cue for a new wave of Soviet adventurism. For Sorensen, as for Winston Churchill at the time of World War II, it might be said that "all his past life had been but a preparation for this hour, and for this trial."

To help devise an American response, the President convened a group that became known as Ex Comm, or the Executive Committee of the National Security Council. Included in its doomsday deliberations were the Secretaries of State, Defense, and Treasury, the Attorney General, the Director of the CIA, the Chairman of the Joint Chiefs of Staff, and the other top officials of the government. Sorensen participated as the President's personal representative and he played a consistently prominent role in the discussions. During thirteen days of unbelievable pressure and grueling debate, his moderate, cautious thinking closely paralleled Kennedy's own.

At the beginning of the discussion, the idea of American jets striking swiftly and suddenly to eliminate the missile complex seemed to have the broadest appeal. No single proposal, however, managed to satisfy everyone and Kennedy wanted a strong consensus before he made the final decisions. JFK personally guided the meetings in their early stages before Sorensen persuaded him that opinions and suggestions would be more freely expressed without the intimidating presence of the President of the United States. Kennedy agreed to leave Washington for previously scheduled campaign appearances —cancellations would have alerted the world to the existence of a crisis—while Ex Comm struggled toward a recommendation. With nuclear holocaust never far from the minds of the participants, the internal debate could be punishing. At one point, Sorensen complained to his colleagues that they were not serving the President well and that his recently healed ulcer "didn't like it much either."

Despite such outbursts, the group gradually swung around to the Special Counsel's point of view. Sorensen opposed the idea of an air strike as a needlessly risky course of action: Russian technicians, as well as Cuban troops, would probably die in the devastation, forcing the Soviets to retaliate. Moral issues also played a part in the discussions. Robert Kennedy passionately declared that the proposed surgical strike would be "a Pearl Harbor in reverse, and it would blacken the name of the United States in the pages of history." Both RFK and Sorensen favored some form of blockade, but numerous questions remained to be answered. As the deliberations dragged on, the President told his Special Counsel and his Attorney General that he counted on the two of them "to pull the group together quickly."

Sorensen finally managed to do just that; his mechanism, characteristically enough, was the preparation of a speech. Still unable to reach final agreement, the members of Ex Comm requested two speech drafts from the Special Counsel, one of them announcing a naval blockade, the other explaining a tactical air strike. With the two alternative statements in hand, some of the persistent disagreements might resolve themselves. Sorensen left the group and went to his office to think and write. He began work first on the blockade speech but doubts about the course he had recommended continued to plague him. A naval "quarantine" posed fewer dangers than an air strike, but it bore only a tangential relationship to the core of the problem. How would interference with Soviet supply ships ensure ultimate removal of the missiles already in place in Cuba? Late that afternoon, Sorensen returned to his colleagues empty-handed. Instead of the speech drafts they had expected, he presented a series of questions. The discussion of these questions led to what Sorensen later described as an "amalgam" of the two prime proposals. The United States would begin by blockading military shipments to Cuba, but would make it clear to the Russians that an air strike would follow if the missiles were not removed. This modified proposal won nearly unanimous support and became the approach that Kennedy ultimately followed.

Sorensen's role in this process deserves special praise. Anyone who has ever worked in a competitive group situation knows the temptation he must have felt when asked by his colleagues to take responsibility for producing workable speeches. Another man would have tried to prove himself, returning with two glittering and accomplished texts. On a matter of such earthshaking importance that temptation was all the greater—Sorensen had been asked to give verbal form to an epoch-making decision. It is hard to imagine Sherman Adams, Clark Clifford, or Harry Hopkins admitting confusion and coming back to the group without a completed speech. Sorensen's thoughtful, unassertive temperament, however, helped him to put the search for truth above any need to impress his associates.

Between Friday and Monday, Kennedy and his aides did the military and diplomatic groundwork necessary to implement the decision they had reached. At noon Monday, October 22, Salinger announced to the press that the President had obtained 7 P.M. network time for a speech of "the highest national urgency." The country immediately adopted a crisis mentality with anxious crowds gathering outside the White House and newsmen clamoring for information. Not even the President's brother Teddy, running for the Senate in Massachusetts, knew the details of what was happening. He called Sorensen to ask if he should go ahead with a planned speech on Cuba to a campaign dinner that evening. Under the circumstances, the Special Counsel suggested that Teddy find another topic.

Two hours before the President's televised address to the nation he met with Congressional leaders of both parties to brief them on the situation. Sorensen waited outside the door with Kennedy's reading copy of the speech while the meeting dragged on past 6 P.M. The Congressmen repeated many of the same questions that JFK had gone through so thoroughly with Ex Comm. Some of them, notably Senators J. William Fulbright and Richard Russell, stubbornly disapproved of Kennedy's course and urged an immediate invasion of Cuba. When the President emerged he seemed visibly irritated. "If they want this job, they can have it," he muttered to Sorensen as they ran up to his private quarters where the President changed his clothes before the broadcast. On the way back down to the office they reviewed the final text of the address. They had worked together on literally thousands of speeches and gone through thousands of such last-minute checks, but both men knew that this situation was unprecedented. With the world on the brink of nuclear war, the speech might be the last public pronouncement Kennedy—or any other American President—ever made. JFK had already asked his wife and children to leave Washington in order to be closer to their assigned bomb shelter; the First Lady refused, preferring to remain at her husband's side. Special arrangements had also been made for those who worked with the President. Members of the staff and their secretaries could sleep in the shelter in the basement of the executive mansion, while the White House cafeteria remained open around the clock to feed them.

The words of the Kennedy-Sorensen speech that reached the world that Monday night made no attempt to conceal the dangers facing humanity. After announcing "a strict quarantine of all offensive military equipment under shipment to Cuba," Kennedy warned that if the Soviets continued work on their missiles "further action will be justified. I have directed the Armed Forces to prepare for any eventualities. . . . The path we have chosen for the present is full of hazards, as all paths are, but it is the one most consistent with our character and courage as a nation and our commitments around the world. The cost of freedom is always high, but Americans have always paid it. And one path we shall never choose, and that is the path of surrender or submission."

During the next six days the public and the policymakers awaited a definitive response from Khrushchev. The atmosphere in the White House developed a surrealistic tinge, as staff members did what had to be done without quite believing the nightmare reality in which they found themselves. Kennedy managed to astonish his associates with his outward display of calm and good humor. "This is the week we earn our salary," he told them. Sorensen tried to emulate his chief, projecting a sense of assurance and determination. He ate and slept haphazardly, but continued to play a leading role in the expanded meetings of Ex Comm.

On Friday night, October 26, a secret message from Khrushchev arrived at the State Department that seemed to point a way out of the crisis. The Soviet leader offered to remove the missiles from Cuba under U.N. inspection in return for an American pledge never to invade the island. The administration greeted this proposal with enormous relief, but before it could be formally accepted another message came in. This time the Soviets released their statement to the press and public and demanded an additional U.S. concession: the removal of American missiles from Turkey. The President and his advisors found this new ultimatum totally unacceptable. Though the Turkish bases had little strategic value, their abandonment under pressure would have given the Russians a major diplomatic and propaganda victory; their experiment in Cuba would have succeeded in forcing a U.S. retreat on another front. At the same time, outright rejection of the new Soviet proposal would be condemned throughout the world and continue the risk of thermonuclear war. In the midst of anguished discussions, Robert Kennedy proposed a solution to the seemingly impossible situation. The Americans should concentrate on the first message they received, pretending that the second communiqué had never arrived. If they went forward and agreed to the terms of Khrushchev's private, more conciliatory letter they could present the Russians with a fait accompli that they might accept. If the Soviets rejected that resolution, the United States would have to go forward with either an air strike or an invasion of the island.

The wording of the American message to the Kremlin could determine war or peace. The United States had to give the Russians the chance to save face while maintaining its own policy of firmness. Ex Comm spent hours struggling over a text, but with tempers badly frayed and energies virtually exhausted the group made little progress. In frustration, the President asked his brother and Sorensen to leave the room and come up with a workable draft. They soon returned with a product acceptable to everyone. With the decision made and a response dispatched to Moscow, the tension quickly subsided. By the time the meeting adjourned at 10 P.M. Saturday night the participants knew that the crisis would be settled, in one direction or another, by the following afternoon.

Sorensen went home to his lonely apartment, collapsed from sheer exhaustion and slept fitfully until Sunday morning. As he stumbled awake to the sound of an alarm, he instinctively flipped the switch on his bedside radio to listen to the 9 A.M. news. In the course of the broadcast a special bulletin came in from Moscow. The reporter announced a new letter from Khrushchev, made public immediately in the interests of speed. The Premier had agreed to accept Kennedy's terms. The missiles would be withdrawn and inspection would be permitted. The crisis had been successfully resolved. The Special Counsel immediately called McGeorge Bundy at the White House, who confirmed the radio account of the Soviet message. It was, as Sorensen put it, "a beautiful Sunday morning in Washington in every way."

At 11 A.M. the members of Ex Comm gathered at the White House in a spirit of triumph and exultation. As they waited for the President to come in, they speculated on what might have happened, "if Kennedy had chosen the air strike over the blockade . . . if both our conventional and our nuclear forces had not been strengthened over the past twenty-one months . . . if the President's speech of October 22 had not taken Khrushchev by surprise . . . if John F. Kennedy had not been President of the United States." When JFK entered the room his colleagues arose in a silent but eloquent tribute.

Twelve years after the crisis, in December 1974, ABC television presented a three-hour dramatization called *The Missiles of October*. Sorensen invited a number of former colleagues to his New York apartment to watch the show.

Jacqueline Kennedy Onassis, McGeorge Bundy, Arthur Schlesinger, and many others attended the party, looking on skeptically as the actors on the little screen tried to recreate the sense of those unforgettable days. It was, as one of them confessed, "an eerie feeling." The host in particular seemed emotionally drained after reliving the experience. He told a reporter from the New York *Times* that he regarded his part in the real-life drama as "the accomplishment of my life."

That statement revealed some of Sorensen's deepest feelings about the years in the White House: he believed that nothing he could do in the rest of the time allotted him on this planet could possibly equal the grandeur and significance of his service to Kennedy. Few Presidential aides have been so totally satisfied with their jobs. "I was very, *very* lucky to be where I was. That was my only thought. To be at the center of influence in world events was the fulfillment of a lifetime's dream. To say that it was somehow depressing for me to subordinate my personality is simply not an accurate way of describing me. I was not the President. I was not in any way equipped to be the President, or the candidate. I knew I had come a very long way as a very young man and I was grateful. None of it would have been possible had it not been for my relationship with President Kennedy."

He looked forward to continuing that relationship during JFK's second term. Like most other political observers, he rated the President's chances of reelection as excellent, especially with Barry Goldwater as the likely Republican nominee. Looking past the election, the President had mentioned to Sorensen the possibility of a future promotion. "We had a general kind of conversation once about the possibility of a Cabinet position in the second term. Very general, and I'm not sure that when it came down to the crunch he would have wanted me any place other than the job I was filling for him. I certainly wasn't looking for anything else. There might have been more theoretical prestige attached to a Cabinet position, but not as much opportunity and challenge as where I was."

With the election still a year away, Kennedy began laying the political groundwork for his anticipated victory. His trip to Texas in November 1963 was part of that effort—an attempt to reconcile the warring factions of the Democratic Party of the Lone Star State. As he boarded his helicopter on the South Lawn of the White House, Sorensen ran out to him with some last-minute suggestions. The President had asked for some ideas on "Texas humor" to include in his upcoming speeches and the Special Counsel managed to come up with a few punch lines. JFK took the material, thanked him, said goodbye, and stepped into the waiting helicopter.

The next day, as Sorensen returned from lunch in a chauffeured White House car, a message came in over the two-way radio that he should return to his office immediately. He rushed back to his West Wing headquarters, expecting some new political crisis. At the door his personal secretary, Gloria Sitrin, met him with the news the President had been shot. Numb, he staggered to the

Secret Service office at the other side of the mansion for up-to-date details on the President's condition. By the time he arrived, John Kennedy was already dead.

In the aftermath of the assassination, Sorensen suffered even more intensely than the other members of the Kennedy circle. Not only had he known JFK longer and worked with him more intimately, but he also lacked a personal support system to help him in coping with his grief. While his associates had wives, family, and close friends to comfort them, Sorensen, according to one of his acquaintances, spent hours "weeping alone." He nevertheless maintained a stoic exterior and worked hard every day, helping Lyndon Johnson adjust to the White House. LBJ wanted Sorensen to stay on indefinitely, but seasoned observers knew it was only a matter of time before he departed. Unlike Kennedy aides such as Larry O'Brien and McGeorge Bundy, his highly personalized working relationship with JFK could not be adapted to another boss. When he resigned on January 15, 1964, he became the first major figure of JFK's Presidency to leave the Johnson administration after the assassination.

After returning to private life, Sorensen concentrated his energies on writing a book about his years with Kennedy. He approached the task as a sacred duty. Several times during his Presidency, JFK had told him, "I just wanted to make sure you got that down for the book we're going to write." With his coauthor gone, Sorensen felt obligated to go ahead with the project on his own. There were also less altruistic reasons for the book: Harper & Row reportedly paid an advance of $200,000 to the former Special Counsel. The resulting best-seller offered a detailed but far from balanced view of the late President. "Without demeaning any of the great men who have held the Presidency in this century," Sorensen declared in one typical passage, "I do not see how John Kennedy could be ranked below any of them."

Though he later described the writing of *Kennedy* as "a catharsis" and "a very healthy thing for me to do at the time" it did not put an end to the prolonged depression caused by the death of his friend. Nor did his marriage to a teacher named Sara Elberry help him to regain his balance. Their union, begun less than a year after the assassination, ended in the divorce courts in 1968. "The trauma of that assassination took a terrible toll on me," Sorensen recalls. "I made some moves and decisions which I would not otherwise have made, I don't think. My personal life would certainly have been different. But there's little point in going into that." His second divorce was only one of a series of disappointments that have plagued him with haunting consistency since 1963.

After finishing his book, Sorensen found it difficult to decide on any of the promising career options open to him. "Ted was undergoing a severe case of the bends," says his brother Tom. "I think he really only wanted one job, and I kept telling him that the job of Special Counsel to John F. Kennedy in the White House was no longer available."

At last he accepted a partnership in one of New York's most prestigious law firms—Paul, Weiss, Rifkind, Wharton & Garrison—but he had no intention of making it a permanent commitment. "When I first came to the office, I thought it would be on an interim basis," he recalls. "I thought that Robert Kennedy would be elected President and I would go back to Washington." He served as a part-time consultant during RFK's 1968 Presidential bid, lending eloquent touches to a few of the candidate's major speeches. If the Senator had succeeded in capturing the White House, Sorensen almost certainly would have received a Cabinet appointment. The events of June 5, however, left his expectations once again shattered by an assassin's bullet.

The Kennedys suffered another sort of disaster a year and a half later and Sorensen, the family's faithful retainer, found himself inevitably implicated in their new misfortune. After Teddy Kennedy made his wrong turn off the bridge at Chappaquiddick, he planned a nationally televised address to explain away the embarrassing details. The atmosphere at Hyannis Port the night before the speech—with lights burning into the small hours of the morning and Kennedy loyalists arriving from across the country—seemed a cruel parody of crises of the past. Whatever his personal view of the situation, Sorensen showed up and did his best for the last Kennedy brother. The speech he prepared was vintage Sorensen—full of heroic phrases, self-dramatization, and calls to idealism. He even quoted at length from *Profiles in Courage,* and in so doing seemed to call much of his own previous work into question. If Sorensen could manipulate stirring rhetoric to win sympathy for Ted Kennedy in the wake of Chappaquiddick, then how many of the golden words he provided for JFK had been sincere or significant in the first place?

Widely blamed for Teddy's ludicrous TV performance, Sorensen watched his national stature sink to a new low. According to *Newsweek,* Democratic liberals viewed him as "a burnt-out case: a man infatuated with technique rather than substance." These charges intensified as Sorensen set his sights on a U.S. Senate seat in 1970. A third marriage to a stylish young former RFK volunteer helped make his candidacy plausible, while the endorsement of New York State's Democratic organization established him as the front-runner for his party's nomination. Attacks by three vigorous primary opponents and Sorensen's own shortcomings as a campaigner soon caused that early lead to evaporate. "I could never become much of a backslapping pol," he admits. "That's just not my style and I don't think I could ever do it very well." Instead of glad-handing the masses, Sorensen attempted to wrap himself in the mantle of his fallen chief, speaking emotionally and incessantly of "the Kennedy legacy." As *The New Yorker* observed after one of his campaign appearances: "Mr. Sorensen spoke less as a Kennedy would speak than as a man would speak who was introducing a Kennedy who had yet to arrive." His dismal showing in the primary—which he lost to Representative Richard Ottinger—effectively ended his career as a practicing politician.

In the years that followed, Sorensen avoided publicity and focused on the practice of law. Then, in the first days of 1977, his name burst once more into the headlines. President-elect Jimmy Carter startled official Washington by nominating Sorensen as the new Director of the CIA. Though he lacked direct experience with intelligence work, it could be argued that his involvement with the Cuban missile crisis and other global emergencies showed an ability to handle matters of vital national security. Moreover, his long-standing liberal credentials might help to neutralize some of the most heated criticism of the intelligence community. Less publicized, but no less important than Sorensen's other qualifications was his early support for Carter in New York and his wife Gillian's participation in the Democratic convention as a Jimmy Carter delegate.

Neither the President-elect nor his advisors were prepared for the avalanche of criticism that greeted Sorensen's appointment. Some of the opposition focused on the personality of the nominee. "There was lots of scar tissue from people who had to deal with him during the Kennedy years," said one Washington veteran. Before long, his critics discovered more substantial reasons to fight his confirmation. The press revealed that when writing the book *Kennedy,* Sorensen had taken seven cartons of classified documents out of the White House. This behavior seemed highly questionable in a man who had been picked to run the government's most sensitive top-secret agency. Even more embarrassing was the story of how Sorensen disposed of the confidential papers after he had finished using them. Donating the documents back to the government, he claimed a tax deduction of $231,900—later reduced by the Internal Revenue Service to $89,000. The transaction had been entirely legal, but for many observers it brought back unsavory memories of the shady personal dealings of Richard Nixon.

As conservatives in the Senate rallied to the attack it became clear that Sorensen's support, even among Democratic liberals, was pathetically thin. The night before the formal hearings on the appointment were scheduled to begin, Sorensen met with Carter. They agreed that even if they managed to win the confirmation fight—which appeared increasingly unlikely—the controversy over Sorensen's selection had permanently undermined his effectiveness. The former Special Counsel agreed to withdraw his name after making an angry statement rebutting the charges against him.

Despite his accumulated frustrations in the years since Kennedy's death, Sorensen today is not a bitter man. "There's been one real change in my life— I have found out how happy private life can be. That's really what's important in this world. And that's at least as important as my job in the White House." Since marrying his third wife in 1969, Sorensen has learned to relax and enjoy his leisure time. "Of course we share a strong interest in politics. She was by far the best campaigner in my Senate campaign. But we also share an interest in paddle tennis, which we play on weekends. And swimming. And outdoor life and sports generally. Of course, we share a tremendous interest in our daughter—which has become the most important thing in our life."

Sorensen also enjoys the work of his law firm, where his income is reported to be in six figures. "Obviously, it does not have the same kind of importance or challenge as work in the White House. I mean, it was an incredible experience for me to be in the center of things with Kennedy. If you're brought up as I was brought up, to really care about what goes on in the world, to be where it all passes across your desk is a remarkable feeling. There is never a boring minute, much less an hour or a day. You have a chance to do something—to really do something. Now, life is very different. I enjoy private life—which I never did then. I have a substantial income—which I never did then. I have an unusual kind of law practice, and my work takes me all around the world. My private life, my private practice, my private income, are all sources of satisfaction to me."

Sorensen remains fiercely proud of everything he wrote and accomplished with John F. Kennedy. He has neither sympathy nor understanding for the revisionist historians and Washington gossips who have tried to tarnish the distant glitter of Camelot. To Sorensen, all the fine words are still fine; the heroic deeds are still heroic. "It's sad in a way when you see what's happened in this country. It's as if people don't want to believe in anything today. Sometimes, they even turn against John Kennedy because he was one of the last men they believed in. I saw it all summed up in a *Doonesbury* cartoon a couple of months ago. I clipped it, and have it somewhere. In the first part of the strip, two of his characters are joking around. One of them puts his finger up in the air and says, 'Ask not what your country can do for you—ask what you can do for your country.' Then they both laugh hysterically—a whole box filled with 'ha-ha-ha.' After that, the two young men look very serious, and one of them says, 'What's so funny about that?' In the last panel, they both cry and cover their faces."

Bill Moyers:
The Protégé

Bill Moyers, TV personality, Baptist preacher, newspaper publisher, and former boy wonder of the White House, sat at the window of his hotel room with his stockinged feet resting on the edge of a bed. "I loved Lyndon Johnson," he said. "As much as a man can love another man, I loved Lyndon Johnson. I had been shaped by him. I had been forged in many crucibles with him. I had a relationship with him that was unusual—personal, deep. But I wish that I had known him later and worked for him at a more mature period of my life. There were mistakes I could have avoided, too much that was just young foolishness."

He sucked thoughtfully on a pencil-thin cigar and slouched deeper into his chair. "I'll give you an example of what I mean. It's an incident I've never talked about before, but I think it illustrates the point. It took place in August 1965, just before the President's birthday on the 27th. He was planning a big birthday party at the LBJ ranch. At the time I had a bad case of the flu but I was still determined to go down there. I had just been made press secretary and I knew it was an important occasion. So I got out of bed and called the President and told him I was going. And Johnson said, 'No, you're not going. You're much too sick.'

"But I said, 'By God, I am going.' So I called up the White House garage and ordered a car to pick me up at home and take me to Andrews Air Force Base where the President's plane was loading with staff and reporters."

Moyers arrived at three o'clock for the 4:00 P.M. departure, but when he tried to board the plane an Air Force guard barred his way. "I'm sorry, Mr. Moyers," he said. "The President has issued specific orders that you are not to get on this plane." The Press Secretary put up a brief argument, then called the White House from the nearest phone. He reached Marvin Watson, the President's Appointments Secretary, who confirmed Johnson's order and refused to alter it. Feeling impotent and humiliated, Moyers marched back to Air Force One. "I ranted and raved and tried to get on the plane again but they forcibly kept me out. And I was furious. Absolutely furious. So I went back to the phone and called Marvin Watson and told him, 'I quit.'

"Then I hung up and got back in the car and told the driver to take me home. As soon as we pulled onto the Belt Loopway, the White House communications office was trying to reach us on the two-way radio. I instructed the driver not to answer it. All the way back to the house, it kept saying, 'Volunteer calling Moyers, Volunteer calling Moyers.' Volunteer was the President's code name, but I didn't answer it. Then four blocks from my house, I said to the driver, 'Let me out here. Because when you get back to the garage they're going to ask if you've taken me home, and I want you to be honest and say that you haven't, that you don't know where I am.' He was nervous, he was sweating, he was scared to death.

"I got out and walked the rest of the way to my house but as soon as I got in the phone was ringing. I knew the President was trying to call because I'd said I was going to quit. And I didn't take the call. I told my wife not to take the call. This went on most of the afternoon. And he kept his plane on the ground, with everyone in it, sitting on the plane. Finally at seven o'clock he sent everyone home and postponed the flight till the next day. He kept trying to call me, literally all night, but I refused to talk with him. It was an impetuous display of adolescent temper, and yet he had been wrong to deny me the chance to do my job. That same night, I picked up the phone and called Robert Kintner, who was then president of NBC. I said, 'Bob, you once told me that when I got ready to leave the White House you would give me a job with the network. Well, I'm ready to leave the White House.' The call scared the purity hell out of Bob, because he didn't want to offend the President of the United States. As it turned out, he called the White House and Johnson talked to him and said, 'If you give that son-of-a-bitch a job, then I'll deny every one of your licenses. I'll have the FCC take back every one of your Owners and Operators licenses across the country and NBC will go broke.'

"The next day he sent everybody else on to Texas but he stayed behind. After lunch I went down to the White House to start cleaning out my desk. The birthday party was scheduled for a few hours later, but he was still there. I didn't want to see him. But finally, as I was cleaning out my office, Watson came in and said, 'He just wants to see you for a minute.' So I said, 'Oh, I'll go in and tell him goodbye.' And I went in. He was hunched over his desk, signing something. And I stood there for two minutes. He was obviously pretending to ignore me. Finally, he looked up and put the pen down and said, 'Well, I guess it's a case of an irresistible force meeting an immovable object.' He stuck out his hand and said, 'We both acted like fools.' And I said, 'You're right'—and after that it was as if nothing had happened. He flew off to Texas that afternoon. I went with him. And I stayed at the White House for another year and a half." Moyers sighed, almost imperceptibly, and ground out his cigar in the ashtray on the arm of the chair. "I worked for him when I was too young, too inexperienced, too impetuous, too superficial. But for a period of time it was a remarkable, satisfying, and painful relationship—for both of us."

To most observers the contours of that relationship seemed to follow the familiar father-and-son pattern, but Moyers denies that LBJ became a substitute parent. He points out that his real father offered a striking contrast to the hard-driving Johnson. Henry Moyers, a gentle, infinitely patient man, never went beyond the fourth grade and earned his living doing various odd jobs. Bill remembers riding along with him in the trucks he drove for Borden's Ice Cream, Doctor Pepper, or a local bakery, and finding that "he had as many friends among the invisible community in our town, the blacks, as he did among the whites. He was a man I never heard speak meanly of anyone."

Bill was born in Hugo, Oklahoma, in 1934 but grew up in the east Texas community of Marshall. "We were poor," he recalls. "My father never made more than $325 a month in his entire working life. I was conscious of not having things. I once thought that he was going to get me a motorbike for my birthday, but it turned out to be a puppy. And there was a disappointment there, but no bitterness about it. That small town in east Texas enabled even a poor boy to have a sense of belonging." One characteristic of his hometown culture was the ability of Moyers' parents to christen their second son "Billy Don" without embarrassment—not William, or even Bill, but "Billy Don." Their fondest hope was that he would someday add the title "Reverend" to his name as a pillar of the Baptist Church.

In school, the boy excelled from the beginning. He racked up a 93.8 scholastic average, wrote about sports for his high school newspaper, and held down a number of outside jobs. Among those impressed by this hard-working, well-mannered young man was Millard Cope, publisher of the Marshall *News Messenger*. Having already employed Moyers' older brother James as city editor, he gave Billy Don a part-time reporter's job at $10 a week. Moyers worked at that position through his last years in high school and pleased his boss so thoroughly that Cope began grooming him as his successor. In order to prepare for that role, the young man enrolled at North Texas State College and majored in journalism. Again he achieved near-perfect grades, while election as freshman class president helped stimulate his interest in politics. By sophomore year, Moyers had decided to specialize in political journalism. "Since I didn't want to write about the subject from a distance, that meant I needed some practical experience. So I sat down and wrote a two-page letter to Senator Lyndon Johnson, asking for a summer job." Moyers had seen LBJ only once in his life, during the summer of 1948. "I was 14 years old at the time, and he came to Marshall to deliver a speech on the courthouse grounds, in the sweltering summer heat, to a large crowd of short-sleeved men, mostly, standing on the courthouse lawn. And I was at the back of the crowd. I remember him speaking without microphone, literally trying through the power of his physical being as opposed to his words, to impress himself upon that crowd. I got a sense of this enormous force, a physical force, of projection, of domination of that audience, of that crowd. And that impression was reinforced when I arrived in Washington to work for him. I remember that Walter Jenkins was taking me over to the Capitol, through the basement, and Johnson was coming over on the subway, and he got off, and Walter introduced me, and I remember the size of his hand. It just engulfed mine. A very large man. A very towering, oversized human being.''

No one knows precisely what appealed to Johnson in the letter he received from young Moyers or what led him to hire the boy as a summer intern. Bill Moyers, however, has his own theory. ''I think what he saw in me was a little Lyndon Johnson. I think that the impudent letter I wrote him recommended me to him as the kind of person he was when he was young. Johnson liked to repeat himself. He believed strongly in duplicating himself, in living forever through his dams and power plants, his assistants and his family and his monuments. And I think he saw me as one of the imitations of Lyndon Johnson that he could both encourage and help nurture. He saw this unformed, ambitious, gangling, awkward but nonetheless prodigious worker of a kid, just 20 years old, and he wanted to live again through me. He thought maybe I could avoid whatever mistakes he made.''

Moyers' Washington education began with a humbling process. The Senator assigned him to the basement of the office where he addressed over 100,000 pieces of mail on a creaking, foot-pedal machine. For weeks, Moyers believed that Johnson had forgotten that he even existed. Then, when the period of trial by addressograph concluded, LBJ suddenly promoted the young intern to a position of responsibility in his mail office, P-38, just off the Senate floor. Moyers still remembers what Johnson told him when he sat him down at his privileged work space for the first time. '''Boy,' he said, 'you're gonna be privy to everything that comes across my desk and everybody I see. Suddenly, you're gonna be very important around here. People who can't even pronounce your last name are gonna say you are a saint. And they're gonna want to buy your lunch, buy your dinner, and take you riding in their convertibles. They're just gonna try to say to you, you are God's gift to Washington. Well, I don't want you to think it's because of you. It's because of where you sit. I just want to give you one piece of advice. I want you to conduct yourself in a way that if it were printed on the front page of the Washington *Times-Herald* tomorrow, you wouldn't be ashamed of it.'''

By the end of the summer, Senator Johnson had given Moyers more than advice: he had adopted the young man as his protégé and made decisions for him that altered the course of his life. LBJ all but ordered Moyers to transfer from North Texas State to the more prestigious University of Texas. In order to finance the move, he offered him a $100 a week job with KTBC, the Johnson-owned television station in Austin. This new position also made it possible for Moyers to wed Judith Davidson, the home economics major he had been dating since their first week together at North Texas.

At KTBC, Moyers' theoretically part-time job turned into a fifty-hour-a-week ordeal. He ran the news department and pinch-hit in all other aspects of the operation as needed. Between errands, he entertained his co-workers by squirting them with a water pistol or composing mock TV commercials for Austin's best-known brothel. ''For a lay preacher he sure had an irreverent sense of humor,'' recalls one female member of the staff. Somehow, Moyers still found time to pursue his journalism studies at the university and to teach a Sunday school class at the First Baptist Church. Small wonder that one of his professors observed that he looked ''tired and pale'' most of the time.

When he graduated near the top of his class in 1956, a recommendation from Lyndon Johnson helped win a Rotary International Fellowship for a year's schooling abroad. He used that opportunity to study church history at the University of Edinburgh while his wife taught school in a nearby coal-mining town, amusing the students with her sweet Texas drawl. The experience in Scotland persuaded Moyers that a quiet life of piety and learning suited him better than the hurly-burly of politics or journalism. Returning to Texas, he refused LBJ's offer of a permanent job at KTBC and enrolled at the Southwestern Baptist Theological Seminary at Fort Worth. There, Moyers and his wife spent two pleasant, low-pressure years while living comfortably on his salary as the school's publicity director. Every other Sunday he drove sixty miles to preach at a small Baptist church in Brandon, Texas. Though he developed a loyal following among the congregants he felt increasingly uncomfortable with the prospect of devoting his life to the ministry. ''In Southern culture there is the assumption that 'the Reverend' is somehow more pietistic and saintly and better than other people. I was just inadequate to what was expected from that title. People depended on me for help that I couldn't give them.'' Nevertheless, he planned to complete his studies at the seminary and to continue his involvement with the church by lecturing in Christian Ethics at Baylor University.

In December 1959, a few weeks before beginning his teaching career, Moyers received a call from Lyndon Johnson in Washington. The Senator described his plans to win the Democratic Presidential nomination in 1960 and asked Moyers to help in the campaign. He assured the young man that he could serve his fellow human beings far more effectively as an aide to a prospective President of the United States than as any sort of preacher or teacher. Moyers hesitated, but Lyndon Baines Johnson, who had successfully twisted the arms of the most powerful figures in the U.S. Senate, eventually had his way.

Beginning as the Senator's ''Personal Assistant,'' the Reverend Moyers quickly won promotion to the post ''Executive Assistant'' and assumed major campaign responsibilities. The other members of Johnson's staff, who initially looked with amusement upon the bespectacled, baby-faced 25-year-old, soon discovered that his Clark Kent exterior concealed some nearly superhuman abilities. As one of them admiringly declared, ''John Connally is a really tough man, but he couldn't organize Lyndon. But that Moyers, who was just a kid, could organize him. He could get him to do things that he should do when none of the rest of us could. I suppose it was his gentle patience that did it.'' During the often chaotic scramble for delegates, Tom Wicker noted that ''a reporter had to latch onto Moyers to know what Johnson would be up to next.''

The young man's importance in the campaign stemmed directly from his personal intimacy with the candidate. ''You see, I actually lived with Lyndon

Johnson for seven of the most intensive and difficult months of his life,''
Moyers remembers. "That was between May and November of 1960, when he
lost the Presidential nomination and then went ahead and ran for Vice-
President. My wife and kids stayed back in Texas and I lived in the basement
of Johnson's house on 30th Place, Northwest. There was a finished den down
there, and a fold-out couch. I was with him day and night, in good and bad
circumstances. I'd ride to work with him in the morning and come home with
him in the evening. I didn't drink then, but he did, and as soon as we came
home I'd sit with him while he had a drink. In the middle of the night he would
usually wake up and come down and talk with me. Or else he would buzz me
on the intercom and I'd go up to him. There wasn't anything in that seven
months that he didn't share with me.'' During this period, their relationship
went well beyond the father-and-son model most observers have imposed on it.
"I knew far more about Johnson than I ever knew about my own father. My
father never talked to me about his sexuality. My father never talked to me
about his wife, my mother. My father never talked to me about his failures.
Johnson would talk about everything—about his relationship with Lady Bird,
about his worries with his daughters growing up, even about his own problems
with his girlfriends. And I won't discuss that even now, because he trusted
me.''

Other Johnson intimates have proven less steadfast in keeping the confidences of the late President. Bobby Baker claims in his memoirs that during the
time Moyers lived with LBJ the Senator was involved in a complex, passionate
affair with the wife of a Congressman. The recollections of TV newswoman
Nancy Dickerson provide further evidence of Johnson's amorous tendencies
and suggest that Moyers occasionally exerted a restraining influence. In *Among
Those Present*, she describes a night in an airport motel in Chicago during the
Vice-Presidential campaign. Johnson, wandering the corridors in pajamas
"after a few drinks," found his way into Ms. Dickerson's room and prop-
ositioned her. "It wasn't very romantic," she recalls. "He kept pacing back
and forth in his bare feet, waving his arms, and I had curlers in my hair."
Before the issue had been finally resolved they were interrupted by a knock at
the door. It was Moyers, who had been sent by Mrs. Johnson to locate the
Senator. In a soft voice, with a sober expression, he made the suggestion "that
everyone get some sleep—alone." The candidate felt constrained to follow that
advice.

After the election, Moyers struggled to escape Johnson's orbit. The Vice-
Presidency has never been noted for the challenges and stimulation it offers and
the prospect of four years as aide to this superfluous officer of government
seemed positively purgatorial. Johnson expected his young aide to share the
misery, but Moyers had other ideas. He hoped to win a place in the administration of the Peace Corps—that glamorous innovation of the Kennedy years that
gave restless idealists the chance to satisfy their altruism and their ambition at
the same time. Moyers frequently reminded his boss that in the 1930's the

young LBJ had left his job with a Congressman to carve out a career with the Federal Youth Administration in Texas, but Johnson resisted the analogy. He continued to insist that Moyers was indispensable until one afternoon, having just returned from a funeral in Texas, he sat slumped at his desk in a somber, introspective mood. Moyers, sensing that the timing might be right, came to him and asked once more about going to the Peace Corps. Johnson lifted his head, glared at his aide, and shouted, "Go, goddamnit, if that's what you want!" Moyers did not wait to ask again.

At the Peace Corps, Moyers began as associate director in charge of public affairs and helped Director Sargent Shriver persuade a skeptical Congress to fund the new agency. He also developed an enormously successful national ad campaign to recruit Peace Corps volunteers. By the end of 1962, he had proven his usefulness in so many areas that Shriver wanted him to take over the agency's number two position—that of Deputy Director. This new job was important enough to require Senate confirmation. Several Capitol Hill conservatives questioned Moyers' youth and inexperience, but he managed to keep a sense of humor and perspective during occasionally stormy hearings on his appointment. When asked by one of the Senators to state his age, the Deputy Director-designate replied, "Twenty eight *and a half,* sir." After the debate concluded, Moyers became one of the youngest appointees ever confirmed by the U.S. Senate.

In later years—particularly during trying times in the White House—Moyers liked to look back on his Peace Corps experience as a tranquil interlude of pure idealism. Actually, the celebrated volunteer agency attracted some of the most competitive of the New Frontiersmen and Moyers paid a bitter price for staying on top of that heap. In January 1963 he spent two weeks in the hospital with a bleeding duodenal ulcer. After his release, a strict soft foods diet and the support of his wife Judith helped to place the problem "under control." To soothe his digestive tract, he developed the habit of consuming as many as four strawberry milkshakes and several vanilla custards every day.

Whatever the tensions of his position, Moyers took special pride in the fact that the Peace Corps job remained officially nonpolitical. He therefore showed little enthusiasm for a special request from Kenny O'Donnell, White House Appointments Secretary, in November 1963. "We are in a mess down in Texas," O'Donnell told him on the phone. "The President is going there in a couple of days. Everybody is fighting with everybody else. Nobody can bring the factions together. You worked for Lyndon. You don't have any enemies down there. Would you just go down and hold hands?"

Moyers refused. "It would be a mistake for this agency," he declared. "We're a fragile operation, only in existence a couple of years. I'm not supposed to be in politics."

Fifteen minutes later the phone rang once again in Moyers' office. This time it was the President of the United States. "I really want you to go," John Kennedy told him. "I am personally asking you to go." With no further choice in the matter, Moyers packed his bags and went off to play his own improbable role in the impending tragedy.

His chief responsibility in Texas involved the coordination of a gala fund-raising dinner for Friday evening, November 22. As he ate lunch in Austin that afternoon, discussing final arrangements with the state Democratic chairman, word spread through the restaurant that Kennedy had been shot. Moyers' only thought was that Lyndon Johnson needed him immediately. He rushed to the Austin airport without a moment's hesitation and chartered a private plane to take him to Dallas. While in the air over the city of Waco, he heard the radio broadcast news of the President's death. As his small craft approached heavily guarded Love Field in Dallas, Moyers persuaded the control tower to grant him emergency permission to land. His plane taxied to within a few yards of Air Force One but Moyers, thinking that Johnson had remained at Parkland Hospital with Kennedy's body, jumped into a state police car and ordered the startled trooper to take him across town. With sirens blaring and lights flashing, they were halfway to the hospital before the police radio revealed that the new President was already on board his plane. Executing a screeching about-face, they sped back to Love Field where Moyers ran unchallenged onto the Presidential jet. A Secret Service agent stopped him at the stateroom door and Moyers scribbled a note for LBJ. It said simply, "I'm here if you need me." Within moments, the President called him in. Moyers' entire performance that afternoon, from the second he heard of Kennedy's shooting, reflected an unquestioning sense of his own importance to Johnson. While most Americans stood paralyzed by events in Dallas, the Deputy Director of the Peace Corps thought nothing of chartering planes and commandeering police cars to rush to the side of his longtime patron.

He began demonstrating his value to the new President during the tense flight back to Washington. The grieving Kennedy entourage looked on Johnson and his men with horror and suspicion, but Moyers, with his Peace Corps credentials and intellectual bent, seemed more acceptable. He acted as a liaison between the two staffs and also helped the President with the brief but moving statement he made upon his arrival in D.C. During the next forty-eight hours, Moyers sat in on some of the key meetings that enabled Johnson to assume command of the government. One encounter in particular forecast his central role in the administration. On Saturday, November 23, Johnson met with Ted Sorensen to review the most pressing items awaiting Presidential attention. As the grieving chief aide to John F. Kennedy ticked off his list of urgent business in a blunt, businesslike tone, Moyers sat beside the new chief executive, quietly taking notes.

In the months that followed, Moyers remained on the Peace Corps payroll and talked wistfully about returning to his former job, but no one believed that Lyndon Johnson would let him go this time. The two men spent six to eight hours a day in each other's company, and Moyers invested countless additional hours running errands for the President or transacting business in his name.

They not only worked together, but ate together, joked together, planned together, and shared those few moments of relaxation that the President allowed himself. In the afternoons, Johnson liked to splash around in the White House pool without submitting to the inconvenience of bathing suits. Moyers joined in these skinny-dipping expeditions and felt not the slightest trace of embarrassment or awkwardness. It was, he insists, "the most natural thing in the world for a boy from East Texas. I didn't think that the ghost of Lincoln was offended."

During one such session in the White House swimming hole, the President talked of his desire for a dramatic new program that would help him emerge from Kennedy's shadow. With the election of 1964 rapidly approaching, the time had come for an ambitious departure to capture the imagination of the public. Out of this casual conversation grew the concept of the Great Society task forces—fourteen august assemblages of academics and officials who drew up specific proposals for sweeping domestic reforms. Moyers coordinated the entire scheme, recruiting the experts, keeping their deliberations harmonious and productive, and giving their recommendations a viable, practical shape. Johnson himself publicly credited his aide as the chief architect of the special messages and legislative packages with which the administration soon began bombarding Congress.

In the summer of 1964, after the Republicans nominated Barry Goldwater for the Presidency, Moyers turned his attention from the work of creating legislation to a task of political destruction. If Goldwater could be thoroughly discredited in the eyes of the public, the resulting LBJ landslide would speed passage of the President's Great Society program. With this goal in mind, Moyers could justify even the most savage electoral tactics. During the campaign he served as chief idea man for the Johnson forces, supervising all speechwriting and the development of national issues. He also acted as the White House contact for advance men in the field. Most importantly, he assembled the devastating Democratic ad campaign that tagged Barry Goldwater as a dangerous fanatic.

Working with advertising professionals at Doyle Dane Bernbach, Moyers found ingenious means to give visual expression to the public's persistent fears about the Arizona Senator. One TV spot, screened again and again before the election, featured two giant hands ripping up a Social Security card while the narrator discussed Goldwater's criticism of the Social Security system. Another ad made use of a foolish Goldwater remark condemning the eastern seaboard: it showed, in animated cartoon form, someone sawing off the eastern states from a map of the United States and letting them float out to sea. Such attacks had already placed the Republicans on the defensive when Moyers unleashed his ultimate weapon: a beautiful, blonde-haired child known as "the Daisy Girl." In this new Democratic ad, she plucked petals off a flower and mumbled happily to herself before dissolving ominously into the rumble and flash of a hydrogen bomb as a mushroom cloud filled the screen. The only line of narration urged the viewer to vote for Lyndon Johnson to keep humanity safe from nuclear war. Goldwater's name was never mentioned, but the message was clear: a vote for the allegedly trigger-happy Republican was a vote to wipe out the Daisy Girl in a global holocaust. After the ad's first showing on nationwide TV, Goldwater's managers immediately cried foul. Moyers agreed to delay further screenings pending public discussion of the controversy, knowing that this discussion would give invaluable free publicity to his anti-Goldwater themes. He barely complained when the Daisy Girl remained off the air.

The ruthless effectiveness of Moyers' TV campaign left a sour aftertaste with many observers. Particularly in view of Johnson's already massive lead, his instinct for the political jugular seemed somewhat overdeveloped. Today, Moyers regrets his excessive zeal. "The use of the television commercials to destroy Goldwater—that was one of my mistakes," he admits. "It was the product of immaturity, of quickness of judgment. Yes, it worked. But was it right? No, I don't think so. I wasn't right, and it wasn't necessary."

Though Moyers' conscience may have been strained by the campaign, he emerged at the end of the ordeal psychologically and physically intact. Unfortunately, the same could not be said for the President's other principal aide at the time, Walter Jenkins. For more than twenty-five years, Jenkins had subordinated his life to Johnson's and become an extension of the LBJ personality. While Moyers concentrated on substantive issues and the shaping of policy, Jenkins handled a mass of administrative details and served as an unobtrusive linchpin in the executive organization. With the extra burdens of the Presidential campaign, he pushed himself to the point of nervous collapse. On the evening of October 7, Washington police arrested this father of six for committing "perversion" with an elderly Army veteran in the men's room of the YMCA. It points up one of the ironies of an aide's position that Walter Jenkins remained totally unknown during his quarter century of devoted and effective service, but became an international celebrity after one night of personal disgrace. In the heat of a national campaign, no one even suggested that he be given another chance. "If Jenkins had remained we would have had a better team operation than we did," Moyers believes. "He was loyal and he was not a homosexual. He broke under immense pressure. I saw it coming. And had he stayed, Johnson would never have made that announcement from the Waldorf in New York—a statement he hadn't even cleared with me—saying, 'Bill Moyers is now Chief of Staff.'"

Such designations meant little to Lyndon Johnson—he had no sooner suggested the title than he seemed to forget about it completely. He never intended Moyers to act as a formal Chief of Staff in the Sherman Adams sense. The euphemism "Staff Coordinator," which Moyers himself used with the press, offered a better description of his role. It suggested the young Texan's unofficial leadership of a free-wheeling constellation of aides even less bound by flow charts than the men around Kennedy. "It is a remarkably cohesive group,'' Moyers told *U.S. News & World Report.* "The staff is like a basket-ball team. No one has a rigid position, and each man is able to handle the ball when it is in our part of the court and move it toward the goal.''

Despite the absence of an official chain of command, no one doubted Moyers' status as the star of the team. "He's in everything,'' the President admiringly declared. "That boy has a bleeding ulcer. He works for me like a dog, and is just as faithful. He never asks for anything—but for more work. . . . He won't go home with that bleeding ulcer until nine or ten o'clock. I don't know what I'd do without him.''

The press also found Moyers indispensable. Feature writers across the country, hungry, as always, for colorful copy, ground out endless stories about the youthful clergyman in the White House. They usually depicted him as a barefoot boy scout who had found his way, seemingly by accident, to Babylon on the Potomac. Some of these early accounts so exaggerated his innocence and piety that fundamentalists howled in protest when he was photographed dancing an energetic if inelegant watusi at one swank Washington bash. They might have been even more surprised to learn that the onetime preacher enjoyed sipping sherry, smoking imported cigars, and spicing his conversation with mild profanity. None of these worldly habits, nor Moyers' demonstrated mastery of political hardball, could stop the breathless paeans to his virtuous idealism. In a famous article in *Atlantic* magazine, Tom Wicker of the New York *Times* described Moyers as "Johnson's good angel" and declared him to be "the most able and influential Presidential assistant I have ever seen or read about.'' The press infatuation with Moyers involved even those reporters who disliked his boss. As one minor White House aide observed: "If Johnson did something the press approved they always assumed it was Moyers who had talked the old S.O.B. into giving Tiny Tim a Christmas present.'' The inflated notions of the assistant's role ultimately reached such a pitch that Art Buchwald felt called upon to satirize them in one of his columns. "Lyndon B. Johnson first came to Bill Moyers' attention about ten years ago when Bill discovered the tall, smiling Texan tucked away in a Senate office on Capitol Hill,'' Buchwald began. "Bill was immediately impressed by Johnson's spirit and willingness to do anything asked of him. 'Senator,' said Moyers, 'I think I can use you. . . .'''

Moyers' favorable coverage reflected the fact that he courted the press more assiduously and more effectively than any other White House aide in history. Over the years, seasoned journalists had become cynical about "the Johnson treatment''—that combination of intimidation, flattery, and sheer force of personality by which LBJ got what he wanted from his fellow human beings—but they seemed oblivious to the equally seductive "Moyers treatment.'' As one of his White House colleagues recalled, "Bill just made you feel so good when you were around him that you didn't care what he was doing.'' Moyers is an absolutely spellbinding talker whose slow, melodious drawl can make even the most mundane observations sound like well-considered pearls of wisdom. When you sit down to speak with him, you feel he is concentrating all of his considerable warmth and intelligence on you, that he cares about who you are and what you want, and that he would like to help you if he possibly can. According to a federal official with more than twenty years' experience, "I never knew anyone in the White House quite like Moyers. You find that most of the Presidential expediters, men like Adams and O'Donnell, get in the habit of running over people. 'I'm the President's man,' they say. 'Do what I tell you.' Moyers was the very opposite of that. He was always receptive, he always made time to discuss an issue, and he wanted to involve himself in issues that other White House people weren't interested in."

This does not mean that the Moyers' treatment worked on everyone. Even within the administration, a few individuals saw his soothing certainty as a form of arrogance and found his personalized attention to be merely patronizing. "I remember once he sat me down and talked to me like a child," recalls one of the Democratic advance men from the Presidential campaign. "He said, 'It's very important that you do a good job on this event, and if you do, I'm sure the President will notice you and he'll appreciate it.' What he was really saying was that I should do a good job so that it would reflect favorably on him. And the point was he never had to tell me anything like that in the first place. I knew. Here was this kid—in his twenties—telling me, an older man, that working for the President was serious and important and I had better do a good job. It was ludicrous."

The most important minority report on Moyers came from the pen of Eric Goldman, the Princeton historian who served on LBJ's staff as an in-house intellectual. Goldman ultimately left the White House in frustration over his own limited role and wrote a bitter, fascinating book called *The Tragedy of Lyndon Johnson*. In it he sketched a Moyers resented by his colleagues and called Elmer Gantry behind his back. According to Goldman, the conspiratorial nature and boundless ambition of the number one aide led him to monopolize the President's time and to isolate Johnson from other members of the staff.

Moyers emphatically denies these charges. "Contrary to wanting to keep people out, we wanted to bring people in. It would have eased the burden on us. It would have given us time to go home. It would have given us time to go drink with somebody else—other than Lyndon Johnson. For Eric, sitting over in the East Wing and waiting for things to happen, maybe it seemed desirable to see the President more often. But those of us who were with him day and night wanted to see him a good deal less. Honest to God! We were desperate to get our work done—and desperate to get away from the President."

The testimony of other White House veterans confirms Moyers' description of the President's consuming relationship with his top aides. "The closer you are to him the tougher it is," said a Kennedy holdover who worked several months for LBJ. "Frankly, he just doesn't recognize that you have a right to a private life." The President ordered all his senior aides to install special white telephones in their homes to connect them directly to the White House switchboard. They also carried two-way radios in their cars so that the boss could reach them at all times. Staff members often complained about the Orwellian, Big Brother atmosphere of the Johnson White House. "You just can't escape him," one of them moaned. LBJ used to wander through the offices of the West Wing late at night, pausing at the desks of his aides to read memos and letters left there at the end of the day.

Bill Moyers bore the brunt of these attentions and of Johnson's incessant demands for companionship. As a consequence, he enjoyed privileged standing with the President. As even Eric Goldman admitted, Moyers acquired the reputation "of being the only man in the inner circle who said no to Lyndon Johnson." His colleagues sometimes blinked in disbelief when this normally gentle-mannered aide stubbornly asserted himself with LBJ. "Bill would really go to the mat with him," one special assistant recalled. "I've seen them fighting like a couple of 10 year olds." These confrontations never threatened the essential security of Moyers' position. "Once you established a relationship with Johnson, even though it had its ups and downs, you knew he would never voluntarily sever it. I never had the fear that anybody else could be what I was to him."

Though Moyers showed little concern about losing his standing with the President he did worry constantly about losing his sense of self. Johnson had a habit of swallowing up those around him and destroying their independent identities. Moyers liked to think of himself as a shaping influence on Johnson, but reality might point to something else. As he sighed to a close friend in 1966: "The trouble is, he doesn't get more like me, I get more like him." To preserve a sense of sanity and wholeness, Moyers resorted to theological speculation. "Going through my mind constantly was the thought that this is transient, I won't be here long. At the most I'll be in the White House maybe four years, maybe eight. I knew, and partly this is the result of Christian teaching, that temporal power is totally transient and impermanent. The self isn't. The self is permanent. It stays. We don't even know what happens to the self when this life is over. I made a lot of mistakes in the White House, but I tried to keep that in mind at all times."

Another factor helping Moyers to keep his independence was the personality of his wife Judith. "My wife is the most remarkable person I've ever met. She is as strong as they come. She is her own person. She is against me. She is against anybody. When they invented the term liberation, they invented her to give it meaning." Naturally, this tough-minded woman resented Lyndon Johnson's attempts to dominate her family life. "There was a real contest of wills there. She liked him. She worked for him. She even campaigned for him. But she refused to be a Johnson girl."

One specific point of tension between Johnson and Judith involved the naming of the Moyers' third son in April 1964. The President wanted the boy named after him—"Lyndon Johnson Moyers" seemed to have a lovely ring to it. LBJ had long made a practice of presenting a calf from his ranch to any friends or employees who chose to name a child in his honor. He had already ordered a particularly beautiful animal for the Moyers family, but Judith had other ideas. She insisted on naming her child for her father and willingly passed up the promised beef.

Feeling cheated and disappointed, Johnson kept his resentment to himself for several months. After some persuasion, Judith had agreed to accompany Lady Bird on a whistle-stop swing through the Southern states, with Lyndon and Bill scheduled to join them for the last leg of the journey. She made the trip though her six-month-old baby remained in Johns Hopkins hospital with severe medical complications. In New Orleans, after the President and his party had boarded the train, Judith received word that her son had taken a turn for the worse. She decided to leave immediately, but that did not sit well with Johnson. He remembered her two previous miscarriages, which had distracted his top aide at inconvenient times, and recalled the controversy over the naming of the boy. As he came over to wish Judith goodbye, he draped a massive arm over her shoulders. "Honey," said the President of the United States, "you've just got to get out of this baby business."

The Moyers' boy eventually recovered but the mother's relationship with LBJ remained testy. "I think Johnson felt a grudging respect for her," Moyers ventures today. "Here was this Texas girl he simply couldn't co-opt or control." This did not mean that the President stopped trying. "He always wanted the wives with us at the state dinners. He'd always invite us. In fact, he became very sensitive to the fact that we didn't go very often. He would always ask us up to Camp David on the weekends, but we didn't want to go. Not because we didn't like him. But because we wanted some time to ourselves.

"Like anybody else who's ever worked in the White House, our relationship was very thin at one time. We were lucky that it survived. *I'm* lucky, because she had every reason to leave. You know, I was absent. I was preoccupied. I was obsessed. I was unreliable. I went through that crisis that every man goes through in regard to his wife, and his life, and all the doubts. And she stuck it out, and helped me a great deal in the most difficult time."

That difficult time began in the summer of '65 when Lyndon Johnson surprised the public and Moyers himself by naming his already overworked aide the new White House Press Secretary. He replaced long-suffering George Reedy, who needed surgery to correct a problem described as "painful hammer toes." It was no secret, however, that Reedy's departure had less to do with the condition of his feet than with the state of Lyndon Johnson's public image. As the escalation proceeded in Vietnam and the press began complaining of what came to be known as "the credibility gap," the President turned, almost inevitably to Moyers. After all, how could they question the word of an ordained preacher? It made instinctive good sense for the President to interpose the aide with the shining image between himself and his critics. Since Moyers had proven such a stunning success in handling his own press relations, he theoretically should be able to do the same for the President.

At first, the new arrangement worked remarkably well. Washington had never seen a Press Secretary like Moyers, who not only explained decisions but had a major hand in making them. As the acknowledged leader of the White House staff, he could speak with authority on any questions that might arise. Even on those rare occasions when he lacked some piece of information, he simply picked up the telephone, called the President, and provided a reporter with an answer straight from the top.

For these direct and authoritative responses, newsmen were grateful. They also liked Moyers' sense of humor about himself and his boss. A morning briefing during a Presidential vacation at the ranch, for instance, contained the following irreverent interchange:

> QUESTION: Where is the President this morning?
> MOYERS: He's out on the lake.
> QUESTION: Is he boating?
> MOYERS: No, he's taking a stroll.

Leading reporters continued to respect Moyers as a man of integrity even while they attacked administration duplicity on Vietnam. In fact, onetime journalist James Fallows, who went on to become Jimmy Carter's chief White House speechwriter, believes that Moyers' slick handling of the press served to prolong the war. "Intentionally or not, he helped to postpone the tide of criticism which finally drove Johnson from office. . . . Knowing what they did about his views on the war and respecting his character and abilities as much as they did, members of the liberal press (that is, the people who started hammering away on the war policies two years later) sensed that, as long as Bill was on the inside, the madmen couldn't have taken over."

As the war dragged on, Moyers found himself increasingly torn between his public role and his private doubts. Looking back, he cannot determine precisely when those doubts began. "You know, Vietnam just happened. That sounds naive to say, because I was there in the White House, making all the easy assumptions, espousing the line about why it was important, but then all of a sudden things happened that none of us knew about. We couldn't shape events in Vietnam. We couldn't shape events in this country. There were riots and all that. I think we'd become—not the actors, but the audience."

Moyers nevertheless continued his efforts to influence key decisions. By 1966 he had painstakingly assembled a network of officials throughout the bureaucracy who shared his doubts about the continuing escalation in Vietnam. Working with second-level appointees who would have been afraid to challenge their superiors directly, Moyers constructed a pipeline to provide the President with information and advice contrary to what he received through official channels. With the President's most trusted assistant in the pivot position, these Vietnam dissenters managed a daring end run around the Walt Rostows and Dean Rusks in the government. They insisted that the conflict could never be won militarily and that a negotiated settlement offered America's only hope. As one participant recalls: "These were people at State and on the NSC staff and elsewhere who were sticking their necks out—risking their jobs—to deal directly with Bill.''

Moyers faithfully presented their views and at the same time worked to curb his chief's emotional outbursts in dealing with critics of the war. One of Lyndon Johnson's most embarrassing public utterances—the speech in Chicago in which he used the term "Nervous Nellies" to describe those who questioned his policies—might well have been avoided had a heel stayed securely fastened to one of Moyers' shoes. Because of the defect in his footwear, the exhausted Press Secretary fell down the White House steps one afternoon and wound up in the hospital. He missed the scheduled trip to the Midwest and lost his opportunity to review the text of the President's speech. "If that phrase about 'Nervous Nellies' had been written into a script, I certainly would have edited it out. I did save LBJ from some of his own worst excesses—probably my biggest influence on him was a restraining influence. But what I don't know is whether that thought occurred to him at the moment, on the podium, or whether he planned it before he got up to speak.''

Moyers saw that Johnson's emotional investment in the war made him increasingly immune to rational argument. "What was happening in Vietnam inflicted great wounds on Lyndon Johnson," he remembers. "He didn't take casually the loss of lives—American or Vietnamese. He agitated and grieved. I saw him. I was there. I was there at 2:30 in the morning when the word came back about the first bombing of the petroleum facilities. We were waiting in the situation room downstairs for the reports. And he was really upset by the loss of two pilots—deeply upset. But in his own conscience he felt that what we were doing was right.''

That conviction eventually led him to view his Press Secretary's doubts as a form of betrayal. Their relationship remained as intimate as before, but Johnson began to express his hurt with bitter teasing. On several occasions, after calling Moyers into meetings already in progress, the President announced his entrance by snickering, "Here comes Stop-the-Bombing Bill." Meanwhile, Moyers watched the Great Society programs he had helped to initiate "paling in significance as they were scorched by the war.''

Wearying of the debilitating trivia of his Press Secretary's job, despairing of success in his efforts to alter policy, by mid-1966 Moyers hoped to move on to another position. When McGeorge Bundy resigned as National Security Advisor he felt he would be a suitable successor, but the appointment went to superhawk Walt Rostow. Moyers waged a more serious campaign for the job of Undersecretary of State following George Ball's departure. For weeks the Washington press—resolutely pro-Moyers, as usual—speculated that he would receive the appointment. But in the end, Lyndon Johnson resisted the idea of giving his young protégé an independent base of operations in the State Department. One morning as he was shaving, LBJ called Moyers on the phone. ''Bill, I don't want you over there,'' he announced. "I want you here with me.'' That settled the matter. With his escape routes blocked, Moyers' only chance to end his servitude was to leave the government entirely.

That radical possibility seemed increasingly attractive after a disaster in his personal life in September 1966. Moyers had always been close to his older brother James and a few months after the election he managed to secure him a job in the White House. James gave up twelve years of security as advertising manager at a Texas sulfur company to share in the excitement of the Great Society. James struck everyone he met as "pleasant," but he obviously lacked his brother's brilliance and drive. He had a difficult time adjusting to Washington life and found himself consigned to relatively trivial White House tasks, such as reviewing the President's mail or backing up Bill at press conferences. As Moyers recalls, "He probably felt somewhat in the shadow of a younger brother, and that is awfully hard to take."

On September 16, before reaching his fortieth birthday, James killed himself. The tragedy could hardly have come at a worse time for Moyers. "Scarcely had his funeral been over than I had to leave to advance Lyndon Johnson's Far Eastern journey. I was gone two and a half weeks. I came back on a Saturday, and that Sunday I had to leave again—this time going with the President on the same trip I had just taken. So there, a few weeks after his death, with scarcely the time to console my kin, much less myself, I was off. I was fatigued. I was physically at the end of my endurance capacity. I was also emotionally wrought. Not only because I had loved him, but because I suddenly realized how, there at the end, he had been reaching out for me and I was so damned busy that I didn't know it. And I was determined that this would never happen to me again. If anyone else had some need of me, I would be there."

Among those who needed Moyers most in the fall of 1966 were his brother's widow and children. Bill felt financially responsible for their support and so for the first time the size of his income became an important consideration. His $30,000 White House salary seemed suddenly inadequate. As Moyers remembers, "It all just came together"—the questions about Vietnam, the frustration in his position, the death of his brother, and the new financial worries—to persuade him to turn his back on the seemingly indestructible relationship with Lyndon Johnson. Some months before, Captain Harry Guggenheim, elderly owner of the Long Island journal *Newsday,* proposed that the Press Secretary leave the White House to take over his newspaper. In November, Moyers decided to accept the offer, and with it a salary nearly three times what he had earned in Washington.

It remained to break the news to Lyndon Johnson. Moyers resolved to do so in writing, sending a letter by courier to the LBJ ranch where the President relaxed over Thanksgiving weekend. Johnson called him immediately, and without making reference to the contents of the letter, ordered him to fly down to Texas for Thanksgiving day. Moyers refused: he had already planned a traditional holiday meal with his family in Washington and his brother's death left him particularly sensitive to the importance of such occasions.

The day after Thanksgiving he flew to the Presidential retreat and spent all of Saturday talking with Johnson. "We rode around in a jeep on the ranch for seven hours. We got out and walked around a lot, looked at the deer, looked at the cattle, and went to a couple of the ranch houses. Mrs. Johnson joined us for a while but the rest of the time we were alone, and the President drove. He rambled on in that inconsistent pattern of his which has a purpose hidden at its devious center. He seemed to be resigned about my leaving, but depressed. As I look back now, it wasn't my leaving. It was the whole developing phenomenon that, as Gabriel says in *Green Pastures,* 'Everything that's tied down is coming loose.' And he said to me, 'A lot of my critics will say I can't keep you. They'll say that you're closest to me and that your leaving is personal.' We talked about the war. I said I was troubled. And he said, 'If what I've done in Vietnam works—that is, if the Communists do not end up in control of South Vietnam—then fifty years from now I will be seen as the President who literally stayed the course of history. But if the Communists wind up in control then I will be seen as the President who gambled and lost.'"

Several times during their long conversation, Johnson discussed Moyers' career. "He kept trying to tell me that I should come back to Texas and make a lot of money. He said, 'Once you are independent you can run for Congress. You know, you can be Senator from Texas one day.'" It was long after dark before the President had talked himself out and parked his jeep in front of the main ranch house. "His last words were, 'If you feel you have to do it, then you go with my blessings.' He said that to me, but he instantly forgot it."

The evening after Moyers' resignation became official, columnist Drew Pearson sat with the President in his bedroom watching the Press Secretary's farewell statement replayed on the network news. According to Pearson, Johnson wept as he saw it, wailing bitterly that his aide had "sold out" to the Kennedys. Within a few weeks, the President had rewritten history to suit his emotional needs. He told a group of *Life* magazine correspondents that Moyers had never been genuinely close to him and had done a miserable job handling the press. "When he became my press secretary, my popularity was at an all-time high, and nobody ever heard of Bill Moyers," the President claimed. "When he left, I was at an all-time low and Bill Moyers was a world hero."

After Johnson retired from the White House, his version of events strayed even further from reality. He began talking with friends about "the day I fired that boy Moyers." During his four years of retirement on the LBJ ranch, he refused to even consider a reconciliation. His stubborn, paranoiac hostility resembled Woodrow Wilson's bitterness toward Colonel House following their break in 1919. For both Presidents, the emotional overreaction to strains in the relationship reflected the depth of their dependence on that one, idolized aide—a dependence that transcended practical and rational considerations. Doris Kearns, LBJ's intimate during the last years of his life and later his biographer, reported: "He just couldn't talk about Bill in the same jaunty tone he would use to denounce other people. . . . He had such feeling and trust and caring for Bill that it was different when he spoke of him. He would talk about Bill as you would talk about a really good person who had fallen into evil hands."

Moyers' feelings for Johnson kept him on the sidelines during the dramatic election of 1968. At one point, key supporters of Eugene McCarthy's antiwar crusade came to the former Press Secretary and asked him to manage their campaign. A few weeks later Robert Kennedy, considering his own challenge to Lyndon Johnson, ate lunch with Moyers and inquired about his availability to run a possible Kennedy campaign. To both offers, Moyers gave an unequivocal no. He refused to lend substance to Lyndon Johnson's fantasies of betrayal.

LBJ's departure from the White House liberated Moyers from guilt and hesitation in opposing the war. Since he entertained no personal affection for Richard Nixon, he could attack the foreign policy of the new administration with abandon. He spoke at the Vietnam Moratorium in 1969 and composed a series of strongly worded editorials, thereby managing to offend his employer, Captain Guggenheim. The owner of *Newsday* admired President Nixon and continued to support American involvement in Southeast Asia. Moyers' management had won the newspaper two Pulitzer prizes and transformed *Newsday* into a nationally respected journal, but Guggenheim could not overlook the young man's liberal heresies. These political differences ultimately led to Moyers' resignation in May 1970. Despite numerous prospects in journalism and politics, Moyers told the press at the time of his departure that he would take time off "to think for a while about what I can do."

This brief interruption in his normally hectic pace resulted in a remarkable book. For several months, Moyers traveled the side roads and superhighways of the heartland talking with citizens in every conceivable situation about their feeling for America and its problems. If any doubt remained about his gifts as a communicator, then the publication of *Listening to America* surely erased it. The book won a substantial popular audience at the same time it pleased the critics as a haunting evocation of the national mood.

In 1971, Moyers discovered the ideal outlet for his conversational skills—a regular show on public television. After long years of travail, the wanderer had finally arrived. The New York *Times* hailed *Bill Moyers' Journal* as "one of the most outstanding series on television," while Richard Schickel wrote in *Time* that its star was "television's best regularly scheduled observer of the American scene." Because of his new media exposure, Moyers emerged as a public personality in his own right and not simply "a former aide to President Johnson." Among previous White House assistants, only Cortelyou and Clifford had achieved a similar state of independent celebrity.

According to Moyers, the secret of his success is his unabashed enjoyment of his work. "I have used television as a postgraduate course in the education of Bill Moyers. There are people handsomer, more charming or more articulate, with a better voice and a better face. But something happens in most of these programs that I do. I'm taking an adventure. I ask the audience to come along with me. I think that's why it's worked." After five years at public television—the longest period of continuous employment in his life—Moyers switched to CBS to accept new challenges. As chief reporter of the *CBS Re-*

ports documentary series, he hoped to win an even larger audience while commanding greater resources for the production of his shows. By 1978, however, disputes with the network over scheduling the series brought about his departure and a return to public TV.

A dazzling array of alternatives confronts Bill Moyers as he contemplates his future. Some of his friends continue to hope that he will someday be a candidate for public office—Senator from New York is the post most frequently mentioned. Appointive office is also a lively possibility, and in the early days of the Carter Presidency his name came up for a variety of top positions. After Ted Sorensen withdrew from consideration as Director of the CIA, Moyers was even rumored to be a potential substitute. Somewhat to his relief, the idea never went beyond a brief flurry of publicity. "My business today is my sense of self, not politics," he says. "Not—'How do you take a policy and shape it into legislation—or a war?' but 'How do you take a life and make something of it?'"

"As a young man I was ambitious, driven by that Protestant, Calvinist ethic which says that success is the result of virtue—that you must do good, you must save the world. It's precisely that sort of compulsion that sometimes worries me about Jimmy Carter. Today, I'm either wise enough or cynical enough to realize that I can't save the world, and can't really make that pivotal difference. There's been an evolution in me from an antiseptic, impersonal sense of contribution to a realization that what really counts are personal relationships."

For Moyers, those relationships are too important to mix them up with politics. "I was too close to Lyndon Johnson. I would have been a far greater servant of the Republic had I been more distant from him and not caught up in all of the nuances of a personal relationship. You may know your brother is a scoundrel, you may know he's a womanizer, you may know he's a misshapen human being. But you never turn on him. And why? Because that's the nature of things. Personal loyalty counts in the long run more than anything else. And I think that probably happened to me with Johnson. Certainly, it reduced my effectiveness. The fact that you are intimate with the President, that you share his innermost life and are part of his personal family and not just his official family, can weaken or obviate your arguments on policy. That's not good. If Jimmy Carter is wise, he will make sure that on his staff, with equal standing and access to him, are people who have not been close to him for the last ten years."

Having dispensed that advice, Moyers will leave it to others to implement it in the White House. He has no desire to repeat himself or to try to recapture the glories of his past. He does not even enjoy looking back, because he is too absorbed with taking the next step on his journey. "Lyndon Johnson used to tell me that I worked too hard. He would always say that just before giving me ten new chores to do! I can hear him now, 'If you keep working the way you do, you're gonna be dead before you're forty.'

"Well," Moyers drawls, and smiles with satisfaction, "I've already proved him wrong by a couple of years."

H. R. Haldeman:
The Zero Defects Man

In the months just before he went to jail Bob Haldeman spent most of his time at home. The reporters who used to camp outside his door had long since departed and the stately, Tudor-revival mansion provided a sense of tranquillity and refuge. On the Monday morning of our interview, his shady street in an exclusive Los Angeles neighborhood was absolutely deserted except for a single Japanese gardener tending the lawn of the house next door.

Haldeman answered the doorbell himself and ushered me through a dining room where an enormous, half-completed jigsaw puzzle covered most of a long oak table. Assembling this idealized vision of the Venice canals from several thousand tiny pieces was, as he described it, "a family project." The den where we sat down looked out on a spacious patio and had clearly been de-signed for comfort rather than for style. It contained an electric organ and a massive, good-natured hound named Rufus. The dog, a purebred Rhodesian Ridgeback, began sniffing and whining to greet the visitor, but when Haldeman snapped his fingers he fell to the floor and cowered. On one wall of the family room hung a framed needlepoint of two opossums kissing one another beneath a vivid red heart; the caption honored "Bob and Jo" on the occasion of their wedding anniversary. This was hardly the sort of art to please Manhattan sophisticates, but even the most cultivated visitor to the Haldeman home would have approved of the titles on the bookshelves. These included well-worn vol-umes by Toynbee, Solzhenitsyn, Dickens, Tolstoy, Pasternak, Dostoyevsky, Malraux, Shaw and even "White House enemy" Gore Vidal. According to Washington gossip, Haldeman read nothing aside from marketing reports, enemy lists and inspirational pamphlets from his Christian Science Church, so the range of his home library seemed somewhat surprising. He laughed out loud at that observation. "What would you expect me to have up there, *Mein Kampf?* It's there too, if you want to look for it. By the way, I also have a copy of *The Rise and Fall of the Third Reich.*"

If there is a bitter edge to his humor Bob Haldeman is entitled. Next to Richard Nixon himself he is probably the most unpopular man in America. On occasion, strangers have recognized him on the street and yelled obscenities and threats of violence as he passed. "I never let that hatred bother me," he says. "I can't let it bother me because it's not personal. It comes from people

304

who don't know me.'' Yet millions of Americans believe they know him—as an arrogant, fanatical California stormtrooper who precipitated the worst scandal in the nation's history. Haldeman makes far too convenient a villain in the Watergate melodrama to allow for subtle shadings in our perceptions of him. When he walks on stage, everyone hisses—even that dwindling band of diehard Nixon loyalists who blame him for the downfall of their chief. *The National Review,* while sharing Haldeman's conservative philosophy, thought nothing of running a review of his memoirs that casually linked him to the Nazis. The author of that piece was none other than Charles Colson, the former master of political hardball who now campaigns for Jesus Christ with the same ruthless intensity he once reserved for Richard Nixon's reelection effort. ''Haldeman's book,'' Colson declared, ''reminds me of what we would have read if Adolf Hitler had survived World War II and written his memoirs from Spandau prison. He knew nothing; the system blew a gasket; and anyway, it was all Goering's fault.'' The trouble with that passage—aside from its questionable source—is its absurd suggestion that Haldeman, and not Richard Nixon, played the role of ''Fuehrer'' in the Watergate White House. This is an idea so manifestly ludicrous that not even the most paranoid connoisseur of conspiracy theories—and not even the ex-President himself—could seriously defend it.

Similar distortions and exaggerations seem to appear whenever Haldeman's name is mentioned in print. Perhaps the most influential portrayal of his White House years was provided by Dan Rather and Gary Paul Gates in their bestseller *The Palace Guard.* This entertaining, partisan polemic heaps contempt not only on Haldeman's political maneuvers but on his professional background, his family attachments, his religion, and even his hobbies. They mention, for instance, that Haldeman used to enjoy sailing, an activity that always seemed wholesome and romantic enough when associated with liberal heroes like John Kennedy and Franklin Roosevelt. But when Haldeman sailed, write Rather and Gates, he did so ''in a style suggesting a man going through brisk close order drill. Friends from Newport Beach say he would often just get in his boat and proceed in a crisp straight line to a predetermined point, then abruptly turn around and sail right back again. Not exactly the way it's done, but at least he could put himself on record as having given himself an outing.'' No matter how distasteful his political philosophy, is it not possible that Bob Haldeman sincerely enjoyed boating with his family on the blue Pacific? Whatever his ethical shortcomings, is it not possible he is an essentially well-meaning person? Unless we approach Haldeman as a human being rather than a caricature we can learn nothing from his White House experience. At last, more than six years after his resignation as Chief of Staff, the time has arrived for a balanced view of the man. We must begin to examine his contributions as well as his crimes, and see him as a complex combination of sanity and blindness, strength and weakness, like all of his predecessors.

One of the ''facts'' that virtually everyone knows about Bob Haldeman is that he springs from German origins. Back in the days when he ruled the White House in collaboration with John Ehrlichman and Henry Kissinger, all America joked about "the Teutonic Trio," "The Berlin Wall," "The Katzenjammer Kids," or "All the King's Krauts." Haldeman notes that such remarks, if directed at Americans of any other nationality, would have been condemned as "ethnic slurs." He also points out that in reality his ancestry isn't German. The Haldemans came originally from Switzerland and they have lived in the United States for at least five generations. During that time they intermarried with Americans of so many backgrounds that the most celebrated of Richard Nixon's "Nazis" could never have met Hitler's standards of Aryan purity.

"There was no sort of ethnic consciousness while I was growing up," he remembers. "My grandparents on both sides were born in Indiana and then came to California. If we had any sense of self-identification it was as Californians—which can be a strong group identity in itself." Haldeman's paternal grandfather established a moderately successful plumbing supply business and helped to found the Better America Foundation, one of Southern California's first anti-Communist organizations. In time, this patriarch passed on to his son Bud the family business and a set of conservative principles. Along with this solid Republicanism, the dominant influence in the Haldeman household was Christian Science. Bud's wife, a recognized leader and practitioner in the church, eventually converted her Presbyterian husband to the teachings of Mary Baker Eddy.

Harry Robbins Haldeman, the oldest of their three children, was born on October 27, 1926. From earliest childhood he was called Bob in much the same way that his father, whose given name was also Harry, had been called Bud. During his early years at school Bob proved something of a problem child, doing consistently poor work despite high scores on his aptitude tests. His teachers cited a lack of self-discipline and recommended that he transfer to a local military academy. In this new, tightly structured environment Bob's performance immediately improved. He particularly excelled at mathematics, Latin, and the sciences. A psychohistorian would point out that this early crisis and its solution—in which crisp, military concepts of order rescued him from indolence and confusion—left a lasting mark on Haldeman's character.

Graduating from high school at the height of World War II, Bob signed up for the Navy's V-12 program and went on to college to prepare himself as an officer. The Navy sent him to the University of Redlands and USC before he settled on UCLA for his last two years. By that time the war was over and Haldeman could devote himself to the pleasures of campus and fraternity life without worrying about his military obligations. Other members of the Class of '48 remember him "running around in saddle shoes and a cashmere sweater, ushering at pep rallies and silly stuff like that." His own recollections highlight his service as "Homecoming Chairman and Chairman of the All-U-Sing, which put on a monthly musical variety show. I was also active in Gold Key, the University Religious Conference, and the California Club Council." These momentous responsibilities naturally left him little time for his studies or for an interest in the larger world beyond the university.

Like most campus leaders of his generation, Haldeman proudly squired one steady girl to all major social events: the pretty, athletic Joanne Horton. She had been a friend of his younger sister and his regular date since he was 17. When they married the year after Bob finished college both families were delighted. Their union, producing four talented children and lasting thirty years, has been the greatest triumph of Haldeman's life. Nevertheless, he finds it difficult to talk about his wife or to say what drew him to her in the first place. "That's the kind of subject I never spend much time analyzing," he declares. For the most part, Joanne Haldeman has played the traditional role of a suburban wife and mother, working as a girl scout leader, member of the junior league, and pillar of a social work agency called the Neighborhood Youth Association.

The career that made possible this volunteer activity, as well as the Haldeman's steady rise through a succession of comfortable homes, began modestly enough. In 1949, Bob went to work for $35 a week as a "tabulator in the consumer panel division" of the J. Walter Thompson advertising agency in New York. He climbed gradually within the organization and was transferred to the San Francisco office and eventually back to Los Angeles. Over the years he administered accounts such as Seven-Up, Blue Chip Stamps, Walt Disney Productions, Blue Cross, and Douglas Aircraft. No one considered him an advertising genius, but his administrative skills impressed his superiors. Eventually, he won promotion to the post of manager of J. Walter Thompson's L.A. office and became a vice-president of the firm. This position of eminence brought with it a salary of $42,500 and entree into a large number of community service activities. Haldeman became a national vice-president of Junior Achievement, chairman of the board of the California Institute of the Arts, and a trustee of the Coro Foundation. The onetime homecoming chairman reserved his best efforts, however, for the service of his alma mater: he was elected president of the UCLA Alumni Association and won a sixteen-year term on the Board of Regents of the University of California.

Haldeman recites these impressive credits almost defensively in an effort to rebut the charge that he was obsessed by Richard Nixon and allowed his devotion to another man's career to dominate his life. "I hardly had any contact with Nixon except during election campaigns. My alumni work at UCLA, my position at Cal Arts, had nothing to do with Nixon. I think I was an unusually well-rounded and diversified person, totally apart from any involvement in politics."

That involvement developed from the same factors that drew Haldeman to his other volunteer commitments: a general sense of restlessness with his job and the desire for involvement in a worthy cause. But why Nixon, of all the politicians he might have chosen as deserving of his help? An enormous amount of nonsense has been written to try to answer this question and explain

Haldeman's allegedly fanatical attraction to his future boss. One of the most persistent stories, repeated in virtually dozens of books and articles, suggests that Haldeman's father contributed $18,000 to the top-secret "Nixon Fund" that played such a controversial role in the campaign of 1952. This account is totally false, but it is easy to understand the origins of the mistake. The official list of contributors to the Nixon Fund includes the name of one Henry E. Haldemen, a well-known car dealer and Republican activist. He bore no relation to Bob or his father—in fact, he spelled his last name differently—but such petty distinctions have not deterred countless enterprising journalists in quest of good copy.

The true story of Haldeman's connection with Nixon is far more prosaic than the lurid accounts of passionate hero worship or inherited admiration. Bob was a California Republican and Richard Nixon was the rising young star of the California Republican Party, so Haldeman inevitably developed a certain interest in his career. What's more, he liked the fighting spirit Nixon displayed during the Alger Hiss affair and in the midst of the controversy over the Nixon Fund in 1952. The night that the Republican Vice-Presidential nominee vindicated himself with the celebrated Checkers Speech, Haldeman joined a crowd outside the TV studio to cheer the candidate and show his support. He found himself so moved by the occasion that he scribbled a note to Senator Nixon offering his services as a volunteer in the campaign. The candidate, who apparently had more important matters on his mind, failed to respond, thereby delaying Haldeman's entry into politics by four years. When he next contacted Nixon in the summer of 1956 the line of approach was more direct: Haldeman happened to know a young lady who worked in the Vice-President's office. She put him in touch with the head advance man, who accepted his offer of help. The question of why he once again went to Nixon poses no deep mysteries. "He was from California. He was the Vice-President. And I didn't know anybody who worked in the office of anybody else."

In the campaign that followed, Haldeman discovered that he was a born advance man. The same gift for organizational detail that had helped make him a success in the advertising business enabled him to do a first-rate job in arranging Nixon rallies and public appearances. "I readily confess to not having done it out of a sense of duty. I did it because I wanted to. I liked the action. The excitement. The feeling of participation in something big and important. It was a change from anything I'd been doing before." His enthusiasm and competence so thoroughly impressed the professionals on Nixon's staff that they asked his help again two years later in arranging the Vice-President's extensive campaign tours for Republican Congressional candidates. By 1960, Haldeman had established himself as the top advance man in the Nixon entourage. With the candidate gearing up for his first run for the Presidency, he recruited Haldeman for the job of "tour director." This meant taking a year's leave of absence from his work at J. Walter Thompson and for the first time accepting a salary for his political efforts. "I was on the campaign plane every inch of the way,'' Haldeman recalls. "I was never more than ten feet away from Richard Nixon during the entire 1960 campaign and I was responsible, minute by minute, for the implementation of his daily schedule.''

After the cliff-hanger loss to John Kennedy, Haldeman remained part of Nixon's personal entourage. "He did some traveling as a private citizen to make speeches and that kind of thing. I handled some of the plans for those trips and traveled with him as an aide. It was a perfectly natural thing, I mean having run his campaign travels. Without the panoply of the Vice-Presidency, without the staff from the campaign, it was just the two of us plodding around the country. Obviously, that sort of proximity builds a strong personal relationship.'' As with Ted Sorensen, who had joined John Kennedy on his lonely pre-primary wanderings in 1959, the role of faithful traveling companion to a future President paved the way to White House power.

When the Nixons finally returned to California, Haldeman helped them in finding a new home and settling down to life in Los Angeles. He naturally hoped that his patron would make a political comeback, but urged him not to run for the California governorship in 1962. "I was still asking him not to run all the way down the corridor to the room where he made his announcement. I lost that one—and, having lost, agreed to manage his campaign.'' It would be wrong to hold Haldeman responsible for the disastrous results of that race— Nixon himself deserves most of the blame—but the campaign manager did concur in nearly all of the fatal mistakes. In the grim aftermath of defeat, following the public humiliation of Nixon's "Last Press Conference,'' Haldeman shared the general assumption that his boss had destroyed himself as a national political figure. Since no other candidates came clamoring for his services, he resigned himself to a return to the world of advertising. Critics later labeled him "a perfect Madison Avenue type,'' but Haldeman could never win the satisfaction he craved by selling soft drinks or cleanser to the gullible public. Nor were his superiors at J. Walter Thompson particularly pleased by his performance. "There was this huge growth period and our L.A. office was stagnant,'' recalls his New York chief. "He knew we were discontented with him.'' It took Nixon's renewed interest in the Presidency to rescue Haldeman's career from the doldrums. After the Republican victory in 1968, his wife expressed her sense of relief. "Thank goodness Nixon won,'' she declared, "because now Bob will have something to devote his life to.''

From the beginning, Haldeman had helped shape the strategies that made that triumph possible. In the fall of 1967, while still toiling full time at J. Walter Thompson, he prepared a memo for Nixon on the use of media in the coming campaign. "The time has come,'' he wrote, "for political campaigning—its techniques and strategies—to move out of the dark ages and into the brave new world of the omnipresent eye.'' He urged Nixon to cut down drastically on coast-to-coast barnstorming and concentrate on reaching the public through the carefully controlled and structured use of television. By following these recommendations, the candidate created the cool, deliverate image of a "New

Nixon'' and managed to bring off what one reporter called ''the most amazing comeback since the Resurrection.'' After Nixon proved himself a viable candidate in the primaries, Haldeman left J. Walter Thompson permanently and joined the campaign. He implemented his public relations ideas as the candidate's personal chief of staff and coordinator of his schedule, while John Mitchell ran the political organization.

After the election Nixon asked Haldeman to continue as his principal aide with the official title ''Chief of Staff.'' This job designation had not been chosen by accident. It had last been used in the White House by Sherman Adams back in the days of the Eisenhower administration; to Richard Nixon, nearly everything about the Presidency of General Ike seemed worthy of emulation. What's more, the Chief of Staff concept particularly suited his own emotional needs. For a politician, Nixon remained strangely uncomfortable in face-to-face interaction with his fellow human beings. He preferred to deal with a single trusted coordinator who would transmit his wishes than to open his office doors to a large group of eager assistants.

Haldeman prepared for his new role more conscientiously than any of his predecessors. He read everything he could get his hands on about the history of the White House staff but found himself frustrated by the lack of comprehensive information, particularly concerning Presidential aides before FDR. His investigations did lead him to restore one suspended practice from the past— formally structured staff meetings to begin each working day. Not surprisingly, Haldeman once again used Sherman Adams as his model; he even referred to these meetings as ''Sherman Adams-type gatherings.'' With the Chief of Staff seated at the head of the table, the senior aides ''went around the room and everybody filled everybody else in on whatever was important in his area.'' The purpose, as John Dean expressed it, was to ''flush up matters the President's top-level aides thought he should be thinking about that day. . . .'' At the conclusion of each meeting, Haldeman went in alone to see Nixon and summarize for him what had been discussed.

Though he admired the ruthless efficiency Sherman Adams brought to the White House, Haldeman did not attempt to duplicate the Eisenhower operation in every detail. Adams, for instance, relied heavily on telephone communication while Haldeman preferred that all information for him or for the President be put in writing. This same desire for a complete and accurate record, this same fear of forgetfulness and human frailty, ultimately led Haldeman and his boss to install an elaborate taping system in the White House with results that the whole world came to know. During the first months of Nixon's Presidency, however, the Chief of Staff contented himself with a yellow legal pad— Nixon's own favorite organizing tool. For important meetings in the Oval Office, Haldeman invariably sat in as official notetaker, leaving a wide margin on the left of his pad for progress notes on the points of business raised. ''It's my role to see that whatever is decided at meetings is followed up,'' he told *Newsweek*. ''I channel the stuff and keep things going.''

In order to "keep things going," Haldeman used memos to ride herd on his subordinates. Any request from his desk always included a specific deadline for response, a procedure that White House speechwriter Bill Safire found "annoying at times, but necessary." Nor did Haldeman waste time in acting on memos that flowed in his direction: the simple procedure of checking the "approved" or "disapproved" box at the top of the paper saved him from countless meetings and explanations. "He had a fetish about memos," recalls his onetime assistant Jeb Magruder. "One of the first ones I sent him was returned with orders that it be retyped because of some minor defect in style—his name wasn't capitalized or something like that. He usually scribbled comments in the margin when he returned a memo to you, and we all awaited his comments like kids awaiting their report card. A 'Good thinking' or 'Excellent' could make your week, while a 'No!' or 'See Me!' could cast you into despair."

Haldeman's terse notes to his underlings became the stuff of White House legend. Once he returned a memorandum to a junior aide with only the cryptic inscription "TL². " It took the young man several days to work up the nerve to ask Haldeman what it meant. "Too little, too late," snapped the Chief of Staff. On another occasion, a carefully prepared memo went to Haldeman suggesting that the President place a personal call to a Republican Senator who lay in the hospital mortally ill. The Chief of Staff concluded it would be a pointless gesture inasmuch as the dying legislator hardly had the strength to talk on the phone. The President could invest his time more wisely, Haldeman reasoned, if he placed a condolence call to the widow after the Senator passed away. The memo went back down through channels, with a brief message in Haldeman's crisp, decisive hand: "Wait until he dies." In every corner of the bureaucracy, officials came to recognize the emphatic "H" with which he signed all his notes and memoranda. According to one of his friends, he used the single letter because his full initials, "H.R.H.," could be too easily ridiculed as an abbreviation for "His Royal Highness."

Haldeman may have avoided the initials of royalty, but he missed few of its other prerogatives. The practical, logistical problems that plagued other mortals never worried Haldeman; he had the constant assistance of the Secret Service and the General Services Administration to make his life smooth and effortless. During visits to California with the President, for example, he liked to stay at a family house on Lido Isle, about 35 miles north of San Clemente. Each morning, a Coast Guard launch picked him up at the island and carried him across a small bay to a waiting car and a short drive to a Presidential helicopter. He then flew to a landing pad within a few miles of the Western White House, where another car picked him up and whisked him to the President's side to begin his working day. This elaborate process employed six men and four government vehicles for nearly an hour. Haldeman continued to travel to San Clemente in this manner until midway in Nixon's first term, when he discovered that simply driving the freeways and dispensing with the helicopter would bring him to work several minutes earlier.

Haldeman received the same privileged treatment in Washington that he did in California. Every morning when he arrived at his spacious White House office he found a cheerful fire crackling in the grate; the White House maintenance crew lit it and tended it at his request. Haldeman believed that the fire gave a homey touch to his office, as did the California-style patio he ordered built beyond the glass doors. He feels a powerful nostalgia for these minor amenities, as he does for the White House desk he designed personally. "I've never liked sitting behind a big, flat desk in the middle of a room. I've always worked with a desk against the wall. So I had the General Services Administration build a special desk to my specifications—a huge thing, that went most of the way up to the ceiling. On top it had bookshelves and closed cabinets, an intercom, built-in speakers for piped-in Muzak, and a special lighting system above the work area. Then on the bottom were a lot of storage drawers designed for the big Presidential certificates which I had to stack up to take in to the President to sign. I also had a system of small drawers—whole rows of them—sort of like in and out boxes. I used them for filing stuff on my action subjects. It was a personalized system and a personalized desk." Haldeman would like to acquire this particular piece of government property and move it into his home, but he believes it is still being used somewhere in the White House. More than one hundred years ago Lincoln's former aide John Nicolay succeeded in buying his White House desk from the government as a memento of his service, but the circumstances of Haldeman's departure would make a similar transaction considerably more difficult.

The external trappings of power—the lavish office, the limousines, helicopters, and armies of personal aides—all seemed deliberately designed to convince skeptics of Haldeman's lordly position at the top of the federal bureaucracy. He had good reason, of course, for insecurity: before beginning work at the White House he had never spent so much as a day in government service. His name was virtually unknown to Washington insiders and during Nixon's first year in office several leading journals even got it wrong. *The New Republic* referred to him as "Robert Haldeman" while *Newsweek* wrote of "Harold Robbins Haldeman"—apparently suggesting that Nixon's Chief of Staff had been named after the best-selling author of *The Carpetbaggers*. After the inauguration, this obscure, soft-spoken advertising man from the provinces was suddenly supposed to assert himself with some of the Capitol's most seasoned politicos. No wonder he felt a need to impress the world with his importance.

Haldeman concedes that his demeanor "changed one hundred per cent" when he arrived at the White House but insists that the transformation was necessary. "I was tough because I had to be tough. In the White House you don't have the luxury of time. You're not building for the long haul, the way you are in business. And I felt that we couldn't tolerate many mistakes. On that basis, I'm sure I created the impression of great hardheartedness and perhaps even joy when I had to come down on people."

Haldeman is certainly correct about the impression he created, though he continues to think of himself as "a nice guy." *Time* magazine pictured him as "Spiky and glaring . . . the 'zero defects' man who bosses the White House staff, the all-knowing assistant President of legendary arrogance, efficiency, and power." Many of the stories about Haldeman's style of command show that he gave the press abundant basis for this sort of portrait. His orders at times had little to do with substantive questions of administration and a good deal to do with building an aura of invincible authority around an insecure newcomer to Washington. Aboard Air Force One, for example, he received a rock-hard dinner roll and immediately decided to do something about it. Scribbling a note of complaint, signed with the single intimidating "H," he stapled it to the roll and sent it to the captain's cabin. The bread on Presidential flights quickly improved.

Such displays of temper had their desired effect. One junior staffer observed that "If Haldeman and the President were making simultaneous demands on me, I'd do what Haldeman asked first." Jeb Magruder, another hard-pressed subordinate, recalls that "He could chew you out with class. . . . Once he had gotten his point across he would proceed to other business. It was nothing personal; just a tactic to keep people on their toes. If you really displeased him you'd simply discover one day that you no longer worked at the White House."

One of the reasons that administration operatives endured Haldeman and his demands so cheerfully was that a good number of them owed their presence on the staff to his sponsorship. Never before in history had one man succeeded in placing so many of his personal protégés in top White House positions. John Ehrlichman, who had been Bob's good friend since college, became the President's Counsel and domestic policy chief. Press Secretary Ron Ziegler and Appointments Secretary Dwight Chapin had both served under Haldeman at J. Walter Thompson. Other alumni of the L.A. advertising firm who found their way to top White House jobs were Larry Higby, Ken Cole, and Bruce Kehrli. Members of the Eisenhower staff may have reveled in their designation as "Sherm's Boys," but they were never beholden to Adams in quite the same way as the battalion of ambitious, clean-cut Californians who surrounded Haldeman. To more sophisticated Washington observers they became known as "The Beaver Patrol"—both for their boy scout enthusiasm and their eagerness to please the Chief of Staff. They even dressed in imitation of Haldeman, favoring conservative ties, gray, thin-lapelled suits, and black shoes with a military shine. All White House aides kept their hair closely cropped and neatly combed, though none of them went as far as Haldeman did with his severe and bristling crew cut.

Haldeman seemed to welcome the public attention that focused on his closely shaven skull: by grooming himself like a Marine drill sergeant he expressed his profound distaste for the antiwar longhairs and everything they stood for. Fortunately, he maintained the ability to laugh at his determinedly unstylish haircut. His son Hank, a student at UCLA, boasted flowing, shoulder-length locks, and Haldeman used to tell reporters that between them they had a normal hair style. When friends urged him to let his hair grow in order to moderate his harsh public image, Haldeman good-naturedly brushed them aside. "Who'd know me?" he asked. After leaving the White House in 1973 he did let his hair grow—and nobody knew him, just as he had predicted.

With or without the famous crew cut, Haldeman in person is a surprisingly attractive man. His towering, athletic build, enormous hands, and warm blue eyes project a sense of All-American stability. As John Dean commented after meeting him for the first time: "He looked like a college football coach recruiting a new player—not like the awesome ramrod of the President's guard I had heard so much about." One of the personal details about Haldeman that intimidated most Washingtonians was his fervent commitment to the Christian Science Church. In the days before Jimmy Carter the combination of awesome power and deep religiosity seemed automatically suspect—especially when the faith in question frowned on alcohol and tobacco. The fact that Bob's old friend John Ehrlichman shared his devotion to Christian Science suggested some sort of smug and sinister conspiracy. These two fanatics didn't fit in; what's more, they didn't want to fit in. They contented themselves with Sunday barbecues and home movies and took no interest in the glittering cocktail parties around them. "With the haughty disdain of Victorian Englishmen forced to live among the Hottentots," grumbled Dan Rather, "they took care not to mingle with the natives except in the line of duty."

Though it is easy to write them off as hopeless squares the Haldemans have always been something more than a typical Middle American family. "We're proud of the way we've raised our children," Bob declares. "Our two older children were both National Merit Scholars. Our oldest, Susan, went to Stanford and then the University of Minnesota, where she graduated summa cum laude. She recently finished UCLA Law School and has been clerking for a federal judge. The next one, Hank—the one with the long hair—graduated from UCLA as a political science major. Our other son has been studying Chinese at Berkeley. Then there's the youngest, Ann, who's still in high school. We're not what you'd call the intelligentsia—not an artsy type family. But I certainly don't think we're lacking in intellectual or cultural pursuits."

Haldeman's pride in his children reflects the unusually close-knit nature of his family. He learned to play tennis—but only as a concession to his wife Joanne. He even took up the game of chess in order to entertain his children. Among the dreariest days he spent in Washington were the first six months after the inauguration when he and his family were forced to live apart. While Joanne remained behind in California so the kids could finish school, Bob lived alone in a Washington hotel. Which hotel did he choose? The Watergate, ironically enough. While another man would have been tempted by these bachelor circumstances into frequent entertainments on the town, Haldeman ate every night at the White House mess and worked in his office till ten or eleven. It was not a question of dedication to his job: with his family away he simply had nothing else to do.

Once his wife and children had settled into a comfortable house in suburban Maryland, Bob made a point of coming home every night in time for dinner. Leaving the premises of the office, however, did not mean an escape from the pressures of his job. Only rarely did a night pass at home without at least one phone call from the President of the United States. These conversations seldom involved pressing business—they had more to do with Nixon's need for reassurance and moral support than with Haldeman's ongoing administrative responsibilities. Bill Safire remembers a dinner party at the Haldemans' in March 1970 which helped to explain why Bob and Joanne so rarely entertained. In the course of the evening the host had to excuse himself five times to take calls from the President. Each of these conversations concerned Nixon's anger at Jewish groups for demonstrating against visiting French President Georges Pompidou. All Haldeman could do to soothe his agitated chief was to listen politely and await the next interruption.

Nixon's habit of disturbing his aide at home reflected a little-known aspect of their relationship. All Washington recognized the President's practical reliance on Haldeman for the day-to-day running of the White House, but few observers would have guessed the intensity of his emotional dependence on the Chief of Staff. Nixon hoped to draw from Haldeman an inner strength that he himself lacked. Throughout his career, Nixon attempted to project the image of a tough, hard-boiled decision maker who could handle any crisis without "losing his cool." In reality, he remained moody, erratic, and painfully vulnerable. Haldeman—the broad-shouldered authoritarian who never registered his emotions—represented the sort of manly self-sufficiency Nixon wanted for himself. In several revealing diary entries during the Watergate crisis, Nixon expressed his respect for Haldeman's ability to "hang tough." "I marvel at the strength of Haldeman," he wrote. "He is really a remarkable man. . . ." The President's administration reached its peak on the day he asked for his aide's resignation. As he reported in his memoirs: "Even at this moment Haldeman's effort was to reassure me. He was proud and secure." When they finally parted after a dramatic conversation and Haldeman stepped into a waiting car, the badly shaken President told him, "I wish I were as strong as you."

One of the reasons that Nixon found it so difficult to fire Bob Haldeman when he had to do so was that he had almost no experience in dismissing or reprimanding his subordinates. The Chief of Staff handled all such chores before his own departure and spared the President the unpleasantness. Even when the victim was Secretary of State William Rogers, technically the administration's highest appointed official and Nixon's longtime personal friend, it was Haldeman—and not the President—who gave him the bad news that he would ultimately be replaced by arch rival Henry Kissinger. Not surprisingly, Haldeman became known as "Nixon's S.O.B."—a designation he accepted "only if you meant Robert Benchley's definition of S.O.B.—that is, 'Sweet Old Bob.'" In his own view, Haldeman performed an indispensable service to the President by acting the part of the heavy. This arrangement allowed disgruntled officials to direct their anger at Haldeman and to continue thinking of Nixon as their friend and protector. According to one frequently repeated tale, a visitor to the Oval Office who had known Nixon before his election made the mistake of addressing the President as "Dick." Nixon barked back, "Don't you dare call me Dick! I am the President of the United States. When you speak to me you call me 'Mr. President.'" It makes a good story, but Haldeman insists it never happened. "If anyone was actually foolish enough to talk to the President that way, he would have just nodded his head and said, 'Thank you very much.' Then as soon as the meeting was over he would have called me in there and said, 'You go tell that son-of-a-bitch if he ever calls me Dick again, he's not going to see the inside of the office.' That's the way it would have happened. And that's the kind of job I had to do."

Haldeman's loyal service as Nixon's "enforcer" encouraged the President to think of them as inseparable. Several times in his memoirs Nixon describes executive decisions as if he and Haldeman were equally responsible for the course of action. Concerning the campaign of '72 for instance, he writes that "Haldeman and I decided to send Fred Malek, then a member of the White House staff, over the CRP [Committee for the Reelection of the President] to bring things under control." This is a strange construction for a President to use: it would be difficult to imagine John Kennedy saying, "Sorensen and I decided," or Lyndon Johnson saying, "Moyers and I decided," regardless of the specific issues involved.

Curiously enough, the Nixon-Haldeman relationship always stopped short of genuine friendship. "Our ages were different enough and our backgrounds were different enough so that there were no particular grounds for anything purely social or purely personal," Haldeman observes. "In a sense, it was the kind of relationship that I would imagine arises between combat personnel, people who undergo an intensive personal experience together. It becomes a very intense connection, but you wouldn't call it affection or friendship or anything of that sort." It is Haldeman's guess that "to this day, he doesn't know how many children I have nor anything else about my private life. He never asked. . . . ."

This situation is particularly surprising in view of the substantial amount of time the two men spent "relaxing" together in San Clemente or Key Biscayne. The Chief of Staff invariably accompanied the President on his vacations; in fact, White House staffers joked that any fading of Haldeman's well-maintained tan served as a signal to Nixon that they should travel to one of the sunny climates that they both loved. "Sometimes we'd go for a long walk up the beach together, or else sit out on the terrace for hours, just kind of talking things through. I understood that just being there was part of a valuable role that I could play for him. A President is in a position where he can't talk freely to many people—both for reasons of confidentiality and because there's an understanding gap. Most people just wouldn't know what he was talking about. With me, he didn't have to explain anything because I knew what was going on and what was in his mind. He could start from wherever he happened to be and spin it out from there, rather than having to go way back and bring me up to speed. It was definitely a form of relaxation—just sitting and chatting and listening.''

Every once in a great while, Nixon allowed little touches of sentiment to peek through the strictly business exterior of his dealings with Haldeman. One such instance occurred on January 20, 1970—the first anniversary of his inauguration. Late in the afternoon of that cold and blustery day, Nixon sat alone in the Oval Office. He watched the shadows lengthen without turning on the lights, then put on his overcoat at six o'clock. Before walking down the outdoor corridor to his residence, he pressed the desk buzzer to summon Haldeman and Rose Mary Woods, his two most trusted associates. They came into the darkened office to find Nixon fumbling on his desk for a small silver music box. When he found it, the President lifted the lid without a word and let the contraption tinkle out a nostalgic, vaguely festive rendition of ''Hail to the Chief.'' The President of the United States, his Chief of Staff, and longtime personal secretary all huddled solemnly around the desk waiting for the melody to wind itself down. Finally Nixon closed the box and nodded. ''Been a year,'' he said, and then walked dramatically through the French doors and into the night.

Later in 1970 the President gave his aides a more explicit gesture of appreciation. After the Cambodia-Kent State crisis he felt particularly grateful to the senior advisors who had stood by him tirelessly and shared the emotional strain. While in Key Biscayne, Nixon asked his confidant Bebe Rebozo if Bebe's girlfriend, Jane Lucke, would mind doing some sewing for the President of the United States. With Betsy Ross no doubt in mind, Ms. Lucke agreed to help Nixon prepare the surprise which he sprang on his aides on the flight back to Washington. Calling Haldeman, Ehrlichman, and Kissinger into his private cabin, he told them, ''You deserve something like the Purple Heart for all the wounds you have sustained in the line of duty over the past few weeks.''

The three men laughed, insisting they had only done their jobs, but Nixon persisted. ''You have done more than your jobs,'' he declared, ''and I have devised a new award—a Blue Heart, for those who are true blue.'' The President handed them each a small, hand-stitched heart cut from navy blue cloth. ''This will be our secret,'' he concluded, ''but I wanted you to know how much I appreciate what you have done.''

The only other recorded instance of Nixon offering sartorial decorations to his staff involved circumstances considerably less heroic. One of the most celebrated fiascoes of his Presidency concerned the chief executive's desire to deck out the White House police in the elegant ceremonial uniforms of a European royal household. The resulting costumes, full of ribbons and glittering braid, reminded more than one observer of the singing soldiers in a Sigmund Romberg operetta. Faced with an avalanche of public abuse, Nixon abandoned this most visible manifestation of his imperial pretensions. He retired the uniforms permanently, but not before he had retrieved two of the gold-ribboned

stovepipe hats as a souvenir for his principal aides. He had the headgear fash-
ionably wrapped in a pair of embossed boxes and then presented as gifts to
Haldeman and Ehrlichman. No note of explanation accompanied this offering,
but the Chief of Staff assumed he was not expected to wear the hat to work.

In a sense, the royal guardsman's helmet may be seen as a symbol of Haldeman's best-known function in the Nixon White House: he was the fierce protector of the Presidential presence, the man the New York *Times* described as "a
latter day Janus . . . a god of the going and the coming." By the middle of
Nixon's first term even the most self-important Washington potentates realized
that in order to see the President they had to go through Haldeman. This arrangement provoked charges from many quarters that the Chief of Staff used
his position to isolate and manipulate Nixon—charges remarkable only for the
fact that they were taken so seriously. Similar attacks have been leveled at
major White House aides for more than a century. By modern standards,
Abraham Lincoln was an astonishingly accessible chief executive who spent
hours each day meeting with politicians, soldiers, diplomats, and ordinary citizens
who showed up at the White House. Yet even in his case, contemporary Congressmen complained that Lincoln's secretary John Nicolay made it unduly difficult for them to see the President. The same complaint has been echoed with
such consistency in every administration that it suggests an immutable rule of
Washington politics. No one likes to believe that he has been denied an audience with the chief executive because his opinion is insignificant or irrelevant;
it is much easier to blame a conspiratorial aide for cutting off advice "the
President needs."

This is not to say that the dark mutterings about a "Berlin Wall" around
Richard Nixon lacked all basis in reality. Haldeman did go further than most of
his predecessors in protecting the President's privacy, particularly when it came
to members of Nixon's own official family. Transportation Secretary John
Volpe tried for months to get an appointment with the President before he
finally managed to slip into the Oval Office on the coattails of a visiting arch-
bishop. After more than two years in office, an assistant secretary in one of
the major federal departments had to be introduced to the President when they
met in a White House receiving line. Most people blamed Haldeman for this
state of affairs, not realizing that he received constant pressure from Nixon to
schedule fewer and fewer appointments. The President demanded long stretches
of open time—quiet hours built into every day for rumination and planning.
Eventually, the order came down for the Chief of Staff to "steal
Wednesday"—to remove the day in the middle of the week from the normal
flow of White House activity. There would be no meetings, no interviews, no
photographs, no public events, so that Richard Nixon could contemplate the
world in serene isolation.

Haldeman's critics believed that his ruthless thinning out of the schedule
reflected an attempt to keep Nixon from conflicting ideas. On the contrary, the
Chief of Staff took great pains to ensure that every memo or recommendation

that went to the President had been thoroughly "staffed out"—that is, that it included dissenting or concurring opinions from all officials affected by the issue. Everyone knew that transmitting thoughts through Haldeman could never be as effective as presenting them in person to the President, but even the Chief of Staff's harshest critics recognized that he tried to be impartial in outlining available alternatives. As one particularly outspoken assistant to the President recalled: "Each of us, telling Haldeman what we thought about a given matter, would be certain that our point of view would get to the Old Man 'with the bark off,' reduced to essentials, and put persuasively—without the tone of voice or added comment that would undercut it in transmission. That was Haldeman's greatest talent, his most important contribution. . . ." Even *Newsweek* magazine, not known for its fond relationship with the Nixon staff, concluded that Haldeman "is scrupulous about getting every side of an argument before the chief and he keeps his own politics largely to himself." As one member of the Cabinet observed, "I'm not aware that he has any politics."

Haldeman's role as a conduit of information to and from the President left him so incredibly busy that he had to delegate many of his administrative chores to subordinates. Before long, it became nearly as hard to get an appointment with the Chief of Staff as with the President himself. Larry Higby, the boyish aide known everywhere as "Haldeman's Haldeman," deflected much of the day-to-day White House business. A charter member of the Beaver Patrol, he first met his future boss at a UCLA alumni dinner honoring the outstanding members of the Class of '67. Haldeman immediately recruited this promising prospect for J. Walter Thompson and then brought him along to the White House. Many elected officials found it difficult enough to adjust to Haldeman, and the powerful position of this inexperienced 24-year-old only added insult to injury. Senator Robert Dole, while serving as Republican national chairman, complained that he would call the White House to talk to the President, be switched to Haldeman's office, and "wind up talking to some kid named Higby." Jeb Magruder estimated that on an average day he would receive one or two calls from Haldeman, but at least ten calls from Higby relaying orders in Haldeman's name. "It became a joke in the White House that there really wasn't any Haldeman," he remembers, "just Higby up there sending all those memos."

Yet Haldeman was there after all, working not only to protect Richard Nixon from the outside world but to protect the outside world from Richard Nixon. He knew the President well enough to understand his darker impulses. Nixon frequently exploded in fits of vindictive temper—outbursts that could severely damage his Presidency if allowed to run their course. Haldeman acted as a buffer to absorb these excessive emotions until the President calmed down and came to his senses. Nixon himself understood and valued this arrangement. Bill Safire believes that he deliberately "placed Haldeman between himself and the rest of the world as a safety catch on a trigger."

In practical terms, this responsibility took up a good deal of Haldeman's energy. "Time and again I would receive petty vindictive orders. 'Hugh Sidey is to be kept off Air Force One.' Or even once or twice, '*All* press is barred from Air Force One.' Or, after a Senator made an anti-Vietnam War speech: 'Put a 24 hour surveillance on that bastard.' And on and on. . . . The President never let up. He'd be on the intercom buzzing me ten minutes after such an order. 'What have you done about Sidey?' I'd say, 'I'm working on it,' and delay and delay until Nixon would one day comment, with a sort of a half smile on his face, 'I guess you never took action on that, did you?'

"'No.'

"'Well, I guess it was the best thing.'"

Of all the members of the Nixon inner circle, Haldeman alone occupied a position of sufficient trust to disregard or alter a Presidential order without fearing the consequences. The story of a disastrous airport rally during the campaign of '68 illustrates that aspect of their collaboration. The exhausted candidate stepped out of his plane at Cleveland to see a sparse crowd, with no signs, no cheering, and no functioning P.A. system. The traveling press, hungry for some novelty to report, filed numerous stories about "the significant lack of turnout" in Ohio.

As the campaign plane took off for the next stop, Nixon struggled to control his temper. Finally, as Haldeman sat down beside him in the forward compartment, Nixon broke his silence and barked out with authority: "There will be no more landings at airports!"

Haldeman dutifully transcribed the order on his yellow legal pad, then began to consider the consequences. If the candidate would permit no further landings at airports, where would he land? In cornfields? Parking lots? Would he parachute into waiting crowds? Shaking his head, Haldeman drew a thick line through what he had written. Obviously, what Nixon had meant was that "there will be no more *rallies* at airports." But this command also made no sense. For months, the technique of airport rallies had been used with telling effect. TV newsmen depended on the action film to use on their evening broadcasts. It would be a major mistake to change the entire campaign strategy because of irritation over the failure of a single rally. Haldeman knew that when the candidate regained his composure he would regret his impetuous decree and approve a free-form interpretation of his words. Therefore the Presidential edict, as it finally filtered down through Haldeman to the advance men, proclaimed: "There will be no more *unsuccessful* rallies at airports." The Chief of Staff enforced that order with a vengeance to make sure that the Cleveland experience would never be repeated.

In addition to restraining the President, Haldeman kept a wary eye on another hotheaded top official—Vice-President Spiro Agnew. On several occasions his timely intervention saved Agnew from embarrassing blunders. When the Vice-President prepared a major address lambasting the press, the Chief of Staff got hold of an advance copy. What he read "made even my short hair stand on end . . . and I'm not easily shocked." He marched the draft directly into the President's office and with Nixon's approval deleted the most offensive passages. "To those who heard or read Agnew's now famous first speech attacking the press and thought it was too strong," Haldeman explains, "all I can say is: you should have seen the first draft." During the Republican convention of 1972, Agnew once again stumbled toward the edge of a public relations disaster. He planned to ask TV psychologist Joyce Brothers to deliver one of the speeches seconding his nomination as Vice-President. To Agnew, this seemed an ingenious way to emphasize the contrast between his own sound mental health and the well-publicized psychiatric problems of Democrat Thomas Eagleton. As John Ehrlichman dryly observed to his friend the Chief of Staff: "That hardly seems to be the gentle touch." Haldeman immediately took on the difficult task of squelching the Vice-President's latest inspiration.

In all of his attempts to prevent mistakes by his superiors, expediency was Haldeman's guiding principle—moral or legal considerations never entered into the equation. The Chief of Staff simply had a better grasp of public relations than did the President. He knew that some of Nixon's crude ideas for wreaking vengeance on his enemies would surely lead to trouble. In other instances, when he felt certain that Presidential abuses would remain undetected by the public, he cheerfully participated in questionable activities. He thought nothing, for example, of ordering an FBI investigation of the harmless comic "Richard M. Dixon"—who capitalized on his striking physical resemblance to the President—while he balked at the idea of denying White House access to hostile correspondent Mike Wallace. In the latter case, a major uproar would surely ensue, but in the former Nixon's combative urges could be indulged with little danger of bad publicity. On balance, the Chief of Staff gave in to Nixon's petty obsessions at least as often as he resisted them. Nevertheless, he argues that the misuse of Presidential power would have been even worse than it was had he not been on hand to exercise an occasionally restraining influence.

His work in curbing or obscuring the President's emotional reactions dovetailed nicely with his general responsibility for Nixon's image—a responsibility that included even the most minuscule details of dress and grooming. Haldeman was the one who advised Nixon that blue suits looked good on television and helped select the right tie for every occasion. When the President went before the cameras for press conferences or major addresses, Haldeman served as combination set designer and stage manager. He selected the telling little props—including the bust of Lincoln, the American flag lapel pin, the colorful charts and maps—while making sure that the entire operation ran smoothly. His greatest triumph in this capacity was Nixon's trip to China in February 1972. From the moment the President stepped off the plane in Peking, which was precisely calculated to coincide with television prime time in all four zones back home, Haldeman artfully orchestrated every minute of the visit for maximum media effect. As one White House staffer observed, "The China trip was Bob's masterpiece, his Sistine Chapel."

It also illustrated dazzling teamwork between Haldeman and Nixon's foreign policy aide, Henry Kissinger. Against all odds, these two powerful and contrasting personalities enjoyed a cordial relationship during their years together in the White House. Aboard Air Force One, Haldeman occasionally killed time playing chess while Kissinger stood behind him as an unofficial advisor, shaking his head and sighing in despair at his friend's lack of skill. On most mornings in the executive mansion, Kissinger would be the first man to stroll down the corridor to Haldeman's office for daily staff meetings. He frequently paid tribute to the Chief of Staff's Hitlerian image with a hearty Germanic greeting. "Guten Morgen, Herr Haldeman," he would say, while his colleague replied, "And a guten Morgen to you, Heinz." Such pleasantries covered a very real potential for rivalry and palace intrigue which, fortunately for both men, never developed. Kissinger deserves most of the credit for this in-house version of détente. As one member of his personal staff reported, "Henry kissed Haldeman's ass—regularly in the beginning, less as time went by, but always some. He did it because he knew he had to." In the all-important matter of paperwork, the Chief of Staff remained firmly in control. Memos from Kissinger to Nixon—like all other memos to the President—passed over Haldeman's desk.

Kissinger shrewdly capitalized on Haldeman's position as an intermediary during a delicate stage of the Vietnam negotiations in 1972. Before making new proposals to the North Vietnamese, he would telephone the Chief of Staff from Paris to report on the latest developments. Haldeman then took his notes to Nixon to get the President's reaction, which he duly relayed back to Kissinger in Europe. By employing this elaborate procedure, the American negotiator could truthfully tell his North Vietnamese counterparts that he had not spoken to the President and that his suggestions lacked official sanction—thus giving the United States additional room for maneuver at the bargaining table.

The apparent success of the Vietnam negotiations, the utter ineptitude of the Democratic nominee, and Nixon's image as a calm, competent manager of the nation's business all contributed to his landslide victory in 1972. Haldeman shared his chief's triumph, but faced an unpleasant responsibility the morning after the election. Bleary-eyed and exhausted from the long night of celebrations, the senior staff gathered in the Roosevelt Room of the White House to hear a statement of appreciation from the President. Nixon spoke briefly of his mandate from the people and his hopes for the second term before leaving the room and turning the meeting over to Haldeman. Moving swiftly to the head of the table, the Chief of Staff went straight to the point. "As the President has indicated, some things are going to change around here. . . . Now, the President and I are meeting with the Cabinet shortly. We are going to direct them to obtain letters of resignation from all appointed sub-Cabinet officers in the government and submit them along with their own resignations. And the President has directed that everyone in this room also hand in a letter of resignation. This doesn't mean that you won't be asked to stay on, of course. We will review each situation individually. We just want to show we mean business." With that he turned on his heel and departed for the Cabinet meeting, leaving the assemblage too stunned for protest.

The timing of this new Nixon-Haldeman move left something to be desired. A post landslide thank-you meeting hardly seemed an appropriate occasion for firing all of the President's personal assistants. Yet Haldeman's apparent madness was not without its method: it played an important part in a long-cherished goal known as "executive reorganization." During his first term the President had been frequently frustrated by the unresponsiveness of the federal bureaucracy. The major departments were filled with Democratic holdovers who had little use for Nixon or his conservative ideas. By demanding resignations from everyone at the beginning of the second term, Nixon and Haldeman won the chance to build a new structure from the ground up. This time, they resolved, only administration loyalists would be granted significant appointments.

Executing this ambitious plan, known in the White House as "our revolution," required an enormous expenditure of time and energy. To review all of the hundreds of major appointees, the Chief of Staff secluded himself with Nixon at the President's mountain retreat at Camp David. Haldeman's assistant Larry Higby offers vivid recollections of those days: "It was a terribly tense time. Haldeman was constantly with the President. I mean for hours. And then he'd get back to his own office and be called right back to the President's office. It was just a yo-yo thing, you know. . . . And it was a madhouse up there. Bob was just bang, bang, bang, all day. . . . It started out as a very exciting kind of thing because we were gonna rip the place apart and put it back together again. But Bob had so much pressure on him that it got to be very depressing, and you almost didn't want to go on with it."

But they did go on with it and made innumerable enemies in the process. In retrospect, Haldeman believes that "reorganization is the secret story of Watergate." The President's challenge to the established order of things "eventually spurred into action against Nixon the great power blocs in Washington. All of them saw danger as the hated Nixon moved more and more to control the executive branch from the White House, as he was constitutionally mandated to do." In reality, Haldeman and his crew scarcely needed an internal revolution to provoke the hostility of the entrenched bureaucracy. As early as July 1969, during Nixon's first six months in office, an unnamed government insider told a national news magazine: "They have enormous power right now, but everybody hates them. So if they ever make one slip, people will go after them like a pack of wolves."

As every schoolchild knows by now, the Nixon staff made more than "one slip." In handling the Watergate affair, they bumbled often enough to mobilize whole armies of wolves who, just as predicted, came howling after them. Haldeman's participation in the chain of crimes and miscalculations that ultimately brought down the Nixon Presidency has been analyzed and debated too often to require detailed elaboration here. Suffice it to say that the American criminal justice system, after extremely lengthy and well-publicized proceedings, found him guilty of perjury and obstruction of justice. Many White House aides of the past have been accused of serious misconduct—including Robert Johnson, Orville Babcock, C. Bascom Slemp, and Sherman Adams—but Haldeman alone has been officially convicted.

In his own defense, Haldeman continues to cite his lack of criminal intent. "I am the only person in the world who knows what my intentions were. I know that I never intended to commit the crimes I am charged with committing, and I know that I don't belong in jail." In his memoirs he points out that "the ultimate irony is that the Watergate break-in stands as the only major scandal in history in which not one of those who brought it about was personally benefited by it in any way—and no one other than those who brought it about was personally hurt by it in any way."

This statement, like so much of Haldeman's thinking on Watergate, avoids the core of the issue. Though "no one other than those who brought it about was *personally* hurt by it" the abuse of power in the Nixon administration threatened one of the conceptual foundations of American government. In a constitutional republic, ordinary citizens and federal officials must be equally bound by the constraints of the law. It may well be true that Haldeman lacked selfish motives, that he stumbled unwittingly into criminal activity, that he remained at all times devoted to "the higher good"—but none of that changes the consequences of his actions. Indeed, the casual, almost thoughtless nature of his participation in the cover-up makes it all the more chilling. His automatic response indicates how deeply ingrained was the dangerous notion that the President and his men could do anything they pleased.

This same concept played a part in Haldeman's most costly disservice to his chief: the fatal mishandling of the Watergate tape recordings. In April 1973, when John Dean began cooperating with the federal prosecutors, Nixon became worried about previous conversations in which he may have compromised himself. At the time, only Haldeman and a few White House technicians knew that elaborate taping equipment recorded all transactions in the Oval Office. The Chief of Staff had persuaded Nixon to install the machines in 1970 as a hedge against precisely the sort of situation that had arisen with Dean, in which the President needed to recall specific details of key meetings. To assure himself that Dean's testimony would not damage his Presidency, Nixon asked Haldeman to listen to the tape of a problematic interchange on March 21 in which he openly discussed hush money for Watergate defendants. The Chief of Staff obediently waded through the mass of recordings that had accumulated in the White House—the first human being to make use of this highly confidential government resource. When he finished his review he offered an optimistic report to the boss. Yes, Nixon had said "We could get the money," but Haldeman believed that the context of the tape made it clear he had merely been "drawing Dean out." Nixon breathed somewhat more easily after hearing this analysis, but remained troubled enough by his own recollections to call

Haldeman twice at home that evening. During one of these conversations, duly recorded on the White House equipment, he told Haldeman that he had always wondered about the taping capacity, "but I'm damn glad we have it, aren't you?"

"Yes, sir," the Chief of Staff snapped back, adding that the section of tape he had reviewed that morning would someday prove "very helpful."

Haldeman maintained his naive belief in the saving value of the tape recordings long after he had resigned from the White House. In July 1973, when Alex Butterfield made his sensational disclosure to the Senate Watergate Committee about the top-secret sound equipment in the Oval Office, Nixon called his former Chief of Staff for advice. As the President recorded in his memoirs, "Haldeman said the tapes were still our best defense and he recommended that they not be destroyed."

The stupidity in this position is positively breathtaking. Haldeman had participated personally in all the crucial conversations which, when finally revealed to the public, forced the President's resignation. He had even reviewed the recording of an obviously damning exchange between Nixon and Dean. Without question, he knew that the President had attempted to use the CIA to block the Watergate investigation, had discussed offering blackmail and clemency to the Watergate burglars, and otherwise implicated himself in literally dozens of different tapes. How then was it possible, barring a massive attack of amnesia, for Haldeman to seriously maintain that the recordings "were still our best defense"?

The answer is that he believed so deeply in the absolute authority of the President that he took it for granted that all other Americans shared his conviction. To Haldeman, it seemed self-evident that a different set of standards would be applied to Richard Nixon than those used for judging ordinary mortals. As long as the President avoided murdering old ladies, robbing grocery stores, or committing other gross criminal acts, Haldeman believed that he remained within his rights. The tapes would show Nixon to be free of any shabby personal motive in the Watergate cases. His only interest in the cover-up had been a sincere desire to protect the effectiveness of his administration for the sake of national security. Surely, the people would support him.

Haldeman reasoned this way because he had been trained never to second-guess his chief in matters of substance. A casual passage in his book *The Ends of Power* speaks volumes about this aspect of their relationship. "I believed in tough campaigning, too," Haldeman writes, "but even from my hard-line standpoint, Nixon went too far at times. But political strategy wasn't my province, only the mechanics." He was, in other words, an administrative extension of the Presidential will, a throwback to the old-time "Secretaries to the President." As Chief of Staff, Haldeman had more in common with Nicolay, Cortelyou, and Loeb than with recent activist advisors like Hopkins, Clifford, and Moyers. It is impossible to imagine Watergate taking place with anyone from this latter group as top aide to the President. Not because Hopkins, Clifford, and Moyers were better human beings than Haldeman; not because their moral standards were necessarily more elevated; but because their relationship to the President was fundamentally different. They were advisors as much as assistants, free to speak their minds and suggest courses of action. They not only carried out decisions, they helped to make them. In a sense, Haldeman's fall came not because his position was too strong—as is generally believed— but because it was too weak. His obsession with competence and smooth administration, his disinterest in virtually all questions of policy, set the pattern for an aide who briskly and unthinkingly followed the outlines of the President's intentions. In his book he compares himself, not without a trace of pride, to an efficient robot, "a metal machine clanking along doing what it's told by a computer-like mind."

Yet Haldeman's status as an impersonal automaton did not make it any easier for Nixon to fire him when it became politically necessary to do so. At the time, the President declared that demanding the resignation of his top aide "was the hardest decision I had ever made." He agonized for weeks before bowing to public pressure and banishing Haldeman and sidekick John Ehrlichman from the White House. The two aides wanted to remain on the job—or to take only temporary leaves of absence—in order to avoid the presumption of guilt. Ehrlichman in particular felt bitter about being forced to leave before he had been formally indicted. In a telephone conversation with the President he charged that Nixon, either directly or indirectly, had been the inspiration behind all illegal acts. If the two senior aides resigned, Ehrlichman implied, then the President himself should resign along with them.

In contrast to his beetle-browed colleague, Haldeman proved a good soldier to the very end: he never squirmed as the axe fell. On Sunday afternoon April 29, 1972, the President summoned both men to Camp David to give them the bad news. He faced Haldeman first in a private meeting at the Aspen Lodge. They stood before a huge picture window, watching a light fog creep along the mountainside. The tall trees beyond the terrace had taken on the fluffy pastel green of early spring and for several minutes Nixon tried to make small talk about the view. Finally he blurted out, "You know, Bob, there's something I've never told anybody before, not even you." Haldeman remembers the hushed quaver in his voice as he continued. "Every night since I've been President, every single night before I've gone to bed, I've knelt down on my knees beside my bed and prayed to God for guidance and help in this job.

"Last night when I went to bed I hoped, and almost prayed, that I wouldn't wake up in the morning. I just couldn't face going on."

As usual, Haldeman rushed to reassure him, to make his job as easy as possible. He told Nixon that he would resign his post without protest. He accepted the decision that had been made, though he didn't agree with it. What's more, the President should always feel that he could call on Haldeman for aid and advice, even after he left the White House. "What you have to remember," the Chief of Staff concluded, "is that nothing that has happened in the Watergate mess has changed our mandate in the non-Watergate areas. That is what matters. That is what you do best.'' He then volunteered to go to another cabin and write out a letter of resignation.

It is easy to spot the manipulative technique in Nixon's exchange with his aide, but the President's depression was real enough. The next day he "tried to make it up" to his fallen comrades in a nationally televised address. He told the American people: "Today, in one of the most difficult decisions of my Presidency, I accepted the resignations of two of my closest associates in the White House—Bob Haldeman, John Ehrlichman—two of the finest public servants it has been my privilege to know.'' In his autobiography, Nixon expresses more profound feelings of guilt about the firing of Haldeman and Ehrlichman than on any other aspect of his Presidency. "They had been my closest aides. They were my friends. . . . I felt as if I had cut off one arm and then the other. The amputation may have been necessary for even a chance at survival, but what I had had to do left me anguished and saddened that from that day on the Presidency lost all joy for me.''

For Haldeman as well, resignation meant the beginning and not the end of a nightmare. Over the next five years he faced an endless round of government investigations, Congressional testimony, trials, appeals, and finally a jail term. Outside of the charmed circle of power and potency, isolated in the glare of hostile and unrelenting publicity, his life had been reduced to a single essential: a losing struggle to clear his name and establish his innocence. Under the circumstances, he derived small comfort from the fact that Richard Nixon still called him periodically, trying to talk out his own troubles and looking, as always, for friendship and moral support. Haldeman received one such call on August 7, 1974, when the President informed him of his decision to resign. To the crumbling chief executive, the familiar voice on the other end of the line sounded "energetic and unself-conscious" as Haldeman urged him to take more time to reconsider. If, however, the President had unequivocally made up his mind, then the former Chief of Staff wished to advance a daring suggestion. "I firmly believe that before you leave office you should exercise your constitutional authority and grant pardons to all those who have been or may be charged with any crimes in connection with Watergate. I think it's imperative that you bring Watergate to an end before you leave—for the sake of the country and especially for your successor.'' He then modestly added, "I realize this is a minor point in contrast to what you are facing, but I think it is very important.''

When Nixon promised to give the matter serious consideration, Haldeman followed up with characteristic efficiency. Through his lawyers in Washington, he presented the President with a written recommendation for a blanket Watergate pardon to be coupled with full amnesty for all Vietnam draft evaders. He argued that the twin acts would clear away the remnants of both major traumas of the Nixon era and allow President Gerald Ford to take office with a fresh slate. Haldeman even drafted a specially typed page for inclusion in Nixon's resignation speech, announcing and justifying the pardons. The President never told Haldeman his reasons for ignoring this last gasp appeal—it seems to have been lost in the shuffle during the chaos of Nixon's last hours in the White House.

Whatever the basis for the failure to act, it eliminated the last real chance for Haldeman to avoid a term in prison. The legal process still had to run its course, but the conviction of the former Chief of Staff had become a virtual certainty. With this prospect ahead of him, Haldeman tried to construct a normal life for his family back in California. While engaged in his complex legal battles, he made notes for a book on the Nixon administration. His wife Joanne helped to relieve their increasingly desperate financial situation by going to work as a residential real estate broker. In his spare time, Haldeman played an active role in the Christian Science Church in his neighborhood, serving for a time as its president. During this period of waiting, he developed a resigned, philosophical attitude toward his predicament. "I don't feel any bitterness, and I guess that's terribly disturbing to some people. It seems to be inconceivable that someone can be had in the sense that I've been had and not be bitter about both the results and the people that brought about the results. But I'm not. I don't know—I guess that's part of my basic approach to anything. I've never dealt much with reaction, with being bitter or elated about something that's past and done with. I have no feelings of great joy that this has all come about. But I can't untangle it, or, as I supposedly said to John Dean once, I can't put the toothpaste back in the tube. So the thing now is to brush my teeth, I guess. You know, if you have a stable base and your own self-confidence you can deal with these things on a day-to-day basis. You could never imagine dealing with them in the abstract, but in the concrete you find that you can deal with each day as it comes."

In June 1977, Haldeman entered the federal minimum security facility in Lompoc, California, to serve a one- to four-year sentence. He actually remained in prison for eighteen months, during which time he proved himself a model inmate. He kept largely to himself and worked as a chemical technician in Lompoc's sewage treatment plant—an assignment that gave rise to some cruel jokes in the press, particularly after the release of his book *The Ends of Power*. This was not the sweeping history of the Nixon years he had hoped to write, but a limited and strangely impersonal review of various theories in the Watergate case. Money, Haldeman freely admits, was his primary motive in writing the book: only a major best-seller would enable him to retire the $450,000 in outstanding legal debts he had accumulated during his trial. In financial terms the project justified his high hopes, despite the overwhelmingly negative critical response. Many writers seemed disappointed that Haldeman had failed to include any sort of blanket apology to the American people. The closest he came to an admission of personal guilt was an intriguing passage on his unfortunate effect on subordinates. "I put on too much pressure," he wrote, "and in the process laid the groundwork for the mental attitude that 'the job must be done' which badly disserved the cause when Watergate struck. . . . My wife, getting glimpses of my operation and relationships with the staff, especially the junior men, very perceptively has since observed that it wasn't *Nixon's* character or moods that allowed Watergate to happen. She points out that *My* character and demands pushed people to become 'little generals' which was out of character for them. . . . I had too much on my mind to realize how far-reaching this was—or how damaging it could be.''

Haldeman reserves his deepest feelings of regret for the missed opportunities of the Nixon administration. He believes that if the President had not been brought down by Watergate "the United States would have celebrated its Bicentennial with joy and enthusiasm, renewed patriotism, and dedication. . . . A solid structure for world peace would have been established, along with a sound internal economy.'' Aside from these grandiose visions of a golden age, Haldeman confided to the author that he would have personally pushed for another sort of accomplishment as a legacy of Nixon's second term. "I planned for a federal initiative in the whole area of cable television—cable communication. It's what's been referred to as 'the Wired Nation' with all the homes in the country linked up with coaxial cable. There would be two-way communication. Through computer, you could use your television set to order up whatever you wanted. The morning paper, entertainment services, shopping services, coverage of sporting events and public events. Technologically it can be done. And I felt that this should be the Nixon legacy, in the sense that the federal highway program was the Eisenhower legacy. Just as Eisenhower linked up the nation's cities by highways so that you could get there, the Nixon legacy would have linked them by cable communications so you wouldn't have to go there. You'd be there without going. It all goes back to my old area of interest in communications and media. And it's going to come—someday. But if I had stayed on for the second term, I believe it would have come much faster.''

All this is vintage Haldeman—not malicious, not slow-witted, but almost hopelessly obtuse. The man who brought the sophisticated taping system to the White House can speak without irony or embarrassment of his dreams for "a wired nation,'' remaining all the while totally oblivious to the "Big Brother'' implications of his plan. As correspondent Daniel Schorr wrote in reviewing Haldeman's book: "He has learned little and, except unintentionally, taught us little. But he remains true to himself, and that's something in a time of born-again sinners.''

Haldeman is only 53, and there is no telling what course his life may take following his release from Lompoc. Nevertheless, nearly all writing about him adopts the past tense, as if obituaries were already in order. Election chronicler Theodore H. White provided one of the best and briefest of these final judgments when he wrote that Haldeman's "entire career can be read as that of a man who swam too far out, beyond his natural depth.'' He was a successful advertising executive and a gifted advance man, but he probably had no business running the White House.

Nevertheless, it is hard not to sympathize with his desire to break out of the confines of his Southern California existence and do something "important" with his life. Haldeman's favorite quote from Richard Nixon came from the first inaugural: "Until he has been part of a cause larger than himself, no man is truly whole." He felt so strongly about those sentiments that his wife asked the President to write out the sentence by hand and then placed the words in a gilt frame as an anniversary gift to Bob. When he first contemplated writing a book on his Washington experiences, he planned to use the title *Truly Whole*.

In happier times, on the day that Jeb Magruder first reported for duty at the White House, Haldeman revealed this side of his nature to the younger man. "Here you're working for something more than just to make money for your company," he mused, tilting back in his chair. "You're working to solve the problems of the country and the world. Jeb, I sat with the President on the night the first astronauts stepped onto the moon. I listened as he spoke to the first men on the moon. . . . When I come back to California and see my old friends, and they all talk about their business problems, those problems seem mundane to me now." He smiled, and let a glow of satisfaction radiate to the very crown of his crew cut. "I'm part of history being made."

CHAPTER NINE

BACK TO ANONYMITY

Richard B. Cheney:
Ford's Secret Weapon

Richard B. Cheney, White House Chief of Staff and top aide to President Gerald Ford, had to pay his own way to the Republican convention in 1976. Post-Watergate morality dictated that government resources could not be used for the trip because of its political nature. At the same time the President's campaign committee, having reached its legally mandated spending limit during the long struggle with Ronald Reagan, could not afford an extra plane fare to Kansas City. So Cheney traveled like any ordinary citizen—on a commercial flight with an unwelcome layover at a midwestern airport. During this break he sat down in a coffee shop and became aware that a man a few tables away was watching him intently. Other public figures had abundant experience in dealing with such occurrences, but strangers *never* recognized Dick Cheney. Nevertheless, the man continued staring and finally came over to Cheney's table as if preparing to ask him for an autograph. This unprecedented development offered balm for the aide's ego, making up for some of the frustrations of his trip.

"Excuse me," the stranger began sheepishly, "I'm sorry to bother you, but, aren't you . . . I mean . . . aren't you John Dean?"

Nearly all stories about Dick Cheney make the same point: in an age of media hype and instant celebrity this youthful assistant maintained an astonishing anonymity. For the better part of Ford's Presidency, he held a job considered by many to be the second most powerful post in government and yet his name, let alone his face, remained unknown beyond the walls of the White House. In previous chapters this book has attempted to rescue from obscurity some of the most important and intriguing Presidential aides of the past—men whose names have been all but erased from the pages of history. It is startling to learn that a gifted Chief of Staff in our own era is in danger of being similarly forgotten. As one senior Democratic Congressman observed: "Nobody talked about him at the time, but if you look back on it, that kid Cheney did a hell of a job. He was probably a better man than Jerry Ford deserved. He was also a damn sight smarter than any of the clowns Jimmy Carter has brought with him." Cheney's contributions to the Ford administration have remained, until now, one of Washington's best-kept secrets.

He was born on January 30, 1941, the son of a career civil servant. His father spent forty years working for the U.S. Department of Agriculture in Nebraska and Wyoming. Cheney attended Natrona County High School in Casper, Wyoming, where he played football and served as president of the senior class. His outstanding all-around record helped him win admission to Yale University, but he found it difficult to adjust to the rigors of the Ivy League. "I didn't relate to Yale at all," he recalls. "I was just at that stage of my life when I wasn't ready to buckle down and get to work. I had some romantic notions about wanting to get out and see the world—or at least traveling all around the west." During his second year of college he dropped out and returned to a job he had first held the summer after high school. Working as a "grunt" on a construction crew, he helped build power and transmission lines in Wyoming, Colorado, and Utah. He also resumed contact with his high school sweetheart—a scholarly, diminutive blonde named Lynne Vincent who had successfully advanced her academic career while Dick pursued his ideal of he-man adventures. At the time of their marriage in 1964, Lynne taught literature at the University of Wyoming while Dick, having returned to school and enrolled at the state university, worked to finish his undergraduate degree. Eventually he went on to a master's in political science before they transferred together to the University of Wisconsin.

At Madison, Lynne completed her Ph.D. in English while Dick won praise from his professors for lucid, probing essays about the Congress of the United States. In 1968 he won a fellowship to work as an intern for a Congressman of his choice. He selected Representative William Steiger, a Wisconsin Republican, and planned to use the practical experience of his year in Washington as the basis for a Ph.D. dissertation. As it turned out, Cheney never returned to the university. In 1969 the Republicans entered the White House and an ambitious young Congressman from Illinois named Donald Rumsfeld took over the Office of Economic Opportunity. He needed help in making the transition and asked his friend Congressman Steiger if he could "borrow" Steiger's energetic aide Dick Cheney for just ten days. Cheney wound up working for Rumsfeld for the next five years. He served as Rumsfeld's executive assistant at OEO and then continued as his top aide when he moved to the Cost of Living Council in 1971. Rumsfeld's progress from one key post to another marked him as a notable "comer" in the Republican Party and in 1973 he won appointment as U.S. Ambassador to NATO. This European post meant temporarily parting company with Cheney and left the younger man without a job. By this time, the Cheneys had become addicted to life in the capital. Their two daughters had no memories of a home away from Washington, and Lynne enjoyed her part-time teaching job at George Washington University. What's more, with his patron's star so obviously on the rise it made sense for Cheney to stay in Washington to see what developed. He accepted a position as an investment counselor—a job in which his governmental experience and connections made up for the lack of a business background.

From this secure vantage point, Cheney watched the Nixon administration going through its death throes in the summer of 1974. On August 8, the eve of the President's resignation, he received an emergency phone call from NATO headquarters in Brussels. "It was Rumsfeld. He told me he was on his way back to the states to head the team of Ford's advisors who were handling the transition. He wanted me to meet his plane at Dulles airport. I did, and agreed to help him." By mid-September these volunteer efforts led to major White House appointments for both men. Rumsfeld became "Staff Coordinator"— or Chief of Staff in all but name—while Cheney signed on as his deputy.

The main task facing Gerald Ford's staff was to clear away the clouds of suspicion that continued to surround the executive mansion. The President's "full and absolute pardon" for Richard Nixon—granted just two weeks before Cheney and Rumsfeld settled into their White House offices—did much to complicate the job. To win back the public's confidence, Rumsfeld made several cosmetic changes in the administration of the White House—symbolic gestures that nonetheless won favorable comment in the press. He decreed, for instance, that the lavish redecorating of staff offices that had characterized the Nixon era would be immediately suspended. All Ford aides would have to be satisfied with the physical facilities as they found them. Rumsfeld also cut down sharply on the number of government cars and "hotline" home phones assigned to White House aides. His frugal influence even penetrated into the inner sanctum of the White House mess, the popular staff cafeteria that had been subsidized for years through the Agriculture Department. The new regime put this establishment on a paying basis, thereby doubling the price of lunch. At the same time, amenities such as glasses of wine and chilled martinis were altogether eliminated.

In more substantive areas, Rumsfeld similarly attacked the left-over apparatus of the Imperial Presidency. In countless press interviews, he announced that the days of a single, all-powerful Chief of Staff had come to an end. Instead of one man positioned, like Bob Haldeman, directly below the President, the Ford staff would array itself like "the spokes of a wheel." The Kennedy administration had used the same metaphor to describe its own internal arrangements in which various assistants or "spokes" shared similar access to the President as the "hub." Ford's speechwriter Robert Hartmann made the point in slightly different terms to a reporter from *Fortune* magazine. "The President doesn't want any Colonel House or Rasputin around here," he declared. "He prefers something analogous to the Knights of the Round Table, where all are equal."

The round table concept may have worked out well in the Camelot of King Arthur's (or Kennedy's) time, but for the White House of the 1970's it left a good deal to be desired. Frequently, Ford's knights rode out in different directions at once, or even crossed swords with one another. Not since the administration of Harry Truman had in-house bickering posed such serious problems for a Presidential staff. As Press Secretary Ron Nessen recalls, "Almost every week someone was squabbling with someone else in the Ford White House."

The peculiar circumstances of Ford's assumption of power contributed to the quarreling among his assistants. Ordinarily, a Presidential candidate has the chance to build up a suitable staff over the long months of a national campaign. The pressures of this shared ordeal can weld even the most disparate personalities into a smoothly functioning team. In Ford's case, a group of strangers found themselves suddenly thrown together at the very center of national power. A certain amount of head bumping was all but inevitable.

Many of the conflicts centered specifically on Bob Hartmann—the portly, pipe-smoking midwesterner who wrote most of the President's speeches. Hartmann had served Congressman Ford for years and held the title "Chief of Staff" during his employer's brief term as Vice-President. After the move to the White House, Hartmann saw no reason why he shouldn't continue in that capacity. To him, Rumsfeld, Cheney, and their colleagues were interlopers more interested in their own careers than the welfare of Gerald Ford. This attitude made him blustery and insecure in dealings with his fellow staff members. Nevertheless, his position of influence remained unassailable because of the President's sense of personal loyalty.

The situation called for an unusually patient and easygoing Chief of Staff—a prescription that Donald Rumsfeld could never fill. Novelist John Hersey, who spent a week closely observing the Ford White House, described the Staff Coordinator as "bright, jealous, crafty and fiercely combative." After all, Rumsfeld had once captained the Princeton wrestling team. Friends knew him by the jovial nickname "Rummy," but reporters and colleagues began calling him "the Haldeman who smiles." They had discovered that Rumsfeld's manner could be as cool and severe as his aviator glasses and immaculately combed, silky brown hair. "If I seem sharp with people," he declared, "it is because my job is to keep things moving around here." At times, however, Rumsfeld ended up slowing things down. He used to take hours of the President's time battling with Hartmann over the wording of major speeches. In retaliation, the White House wordsmith boycotted the staff meetings that Rumsfeld chaired each morning.

Dick Cheney succeeded in keeping his distance from these feuds. No one, not even the hypersensitive Hartmann, could feel threatened by the Deputy Staff Coordinator's quiet, self-effacing style of operation. His low profile corresponded perfectly with his Secret Service code name—"Backseat." While Rumsfeld handled the outside world, talking with reporters, Congressmen, and Cabinet members, Cheney concentrated on the 480 people within the White House staff. If the President gave an order, he would be the one "to farm it out and get it done." In a superficial sense, his job resembled that of Larry Higby, who had been "Haldeman's Haldeman" in the last administration, but unlike Higby, Cheney enjoyed free and direct access to the President. He became not so much a Deputy Staff Coordinator as an alternate staff coordinator—standing in for Rumsfeld not only in dealings with junior aides but in private meetings with the President. The Chicago *Tribune* reported that Ford never knew which of his top aides, Rumsfeld or Cheney, would pop into the Oval Office at 8:30 each morning for his "one-on-one" preview of the day ahead. "He is as comfortable with Cheney as he is with Rumsfeld," said one senior aide. "He doesn't hesitate to say, 'Get me Cheney,' if something comes up and Dick is the one close at hand." In arranging Ford's foreign and domestic journeys, Cheney and Rumsfeld roughly split the time on the road with the President. "Whoever stayed behind in the White House ran that end of the operation," Cheney recalls, "and whoever was with the President ran that end of the operation."

When Ford rearranged his official family in November, Cheney, along with Rumsfeld and Kissinger, was among the bare handful of insiders who knew what was coming in advance. The President planned a complex series of appointments and reassignments: firing James Schlesinger as Defense Secretary and replacing him with Rumsfeld; dropping Kissinger as National Security Advisor while retaining him as Secretary of State; replacing William Colby as Director of the CIA; and arranging for Nelson Rockefeller to announce that he would not seek a full term as Vice-President. With all the excitement and confusion, reporters took small note of Cheney's quiet assumption of the top job in the White House. In fact, he began unobtrusively but unequivocally performing that function on the weekend before the formal announcement. Traveling with Ford to Florida for a meeting with Egyptian President Anwar Sadat, Cheney learned that Rumsfeld had developed last-minute cold feet about taking the job at the Defense Department. Ford, preoccupied with his diplomatic mission, delegated to Cheney the responsibility of persuading Rumsfeld to go along with the plan. "Frankly, I had to talk him into it—long distance. We spent quite a while on the phone. It was a strange situation. I went from a position where on Saturday I was Rumsfeld's deputy, to a place where on Sunday I was working for Ford trying to get Rumsfeld to do something the President wanted him to do. And I was clearly the President's man from that point forward."

To prepare for the news conference announcing his "big shake-up," Ford huddled with advisors in the Oval Office. As he worked his way through a stack of likely questions, he suddenly paused, blinked, and burst into laughter. A White House jokester had inserted a sheet demanding, "Who in the Hell is *Richard Cheney*?"

Many Washingtonians never learned a satisfactory answer to that question, despite Cheney's formidable impact. Within weeks of the young aide's promotion, John Osborne of *The New Republic*, Jules Witcover of the Washington *Post*, and several other reporters noticed a dramatic improvement in the Ford White House, though none of them could explain why it had taken place. In conversation with the author, a veteran aide to House Speaker Carl Albert reached similar conclusions about Cheney's beneficial, though somewhat mysterious effect on the Presidential staff: "You could really tell the difference after he took over, just in terms of simple competence. Not that Rumsfeld wasn't good. He was. But he was too concerned with publicity, with his own image. He didn't want to be seen as another Haldeman, so things were a little rocky, a little sloppy. Then Cheney took over and they started shaping up. It's amazing how much better Ford performed after he had Cheney in there." This boost in morale and efficiency seemed equally obvious to those who toiled inside the White House. Three weeks after the shake-up, Press Secretary Ron Nessen wrote in a note to himself: "There has been a real change at the White House since Rumsfeld left, a change of mood, almost like a fresh breeze blowing through."

In retrospect, most observers agree that this seemingly magical transformation had something to do with Cheney's personality. In contrast to Rumsfeld's brusque, edgy style of command, Cheney offered an amiable presence at the eye of the ongoing White House storm. He is a compact, bull-necked man with sandy hair, flinty green eyes, and a peculiar, jagged smile. That smile—with the teeth clenched together and the bright eyes narrowed by little creases of merriment—suggests boyish energy and total guilelessness. In conversation, Cheney swivels restlessly in his chair, chain-smokes, and occasionally cocks his short, muscular arms behind his head. He represents a combination seldom seen in Washington—part of him reflective grad student, part of him straight-shooting, blunt Wyoming cowboy. After meeting Cheney, advertising man Malcolm MacDougall, who had been asked to help the President's campaign, "suddenly realized that I was beginning to like President Ford." He saw Cheney as "the kind of guy . . . who usually winds up at the head of the best-run American businesses—straightforward, competent, quick, humorous, pleasant people to be with. . . . Confident but not imperious." Under Cheney's soothing influence, staff rivalries at the Ford White House began fading into the background. Even Bob Hartmann came around and started attending the morning staff meetings he had boycotted for a year.

This increase in harmony did not mean that Cheney stepped back from the role of an active Chief of Staff; in fact, he wielded power far more aggressively than had his predecessor. The secret of his White House success was that the easygoing style accompanied an unquestioning sense of his own authority—the proverbial iron hand within a velvet glove. That strong hand seemed increasingly necessary in response to chronic administrative problems at the Ford White House. More than two decades of Congressional experience had conditioned Jerry Ford to an informal and personalized approach to his job. Unlike Nixon, who had received all suggestions in writing and then pondered them alone in solitude, Ford enjoyed the give and take of face-to-face encounters. These sessions allowed him to use some of the skills at negotiation, persuasion, and compromise that he had developed as House minority leader. Unfortunately, these free-wheeling meetings with top aides and others often degenerated into mere "brainstorming sessions" that produced nothing of value. According to one participant, "too many people were popping off with ideas that obviously came right off the top of their heads." As a result, difficult decisions frequently remained unresolved.

This quality of genial indecisiveness, spreading from the President outward through his subordinates, had become a hallmark of the Ford administration by the time Richard Cheney took on the top White House job. An illustration of this crippling tendency is provided by an astonishing exchange between Cheney and the President, duly recorded by eyewitness John Hersey. Ford had just finished personal interviews with a series of candidates for the relatively trivial position of White House military aide. When Cheney came into his office to ask his preferences, the President paused, then wanted to know which members of the staff had previously met with the applicants. Cheney rattled off a list of five senior aides, including himself.

"I'd rather wait and get your recommendations," declared the President of the United States. "I don't want to prejudice you."

Such cautious deference may have endeared Ford to his subordinates, but it hardly made for efficient administration. It became clear to Cheney that confusion and delay would occur time and again unless someone took charge decisively at the White House. He knew that he ran certain risks by asserting himself with his colleagues and the President. For one thing, he might compromise the image of "openness" and accessibility that had been such a public relations plus in the early days of Ford's Presidency. To Cheney, it seemed necessary to take that risk. "It's really a matter of trade-offs," he believes. "There is no question that to the extent that you involve a number of people in the consultative process before you make a decision, you raise the level of noise in the system. You enhance the possibility of premature disclosures and leaks. You also take more time, cut down in efficiency. On the other side, by encouraging different viewpoints you make sure that the President's got a wide variety of options so he won't be blindsided. But it's a very risky business to classify an open system with a lot of consultation as all good, and a very tightly run system with little consultation as all bad."

Cheney soon managed to establish the tightly run system he wanted with only a minimum of grumbling from his associates. Press Secretary Nessen concluded that the top aide's "easygoing manner and low public profile hid his steely control over the White House staff and the campaign organization." Several White House reporters reached the same conclusion. They began calling Cheney "the Grand Teuton"—a double-barreled pun alluding to the Teton Mountains of his native Wyoming and a command of the staff structure that was increasingly reminiscent of the departed Prussian, H. R. Haldeman.

Whatever traits he may have shared with his controversial predecessor, Cheney remained uncomfortable with the physical remnants of Haldeman's reign. In particular, he disliked the enormous, custom-built desk that Haldeman had installed in his West Wing office. "That thing has got to be at least eight feet tall. It's got so many drawers, so much wood in there that it takes ten men just to move it. I'm told that when they first brought it in, there was only one door in the whole building that was big enough to accommodate it: that was the door from the Rose Garden through the Oval Office. I never liked the thing, it wasn't the kind of desk I would have chosen. The problem was that it faced a wall. Maybe it's my own background, my nearness to open spaces, but I like to be able to see daylight. But it was so big, so difficult to move, that it would have been more trouble to take it out than it was worth. So we just left it there. I believe it's still there now, for Carter's people."

Despite the continued presence of Haldeman's cherished desk, his memory had begun to fade by the time Cheney took over the White House. Unlike Rumsfeld, he did not have to glance over his shoulder at every turn in flight from Haldeman's shadow, nor did he struggle consciously to avoid comparison with the disgraced Chief of Staff. People had been far more suspicious of Rumsfeld—the former Congressman and top federal officeholder noted for his ambition—than they were of the obscure Cheney. This meant that he could take up the slack in the White House staff system without provoking anguished cries about an "Imperial Presidency." Cheney's experience illustrated a classic paradox of White House service: by avoiding the appearance of power and potency, he actually increased his influence. Cheney even felt free to drop Rumsfeld's euphemism, "Staff Coordinator," and openly used the title "Chief of Staff" in describing his responsibilities.

The invisibility that contributed to Cheney's success resulted from a series of conscious decisions. As Chief of Staff, he turned down all of the hundreds of speaking invitations he received and agreed to only a handful of press interviews. When he spoke with reporters, he did so primarily on a "background" basis—providing information without giving them the right to quote him by name. He also frowned on human interest stories about his personal life. "At one point the 'Style' section of the Washington *Post* wanted to send a team out to take pictures of my family and my wife and myself. It sounded awful, so I said no. The *Post* did a profile anyway, but it was about the way the President worked with his staff and what he was trying to do, not about Dick Cheney the man. I had made a very determined decision to keep my head down, and I stuck to it. I thought I could get a hell of a lot more done if I was not a public figure."

This same thinking led him to avoid the cocktail parties on embassy row and elsewhere at which White House aides were always in demand. "My experience has been that people who show up at those things on a continuous basis don't have enough to keep them busy," he says. Cheney, like Haldeman and Ehrlichman before him, preferred to spend his free time with his family.

The President treated his principal aide with respect in the context of the working relationship. Cheney learned that he could always speak his mind and even argue with Ford over issues of policy. "No matter how much you might disagree in a particular instance, you were always free to come back two hours later and do it again. I mean, you would never find your access reduced as a result of having fought him on a particular point. I know that hasn't been true with some of the other Presidents we've had." Ford never stood on ceremonies with his Chief of Staff. The hardworking assistant felt free to break in on the

President at night, walking up to his private residence on the second floor of the White House. Neither Jerry nor Betty Ford seemed to mind when Cheney disturbed their few moments of privacy. On occasion, Cheney even transacted business with his boss while the Commander in Chief showered and dressed. The President, above all, maintained a sense of humor about his aide and about himself. During the first months of 1976, Cheney suffered a nasty household accident while running upstairs to catch a phone. He appeared at the White House late the next morning, leaning on crutches and with a huge cast on his foot. As he hobbled into the Oval Office to tell the President what had happened, Ford shook his head sadly. "I thought I was supposed to be the clumsy one," he said, then leaned back and roared with laughter.

Such friendly interchanges were typical of the President's dealings with Cheney. The two men had not known each other long enough to develop the intense personal connection that characterized the Nixon-Haldeman or Johnson-Moyers relationships; nor did Cheney stand in awe of his chief as had Ted Sorensen with Kennedy. What he felt for Ford was down-to-earth affection, not adulation. "It was always the little things he did," Cheney recalls. "You know, you never went out the door of the Oval Office without him saying 'goodbye' and 'thank you.' And just the way, on the Presidential helicopter, he'd always go up to the front to thank the pilot and crew for getting him there safely. He is, very simply, the nicest man I've ever met."

Ford needed all of his patience and decency to survive the bitter duel with Ronald Reagan for the Republican Presidential nomination in 1976. As the only chief executive in history to hold office through appointment rather than election, his vulnerability was obvious, especially in the face of a spirited challenge from his party's conservative wing. In the early stages of the struggle, Ford hoped to maintain a clear distinction between his campaign organization and the White House operation. Presidential aides were supposed to concentrate on the business of government, keeping the White House above the battle and letting campaign professionals supervise the political wars. This division seemed fine on paper, but in practice the incompetence and indecision of "The President Ford Committee" forced Cheney to play an increasingly important role in running the campaign. Whenever disagreements arose between the Chief of Staff and Ford's political handlers, Cheney's closer proximity to the President meant that his will prevailed. By the time of the Republican convention, his control over all major campaign decisions paralleled his absolute dominance of the White House staff.

A milestone in Cheney's emergence as the President's de facto political manager occurred shortly after the Florida primary when Howard ("Bo") Callaway, Ford's official campaign chairman, ran into trouble with the press. The newspapers charged that Callaway, who owned a profitable ski resort in Colorado, had used his former position as Secretary of the Army to win special favors from the Agriculture Department involving the use of federal lands. With the pardon of Richard Nixon an unspoken issue in the public's mind, the

Ford campaign could ill afford even the appearance of impropriety. Cheney knew that Callaway would have to go and that delaying his departure would only compound the political damage. Yet the campaign chairman had begun protesting his innocence and his anguished pleas might win sympathy from the President. Cheney decided to take matters into his own hands and met with Callaway over breakfast. Press aide Peter Kaye came along as an interested observer. "Cheney played him like a guy landing a fish," Kaye recalls. "Bo was flopping around, then lying there for awhile, amid long, awkward silences, and then would start flopping around again. Finally, Bo asked, 'What should I do?' 'Better get a lawyer, Bo,' Cheney told him." With Callaway's resignation in hand, Cheney presented the President with a fait accompli. Ford did not complain: he welcomed the fact that his top aide had relieved him of an unpleasant responsibility.

If, without prior authorization from the President, Cheney could effectively fire the campaign manager, then he could do anything. His associates took careful note of the situation and also learned to respect the Chief of Staff for his political judgment. His mastery of preconvention strategy seemed little short of amazing in a man with no prior campaign experience. In "The Battle of Mississippi," for instance, he overruled some of the most seasoned politicos in his party and went on to see his point of view dramatically vindicated. For weeks, President Ford's southern coordinator Harry Dent had tried to interest the campaign committee in a daring raid on Reagan's presumed stronghold in Mississippi. The delegation remained officially uncommitted and Dent believed that pressure on a few key delegates could swing the whole state, under the unit rule, into Ford's column. When the campaign staff dismissed his scheme as a waste of time and effort, Dent turned to the White House. There, Cheney perceived the chance for a crucial breakthrough in the tight intraparty struggle and resolved to take charge personally of efforts to turn the tide in Mississippi. The President Ford Committee resented this meddling in "their business," but the Chief of Staff easily triumphed in the jurisdictional tug of war. He began making phone calls to leaders of the Mississippi delegation and even flew to Jackson to address a preconvention caucus. A few weeks later, Cheney pressured the President himself to make a similar trip and to place a personal call to the delegation's chairman—despite Ford's well-developed distaste for such conversations. At the convention, the Chief of Staff's painstaking efforts paid off handsomely when Mississippi gave Ford the key votes he needed to nail down the nomination. Had Cheney failed to act in backing up Dent's audacious and timely maneuver, it is entirely possible that the Republican Party would have rejected Gerald Ford in 1976.

Certainly, a majority of the delegates seemed more philosophically attuned to Reagan—particularly on the issue of Henry Kissinger's foreign policy. On the very eve of the climactic balloting, Reagan forces tried to mobilize that sentiment in a last-ditch maneuver on the convention floor. They introduced a hard-line amendment to the party platform that called for "Morality in Foreign Policy" and implicitly criticized the record of the Ford administration. If the President's managers chose to accept the gauntlet that had been thrown down to them and wage a floor fight over these ideological questions, some of the conservative delegates pledged to Ford might well be shaken loose. The President, strongly backed by Vice-President Rockefeller, nevertheless wanted to take a stand on principle. "I don't like it. I'll fight it," he snapped, when he first read the proposed amendment to the party platform.

Fortunately for Ford's cause, cooler heads—with Dick Cheney's prominent among them—ultimately prevailed. The Chief of Staff urged the President to accept the plank without a fight, thereby deflating Reagan's efforts to provoke a test of strength on the issues. "Principle is okay up to a certain point," he declared to National Security Advisor Brent Scowcroft, "but principle doesn't do any good if you lose the nomination." Besides, "platforms don't mean anything; they are forgotten the day after the convention." When the proposed amendment finally came to the floor, the Ford forces had decided, as Cheney put it, "to take a dive." They accepted the conservative plank without protest, then swept on to the nomination the following evening. On a tricky tactical question, the instincts of the novice Richard Cheney had proven more reliable than those of the President himself.

Ford's uphill struggle against Jimmy Carter began on the last night of the Republican convention when he delivered his dramatic acceptance speech. The highlight of that address was a surprise challenge to debate the Democratic nominee—a challenge that had been researched and prepared nearly a month before by Dick Cheney and his assistants. For the Chief of Staff, who had spent the entire convention in Ford's command suite in a Kansas City hotel, the speech offered his first chance for a glimpse of the convention floor. He rode over to the hall with the President and waited backstage while Ford walked out into the glare of the lights and the cheers of the crowd. Once the speech had begun, Cheney managed to slip unnoticed onto the floor. He felt a sense of dreamlike unreality: after a week of watching this setting so intently on TV, of phoning endless orders and questions to his representatives in the thick of the action, he stood at the center of the listening crowd himself and looked up at the President. "It was an extremely emotional moment. I mean, we'd worked hard for months to get to this point. I'd put in long days, and the night before I'd been up all night on the whole thing of picking a Vice-President. I knew we'd be running as the underdog against Carter—according to Gallup we were down 33 points—but that position can give you a certain spark and a certain fire. We felt it that night. For the President, for the rest of us, it all came out that night."

Cheney now faced the job of keeping that spirit alive through the course of the fall campaign. From the beginning, he recognized that the televised debates with Carter might well prove decisive and represented the President's best hope for closing the gap with his Democratic rival. Having read the history of the campaign of 1960, Cheney knew that superior preparation by Kennedy's aides had given JFK his edge in the all-important first debate with Richard Nixon. Since Ford lacked Kennedy's natural facility, the briefing and practice sessions loomed even more important in his case. The press unanimously assumed that the bright, aggressive Carter would make mincemeat out of a President thought to be a slow-witted bumbler "who had played too much football without a helmet." Cheney remained confident that given the right sort of preparation, Gerald Ford could prove them wrong.

Two weeks before the first debate, the Chief of Staff directed that the family theater in the White House basement be converted into a mock-up of the actual set that would be used for the telecast from Philadelphia. The lectern was identical in every detail, so that the President's television advisor could check the camera angles and recommend the most appealing positions for Ford to assume. As the President stood at the podium practicing his remarks, aides held up warning cards showing "one minute to go" or "thirty seconds" so he could develop his timing. Cheney and other top assistants took turns sitting on "the reporters' panel" and fired questions at Ford for hours on end. After each session, the President and his men reviewed complete videotapes of the proceedings to critique what had been said and Ford's style of delivery.

In place of Ford's intensive training, Carter tried to relax before the first debate and the difference in approach became apparent in his answer to the opening question. When asked about unemployment, the former Georgia governor addressed his national audience with a bland, nervous lecture full of statistics. Ford, on the other hand, jumped immediately to the attack. "I don't believe that Mr. Carter has been any more specific in this case than he has been in many other instances," he growled, and began punching away relentlessly at his opponent. The staff had prepared him for precisely this role, so that his stumbling "Nice Guy" reputation could be replaced by the image of a determined fighter. As reporter Jules Witcover observed in his excellent book on the campaign, Ford gripped the edge of his podium and glared at Carter "like some big menacing bear straining to leap at his adversary. Carter in contrast seemed somewhat disoriented, tentative and deferential." Not surprisingly, the public opinion polls conducted immediately following this first encounter showed the President gaining dramatically on his rival.

The second debate—featuring Ford's celebrated gaffe about "no Soviet domination of Eastern Europe"—served to reverse the Republican trend. Neither Ford nor Cheney recognized the magnitude of the blunder until hours after the live telecast when hysterical calls began coming in from politicians and the press. The Chief of Staff quickly concluded that the President should admit that he had misspoken, correct himself, and go on to other issues. Ford, however, insisted on trying to justify his statement and thereby magnified its damaging effects. In a blunt, private conversation in the forward cabin of Air Force One, Cheney attempted to push the President into changing his approach but found that Ford wouldn't budge. "His feet were in concrete on this one," recalls campaign official Stuart Spencer, "and he was sore at us for putting the heat on him.'' Ford could withstand pressure from the members of his staff but he could not indefinitely ignore the furious attacks from Polish-Americans, Jimmy Carter, and the press. After several days of intense public criticism, the President swallowed his pride and issued the retraction his top aide had known to be inevitable.

Despite inept handling of this situation, Ford's campaign managed to regain its momentum in the last two weeks before the election. The final Gallup poll showed that the President had actually pulled ahead of his opponent for the first time—46 percent to 45 percent. Buoyed by the news, he arrived in Grand Rapids on the day before the balloting for a tumultuous welcome from his hometown. Bleary-eyed, exhausted, with his voice reduced to a husky whisper, Ford tearfully acknowledged the good wishes of his longtime neighbors. For Cheney, himself worn down by the long months of tension and uncertainty, that emotional moment marked the high point of the campaign.

The next day the Presidential party returned to Washington in the early afternoon. Cheney drove out to his home in Bethesda to vote, then reported to the White House. A number of people were waiting to see him when he arrived, and reports about the voting had already begun coming in from around the country. A poll of people leaving the voting booths showed an extremely close race. "It was nothing definitive," Cheney remembers, "but it did not look good. The way we put it was that we should prepare ourselves for either outcome. And then . . . well, it just went down from there." For Ford and Cheney, two men accustomed to making news and controlling events, there was a haunting feeling of helplessness as they waited for the final numbers to accumulate. The mood at the White House remained subdued through the night—certainly the early returns offered little ground for rejoicing. Shortly before three A.M., Cheney and pollster Bob Teeter went up to the President's private quarters to review the gloomy news with him. "We made a decision to fold up for the night, not to issue a statement either claiming victory or conceding defeat." The weary President staggered into his bedroom, while Cheney returned to his own office downstairs in the West Wing to continue his vigil and his conferences.

At eight the next morning, November 3, 1976, the Chief of Staff called a meeting of Ford's senior aides. They meticulously reviewed the returns, state by state, and satisfied themselves that the race was over. The President agreed that the time had come to make a statement of concession and asked his Chief of Staff to prepare a text. A few moments later the two men were on the phone with Jimmy Carter in Plains. The President spoke first, rasping out congratulations and explaining that because of the sorry condition of his voice he would put Cheney on the line. The Chief of Staff read the formal statement to the President-elect and received his thanks.

In the ten weeks between the election and the inauguration, Cheney found his White House job suffused with the glow of advance nostalgia. Every day, as he went through his normal routine, he could not help thinking how he would miss the place after January 20. On the morning of the inauguration he supervised an informal breakfast for the Cabinet and the senior staff in Ford's residence. The President exchanged a few mementos with his aides and said his goodbyes. Afterward, Cheney and Ford went downstairs alone. "He walked back over to the Oval Office for the last time. We went in and looked around for one last time. He and I had a talk. No, I won't say what we talked about—it was private." When they had finished, Ford went back to the residence to await Carter and Mondale while Cheney continued to wander through the familiar halls of the West Wing. "I went over to my office, to make sure it was cleared out and everything. I remember I went through the room and collected the pictures—the personal things. Then we all went up to the Hill together. After the ceremony, I rode with Ford on the helicopter to Andrews Air Force Base. I watched him walk down a red carpet, get on a plane and head for California. Then my wife came and picked me up with our daughters. We drove down the street and stopped at MacDonald's, got a hamburger for lunch, and rejoined the private sector."

During the next six months, Cheney stayed on in Washington and pondered his future. He returned to his pre-White House job as an investment counselor more out of convenience than as a career solution. "It pays the mortgage and buys the beans while I decide what I want to do next," he said. Though both he and Lynne continued to enjoy life in the nation's capital, Cheney did not want to remain there indefinitely. "I've got a feeling that this town is full of ghosts from prior administrations, and I'm not eager to become one. Too many people, after they have once served in the White House, can't get it out of their system. They just sit around, maybe for the next thirty or forty years, waiting for lightning to strike again. And that's sad." One option he never considered was writing a book about his experiences inside the Ford administration. "I feel very, very strongly that I couldn't do it. The guy who holds that particular job—the job I held—has to be an individual to whom the President and everybody else can express himself freely, knowing that it's a privileged communication. If I were going to write a book, I would have felt an obligation while I was there to tell everyone, 'You know, I'm writing a book.' That would be the only ethical way to handle it. But I never did that, and I had a relationship with the President that was a private one—it had to be. I have never violated the confidences he shared with me, and I never will." Cheney understands that his silence contributes to the understatement of his role in the historical record, but he is willing to accept those consequences. "My satisfaction with the job came from doing the job. I know what my relationship was with Ford. I think he has a good understanding of the role I played. I think other people inside, whose judgment I also respect, have similar feelings. And if I'd wanted a public job, or one where I was trying to make a mark in the history books, then I should have run for office myself."

In the first months of 1978 that is precisely what he decided to do. When the Congressman from his home district in Wyoming announced his retirement,

Cheney returned to Casper and declared his candidacy for the open seat. In a state where Reagan sentiment ran high, his close association with Gerald Ford was not an unmitigated blessing. He faced a tough fight for the Republican nomination, but showed a genuine flair for person-to-person campaigning. On June 18, in the midst of his hectic schedule, the 37-year-old candidate suffered a mild heart attack. His doctors blamed heavy smoking (often totaling more than three packs a day) and a lack of regular exercise. After several weeks of rest and recuperation, he returned to the hustings, promising the voters that he had learned his lesson and that his health should not be considered a factor in the campaign. On September 12 he won the Republican primary by a surprisingly decisive margin and became the odds-on favorite to capture the seat in Congress. His ultimate triumph made him the first major aide in American history to succeed in using White House service as a stepping-stone to elective office.

Whatever glories Cheney achieves in Congress, it is unlikely that he will ever again hold the power he enjoyed at Gerald Ford's right hand. That can be sobering knowledge for a man not yet 40, and Cheney must console himself with the certainty that he was one of the most effective, though least publicized, Presidential assistants of our time. He also has his store of personal memories to fall back on. "In December of 1976, a couple of weeks before the inauguration, some of the guys on the staff gave a private party for me. There were 40 people there—all of the people who knew me best. It was done basically as a roast, with Don Rumsfeld as M.C. At the end of the party, I was presented with a gift from the assembled group." The object in question had a mysterious air: on a large piece of plywood, painted black, a black felt flap obscured something round. At the bottom of the board, a neatly lettered sign proclaimed, "THE SPOKES OF THE WHEEL—A Rare Form of Artistry as Conceived by Don Rumsfeld—but Modified by Dick Cheney." As the Chief of Staff lifted the flap, he saw a bicycle wheel with most of its spokes appropriately "modified"—that is, smashed, broken, clipped, or twisted—except for a single strand of metal connecting the hub to the rim. "On the twentieth of January the only thing I left in my office besides the furniture was that board with 'the Spokes of the Wheel.' I set it up on the bare desk so Ham Jordan could find it, and I put a little handwritten note right beside it. It said, 'Dear Ham: Beware of the Spokes of the Wheel.' Well, by this time I think they're learning."

If they had learned somewhat faster, the first years of Jimmy Carter's Presidency might have been considerably more successful.

CHAPTER TEN

THE PAST, JIMMY CARTER, AND THE FUTURE

Suffering schoolchildren in every generation have demanded to know why they are forced to study history. In answer, their parents and teachers frequently resort to a trusty old saw attributed to the philosopher George Santayana. "Those who cannot remember the past," declared the sage, "are condemned to repeat it."

The simple wisdom of this statement has penetrated every corner of our national consciousness. Football coaches, stockbrokers, and movie producers all quote it approvingly. Its essential truth is recognized everywhere—except, it seems, at the Jimmy Carter White House.

There, the President's top aides see themselves as a totally new breed and view the experience of their predecessors as frankly irrelevant. Mary McGrory, a columnist generally sympathetic to the administration, accuses Carter's men of "an aggressive ignorance of recent history" and wonders "where they were while it was all going on." When this writer asked one of the President's ranking aides what he had learned from Richard Cheney's White House experience, he proudly announced: "The only thing I know about Dick Cheney is that he has a nice wife."

This sort of arrogance would be easier to accept had the President's Georgia Mafia lived up to its own expectations. After all, these were the young miracle workers who had masterminded Jimmy Carter's astonishing march to the Presidency and who were supposed to raise White House operations to a new level of responsiveness and efficiency. By the end of the President's first year in office, however, it had become clear to everyone that his aides had failed—and failed miserably. Despite more publicity than any other White House staff in memory, despite the hiring of 140 new full-time employees to supplement the more than 500 already in place when Ford left office, despite the frequent discussions of the President's "unique approach to public administration," chaos reigned at the White House. One of Carter's senior assistants told *Newsweek* magazine that "things run wild and fly crazily because there's no coordination." A junior-level aide, worried over a major slip for which he would have to take personal responsibility, sought advice from former Democratic national chairman Robert Strauss. "What are you worried about?" Strauss replied. "The administration is unique in that there's no penalty for fouling up.'' Even Jody Powell, the President's loyal Press Secretary, conceded after fifteen months in power that ''we need to get our house in order.'' Various charges have been leveled at White House assistants over the years—from influence-peddling to political manipulation, to plots to undermine the Constitution—but not since the administration of Warren Harding has the fundamental competence of the President's top aides been called so frequently into question.

Many of the problems in the current White House could surely have been avoided by a careful examination of the mistakes and successes of the past. One hundred twenty years have gone by since the establishment of an official White House staff, and twenty-three Presidents have grappled with the question of how to use their personal assistants most effectively. Inevitably, certain patterns have emerged and certain lessons can be learned about what works and what does not. In four specific areas, Jimmy Carter has ignored these lessons and in each case his administration has suffered for it. Any list of ground rules for future Presidents and their assistants ought to include the following:

1. A President should select as his principal aide a man whose goals and experience involve more than the service of a single politician.

2. Presidential assistants must do everything in their power to escape publicity.

3. Emotional dependence by a President on his top aide should be avoided as far as possible.

4. The emergence of a central figure on the staff—whether he is called White House Secretary, Staff Coordinator, Assistant President, or Chief of Staff—is necessary for the efficient functioning of the White House.

Each of these points deserves consideration in depth.

On the first conclusion, the historical record could hardly be more clear: when a President selects as his senior aide a man whose whole sense of purpose in life has been wrapped up with that President's career, he is asking for trouble. Nearly all of the most disastrous assistants have fallen into this category, including Robert Johnson, William Rogers, George Christian, Lawrence Richey, and Bob Haldeman. On the other hand, an inordinate number of the most talented and distinguished Presidential aides—John Nicolay, George Cortelyou, Colonel House, Clark Clifford, and Richard Cheney—went to work as full-time personal assistants only after their patrons had been nominated for the nation's highest office. This pattern is easy to understand. A President of the United States has available to him a far larger pool of talent than does, say, a candidate for Congress, a mayor of Buffalo, or a governor of Georgia. If he is willing to move beyond the small band of trusted foot soldiers who have served him selflessly for years and consider "new blood" in staffing the White House, his chances of selecting an aide of truly national ability are greatly increased. Every President will feel the temptation to use loyalty as his sole criterion in choosing a top aide—especially after an arduous national campaign has forged his staff into a tightly knit combat unit. That temptation should be resisted. As one hard-bitten veteran lobbyist observes: "Hell, if loyalty is all a President is looking for in his aides, then he ought to get a chief of staff named Fido." As Shakespeare's Prince Hal discovered long ago, the responsibilities of leadership often demand a new circle of friends. Sir John Falstaff might be a pleasant companion for a Prince, but a King needs advisors of a different caliber.

This does not mean that a President-elect must automatically reject all of his most familiar helpers when he looks for a top White House aide. In some cases, an especially talented veteran assistant can provide the support a President needs—so long as his length of service is balanced by a breadth of vision. Ted Sorensen identified intensely with JFK and devoted most of his career to advancing Kennedy's fortunes, but his ideological commitment to liberal principles gave him a sense of perspective. Bill Moyers, another effective aide who spent long years working for a future President, similarly viewed service to his chief as a means to an end rather than an end in itself. Several times in his intimate association with Lyndon Johnson, this preacher in politics showed a streak of stubborn independence, most notably when he deserted Vice-President Johnson in 1961 to accept a challenging post at the Peace Corps.

That sort of tension is totally absent from the relationship between Jimmy Carter and his chief aide, Hamilton Jordan. Jordan and his sidekick and counterpart, Press Secretary Jody Powell, are the President's creatures in a way never quite seen before in the White House. Both men have spent their entire working lives toiling in the vineyards of Jimmy Carter—Jordan since his junior year at the University of Georgia, Powell since his days as a 26-year-old graduate student in political science. Working day and night for this one man is quite literally the only life they know and, it would seem, the only life they ever hope to know.

His long-term dedication, Hamilton Jordan makes clear, has nothing to do with ideology. As he bluntly told the New York *Times* during the Presidential campaign, "My commitment to politics is a commitment to Jimmy Carter." Jordan has been accurately described as "a power mechanic." In sharp contrast to Sorensen and Moyers, he shows little concern for policy or programs; he has always been more interested in acquiring power than in using it. A former Atlanta reporter recalls: "After Jimmy became governor and Hamilton was his executive secretary, Hamilton was like the dog who chased the car and caught it. He didn't know what to do." Eventually, the governor's assistant found something to occupy his time: planning his chief's improbable drive for the Democratic Presidential nomination, the next hurdle on the path to ultimate power.

Jordan (pronounced "Jerd'n") came by his interest in politics through inheritance. His maternal grandfather, Hamilton McWhorter, served as president of the Georgia State Senate. His father, a well-to-do insurance agent, provided him with economic security and the privilege of growing up in one of the "better families" in Albany, Georgia. In high school, Hamilton received "gentleman's C's" while spending most of his time as a behind-the-scenes mover and shaker in campus politics. Severely bowed legs spoiled his dreams of athletic glory; later, the same physical defect won him a IV-F deferment at the height of the Vietnam War.

Jordan graduated from high school with the "American Graffiti" Class of '62 and proceeded to the University of Georgia. There, his stated goal was "to have a good time" and by all accounts he succeeded. As a hard-drinking member of Phi Delta Theta, his rollicking good spirits led to occasional clashes with the authorities and a leisurely 5½ year cruise toward a bachelor's degree. During this period he had little contact with the world outside the campus except for one summer as a Washington intern licking stamps for his grandfather's old friend, Senator Richard Russell. Jordan respected Russell, but the elderly Senator never sparked his imagination as did one of the candidates for the governor of Georgia in the Democratic primary of 1966. Even today, Hamilton Jordan finds it difficult to say with precision what first attracted him to then State Senator Jimmy Carter. At the time, when asked by friends why he suddenly began devoting so many hours to this particular candidate, he said simply: "This is a man who goes to church on Sunday and believes it. . . ."

Such logic may have convinced Jordan, but the majority of Georgians remained skeptical and Carter lost the election. Jordan nonetheless maintained his faith in the politician from Plains. As one of his acquaintances observed: "Jimmy Carter's got God, and Hamilton Jordan's got Jimmy Carter." In his spare time, the young man began driving to Carter's home for afternoon visits. Jordan helped his hero with occasional paperwork or engaged in long, intimate conversations with the once and future candidate. Their relationship suffered only a temporary interruption when, following college graduation, Jordan spent ten months working with civilians in Vietnam as part of an organization known as International Voluntary Services. He returned home in a badly weakened condition with a case of blackwater fever. After a few weeks recuperating, he took a job at a local bank which he soon found insufferably boring. Fortunately for Jordan, by this time Jimmy Carter had begun gearing up for his next run at the governorship and that effort occupied more and more of the younger man's time and attention. He eventually quit his job, signed on as campaign manager for Carter's 1970 drive, and helped devise the sophisticated and hard-hitting strategy that brought his candidate victory. This triumph took Jordan, age 24, to the state capital as executive secretary to the governor of Georgia. His greatest achievement in this new capacity was not a piece of legislation or an administrative reform, but a political memo dated November 4, 1972. This remarkable seventy-two page document, composed on the eve of George

McGovern's disastrous loss to Richard Nixon, set out a step-by-step plan with which Governor Carter could capture his party's nomination for the Presidency. Clark Clifford in 1948 and Bob Haldeman in 1968 also turned out famous memos that helped engineer political upsets, but neither of these previous efforts could match Jordan's in terms of uncanny prescience or attention to detail. Immediately following Carter's departure from the governor's mansion in 1974, his aide concentrated his efforts on putting the master plan into operation. As campaign manager during the marathon struggle that followed, Jordan drew frequent criticism for his haphazard administrative style and had to beat back several concerted attempts to remove him from a position of authority. All the same, he looks back on the Presidential campaign as the peak experience of his life. "I wish I were back there," he told one reporter after he had settled into the White House. "Life was a whole lot easier then."

One of the reasons that life seemed easier was that he could function without the glare of national publicity. Since his arrival in Washington, Hamilton Jordan's every move has been viewed as a newsworthy event—a situation for which he has no one to blame but himself. In succumbing to the temptations of sudden fame he violated a second of the cardinal rules for Presidential aides.

John Kennedy stated it as clearly as anyone. "The best way to stay out of trouble," he once told Ted Sorensen, "is to stay out of sight." Sorensen scrupulously followed that advice, as did most other successful White House assistants. Extensive publicity has always spelled trouble for Presidential advisors. In most cases it precedes a spectacular fall from power. Alone among major aides, Harry Hopkins maintained his effectiveness despite emergence as a genuine national celebrity. Yet even in his case there can be no doubt that the constant newspaper stories about his flamboyant lifestyle made his role as an international negotiator and intimate companion to President Franklin Roosevelt far more difficult than it need have been.

There are several reasons why most White House aides have preferred to go about their business in the shadows. As Bill Moyers explains: "The more visible the staff, the more likely is to be the impression that someone other than the President is making the decisions. . . . And much is at stake in the public's confidence that the President whom they have elected, not the men around him, is responsible for the decisions by which their course is charted." Unfortunately, Moyers failed to follow his own advice, allowing numerous writers to sing his praises in the pages of national magazines. His experience illustrates another danger of overexposure. These glowing accounts came to disturb Lyndon Johnson, who had been deeply wounded by his own negative press, and placed an unnecessary strain on the relationship between the two men. Similarly, public hosannas concerning the diplomatic triumphs of Edward House contributed to the Colonel's final break with Wilson. The President felt the need to prove to the world that he could succeed on his own, without the help of his celebrated advisor. Even the most secure and self-assured Presidents have felt twinges of irritation when the importance of their aides is exaggerated. After the press made much of the power of Kennedy's National Security Advisor McGeorge Bundy, JFK wryly observed: "I will continue to have some residual functions."

Of all the negative consequences of intensive publicity for a White House assistant, perhaps the most serious involves his reduced effectiveness in dealing with other members of the power structure. That distinguished observer of American manners and morals, Art Buchwald, understands this point particularly well. "The real problem is that the aide who sits next to the Oval Office is supposed to be taken seriously," he wrote after Hamilton Jordan had embarrassed himself by allegedly spitting his drink at one of the patrons of Sarsfield's bar. "If the aide calls up a union official and says, 'I'm speaking for the President. He wants you to start mining coal right away,' and the person on the other end says, 'Yeh, tell it to the boys at Sarsfield's' this country is in a lot of trouble."

In self-defense, Carter's top assistants insist that they are not to blame for the media hype surrounding their official and off-duty conduct. According to this argument, the journalistic apparatus of contemporary Washington rules out the sort of understated behind-the-scenes role favored by nineteenth-century aides. Gossip magazines and electronic media make sure that anyone next to the center of power will become an instant celebrity. The only problem with this otherwise plausible line of reasoning is that it totally ignores the example of Richard Cheney who, despite his position as Gerald Ford's Chief of Staff, succeeded in maintaining a remarkable anonymity. As even Carter partisans will admit in their more candid moments, the members of the current White House staff have not exactly played the role of shrinking violets in their dealings with the press. In the words of one embittered Congressman: "Hamilton and Jody have acted exactly like two Georgia country boys coming up to the big city for the first time. They've tried to get their names in the papers as much as possible so they can send all the clippings to the folks back home."

It is easy to see what the Congressman had in mind. During Carter's first six months in the White House, Jordan and Powell volunteered to pose for the cover of *Rolling Stone* magazine dressed as Butch Cassidy and the Sundance Kid. This gesture may have endeared them to a handful of Robert Redford fans, but it could hardly have encouraged official Washington to take them seriously. Nor was the collective image of the President's men aided by the juicy tidbits that began emerging concerning some of the more intimate details of their personal lives. Shortly after Jordan arrived in Washington, a local gossip columnist scooped the world with the earth-shattering revelation that the President's top aide "never wears—in fact, has never owned—a pair of underwear in his whole life." Two full years after Carter himself had suffered significant political damage from an interview in *Playboy* magazine, Jody Powell, supposedly an expert in public relations, inexplicably submitted to a similar interview in *Playgirl*. There, alongside full color photographs of male genitalia, the Press Secretary to the President of the United States answered insinuating questions about his extramarital affairs and the sexual temptations of his office. "The main problem of the current staff is the tendency to talk too much to the press. It's almost as if they can't help themselves," admits Patrick Anderson, who served through most of the campaign as Carter's chief speechwriter and has written brilliantly about Presidential aides of the recent past. "The camaraderie of reporters can be very seductive and Carter's people have no experience in resisting that seduction."

By the middle of the President's second year in office, his aides' public image problems had begun to approach crisis proportions. Unhappy developments in the personal life of Hamilton Jordan contributed significantly to these difficulties. In January 1978, Jordan and his wife Nancy, who had been described during the campaign as resembling "the Homecoming King and Queen," announced their separation. Two highly publicized incidents at the time of their breakup reflected Jordan's emotional strain. First came his boozy insult to the wife of the Egyptian ambassador at a dinner for Middle Eastern diplomats, then the celebrated spitting confrontation with an unidentified young lady at a Washington singles bar. Public assaults on the feminine neckline, whether uninvited explorations of "the twin pyramids of the Nile" or sudden showers of Amaretto and cream, seemed decidedly out of place for the principal aide to a born-again President. In the face of a rising public clamor, the White House mounted a spirited defense of the beleaguered aide. Press Secretary Powell released to the press a carefully detailed memorandum denying that Jordan had ever spit his drink at anyone. This thirty-three page document, meticulously prepared by the office of the President's counsel, stands as one of the most remarkable state papers of Jimmy Carter's Presidency. It features deadpan transcriptions of lengthy interviews with bartenders and patrons who happened to be present on the fateful evening, and concludes that Jordan had been the innocent victim of an aggressive female who tried unsuccessfully to get his attention and then slapped his face in frustration. For those who had accused the White House staff of incompetence or disorganization, this effort stood as eloquent testimony that on truly important issues, such as Ham Jordan's conduct in a Washington singles bar, the President's aides could move swiftly and decisively.

The official overreaction only intensified the discussion of Jordan's personal problems and destroyed what remained of his public image. Whether or not he actually behaved as alleged, his name became a national synonym for boorish behavior. In one memorable cartoon, Jim Berry showed a schoolgirl complaining to her teacher about a naughty classmate beside her. "He's acting exactly like Hamilton Jordan!" the child whined.

While most Americans could laugh at the troubles of the chief aide, the next front-page scandal involving the President's men raised far more serious questions. In July 1978, Dr. Peter Bourne, Carter's advisor on drug abuse and a longtime Presidential confidant, was charged by Virginia police with writing a false prescription for Quaaludes to facilitate the indulgence of a female White House employee. Carter and his top aides went along with a brief and feckless attempt to explain Bourne's actions, but when confronted with a huge public outcry decided to throw him overboard. Embittered by what he considered shabby treatment, the good doctor delivered a parting salvo at his colleagues along with his letter of resignation. Without fully realizing the consequences of his words, he told James Wooten of the New York *Times* that he left behind him a "high incidence" of marijuana smoking and "occasional" cocaine sniffing by members of the White House staff. This declaration served as a careless match tossed onto tinder-dry brush: reporters had known for months about drug use in the White House, but prior to the Bourne affair had felt restrained by a code of gentlemanly discretion from sharing that knowledge with the public. Once the initial charges had been leveled by the President's disgraced advisor, reporters felt free to step forward and discuss their personal experiences smoking pot with White House aides. A flood of stories suddenly appeared concerning various illegal and risqué activities within the recesses of the executive mansion. "Sure, there's a certain amount of partying and a certain amount of sexual adventure," conceded one veteran Carter aide. "That's not abnormal. The White House is a very high-pressure place and people need a way to let off steam. In the campaign, we used to have a saying: 'It's better to shack up than to crack up.' It's like a war when you work in politics. You don't know if you're going to die tomorrow and so you go ahead and have a good time tonight. Everything is temporary and chancy. It's a gypsy life, and for some of our people it's the only life they've had for the last ten years. I don't know if Jimmy either knows or cares about what's going on."

Obviously the President should care—not because the human frailties of his top aides necessarily disqualify them from doing their jobs, but because the merciless publicity surrounding these excesses inevitably compromises their effectiveness. The standard of conduct for a successful White House aide, particularly after Watergate, should approximate that for Caesar's wife: he must be above suspicion. Though no one has yet suggested that Jimmy Carter is a secret pothead, Americans have begun to wonder why their President doesn't clean house at the executive mansion. Surely, among his millions of fellow citizens he could find people better qualified to help him than the men he has there now. As Senator Henry Jackson succinctly states the case: "What the President needs most is to get better people around him."

Despite all the criticism and the bad publicity, Carter stubbornly refuses to alter the personnel of his inner circle. In so doing, he demonstrates his ignorance of a third key lesson from White House aides of the past.

The accounts in this book highlight the risks a President takes whenever his connection with a key assistant transcends practical day-to-day interaction and becomes a highly charged psychological bond. That sort of bond can lead a chief executive to protect an unworthy assistant who should be replaced—as with Grant and Babcock, Hayes and Rogers, Nixon and Haldeman. It might cause him to overreact to the unavoidable strains that crop up in the course of a working relationship, as Wilson did when his passionately felt friendship with Colonel House exploded in the midst of the Versailles Conference. This intense dependence on a single aide may also encourage the darker sides of a President's personality, such as Herbert Hoover's paranoid reliance on his hired sleuth Lawrence Richey at the height of the Depression. The common problem in each of these cases is easily stated: when the basis for a relationship is nonrational, it can cause the participants to act in an irrational manner. Judgment is inevitably clouded, and the internal dynamics of a relationship take precedence over the needs of the Presidency and the country. Hardheartedness can be a positive trait for the President of the United States—he ought to be selfish in using the men who serve him. Yes, there is room for friendship in the White House—as with Lincoln and Nicolay, Cleveland and Lamont, Roosevelt and Hopkins—but only if the core of the relationship remains essentially ruthless.

In dealing with his major aides, Jimmy Carter has given few hints of ruthlessness. Certainly, their continued presence in the top White House job serves their interests far more conspicuously than it does his. In return for friendship with the President, Jordan and Powell enjoy annual salaries in excess of $50,000, international fame, and enormous power. Carter, for his part, is rewarded with recurrent staff problems and embarrassing headlines. It is obvious that he stands by his principal aides not because of their record of performance or possession of special skills, but because of personal factors that go beyond logical explanation. Hamilton Jordan himself confessed to *Newsweek*: "Jimmy is terribly loyal and he defended us and really suffered because of my inexperience and immaturity and Jody's the first six or eight months when he was governor." This determination may show Carter's praiseworthy qualities as a friend, but it reflects badly on his judgment as an administrator. Why would a clear-thinking public servant spend six or eight months of his precious four-year term "suffering" with aides who were ill-suited to their jobs?

Carter displayed the same tendency to place personal ahead of political considerations in his handling of the Bert Lance affair. By doggedly supporting his Budget Director long after the man's history of shady dealings had made him a political liability, the President shook public confidence in the new administration. His relationship with Jordan may cost him even more dearly in the long run. The young aide has never been Carter's friend in the ordinary sense of the word. He is twenty years the President's junior and except for an occasional game of tennis on the White House courts, they seldom relax together. Nevertheless, the intensity of their interaction sometimes startles third parties. "The chemistry between them is unbelievable to watch," reports Robert Strauss. Like Nixon with Bob Haldeman, their mutual dependence is all the more compelling for its mysterious, almost impersonal qualities.

The origins of that dependence go back to Carter's long, lonely drive for political power. Jordan believed in his boss when no one else did, and so became a talisman, a symbol of luck, destiny, invincibility. No matter that the President's popularity plummets in the polls or that the chief aide becomes an object of derision in the press; if the two men stick together they simply cannot fail. Carter remembers the snickers that greeted him when he first ran for President and the way that Jordan magically transformed that laughter into cheers. Sudden spurts of popular support and newspaper praise—such as that which followed the Camp David summit—strengthen the President's conviction that his problems will pass without a rearrangement of his staff, Jordan had little to do with that diplomatic triumph, but the optimism surrounding it fortified his position. It helped restore Carter's faith in the inevitability of his own political redemption.

Public criticism of Jordan only intensifies the President's identification with the fate of his top aide since these attacks generally echo charges that have been leveled at Carter himself. Administration opponents complain about Jordan's lack of Washington experience, his unwarranted arrogance, and his Georgia provincialism. The President could not recognize these traits as shortcomings in his top aide without, in effect, conceding his own inadequacy. "We need someone who understands Capitol Hill and understands this town," declared one of Carter's senior advisors. "But that would require an admission that the Georgians haven't been able to hack it and that could never be tolerated." Jimmy Carter therefore persists in tackling the most complex and demanding job in the world with a staff in which six of the eight senior aides are Georgians.

In addition to this geographic preference, another factor that limits Carter's options emerged in conversation with one of the leading White House assistants. After a long, taped interview for this book in which he stoutly defended the staff as "one of the finest—and cleanest—White House teams in history," this Assistant to the President asked that the recorder be put aside and went suddenly "off the record." "There is one problem with Jimmy that you should know about," he began in a conspiratorial near-whisper. "He likes to be smarter than the people around him. That's just his way. A lot of people here are bright and sharp, but there's nobody who's really brilliant. Maybe Brzezinski is the exception, but he's a specialist and he's not really that close to the President. As for the rest of us—we happen to be the people he feels comfortable with."

In short, Carter's emotional needs cause him to confine himself to aides of limited ability. His experiments with the staff structure of the White House, ignoring the fourth fundamental conculsion from the past, cannot make up for this lack of talent.

In the aftermath of the Watergate disaster, the nation's leading pundits reached nearly unanimous conclusions about the best way to organize the White House. According to this conventional wisdom, the "Berlin Wall" which

H. R. Haldeman had constructed around his master played a major role in Nixon's undoing. By allowing one man to dominate his staff and to lord it over all the other assistants, Nixon stifled creativity and prevented dissent. "As a rule of life, people will generally conceal things that make them look bad," argues James Fallows, Carter speechwriter and a former editor of *The Washington Monthly*. "The big peril is having one person everything flows through. You are far more likely to get out of trouble if you have a lot of people who report to you all the time. It's inherently weaker to have one person controlling things than to have several." This popular thesis maintains that a properly structured White House has no room for a Chief of Staff or a single "Shadow President." Instead, the President should depend on a half-dozen or more coequal and competing aides. It is the old "spokes of the wheel" idea, first articulated by the Kennedy administration and cited with approval in the early months of Ford's Presidency, in which the chief executive himself makes all the decisions and mediates every dispute.

Carter and his men publicly committed themselves to this concept long before they arrived in the White House. It certainly made good political sense for them to do so. The candidate could promise the American people that there would be no more Haldemans and no more Watergates, that the President would be open and accessible as never before. Carter also pledged to scale down "The Imperial Presidency" by cutting the number of federal employees at the White House by nearly one third. For the first time in history, the internal organization of the President's staff became something of a campaign issue and Carter used it skillfully in appealing to the voters.

Once he settled into office, however, the new President followed the time-honored American tradition of ignoring much of his own previous rhetoric. Far from trimming the White House staff, he expanded its numbers by more than 25 percent within three months of taking power. Perhaps sensing his political vulnerability on this score, the President and his men clung all the more tenaciously to the other key article of their organizational faith: that the White House would function more effectively without a Chief of Staff. They reacted to any and all suggestions of a formal, pyramidal structure as if they had been urged to establish a leper colony in the West Wing. Hamilton Jordan, by all accounts the most influential aide, went to great lengths to avoid public designation as the staff's leader. Officially, he handled "political affairs" for the President, spending most of the first months in the White House supervising the distribution of federal patronage. To emphasize the diffusion of authority, the daily 8 A.M. meetings of the senior aides were chaired not by Jordan or Powell, but by the soft-spoken and relatively powerless Counsel to the President, Robert Lipshutz. Only once, in a preinaugural trial balloon, did Carter allow the forbidden phrase "Chief of Staff" to sully his lips. In a preposterous move, he suggested that Walter Mondale would serve him in that capacity—presumably because the Vice-President had nothing better to do with his time. Fortunately for all concerned, this novel suggestion never developed into anything more than a public relations gimmick, and Mondale concentrated on such traditional and scintillating Vice-Presidential duties as political "goodwill" tours and attending the funerals of foreign dignitaries.

Meanwhile, back at the White House, the Carter administration made a sincere and determined effort to implement the "spokes of the wheel" approach they had endorsed in the campaign. The main problem, as they soon learned, was that the hub of the wheel—President Carter—found himself hopelessly swamped with work. Information flowed into the Oval Office from every direction, without the slightest attempt at coordination. In the middle of 1977 speechwriter Fallows estimated that the President attempted to digest at least 700 pages of memos every day. His aides insist Carter enjoys working that way and reporter John Osborne notes a preference for "lone immersion in detail and paperwork that most Presidents have left to others." In this, he resembles no one so much as Herbert Hoover. Interestingly enough, Hoover and Carter are the only two Presidents of the century with backgrounds in technical subjects—Hoover in engineering, Carter in nuclear physics. Both men came to office with overdeveloped reputations as administrative experts and proceeded, with much fanfare, to institute new staff arrangements in which several coequal aides with clearly delineated responsibilities replaced a strong staff leader. In both cases the results were the same: a crushing burden on the President himself as even the smallest issues went to him for final decision. A former Nixon aide and convicted felon, not widely noted for his sense of humor, stated the problem in particularly pithy form. "We tried to keep the President from the daily trivia so he could concentrate on the big issues," he recalled. "Now the Carter people are doing exactly the opposite. They're keeping him from the big problems so he can concentrate on the trivia."

The absence of a staff coordinator also contributed to a lack of discipline and consistency among Carter's various aides. As in the Ford administration before Richard Cheney took firm control, top aides often duplicated one another's efforts or found themselves working at cross-purposes. Near the end of his first year in office, a deeply troubled Carter addressed a top-secret meeting of his senior staff. According to one of the participants, the President came close to losing his temper. "Once a decision is made," he said, "I will not tolerate opposition or unenthusiastic support from people involved in that decision." There is something almost pathetic in the Commander in Chief of the world's most powerful nation having to direct these words at men and women who were specially chosen to do his bidding.

A solution to the problem seemed obvious to unbiased observers. In the first part of 1978, Harrison Welford and A. D. Frazier completed a detailed plan for the reorganization of the White House and the executive office and discussed their findings with Hamilton Jordan. Their investigation, never fully revealed to the public, "led inescapably" to the conclusion that Carter needed a Chief of Staff. Despite the President's stubborn resistance to that idea, he did authorize Jordan to expand substantially his area of responsibility. As one junior assistant elegantly described the situation: "It's time Jimmy Carter kicked ass, and Hamilton is his chief ass-kicker."

Two confidential written orders which circulated in the White House during the week of January 23, 1978, gave clear indication of a new direction for the administration. The first order declared that the President would hereafter expect Jordan to involve himself directly in the formulation and implementation of foreign policy. To that end, he would begin attending confidential breakfast meetings held every Friday morning with the President, Secretary of State Cyrus Vance, and National Security Advisor Zbigniew Brzezinski. The second executive order involved an even more striking departure from Carter's previously articulated philosophy. It decreed that Jordan would take broad responsibility for "coordination of White House staff activities." Future meetings of the major aides would be convened and conducted exclusively by Jordan and he alone would report to the President on the substance of those meetings.

When these developments became known to the public, official spokespersons went through elaborate verbal gymnastics to convince reporters that things were not what they seemed to be and that Jordan was not actually following in the footsteps of Haldeman and Cheney. Carter apologists continued to make much of superficial changes of style at the White House, pointing to the absence of neckties and the presence of Hush Puppies on several of the President's aides as significant signs of virtue. Jordan's grooming habits, however, could not conceal the change in his position. Everyone recognized that he had won the structural authority to whip his colleagues into shape if he ever chose to exercise it. By the time Carter entered the second half of his term, Jordan had begun functioning as Chief of Staff in fact, if not in title. "Power blocs at the White House?" snorted one veteran observer. "Hell, the only power bloc I know is Hamilton Jordan."

Does the emergence of a single preeminent aide stand as an indictment of Jimmy Carter's leadership? Not in the least. If anything, the President should be praised for showing enough flexibility to abandon his naive preconceptions about running the staff, and adjusting himself to reality. Carter and his aides have shown an ability to learn from personal experience what they have failed to learn from history. They wasted valuable time in the process, but their midstream readjustments may yet rescue them from the threat of administrative chaos and political disaster.

Carter's people need not apologize for their current attempts to tighten the screws of the White House operations. Far from being an aberration, Jordan's powerful position at the President's right hand is as American as Georgia peach pie. Nearly all of our chief executives have depended on one man as a principal aide, an extension of themselves, and a buffer to the rest of the world. Long before Dwight Eisenhower injected the military term "Chief of Staff" into the White House vocabulary, this reality existed under various titles. Only a handful of Presidents have tried to run the White House without a strong central figure as focal point on the staff. The administrations in which these attempts have been made—those of Andrew Johnson, Rutherford B. Hayes, Chester Arthur, Warren G. Harding, and Herbert Hoover—do not stand out as glittering examples of executive achievement. It is surely no accident that each of our great or near-great Presidents has been able to rely on an energetic individual aide, on a "generalist in chief," to oversee all the complex activities of the White House. At times, as with FDR and Harry Hopkins, this arrangement never appeared on formal organization charts. Yet Hopkins, like Clark Clifford after him, achieved through force of personality a preeminence that he lacked on paper. Even when Presidents have begun their terms with a commitment to a loosely structured staff, as with Kennedy, Ford, and Carter, the demands of White House life have forced a single assistant to the foreground. The chief executive needs someone to share his across-the-board responsibilities, or the post can truly become "the loneliest job in the world." Without a Shadow President his task would be both psychologically and practically unendurable.

Future Presidents should not be scared away from the idea of a tightly run White House organization by the single baleful example of H. R. Haldeman. The by now commonplace assumption that his position as Chief of Staff somehow contributed to Nixon's misfortunes cannot withstand logical examination; it involves a simplistic misreading of the entire Watergate experience. Let us say, for the sake of argument, that Richard Nixon had arrayed his aides in the preferred "spokes of the wheel" configuration. Given the sort of men he had gathered around him, would they have been any more likely to save him from disaster? Who among the inner circle would have given him the bad news about Watergate—even if Haldeman had not been there to guard the door? Would Chuck Colson have told him? Dwight Chapin? John Ehrlichman? When John Dean finally decided to blow the whistle in his famous "cancer on the Presidency" presentation to Nixon in March 1973, Haldeman made no attempt to block his access to the President. The problem then, as always, remained Nixon himself. There is absolutely no evidence to suggest that even the most unlimited communication between this particular President and all of his chosen aides could have rescued him from his self-destructive course.

If anything, a loosely structured White House organization makes it even less likely that a single aide will step into the Oval Office for an unpleasant but necessary confrontation with the President. When responsibility is shared equally among a half-dozen assistants the temptation becomes irresistible to simply shrug one's shoulders and leave the most distasteful assignments to someone else. As Jody Powell admitted concerning the initial arrangement of the Carter staff: "That's the problem with all of us having our own specific areas—things tend to fall in between the cracks." At least under a system with a Chief of Staff, one man is unequivocally responsible for bringing grim tidings to the President's attention. Presumably, he will feel secure enough in his position to do so without fear of negative consequences to himself. The fact that Bob Haldeman failed to perform effectively in that role reflects badly on

Haldeman the man but by no means discredits the theory of organization under which he worked.

As former Chief of Staff Richard Cheney observed: "There's too much of a tendency now to look for formalized answers for avoiding Watergates. It's part of the same characteristic in our nature that led us to pass Prohibition. If we've got a problem, we think we can pass a law to solve it. And when we've got a problem in the White House, we think we can organize our way out of it. I just think that's not getting at the root cause of the difficulty. Ultimately, the place turns on the quality of the people who are there." And that—to use a Watergate phrase—is the bottom line.

A thoughtful chief executive expressed much the same sentiments as long ago as 1881. "I am more at a loss to find just the man for Private Secretary than for any place I should have to fill," wrote President-elect James A. Garfield. "The man who holds that place can do very much to make or mar the success of an administration." Garfield proved fortunate in his selection of a principal assistant—though the man he chose, Joseph Stanley Brown, was a 22-year-old stenographer with no executive experience. Character, rather than specialized skill or a record of accomplishment, is the key criterion for a successful Presidential aide. His effectiveness will be determined by the personal chemistry between two human beings. Despite our efforts to understand that interaction and establish absolute guidelines, the nature of his work will remain essentially private and mysterious.

Nevertheless, a sense of historical perspective can prove useful for the future. Several of our chief executives, including Jimmy Carter, have suffered setbacks in running the White House because of the fog of myth and misunderstanding that clings to the institution of the staff. That fog must be cleared away and the lost chapters of our past recovered. Presidents will remain nothing more than two-dimensional demigods until we understand that they, even more than most mortals, need assistance and support. The next time we read hints of some invisible aide wielding enormous power behind the scenes and acting decisively in the President's name, we need not suspect a sinister departure from tradition. These men are playing their part in a necessary and absorbing American pageant. Our Shadow Presidents may not make headlines, but they will always make history.

SOURCES

CHAPTER ONE: NOBLE BEGINNINGS
The White House Before 1861

Books

Adams, John Quincy. *Memoirs*. Philadelphia, 1874−1877.
Ketchum, Richard M. *The World of George Washington*. New York, 1974.
Klein, Philip S. *President James Buchanan*. University Park, Pa., 1962.
Millett, John D. *Government and Public Administration: The Quest for Responsible Performance*. New York, 1959.
White, Leonard D. *The Jeffersonians: A Study in Administrative History 1801−1929*. New York, 1951.
——. *The Jacksonians: A Study in Administrative History 1829−1861*. New York, 1954.

Articles

Marx, Rudolph. "A Medical Profile of George Washington." *American Heritage*, Vol. VI, No. 5 (August 1955).
Price, W. W. "Secretaries to the Presidents." *Cosmopolitan*, Vol. 30 (March 1901), pp. 487−92.

John Nicolay

Papers and Documents

Abraham Lincoln Papers. Library of Congress, Washington, D.C.
John G. Nicolay Papers. Library of Congress, Washington, D.C.

Books

Dennet, Tyler. *John Hay: From Poetry to Politics*. New York, 1934.
Nicolay, Helen. *Lincoln's Secretary*. New York, 1949.
Nicolay, John George, and Hay, John. *Abraham Lincoln: A History* (10 Vols.). New York, 1890.
Randall, Ruth. *Mary Lincoln: Biography of a Marriage*. Boston, 1953.

Ross, Ishbel. *The President's Wife*. New York, 1973.
Stoddard, William O. *Inside the White House in War Times*. New York, 1890.
Thayer, William Roscoe. *The Life and Letters of John Hay*. Boston, 1915.
Thomas, Benjamin. *Abraham Lincoln*. New York, 1962.
Villard, Henry. *Lincoln on the Eve of '61*. New York, 1941.
Welles, Gideon. *Diary of Gideon Welles*. Boston and New York, 1911.

Articles

Barbee, David Rankin. "The Musical Mr. Lincoln." *Abraham Lincoln Quarterly,* December 1949.
Bernard, Kenneth. "Lincoln and the Music of the Civil War." *Lincoln Herald,* Spring 1964.
Grimsley, Elizabeth Todd. "Six Months in the White House." *Journal of the Illinois State Historical Society,* October 1926.
Hay, John. "Life in the White House in the Time of Lincoln." *Century Magazine,* November 1890.
Wight, Grace Cheney. "Lincoln's Farewell Address." *Lincoln Herald,* Summer 1953.

CHAPTER TWO: SCOUNDRELS AND LOSERS

Robert Johnson

Papers and Documents

Andrew Johnson Presidential Papers. Library of Congress, Washington, D.C.
The Papers of Andrew Johnson, edited by LeRoy P. Graf and Ralph Haskins. University of Tennessee, Knoxville, 1967–1976.

Books

Lomask, Milton. *Andrew Johnson: President on Trial*. New York, 1960.
McKitrick, Eric L. *Andrew Johnson: A Profile*. New York, 1969.
Perling, Joseph Jerry. *Presidents' Sons*. New York, 1947.
Smith, Gene. *High Crimes and Misdemeanors: The Impeachment and Trial of Andrew Johnson*. New York, 1977.
Thomas, Lately. *The First President Johnson*. New York, 1968.
Welles, Gideon. *Diary of Gideon Welles*. Boston and New York, 1911.
Winston, Robert W. *Andrew Johnson: Plebeian and Patriot*. New York, 1928.

Correspondence

Lawing, Hugh A., Park Historian, the Andrew Johnson National Historic Site, Greeneville, Tn.

Newspapers and Periodicals

Cincinnati *Commercial* (1865)
Cincinnati *Daily Enquirer* (1878)
Greeneville *Intelligencer* (1874)
Nashville *Banner* (1861)
Nashville *Daily Press and Times* (1865)
Nashville *Dispatch* (1865)
Nashville *Union and American* (1865, 1875)

New York *Post*
New York *Times*

Orville Babcock

Papers and Documents

U. S. Grant Presidential Papers. Library of Congress, Washington, D.C.
House Miscellaneous Documents, 44th Congress, 1st Session, No. 186.

Books

Babcock, A. Emerson, compiler. *Babcock Genealogy,* Part II. New York, 1903.
Badeau, Adam. *Grant in Peace.* Hartford, Ct., 1887.
Ben: Perley Poore. *Perley's Reminiscences of Sixty Years in the National Metropolis.* Philadelphia, 1886.
Cadwallader, Sylvanus. *Three Years With Grant.* New York, 1935.
Crook. William H. *Through Five Administrations: Reminiscences of Colonel William H. Crook,* edited by Margarity S. Gerry. New York, 1907.
Cullum, George W. *Biographical Register of the Officers and Graduates of the U.S. Military Academy,* Vol. 2, 1867 and Vol. 3, supplement, 1879.
Donald, David. *Charles Sumner and the Rights of Man.* New York, 1970.
Furman, Bess. *White House Profile.* New York, 1951.
Grant, Jesse R. *In the Days of My Father General Grant.* New York, 1925.
Grant, Ulysses S., III. *Ulysses S. Grant, Warrior and Statesman.* New York, 1969.
Hesseltine, William B. *Ulysses S. Grant, Politician.* New York, 1935.
Josephson, Matthew. *The Politicos.* New York, 1938.
McDonald, General John. *Secrets of the Great Whiskey Ring.* St. Louis, Mo., 1880.
Nevins, Allan. *Hamilton Fish: The Inner History of the Grant Administration.* New York, 1936.
Porter, General Horace. *Campaigning With Grant.* New York, 1897.
Ross, Ishbel. *The General's Wife: The Life of Mrs. Ulysses Grant.* New York, 1959.
Woodward, William E. *Meet General Grant.* Garden City, N.Y., 1928.

Articles

Guese, Lucius E. "St. Louis and the Great Whiskey Ring." *Missouri Historical Review,* Vol. 36, No. 2 (January 1942).

Newspapers and Periodicals

Chicago *Inter-Ocean*
Chicago *Tribune*
New York *Times*
New York *Tribune*

William K. Rogers

Papers and Documents

Diary and Letters of Rutherford Birchard Hayes (5 Vols.), edited by C. R. Williams. Ohio State Archaeological and Historical Society, 1922.
Rutherford B. Hayes Papers. R. B. Hayes Library, Fremont, Oh.

Books

Barnard, Harry. *Rutherford B. Hayes and His America*. New York, 1954.

Ben: Perley Poore. *Perley's Reminiscences of Sixty Years in the National Metropolis*. Philadelphia, 1886.

Crook, William H. *Through Five Administrations: Reminiscences of Colonel William H. Crook,* edited by Margarity S. Gerry. New York, 1907.

——. *Memories of the White House*. Boston, 1911.

Polakoff, Keith I. *The Politics of Inertia: The Election of 1876 and the End of Reconstruction*. Baton Rouge, La., 1973.

Articles

Price, W. W. "Secretaries to the Presidents." *Cosmopolitan,* Vol. 30 (March 1901), pp. 487–92.

Newspapers and Periodicals

Cincinnati *Commercial*
Fremont (Ohio) *Weekly Journal*
New York *Times*
New York *World*

CHAPTER THREE: THE SILENT PARTNERS

Joseph Stanley Brown

Papers and Documents

"Introduction" to *Index to the James A. Garfield Papers* by Kate M. Stewart, Library of Congress, Washington, D.C.

Books

Balch, William R. *The Life of James Abram Garfield*. Philadelphia and Boston, 1881.

Brown, Harry J. and Williams, Frederick D. *The Diary of James A. Garfield*. East Lansing, Mi., 1967–1973.

Cortissoz, Royal. *The Life of Whitelaw Reid*. New York, 1921.

Crook, William H. *Memories of the White House*. Boston, 1911.

——. *Through Five Administrations: Reminiscences of Colonel William H. Crook,* edited by Margarity S. Gerry. New York, 1907.

Feis, Ruth Stanley-Brown. *Mollie Garfield in the White House*. New York, 1963.

Smith, Theodore Clark. *James Abram Garfield, Life and Letters* (2 Vols.). New Haven, Ct., 1925.

Articles

Anonymous, "Joseph Stanley Brown." *Bulletin,* Geological Society of America, Vol. 44, p. 36 ff.

Stanley-Brown, Joseph. "My Friend Garfield" (based on unpublished manuscript of the 1880's). *American Heritage,* Vol. XXII, No. 5 (August 1971), pp. 49–53, 100–01.

Newspapers and Periodicals

New York *Herald*
New York *Times*

Daniel Rollins

Papers and Documents

Chester A. Arthur Papers. Library of Congress, Washington, D.C.
Chester A. Arthur Papers. New York Historical Society, New York.

Books

Crook, William H. *Through Five Administrations: Reminiscences of Colonel William H. Crook,* edited by Margarity S. Gerry. New York, 1907.
Howe, George F. *Chester A. Arthur: A Quarter-Century of Machine Politics.* New York, 1934.
Reeves, Thomas C. *Gentleman Boss: The Life of Chester A. Arthur.* New York, 1975.

Articles

Reeves, Thomas C. "President Arthur in Yellowstone Park." *Montana, the Magazine of Western History,* XIX (1969), pp. 18–29.
Richardson, Joe M. "The Florida Excursion of President Chester A. Arthur." *Tequesta,* 24 (1964), pp. 41–47.

Newspapers and Periodicals

Harper's Weekly
The Nation
New York *Times*
New York *Tribune*
New York *World*

Daniel Lamont

Papers and Documents

Grover Cleveland Papers. Library of Congress, Washington, D.C.
Daniel Scott Lamont Papers. Library of Congress, Washington, D.C.

Books

Clark, Champ. *My Quarter Century of American Politics,* Vol. I. New York, 1930.
Eggert, Gerald G. *Richard Olney: Evolution of a Statesman.* University Park, Pa., 1974.
Hudson, William C. *Random Recollections of an Old Political Reporter.* Brooklyn, 1911.
Josephson, Matthew. *The Politicos.* New York, 1938.
Lindsey, Almont. *The Pullman Strike.* Chicago, 1942.
McElroy, Robert. *Grover Cleveland: The Man and the Statesman.* New York, 1932.
Nevins, Allan. *Grover Cleveland: A Study in Courage.* New York, 1932.
——, and Preston, Frances F. C. *Letters of Grover Cleveland.* New York, 1933.

Articles

Price, W. W. "Secretaries to the Presidents." *Cosmopolitan,* Vol. 30 (March 1901), pp. 487–92.
Stewart, Kate MacLean. "The Daniel Scott Lamont Papers." *U.S. Library of Congress Quarterly Journal,* November 1959–August 1961.
American Monthly Review of Reviews. Vol. 30 (September 1904), p. 264.

Newspapers and Periodicals

New York *Times*
New York *Tribune*
New York *World*

Elijah Halford

Books

Josephson, Matthew. *The Politicos.* New York, 1938.
Sievers, Harry J. *Benjamin Harrison: Hoosier Statesman.* New York, 1959.
——. *Benjamin Harrison: Hoosier President.* New York, 1968.

Articles

Halford, Elijah W. "Recollections of a White House Secretary." *Leslie's Illustrated Weekly,* March 1, March 8, May 3, May 31, June 7, June 21, July 12, August 2, August 30, September 20, and October 11, 1919.
——. "General Harrison's Attitude Toward the Presidency." *Century Magazine,* June 1912.

Newspapers and Periodicals

Baltimore *Sun*
Chicago *Tribune*
New York *Times*
New York *Tribune*
New York *World*

CHAPTER FOUR: THE EFFICIENCY EXPERTS

George B. Cortelyou

Papers and Documents

Index to the William McKinley Papers, Library of Congress, Washington, D.C.

Books

Hoover, Irwin Hood. *Forty-two Years in the White House.* Boston, 1934.
Koenig, Louis W. *The Invisible Presidency.* New York, 1959.
Kohlsaat, H. H. *From McKinley to Harding.* New York, 1923.
Morgan, H. Wayne. *William McKinley and His America.* Syracuse, N.Y., 1963.

Olcott, Charles S. *The Life of William McKinley*. Boston, 1916.

Pell, E. L., Buel, J. W. and Boyd, J. F. *McKinley and the Men of Our Times*. Historical Society of America, 1901.

Penrose, Charles. *George B. Cortelyou: Briefest Biography of a Great American*. Princeton, N.J., 1955.

Pringle, Henry F. *Theodore Roosevelt*. New York, 1931/1956.

Pulitzer, Margaret Leech. *In the Days of McKinley*. New York, 1959.

Articles

Anonymous. "When Presidents Collide." *American Heritage,* Vol. XXVII, No. 5 (August 1976).

Price, W. W. "Secretaries to the Presidents," *Cosmopolitan,* Vol. 30 (March 1901), pp. 487–92.

Newspapers and Periodicals

American Monthly Review of Reviews
Arena
Collier's National Weekly
Current Literature
Harper's Weekly
Independent
Living Age
McClure's
The Nation
New York *Times*
New York *World*
North American Review
Outlook
World Today
World's Work

William Loeb

Papers and Documents

Theodore Roosevelt Papers. Library of Congress, Washington, D.C.

Books

Blum, John Morton. *The Republican Roosevelt*. Cambridge, Ma., 1954.

Butt, Archibald. *The Letters of Archie Butt*. New York, 1924.

Cash, Kevin. *Who the Hell Is William Loeb?* Manchester, N.H., 1975.

Hagedorn, Hermann. *The Roosevelt Family of Sagamore Hill*. New York, 1954.

Hale, William B. *A Week in the White House With Theodore Roosevelt*. New York, 1908.

Hoover, Irwin Hood. *Forty-two Years in the White House*. Boston, 1934.

Koenig, Louis. *The Invisible Presidency*. New York, 1959.

Manners, William. *T. R. and Will: A Friendship that Split the Republican Party*. New York, 1969.

Mowry, George E. *Theodore Roosevelt and the Progressive Movement*. Madison, Wi., 1946.

Pringle, Henry F. *The Life and Times of William Howard Taft*. New York, 1939.

——. *Theodore Roosevelt: A Biography*. New York, 1931/1956.

Riis, Jacob. *Theodore Roosevelt the Citizen*. New York, 1904.

Robinson, Corinne Roosevelt. *My Brother Theodore Roosevelt*. New York, 1921.
Straus, Oscar S. *Under Four Administrations*. Boston, 1922.
White, William Allen. *Masks in a Pageant*. New York, 1928.
Willets, Gilson. *Inside History of the White House*. New York, 1908.

Articles

French, Willard. "Private Secretaries to the Mighty." *The World of Today*, March 1907.
Willey, Day. "The Men About the President." *Munsey's Magazine*, July 1903.

Newspapers and Periodicals

The Nation
New York *Herald Tribune*
New York *Times*
Outlook

Charles Dyer Norton

Books

Anderson, Donald F. *William Howard Taft*. Ithaca, N.Y., 1968.
Butt, Archibald. *Taft and Roosevelt: The Intimate Letters of Archie Butt*. Garden City, N.Y., 1930.
Coletta, Paolo E. *The Presidency of William Howard Taft*. Lawrence, Ks., 1973.
David, Oscar King. *Released for Publication*. Boston, 1925.
Dulles, Foster Rhea. *The American Red Cross*. New York, 1950.
Hammond, John Hays. *Autobiography* (2 Vols.). New York, 1935.
Hines, Thomas S. *Burnham of Chicago*. New York, 1974.
Holt, James. *Congressional Insurgents and the Party System 1909–1916*. Cambridge, Ma., 1967.
Hoover, Irwin Hood. *Forty-two Years in the White House*. Boston, 1934.
Lamont, Thomas W. *Henry P. Davidson*. New York, 1933.
Manners, William. *T.R. and Will: A Friendship That Split the Republican Party*. New York, 1969.
Mowry, George E. *Theodore Roosevelt and the Progressive Movement*. Madison, Wi., 1946.
Pringle, Henry F. *The Life and Times of William Howard Taft*. New York, 1939.
Ross, Ishbel. *An American Family*. New York, 1964.
Smith, Ira R. T. with Joe Alex Morris. *"Dear Mr. President . . . ."* New York, 1949.
Villard, Oswald Garrison. *Fighting Years*. New York, 1939.

Newspapers and Periodicals

Chicago *Tribune*
New York *Times*
Outlook
Review of Reviews (1909)
World Today (1907)

CHAPTER FIVE: A SINGULAR FRIENDSHIP

Edward M. House

Papers and Documents

Edward M. House Papers. Yale University Library, New Haven, Ct.
Woodrow Wilson Papers. Library of Congress, Washington, D.C.

Books

Bailey, Thomas A. *Woodrow Wilson and the Great Betrayal*. New York, 1945.
Barber, James David. *The Presidential Character*. Englewood Cliffs, N.J., 1972.
Blum, John Morton. *Joe Tumulty and the Wilson Era*. Boston, 1951.
Coit, Margaret L. *Mr. Baruch*. Boston, 1957.
Cotner, Robert C. *James Stephen Hogg*. Austin, Tx., 1959.
Daniels, Josephus. *The Wilson Era: Years of Peace*. Chapel Hill, N.C., 1944.
Freud, Sigmund, and Bullitt, William C. *Thomas Woodrow Wilson*. Boston, 1967.
George, Alexander and George, Juliette. *Woodrow Wilson and Colonel House*. New York, 1956.
Gerard, James W. *My First Eighty-three Years in America*. New York, 1951.
Grayson, Cary T. *Woodrow Wilson*. New York, 1960.
Hammond, John Hays. *Autobiography* (2 Vols.). New York, 1935.
Hoover, Herbert C. *The Ordeal of Woodrow Wilson*. New York, 1958.
Hoover, Irwin Hood. *Forty-two Years in the White House*. Boston, 1934.
Josephson, Matthew. *The President Makers*. New York, 1940.
Koenig, Louis. *The Invisible Presidency*. New York, 1959.
Link, Arthur. *Wilson: Campaigns for Progressivism and Peace, 1916—1917*. Princeton, N.J., 1965.
———. *Wilson: Confusions and Crises, 1915—1916*. Princeton, N.J., 1964.
———. *Wilson: Road to the White House*. Princeton, N.J., 1947.
———. *Wilson: The New Freedom*. Princeton, N.J., 1956.
———. *Wilson: The Struggle for Neutrality, 1914—1915*. Princeton, N.J., 1960.
Lippmann, Walter. *Men of Destiny*. **New York, 1928.**
MacPhail, Sir Andrew. *Three Persons*. New York and Montreal, 1929.
McAdoo, William G. *Crowded Years*. Boston, 1931.
McCombs, William F. *Making Woodrow Wilson President*. New York, 1921.
Moley, Raymond. *After Seven Years*. New York, 1939.
Richardson, Rupert N. *Colonel Edward M. House: The Texas Years*. Abilene, Tx., 1964.
Seymour, Charles. *The Intimate Papers of Colonel House*. Boston, 1926—1928.
Smith, Arthur D. Howden. *Mr. House of Texas*. New York, 1940.
———. *The Real Colonel House*. New York, 1918.
Smith, Gene. *When the Cheering Stopped: The Last Years of Woodrow Wilson*. New York, 1964.
Starling, Edmund W., as told to Thomas Sugrue. *Starling of the White House*. New York, 1946.
Stoddard, Henry L. *As I Knew Them*. New York, 1927.
Trevelyan, G. M. *Grey of Fallodon*. New York, 1937.
Tumulty, Joseph P. *Woodrow Wilson as I Know Him*. New York, 1921.
Viereck, George S. *The Strangest Friendship in History*. New York, 1932.
Wilson, Edith Bolling Galt. *My Memoir*. New York, 1938.

Articles

Anonymous. "The Real Colonel House." *New York Times Magazine*, December 8, 1912.
Grayson, Cary T. "The Colonel's Folly and the President's Distress." *American Heritage*. Vol. XV, No. 6 (October 1964).
Lippmann, Walter. "Philip Dru, Administrator." New York *Times*, December 8, 1912.
MacFarlane, Peter Clark. "The President's Silent Partner." *Collier's*, May 3, 1913.
Rifkind, Robert S. "The Colonel's Dream of Power." *American Heritage*, Vol. X, No. 2 (February 1959).
Thompson, Charles Willis. "Colonel House, President's Envoy." New York *Times*, June 20, 1915.

Newspapers and Periodicals

New York *Times*
Washington *Post*

CHAPTER SIX: DUBIOUS COMPANY

George B. Christian

Books

Adams, Samuel Hopkins. *Incredible Era: The Life and Times of Warren G. Harding.* Columbus, Oh., 1970.

Britton, Nan. *The President's Daughter.* New York, 1927.

Cotrill, Dale E. *The Conciliator: A Biography of Warren G. Harding.* New York, 1969.

Downes, Randolph C. *The Rise of Warren Gamaliel Harding.* Columbus, Oh., 1970.

Hoover, Herbert C. *The Memoirs of Herbert Hoover: The Cabinet and the Presidency.* New York, 1952.

Hoover, Irwin Hood. *Forty-two Years in the White House.* Boston, 1934.

Lowery, Edward G. *Washington Close-ups.* Boston, 1921.

Murray, Robert K. *The Harding Era: Warren G. Harding and His Administration.* Minneapolis, 1969.

——. *The Politics of Normalcy: Governmental Theory and Practice in the Harding-Coolidge Era.* New York, 1973.

Russell, Francis. *The Shadow of Blooming Grove: Warren G. Harding in His Times.* New York, 1968.

Sinclair, Andrew. *The Available Man.* New York, 1965.

Smith, Ira R. T. with Joe Alex Morris. *"Dear Mr. President . . . ."* New York, 1949.

Starling, Edmund W., as told to Thomas Sugrue. *Starling of the White House.* New York, 1946.

Articles

Christian, George B. "Warren Gamaliel Harding." *Current History,* September 1923.

——. "Why Presidents Break." *Saturday Evening Post.* October 13, 1923.

Duckett, Kenneth W. "The Harding Papers: How Some Were Burned." *American Heritage,* Vol. XVI, No. 2 (February 1965).

Newspapers and Periodicals

New York *Times*
New York *World*
Washington *Post*

Unpublished Studies

Alderfer, H. F. "The Personality and Politics of Warren G. Harding." Ph.D. Dissertation, Syracuse University, 1935.

C. Bascom Slemp

Books

Coolidge, Calvin. *The Autobiography of Calvin Coolidge.* New York, 1929.

Fuess, Claude M. *Calvin Coolidge: The Man From Vermont.* Hamden, Ct., 1965.

Gilbert, C. W. *You Takes Your Choice.* New York, 1924.

Lathem, Edward Connery, editor. *Meet Calvin Coolidge: The Man Behind the Myth.* Brattleboro, Vt., 1960.

McCoy, Donald R. *Calvin Coolidge: The Quiet President.* New York, 1967.

Slemp, C. Bascom. *The Mind of the President: As Revealed by Himself in His Own Words.* New York, 1926.

Smith, Ira R. T. with Joe Alex Morris. *"Dear Mr. President . . . ."* New York, 1949.

Articles

Anonymous. "A Right Handy Man is the New Secretary to the President." *Current Opinion,* Vol. LXXV (October 1923), pp. 413–15.

Anonymous. "Three Wise Men Who Work for Coolidge." *The Literary Digest,* LXXX, 38 (January 5, 1924).

Hathorn, Guy B. "C. Bascom Slemp—Virginia Republican Boss, 1907–1932." *Journal of Politics,* Vol. 17, No. 12 (May 1955).

Sanders, Everett. "The Secretary to the President." *Saturday Evening Post,* 203 (December 6 and 20, 1930; February 28, 1931).

Slemp, C. Bascom. "Inside the President's Office." *Collier's,* LXXV (April 25, 1925).

Strother, French. "A Week in the White House with President Coolidge." *World's Work,* XLVII (April 1924), pp. 575–90.

Newspapers and Periodicals

New York *Times*
New York *World*
Washington *Post*
Washington *Star*

Unpublished Studies

Hathorn, Guy B. "The Political Career of C. Bascom Slemp." Ph.D. Dissertation, Duke University, Durham, N.C., 1950.

Lawrence Richey

Papers and Documents

Herbert Hoover Papers. Herbert Hoover Presidential Library, West Branch, Ia.; Lawrence Richey Files; White House Secretaries Files.

Books

Abell, George, and Gordon, Evelyn. *Let Them Eat Caviar.* Garden City, N.Y., 1936.

Allen, Robert S. and Pearson, Drew. *Washington Merry-Go-Round.* New York, 1932.

Barber, James David. *The Presidential Character.* Englewood Cliffs, N.J., 1972.

Eisenhower, Milton S. *The President is Calling.* Garden City, N.Y., 1974.

Hoover, Herbert C. *The Memoirs of Herbert Hoover: The Cabinet and the Presidency.* New York, 1952.

Ickes, Harold. *The Secret Diary of Harold L. Ickes: The First Thousand Days, 1933–1936.* New York, 1954.

Joslin, Theodore G., editor. *Hoover After Dinner.* New York, 1933.

Liggett, Walter W. *The Rise of Herbert Hoover.* New York, 1932.

Lloyd, Craig. *Aggressive Introvert: A Study of Herbert Hoover and Public Relations Management, 1912–1932.* Columbus, Oh., 1972.

Robinson, Edgar Eugene, and Edwards, Paul Carroll, editors. *The Memoirs of Ray Lyman Wilbur, 1875–1949.* Stanford, Ca., 1960.

Smith, Gene. *The Shattered Dream: Herbert Hoover and the Great Depression.* New York, 1970.

Warren, Harris Gaylord. *Herbert Hoover and the Great Depression.* New York, 1959.

Articles

A.F.C. "Backstage in Washington." *Outlook,* January 2, 1929.

Gilfond, Duff. "The President's Secretaries." *The New Republic,* October 9, 1929.

Marcosson, Isaac F. "The President Gets Down to Business." *Saturday Evening Post,* December 21, 1929.

Richey, Lawrence. "Airplanes and Sailfish." *Review of Reviews,* October 1931.

A Washington Correspondent. "The Secretariat." *American Mercury,* December 1929.

Newspapers and Periodicals

New York *Times*
Washington *Post*

CHAPTER SEVEN: ACTIVIST ASSISTANTS

Harry Hopkins

Books

Adams, Henry H. *Harry Hopkins.* New York, 1977.

Anderson, Patrick. *The President's Men.* Garden City, N.Y., 1968.

Bishop, Jim. *F.D.R.'s Last Year, April 1944 –April 1945.* New York, 1974.

Childs, Marquis W. *I Write From Washington.* New York, 1942.

Churchill, Winston S. *The Grand Alliance.* Boston, 1950.

——. *The Hinge of Fate.* Boston, 1950.

——. *Triumph and Tragedy.* Boston, 1953.

Hassett, William D. *Off the Record With FDR.* New Brunswick, N.J., 1958.

Ickes, Harold. *The Secret Diaries of Harold Ickes,* Vols. II & III. New York, 1954.

Koenig, Louis. *The Invisible Presidency.* New York, 1959.

Perkins, Frances. *The Roosevelt I Knew.* New York, 1946.

Roosevelt, Eleanor. *This I Remember.* New York, 1949.

Roosevelt, Elliot, and Brough, James. *An Untold Story: The Roosevelts of Hyde Park.* New York, 1973.

Sherwood, Robert E. *Roosevelt and Hopkins: An Intimate History.* New York, 1948.

Articles

Anonymous. "Harry Hopkins." *Fortune,* July 1935.

Childs, Marquis W. "The President's Best Friend." *Saturday Evening Post,* April 19 and April 26, 1941.

Creel, George, "One-Round Hopkins." *Collier's,* November 9, 1935.

Flynn, John T. "Mr. Hopkins and Mr. Roosevelt." *The Yale Review,* Vol. 28 (1938—1939).

Hellman, Geoffrey T. "House Guest: Harry L. Hopkins." *The New Yorker,* August 7 and August 14, 1943.

Hurd, Charles. "Hopkins: Right Hand Man." *New York Times Magazine,* August 6, 1940.

Kluckhohn, Frank L. "The Men Around the President." *New York Times Magazine,* March 29, 1942.

——. "Washington Success Story." *New York Times Magazine,* July 26, 1942.

Mitchell, Jonathan. "Alms-giver: Harry L. Hopkins." *The New Republic,* April 10, 1935.

Price, Clair. "Hats New, Old, Shabby." *New York Times Magazine,* September 7, 1941.

Sugrue, Thomas. "Hopkins Holds the Bag." *American Magazine,* March 1936.

Swing, Raymond. "Harry Hopkins: Whipping Boy or Assistant President?" *Atlantic Monthly,* November 1948.

Newspapers and Periodicals

Newsweek
New York *Times*
Time
Washington *Post*

Clark Clifford

Interview with Clark Clifford, March 17, 1976, Washington, D.C.

Books

Allen, Robert S., and Shannon, William V. *The Truman Merry-Go-Round.* New York, 1950.

Anderson, Patrick. *The President's Men.* Garden City, N.Y., 1968.

Clifford, Marny. *Marny Clifford's Washington Cookbook.* New York, 1972.

Cochran, Bert. *Harry Truman and the Crisis Presidency.* New York, 1973.

Donovan, Robert J. *Conflict and Crisis: The Presidency of Harry S. Truman, 1945—1948.* New York, 1977.

Freeland, Richard M. *The Truman Doctrine and the Origins of McCarthyism.* New York, 1972.

Goldman, Eric F. *The Crucial Decade—and After: America, 1945—1960.* New York, 1960.

Goulden, Joseph C. *The Superlawyers.* New York, 1972.

Halberstam, David. *The Best and the Brightest.* New York, 1972.

Hartmann, Susan M. *Truman and the 80th Congress.* Columbia, Mo., 1971.

Lilienthal, David E. *The Journals of David E. Lilienthal.* New York, 1964.

McCoy, Donald R. *Quest and Response: Minority Rights and the Truman Administration.* Lawrence, Ks., 1973.

Articles

Clifford, Clark. "Recognizing Israel." *American Heritage,* Vol. XXVIII, No. 3 (April 1977).

Havemann, Ernest. "Clark Clifford." *Life,* January 27, 1947.

Horowitz, David, and Welsh, D. "Clark Clifford, Attorney at Law." *Ramparts,* Vol. 7 (August 24, 1968).

Newspapers and Periodicals

Los Angeles *Times*
Newsweek
New York *Times*
Time
Washington *Post*

CHAPTER EIGHT: THE SUMMIT OF POWER

Sherman Adams

Interview with Sherman Adams, March 23, 1976, Lincoln, N.H.

Books

Adams, Sherman. *Firsthand Report*. New York, 1961.
Anderson, Patrick. *The President's Men*. Garden City, N.Y., 1968.
Donovan, Robert J. *Eisenhower: The Inside Story*. New York, 1956.
Eisenhower, Dwight David. *Waging Peace*. New York, 1965.
Gray, Robert Keith. *Eighteen Acres Under Glass*. New York, 1962.
Hughes, Emmet John. *The Ordeal of Power: A Political Memoir of the Eisenhower Years*. New York, 1963.
Koenig, Louis. *The Invisible Presidency*. New York, 1959.
Parmet, Herbert S. *Eisenhower and the American Crusades*. New York, 1972.
Pusey, Merlo J. *Eisenhower the President*. New York, 1956.
Rovere, Richard. *Affairs of State: The Eisenhower Years*. New York, 1956.

Articles

Anonymous. "A Day With Sherman Adams." *U.S. News & World Report*, August 15, 1958.
Anonymous. "O.K., S.A." *Time*, January 9, 1956.
Adams, Mrs. Sherman. "Our Six Years in Washington's Whirlpool." *Life*, May 25, 1959.
Donovan, Robert J. "The Man at Ike's Right Hand." *Collier's*, October 14, 1955.
Rovere, Richard. "Boss of the White House Staff." *New York Times Magazine*, January 25, 1953.
Smith, Beverly. "Ike's Yankee Lieutenant." *Saturday Evening Post*, January 24, 1953.
Strout, Richard. "The Administration's 'Abominable No-Man.'" *New York Times Magazine*, June 3, 1956.
White, William S. "Sherman Adams Looks Back: Another View." *New York Herald Tribune Lively Arts and Book Review*, June 25, 1961.

Newspapers and Periodicals

Newsweek
New York *Times*
Time
U.S. News & World Report

Ted Sorensen

Interview with Theodore C. Sorensen, March 19, 1976, New York City.

Books

Anderson, Patrick. *The President's Men*. Garden City, N.Y., 1968.
Fairlie, Henry. *The Kennedy Promise*. New York, 1972.
Halberstam, David. *The Best and the Brightest*. New York, 1972.
Hess, Stephen. *Organizing the Presidency*. Washington, D.C., 1976.
Johnson, Richard Tanner. *Managing the White House: An Intimate Study of the Presidency*. New York, 1974.
Lasky, Victor. *J.F.K.: The Man and the Myth*. New York, 1963.
Opotowsky, Stan. *The Kennedy Government*. London, 1961.
Salinger, Pierre. *With Kennedy*. Garden City, N.Y., 1966.
Schlesinger, Arthur. *A Thousand Days*. Boston, 1965.
Sidey, Hugh. *J.F.K., President*. New York, 1964.
Sorensen, Theodore C. *Decision Making in the White House: The Olive Branch and the Arrows*. New York, 1963.
———. *Kennedy*. New York, 1965.
———. *The Kennedy Legacy*. New York, 1969.
Tanzer, Lester, editor. *The Kennedy Circle*. New York, 1961.
White, Theodore H. *The Making of the President 1960*. New York, 1961.

Articles

Anonymous. "Candidates." *The New Yorker*, June 20, 1970.
Anonymous. "How the President Runs the White House: An Inside Account." *U.S. News & World Report*, June 3, 1963.
Anonymous. "Profile in Courage: Ted Sorensen's Finest Hour." *National Review*, April 7, 1970.
Burns, James MacGregor. "A Hero to His Aide." *New York Times Book Review*, December 31, 1965.
Kempton, Murray. "Sorensen's Kennedy." *Atlantic*, October 1965.
Miller, William Lee. "Ted Sorensen of Nebraska." *The Reporter*, February 13, 1964.
Sidey, Hugh. "Departure of John Kennedy's 'Deputy President.'" *Life*, March 6, 1964.
Smith, Terence. "The New Frontier of Ted Sorensen." *New York Times Magazine*, March 26, 1967.

Newspapers and Periodicals

Los Angeles *Times*
Newsweek
New York *Times*
Time

Bill Moyers

Interview with Bill D. Moyers, June 17, 1976, Beverly Hills, Ca.

Books

Anderson, Patrick. *The President's Men*. Garden City, N.Y., 1968.
Baker, Bobby. *Wheeling and Dealing: Confessions of a Capitol Hill Operator*. New York, 1978.
Evans, Rowland and Novak, Robert. *Lyndon B. Johnson: The Exercise of Power*. New York, 1966.
Goldman, Eric. *The Tragedy of Lyndon Johnson*. New York, 1969.

Halberstam, David. *The Best and the Brightest.* New York, 1972.
Hess, Stephen. *Organizing the Presidency.* Washington, D.C., 1976.
Johnson, Lady Bird. *A White House Diary.* New York, 1970.
Johnson, Lyndon B. *The Vantage Point: Perspectives of the Presidency.* New York, 1971.
Kearns, Doris. *Lyndon Johnson and the American Dream.* New York, 1976.
Lasky, Victor. *It Didn't Start With Watergate.* New York, 1977.
Manchester, William. *The Death of a President.* New York, 1967.
McPherson, Harry. *A Political Education.* Boston, 1972.
Roberts, Charles. *L.B.J.'s Inner Circle.* New York, 1965.
Sherrill, Robert. *The Accidental President.* New York, 1967.
Sidey, Hugh. *A Very Personal Presidency.* New York, 1968.
Steinberg, Alfred. *Sam Johnson's Boy.* New York, 1968.
Valenti, Jack. *A Very Human President.* New York, 1975.
White, Theodore H. *The Making of the President 1964.* New York, 1965.

Articles

Anonymous. "A Look at the Inner Workings of the White House: Interview with Bill D. Moyers, Top Aide to the President." *U.S. News & World Report,* June 13, 1966.
Anonymous. "The President's Right Hand Man." *U.S. News & World Report,* May 30, 1966.
Anonymous. "28 Year Old Under Fire." *U.S. News & World Report,* March 4, 1963.
Anderson, Patrick. "Number Two Texan in the White House." *New York Times Magazine,* April 3, 1966.
Deakin, James. "Moyers." *The New Republic,* June 25, 1966.
Fallows, James. "Bill Moyers: His Heart Belongs to Daddy." *Washington Monthly,* July 1974.
Kempton, Murray. "Johnson's Young Helper." *The New Republic,* December 21, 1963.
Moyers, Bill and Sidey, Hugh. "The White House Staff Versus the Cabinet." *Washington Monthly,* February 1969.
Moyers, Judith. "Confessions of an American Wife." *Vogue,* June 1972.
Wicker, Tom. "Bill Moyers: Johnson's Good Angel." *Harper's,* October 1965.

Newspapers and Periodicals

Los Angeles *Times*
Newsweek
New York *Times*
Time
Washington *Post*

H. R. Haldeman

Interviews with H. R. Haldeman, June 10 and December 7, 1976, Los Angeles, Ca.

Books

Dean, John W., III. *Blind Ambition.* New York, 1976.
Evans, Rowland and Novak, Robert. *Nixon in the White House.* New York, 1971.
Haldeman, H. R., with Joseph DiMona. *The Ends of Power.* New York, 1978.
Magruder, Jeb Stuart. *An American Life: One Man's Road to Watergate.* New York, 1974.
McGinniss, Joe. *The Selling of the President 1968.* New York, 1969.

Nixon, Richard. *RN: The Memoirs of Richard Nixon*. New York, 1978.
Rather, Dan, and Gates, Gary Paul. *The Palace Guard*. New York, 1974.
Safire, William. *Before the Fall*. New York, 1975.
White, Theodore H. *Breach of Faith*. New York, 1975.
——. *The Making of the President 1972*. New York, 1973.

Articles

Anonymous. "How Nixon Handles World's Biggest Job: Interview with H. R. Haldeman, Assistant to the President." *U.S. News & World Report,* September 14, 1970.
Apple. R. W. "Haldeman the Fierce, Haldeman the Faithful, Haldeman the Fallen." *New York Times Magazine,* May 6, 1973.
Colson, Charles. "The Pied Piper of Mediaville." *National Review,* April 14, 1978.
Dean, John. "Haldeman is No More Innocent than I Am." New York *Times,* April 13, 1973.
Drew, Elizabeth. "The Understanding of H. R. Haldeman." *New York Times Book Review,* March 12, 1978.
Ehrlichman, John. "Ehrlichman Reviews Haldeman." *Time,* March 6, 1978.
Hughes, John. "Assaying the Haldeman Version of Watergate." *Christian Science Monitor,* March 1, 1978.
Schorr, Daniel. "Stones from the Wall." *Village Voice,* February 27, 1978.
Wheeler, Charles. "Black Days in the White House." *The Times* (London) *Literary Supplement,* April 21, 1978.

Newspapers and Periodicals

The New Republic
Newsweek
New York *Times*
Time
Washington *Post*

CHAPTER NINE: BACK TO ANONYMITY

Richard Cheney

Interview with Richard Cheney, April 21, 1977, Washington, D.C.

Books

Hersey, John. *The President*. New York, 1975.
Macdougall, Malcolm D. *We Almost Made It*. New York, 1977.
Nessen, Ron. *It Sure Looks Different From the Inside*. New York, 1978.
Osborne, John. *White House Watch: The Ford Years*. Washington, D.C., 1977.
Witcover, Jules. *Marathon: The Pursuit of the Presidency 1972–1976*. New York, 1977.

Articles

Anonymous. "An Inside Look at How the White House Is Run." *U.S. News & World Report,* March 17, 1975.

Bonafede, Dom. "Inside the White House." *Washingtonian,* 1975.
Cameron, Juan. "The Management Problem in Ford's White House." *Fortune,* June 1975.
Shearer, Lloyd. "Don Rumsfeld—He's President Ford's Number One." *Parade,* February 2, 1975.
Walker, Connecticut. "Young Men at the Top in Washington." *Parade,* June 1, 1975.

Newspapers and Periodicals

Newsweek
New York *Times*
People
Time

CHAPTER TEN: THE PAST,
JIMMY CARTER, AND THE FUTURE

Off-the-Record Interviews with Members of the Carter White House Staff, February—June 1977,
     August 1978, Washington, D.C.

Newspapers and Periodicals

Christian Science Monitor
Commentary
Los Angeles *Times*
The New Republic
Newsweek
New York *Times*
People
Rolling Stone
Time
U.S. News & World Report
Wall Street Journal
Washington *Post*
Washington *Star*

INDEX